Oxford Studies in European Law

General Editors: Paul Craig and Gráinne de Búrca

COMITOLOGY

Comitology

Delegation of Powers in the European Union and the Committee System

CARL FREDRIK BERGSTRÖM

Head of Legal Research at the Swedish Institute for European Policy Studies and Associate Professor at Stockholm University Law Faculty

OXFORD
UNIVERSITY PRESS

*This book has been printed digitally and produced in a standard specification
in order to ensure its continuing availability*

OXFORD
UNIVERSITY PRESS

Great Clarendon Street, Oxford OX2 6DP

Oxford University Press is a department of the University of Oxford.
It furthers the University's objective of excellence in research, scholarship,
and education by publishing worldwide in

Oxford New York

Auckland Cape Town Dar es Salaam Hong Kong Karachi
Kuala Lumpur Madrid Melbourne Mexico City Nairobi
New Delhi Shanghai Taipei Toronto
With offices in
Argentina Austria Brazil Chile Czech Republic France Greece
Guatemala Hungary Italy Japan South Korea Poland Portugal
Singapore Switzerland Thailand Turkey Ukraine Vietnam

ISBN 978-0-19-928001-8

For Maria, Gilbert, and Anna Eleanore

GENERAL EDITORS' PREFACE

Legal systems differ in a variety of ways, but they also face certain endemic problems, a classic example being the interplay between primary and secondary legislation, or, if you prefer different terminology, the interplay between legislation and implementing norms. It is clear that primary legislation cannot cope with all eventualities. This is in part because of problems of time, in part because of the need to act expeditiously which precludes recourse to the normal legislative process, and in part because of the desire to draw on expertise outside the legislature. It is therefore common for secondary rule-making or implementing powers to be delegated by the legislature to a different body or indeed to a variety of bodies or agencies. While the need to delegate is therefore common in all developed legal systems, the practice of delegation gives rise to a number of problems. There are issues of principle, raised by the very fact that norms of a legislative nature will be made by bodies or agencies that are separate from the legislature itself, and hence questions will arise as to how to legitimate such norms. There are important issues concerning the bodies to whom the power is delegated, and the conditions on which the delegation takes place. There are equally pressing concerns about the extent to which there can be participatory input from interested parties when secondary norms or rules are made.

The EU has of course not escaped these problems and dilemmas, and the response has been to develop the comitology system. The very nature of the primary legislative process in the EU has however meant that the difficulties of structuring an acceptable system for secondary or implementing rules has been particularly acute. The nub of the problem was that comitology concentrated power in the Commission and the Council to the exclusion of the European Parliament. It was therefore unsurprising that the European Parliament should come to object ever more forcefully to this regime as its power in the primary legislative process increased. The EP felt with justification that where regulations or directives were enacted pursuant to co-decision there was something amiss in a system that largely excluded it from secondary or implementing norms made thereafter. There have in addition been concerns raised about the transparency of the process, and about the nature of the elite and expert participation which it facilitates.

While there has been a good deal of literature on comitology we are very pleased to have this book in our series. Carl Fredrik Bergström tells the full story about the emergence and development of the comitology system, placing it in its historical context and against the background of political changes taking place over time in the European Union. He examines the role of both the main political actors and the European Court of Justice in shaping this system. The book includes astute reflections on the probable impact of the Constitutional Treaty and it will be of interest to all those concerned with governance in the EU.

Paul Craig
Gráinne de Búrca

PREFACE

This book is the final result of several years of work during which I was a researcher at Stockholm University and at the European University Institute in Florence. A final part, discussing the most recent proposals for reform of comitology and the implications for comitology of the new Constitutional Treaty, has been added at a later stage, during my time at the Swedish Institute for European Policy Studies (Sieps). It is my sincere hope that the book will do them all honour. Many thanks are due to friends, colleagues, teachers, and, not least, to students who have listened to my ideas—at various stages of development—and given me their comments. More specifically, grateful acknowledgement is made to:

Ulf Bernitz and Nils Wahl at Stockholm University, Adrienne Héritiér, Gráinne de Búrca, Helen Wallace, Renaud Dehousse, and Emir Lawless at the European University Institute, Josefin Almer and Charlotte Vandercam at Sieps, Joakim Nergelius at Örebro University, Per Cramér at Gothenburg University, Kieran Bradley at the European Parliament, Willem Stols, Jean-Paul Jacqué, and Anders Kjellgren at the Council of Ministers, Koen Lenaerts at the Court of First Instance, Anna Rasponi at Fontallerta, Florence, and, finally, Gwen Booth and Amanda Greenley at Oxford University Press.

Carl Fredrik Bergström
Lidberga 20 February 2005

CONTENTS

TABLE OF CASES

Court of Justice

Court of First Instance

German *Bundesverfassungsgericht*

TABLE OF LEGISLATION

Treaties and Protocols

Regulations

Directives

Decisions

Introduction

1.1 The exercise of implementing powers

1.1.1 A principle of division of responsibility

In almost all fields of co-operation covered by the EC Treaty, the formal competence to adopt legislation has been assigned to the Council (which must normally collaborate, in one way or another, with the European Parliament).[1] Likewise, the formal competence to prepare the necessary proposals, the right to initiate legislation, has been assigned to the Commission. The Commission has also been assigned the rather extensive competence to monitor the application of the legislation at the national level. But over the years it has become clear that the reality is a lot more complex than suggested by the above scheme for distribution or separation of competence.[2]

In this book, the focus will be on the fact that the Council is passing on a substantial part of its responsibility for adoption of legislation to the Commission. An early expression of this can be found in a ruling from 1970 where the Court of Justice manifested its support for the idea that

[1] It may be noted, here, that in the legal sense acts adopted under the so-called co-decision procedure (see e.g. below Ch 4, n 230) are also acts adopted by the Council. This follows directly from the wording of the various legal bases laid down in the EC Treaty ('the Council, deciding in accordance with the procedure referred to in Article 251'). See also Case C-378/00 and Case C-259/95, both below Ch 4, n 144. For the notion of legislation, see further below 1.2.1.

[2] The clearest examples of this are found in an increasing number of inter-institutional arrangements. See, for example, Farrell, H. and Héritier, A., *The Invisible Transformation of Codecision: Problems of Democratic Legitimacy*, Swedish Institute for European Policy Studies (SIEPS) 2003:7 (at internet http://www.sieps.se); Christiansen, T., Intra-Institutional Politics and Inter-Institutional Relations in the EU: Towards Coherent Governance (2001) 8 *JEPP* 747; and Gozi, S., Does the EU Institutional Triangle have a Future? (2001) 36 *IntSpec* 39.

the Council should delegate 'a general implementing power' to the Commission (see below 2.4.5.2).[3] Another expression can be found in the 1986 reform of the EC Treaty which emphasized the need for the Council to apply great selectivity in the choice of cases for action. For this reason, a new rule was introduced which stated that the Council should no longer only be permitted but *obliged* to confer 'powers for the implementation of the rules which [it] lays down' on the Commission (see below 3.4.2).[4] If this rule is complied with, which it normally is, the legislation adopted by the Council will only establish a basic framework and leave it to the Commission both to prepare and adopt the legislation that shall give this framework an operative meaning.

In order to appreciate the full significance of this principle of division of responsibility, it should be noted that it is subject to two qualifications (cf. below 3.4.2.2). The first is that the Council may reserve the responsibility for exercise of implementing powers to itself. According to the EC Treaty, this possibility exists only in 'specific' cases.[5] The second qualification is that the Council may impose 'certain requirements' on the Commission. In practice this provides the formal basis for a systematic use of committees which obliges the Commission to act in close co-operation with representatives of the national administrations. The basic features of the relationship between the Commission and these

---

[3] See Case 25/70, below Ch 2, n 244.   [4] See Article 202 EC.

[5] See Article 202 EC. As repeatedly emphasized by the Court of Justice, the Council will have to explain the grounds for a decision to reserve implementing powers to itself. See e.g. Case 16/88, below Ch 4, n 77, at p. 3485 (paragraph 10); and Case C-240/90, below Ch 4, n 54, paragraph 39. The requirement was later codified in Article 1 of Council Decision 99/468/EC (see below Ch 4, n 275). Here it is explained that: '[o]ther than in specific and substantiated cases where the basic instrument reserves to the Council the right to exercise directly certain implementing powers itself, such powers shall be conferred on the Commission in accordance with the relevant provisions in the basic instrument.' Quite clearly, when the possibility to reserve the responsibility for exercise of implementing powers is used by the Council, this indicates that matters involved are considered particularly sensitive and that it is unable, therefore, to reach agreement on the conditions for a conferral of powers on the Commission. See the Better Law Making Report 1997 COM (97) 626 final, at p. 2; and Commission Communication of 10 January 1991, below Ch 4, n 85, at p. 8. The conclusion has been supported in the doctrine. See e.g. Jacqué, J.-P., Implementing Powers and Comitology, in Joerges and Vos, below Ch 1, n 76, at p. 62; Snyder, F., The Use of Legal Acts in EC Agricultural Policy in Winter, G., *Sources and Categories of European Union Law: a Comparative and Reform Perspective* (Nomos 1996), at p. 382; and Blumann, C., Le pouvoir exécutif de la Commission à la lumière de l'Acte unique européen (1988) 24 *RTDE* 23, at p. 41.

committees, which is the central concern of this book, will be explained below (see below 1.1.2).

As repeatedly stated by the Court of Justice, the principle of division of responsibility rests on the idea that it is possible and, indeed, desirable to 'distinguish between rules which, since they are *essential* to the subject matter envisaged, must be reserved to the Council's power, and those which being merely of an *implementing* nature may be delegated to the Commission' (emphasis added).[6] Clearly, this has many similarities with the idea of a hierarchy of legal acts such as that which is often stated in national constitutional law, making a clear distinction between the different types of legal acts that stem from the legislative authority and those that stem from the executive.[7]

In spite of such similarities one must be careful when comparing acts adopted by the Council with those of a national parliament and acts adopted by the Commission with those of a national government. Article 249 EC, which lists the instruments that may qualify as legislation, contains no indication that it is intended to be read as a principle of separation of powers or correspond to a hierarchy which, in the legal sense, would make acts adopted by one institution superior to those of another (see further below 1.2.1).[8] Instead, it is explicitly provided that the Commission may make use of the same instruments as the Council and that the legal effects of those instruments are the same. This means,

---

[6] See Case C-240/90, below, Ch 4, n 54, paragraph 36; and Case 25/70 below Ch 2, n 244, paragraph 6.

[7] This was acknowledged by the Court of Justice in its ruling in Case 25/70 (see below Ch 2, n 244), paragraph 6. As reasoned by the Court, '[b]oth the legislative scheme of the Treaty . . . and the consistent practice of the Community Institutions establish a distinction, according to the legal concepts recognized in all the Member States, between the measures directly based on the Treaty itself and derived law intended to ensure their implementation.' It may be noted also that the Commission has argued that the principle of division of responsibility (the conferment of implementing powers) 'mirrors standard practice in the Member States where the executive is responsible for adopting decisions to implement laws passed by the legislature.' See Commission Communication of 10 January 1991, below Ch 4, n 85, at p. 2.

[8] See e.g. Case 188–190/80 *France et al. v Commission* [1982] ECR 2545, paragraphs 5 and 6. Here the argument was advanced (by the British Government) that directives adopted by the Commission were not of 'the same nature' as those adopted by the Council: only the latter could contain general legislative provisions and the former should merely deal with a specific situation. The argument was not accepted by the Court. In its view it followed from Article 249 EC (2003) that 'the Commission, just as the Council, has the power to issue directives in accordance with the provisions of the Treaty.'

for example, that acts adopted by the Commission can claim *direct effect* and *supremacy* as forcefully as acts adopted by the Council.[9]

Of course, the fact that the same type of instruments may be used with the same legal effects does not mean that there is not a qualitative difference with respect to content and that matters dealt with by the Council are not of another 'calibre' than those dealt with by the Commission. On the contrary, this must be seen as a logical consequence of the distinction between 'essential' and 'implementing' rules. But it must not be forgotten that this distinction is not so easy to uphold in practice, since the exact meaning of 'essential' and 'implementing' rules is uncertain. The closest one gets to an authoritative statement, in this respect, is the Court's explanation that the classification of rules as 'essential . . . must be reserved for provisions which are intended to give concrete shape to the fundamental guidelines of Community policy.'[10] But this includes a political evaluation which the Court itself has been reluctant to make.[11] The conclusion this leads to is that the potential scope of implementing rules is not so much determined by legal criteria as by political necessity and, therefore, that it can only be ascertained through a careful analysis of each individual case.[12]

---

[9] This, indeed, was confirmed by the spectacular Solange ruling of 1987. See Case 2 BvR 197/83 *Wünsche Handelsgesellschaft* [1987] 3 CMLR 225 (Decision of 22 October 1986). Here the German *Bundesverfassungsgericht* refrained from examining whether Commission Regulation 3429/80/EEC of 29 December 1980 adopting protective measures applicable to imports of preserved mushrooms (OJ 1980 L 358/66) was not in conflict with the German Constitution. For an explanation of the legal principles of direct effect and supremacy, see Craig, P. and Búrca, G. de, *EU Law—Text, Cases and Materials* (Oxford University Press 2003), at pp. 178–227 and 275–315.   [10] Case C-240/90, below Ch 4, n 54, paragraph 37.

[11] See e.g. Falke, J. and Winter, G., Management and Regulatory Committees in Executive Rule-making in Winter, G., *Sources and Categories of European Union Law: a Comparative and Reform Perspective* (Nomos 1996), at p. 549; Snyder, above Ch 1, n 5, at pp. 381–383; and Türk, A., Case Law in the Area of Implementation of EC Law, in Andenaes, M. and Türk, A. (Eds.), *Delegated Legislation and the Role of Committees in the EC* (Kluwer Law International 2000), at p. 173. See also Bieber, R. and Salomé, I., Hierarchy of Norms in European Law (1996) 33 *CMLRev* 907, at p. 927; and Dehousse, R., Completing the Internal Market: Institutional Constraints and Challenges, in Bieber, R., Dehousse, R., Pinder, J., and Weiler J. H. H. (Eds.), *1992: One European Market? A Critical Analysis of the Commission's Internal Market Strategy* (Nomos 1988), at p. 322.

[12] A number of attempts have been made to clarify the scope of implementing rules. See e.g. Kalbheim, J. and Winter, G., Delegation Requirements for Rule-making by the Commission in Winter, G., *Sources and Categories of European Union Law: a Comparative and Reform Perspective* (Nomos 1996) and Falke and Winter, above Ch 1, n 11, at p. 542. It may be noted also that the Commission has explained that its exercise of implementing powers affects three main

1.1.2 A close co-operation with the national administrations

It has already been emphasized that the principle of division of responsibility expects and, indeed, requires the Council to transfer a considerable part of its responsibility for adoption of legislation to the Commission. As manifested in the discussions which led to the signing of the Single European Act in 1986, it is hoped that this above all will make it easier for the Council to focus its efforts and to improve the rate of successful decision-taking (see below 3.3.3 and 3.4.1). But, in order to appreciate the full significance of that principle, it must be observed that the EC Treaty contains also an authorization for the Council to 'impose certain requirements' on the Commission. It has already been pointed out that this provides the legal basis for a systematic use of committees which obliges the Commission to act in close co-operation with representatives of the national administrations.

The idea that the Commission must work together with such committees was formalized for the first time in 1961, when the first attempts were made to establish a common commercial policy (see below 2.2.2.1). One year later, in 1962, it had become the 'balanced solution' for future management of the common agricultural policy (see below 2.2.2.3) and in 1968 it was classified as a 'solution in principle' for progress with respect to the free movement of goods (see below 2.4.3 and 3.3.2.2). Following the amendments to the EC Treaty which were introduced by the Single European Act (see below 3.4.2.2), the idea is now 'constitutionalised' and generally applied in all fields of co-operation. Today, there are at least 257 committees which assist the Commission in the exercise of implementing powers.[13]

During the period before 1986 much time was spent in the Council debating the terms of the procedures which regulated the relationship between the Commission and the committees. Whereas some governments favoured procedures that left the Commission room for discretion and autonomous responsibility others insisted that more restrictive procedures should be used. In order to come to terms with that, in the

areas: quasi-legislation; adaptation to technical progress; and management. See Commission Communication of 10 January 1991, below Ch 4, n 85, at p. 2.

[13] See the Report from the Commission on the working of the committees in 2002, below Ch 1, n 44. See also Information from the Commission of 8 August 2000—List of committees which assist the Commission in the exercise of its implementing powers (OJ 2000 C 225/2).

discussions which led to the adoption of the Single European Act the solution was finally arrived at that the Council should only be permitted to choose between a limited number of fixed procedures. These were established for the first time in 1987, in Council Decision 87/373/EEC (see below 4.2.2), and updated in 1999, in Council Decision 99/468/EC (see below 4.4.2).

The details of the fixed procedures—ranging from the most liberal advisory committee procedure via the management committee procedure to the regulatory committee procedure—will be explained in subsequent parts of this book (see below 4.2.2.2 and 4.4.2.2). Here it is sufficient to note that they all require the Commission to discuss the framing of its implementing measures with representatives of the national administrations within a committee which is expected to deliver an opinion. Essentially, the difference between the procedures relates to the coerciveness of this opinion and the effects it will have on the Commission's right to proceed.

The expression commonly used to denote the relationship between the Commission and this type of committee is 'comitology' (French: *comitologie* and German: *komitologie*). The spelling follows the usage of the Court of Justice, first established by Advocate General Marco Darmon in Case 302/87 *European Parliament v Council*.[14] It is not completely clear where the expression comes from and a great many jokes have been made about its origins.

One explanation which seems to circulate in the corridors of the European Parliament is that it has developed from the French expression *kremlilogie*, often heard in the 1970s as a depreciatory label for a highly politicized bureaucratic system. Entirely different from this explanation, with its obvious link to the word 'committee',[15] is the one advanced in the British House of Lords: that 'comitology' is 'a Brussels-created word deriving, not from the word "committee" but from the word "comity"'.[16] This, in turn, is a sixteenth-century term for courtesy which is used in

---

[14] See Case 302/87, below Ch 4, n 71, at p. 5627.

[15] It should be pointed out that in order to emphasize this link to the word committee, the European Parliament has often adopted the alternative spelling 'commitology'. See e.g. European Parliament Resolution of 16 December 1993 below Ch 4, n 122; and European Parliament Resolution of 16 September 1998 below Ch 4, n 256.

[16] See House of Lords Select Committee on the European Communities, Delegation of Powers to the Commission: Reforming Comitology, Session 1998–99, 3rd Report (2 February 1999), at p. 5.

diplomatic circles in the phrase 'comity of nations' (i.e. the mutual recognition among nations of one another's laws, customs, and institutions[17]).[18]

But even if both these explanations may be appropriate today, none of them can claim the same historical accuracy as the one which traces the expression back to the writings of Professor Cyril Northcote Parkinson and his classical parody from 1958: *Parkinson's Law or The Pursuit of Progress*. Here, the term 'comitology' is introduced to denote the study of public committees and the way they operate.[19] According to his colourful description:

The life cycle of the committee is so basic to our knowledge of current affairs that it is surprising more attention has not been paid to the science of comitology. The first and most elementary principle of this science is that a committee is organic rather than mechanical in its nature: it is not a structure but a plant. It takes root and grows, it flowers, wilts, and dies, scattering the seed from which other committees will bloom in their turn. Only those who bear this principle in mind can make real headway in understanding the structure and history of modern government.

In the functional, rather than etymological, sense the term comitology is not intended to cover all types of committees with which the Commission interacts. Excluded, first and foremost, are the 'grand' committees: the Economic and Social Committee and the Committee of the Regions, and also a variety of bodies which prepare the work of the other institutions, for example the Committee of Permanent Representatives and the specialized committees of the European Parliament.[20] Importantly, there are also a number of consultative bodies which have been set up by the Commission itself in the form of committees (see below 1.3.3). Even if these are a living part of the rather complex structures of comitology, in

---

[17] See *Encarta World English Dictionary* (Microsoft 1999).

[18] See *Oxford Concise Dictionary of English Etymology* (Oxford University Press 1996).

[19] See Northcote Parkinson, C., *Parkinson's Law or The Pursuit of Progress* (John Murray 1958), at p. 31.

[20] For a recent study of the various types of committees with which the Commission interacts, see Larsson, T., Precooking in the European Union—the World of Expert Groups, Ds 2003:16 (at internet http://www.regeringen.se/eso). Cf. the Preamble of Council Decision 99/468/EC (below Ch 4, n 275) which excludes also some 'specific committee procedures created for the implementation of the common commercial policy and the competition rules laid down by the Treaties'.

the strict sense they fall outside. The major reason for this is that their participation cannot be derived from the Council's right to impose 'certain requirements' but from the Commission's willingness to involve other interests than those of the national administrations. The distinction is illustrated by the General Budget of the European Union, in which these consultative bodies are classified as 'committees whose consultation is not compulsory for the Commission' (as opposed to the comitology committees which are classified as 'committees whose consultation is compulsory for the Commission').[21]

1.1.3   A fundamental conflict of interests?

Since it provides the Council and the Governments with a mechanism for control over the Commission, the committee system is often thought to manifest a conflict of interests. This, indeed, is a fundamental assumption for many of those who are most critical. A leading example, in that respect, is P. J. G. Kapteyn and Pieter VerLoren van Themaat who have taken the fact that 'committee procedures afford a means of ensuring that the Commission takes account of national views' to mean that they are also 'a means of tying down its freedom to act in the wider Community interest . . .'.[22]

The same assumption is also central for those who promote the use of committee procedures: the more sensitive the matter involved, the greater the demand that procedures should be used which will make it possible to intervene and correct the final result. An illustration of this can be taken from the Swedish Government's Guidelines for the Administration of EU-matters.[23] Here it is explained that the different committee procedures 'reflect the division of powers' between the Council and the Commission, and that the choice of one procedure rather than another is decisive for the possibility to exercise 'a direct influence' over the Commission's work. For that reason, the Swedish position with respect to the choice between the different procedures should be established in each

---

[21]   See Annex I (Part A) of the General Budget of the European Union for the Financial Year 2000 (OJ 2000 L 40/1).

[22]   See Kapteyn, P. J. G. and VerLoren, van Themaat, P., *Introduction to the Law of the European Communities* (Kluwer Law International 1990), at pp. 180 and 243–244.

[23]   See Swedish Ministry of Foreign Affairs, *Riktlinjer för handläggningen av EU frågor*, UD PM 2003:5 (at internet http://www.regeringen.se), at pp. 2–3.

case on the basis of '[a]n analysis . . . of the Commission's capability and possibility to make use of the resources intended for a specific purpose in a manner which is beneficial to Swedish interests.'

But even if there is much support, in principle, for the assumption that the committee system entails a conflict of interests, in practice, it is characterized by the opposite. In 1968, findings were presented which demonstrated that the role of committees did not cause as much of a problem with inaction as one might have feared: of more than 1,000 opinions which had been issued so far only five had not been positive (see below 2.4.4).[24] The findings were confirmed by the Commission itself in 1989 in a special report which stressed that 'instances of [it] having to refer proposed measures to the Council in the absence of support from national experts are virtually non-existent.' (see below 4.3.1.1). A more recent example can be found in a report from 1998 where the Commission explains that only in 32 of 3,000 situations dealt with under the regulatory committee procedure during the period 1993–1998 had 'difficulties' arisen over the adoption of a decision.[25] The conclusion this leads to is remarkable. Judging from the statistics, the committee system does not give rise to the type of conflicts many expect or fear but appears to be 'a fruitful collaboration between [the Commission] services and those Member State administrations which are most often faced with having to apply, on the ground, the implementing measures adopted at Community level.'[26]

Against this background, anyone who wishes to understand more about comitology is forced to listen to those who warn against 'excessive legalism' and ask for a better understanding of how legal rules correspond with the ways in which powers are actually exercised (cf. below 1.4.2).[27]

---

[24] See the Jozeau-Marigné Report (below Ch 2, n 216), at p. 25 (paragraph 42). See also Bertram, C., Decision-making in the EEC: the Management Committee Procedure (1967–68) 5 *CMLRev* 246, at p. 263.

[25] See Commission Document SG.B1/D (98)34174. Reference in the Swedish Government's (Ministry of Foreign Affairs) Position PM of 20 November 1998 on the Commission Proposal for a Council Decision laying down the procedures for the exercise of implementing powers conferred on the Commission, *Ståndpunkts-PM om kommissionens förslag till rådsbeslut om närmare villkor för utövandet av kommissionens genomförandebefogenheter* (at internet http://www.regeringen.se). The findings with respect to the management committee procedure were more or less identical.

[26] Quote from Ciavarini-Azzi, G. (Chief Adviser of the Commission Secretariat-General), Comitology and the European Commission, in Joerges and Vos, below Ch 1, n 76, at p. 53.

[27] See e.g. Búrca, G. de, The Institutional Development of the EU: a Constitutional Analysis, in Craig, P. and Búrca, G. de (Eds.), *The Evolution of EU Law* (Oxford University Press 1999), at pp. 50–81.

The implication is that both reformers and scholars have to go beyond the judicial realm and that empirical studies are called for: 'there is a need for knowledge about the relationship between, on the one hand, formal-legal institutions, legally binding decisions, and authorised texts and, on the other hand, rule implementation, "living institutions" and actual political conduct and outcomes.'[28]

In an initial reply to the call for empirical studies, a statistical assessment will be made which is intended to clarify the quantitative significance of legislation adopted by the Commission subject to committee procedures. Then, in order to provide some basic understanding of the way in which the committee system actually functions, reference will be made to a previous study of two specific pieces of implementing legislation. The study, which was carried out by the author himself for *Statskontoret*, the Swedish Agency for Public Management, is based on interviews with the Swedish representatives who were involved in the negotiations which led to the adoption of that legislation.[29]

1.2   The legislation: facts and figures

1.2.1   *Regulations and directives 1970–2003*

According to Article 249 EC, in order to carry out their task the Council, the European Parliament, and the Commission 'shall make regulations and issue directives, take decisions, make recommendations or deliver opinions.' Of these different types of legal instrument only the first three, regulations, directives, and decisions, have binding force and, for that reason, are popularly referred to as 'legislation'.[30] In the following the

[28] See e.g. Olsen, J. P., Reforming European Institutions of Governance (2002) 40 *JCMS* 581, at p. 593. For examples of legal scholars who have reached the same conclusion with respect to the study of comitology see Joerges, C. and Neyer, J., From Intergovernmental Bargaining to Deliberative Political Processes: The Constitutionalisation of Comitology (1997) 3 *ELJ* 273; Falke and Winter, above Ch 1, n 11; Snyder, above Ch 1, n 5; and Schmitt von Sydow, H. and von Rosenbach, G., *Organe der Erweiterten Europäischen Gemeinschaften: Die Kommission* (Nomos 1980).

[29] See Bergström, C. F., *Genomförandekommittéer: En expertstudie av svenska departements och myndigheters ansvar för antagande av gemenskapslagstiftning*, report to the Swedish Agency for Public Management, Statskontoret 2000:20C (at internet http://www.statskontoret.se).

[30] See, for example, CELEX at internet http://europa.eu.int/celex or EUR-Lex at internet http://europa.eu.int/eur-lex.

focus will be only on regulations and directives. One major reason for that is found in the fact that decisions, in contrast to regulations and directives, are not subject to any requirement for publication (but only for notification to those to whom they are addressed) and that it is not possible, therefore, to make reliable observations about the way in which they are being used.[31] For regulations and, normally, directives, by contrast, publication is compulsory. Another reason is that decisions are only binding upon those to whom they are addressed and that regulations and directives alone are available for the framing of matters 'which might be regarded as having a legislative bearing.'[32]

The statistical data on which the following assessment is based has been obtained from the computerized documentation system CELEX which includes regulations and directives published in the Official Journal (see Figures 1.1–1.3). Since there is considerable concern with respect to the accuracy of data from the so-called Transitional Period, the assessment has been limited to the period 1970–2003. Furthermore, a number of regulations have been excluded which relate to the day-to-day management of the common agricultural policy and are valid only for a limited period.[33]

On the basis of this at least three observations may be made. Firstly, the most frequently used type of legislation, by far, is not the directive but the regulation, binding in its entirety and directly and generally applicable. Secondly, even if the principal responsibility for adoption of legislation lies with the Council, a considerable proportion is adopted by the Commission. Thirdly, and most importantly for present purposes, the proportion of legislation adopted by the Council is in constant decline in

---

[31] See Article 254 EC. Publication is compulsory for all regulations and the bulk of directives. The only directives for which publication is not compulsory are those which are addressed to a limited number of Member States and, at the same time, have not been adopted by the Council in collaboration with the European Parliament subject to the co-decision procedure (see e.g. below Ch 4, n 230). According to the General Report of the Activities of the European Union 1996 (Office for Official Publications 1997), in that year the Council adopted 179 decisions (at p. 424, point 1057) and the Commission adopted 2,086 (at p. 426, point 1063). Unfortunately, this is one of the few years for which complete statistical information is available.

[32] Winter, G., *Reforming the Sources and Categories of European Union Law: A summary*, in Winter, G., *Sources and Categories of European Union Law: a Comparative and Reform Perspective* (Nomos 1996), at pp. 22–23. According to Article 249 EC (2003): '[a] decision shall be binding in its entirety upon those to whom it is addressed.' Cf. also Article 230(4) EC (2003).

[33] Excluded also are so-called *corrigenda* (corrections to the text of a legal act, caused for example by an error of translation, which do not amount to amendments) and a number of regulations exceptionally adopted by the European Central Bank.

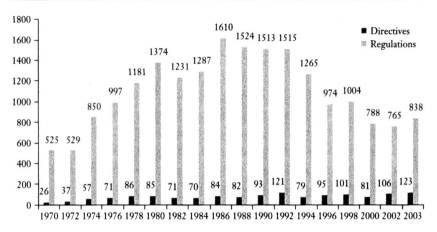

Figure 1.1   Total 1970–2003

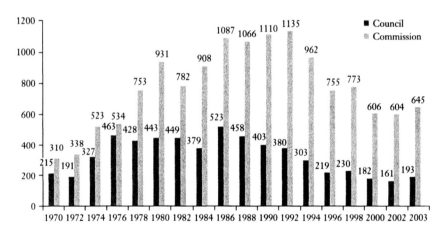

Figure 1.2   Regulations 1970–2003

comparison with the proportion of legislation adopted by the Commission. In 1970 the Council adopted 41% of the regulations and 92% of the directives. Thirty-three years later, in 2003, the Council adopted only 23% of the regulations and slightly less than 50% of the directives.

In an attempt to enhance the understanding of the qualitative difference, the focus shall be on the regulations and directives adopted in 2003. The limited ambition is, first, to make a formal determination of the subject-matter involved and, second, to comment on the content in general by means of some observations. A more detailed explanation of the content in two specific cases will be presented further on (see below 1.3.1).

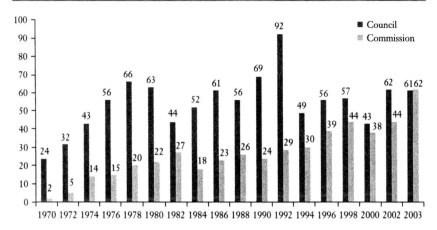

Figure 1.3 Directives 1970–2003

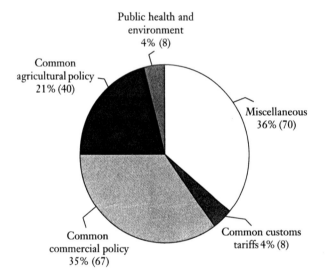

Figure 1.4 Council Regulations 2003 (193)

In order to make a formal determination of the subject-matter involved, a starting point has been taken in the so-called legal basis (stated in the preamble of each legal act). This refers to the specific provision of the EC Treaty and, thus, the main field of co-operation, from which the necessary competence has been derived.[34] Unsurprisingly, the assessment shows that all regulations and directives adopted by the

---

[34] The legal basis shall be indicated in the preamble of all legislation. See Article 253 EC (2003) and Case 45/86 *Commission v Council* [1987] ECR 1493.

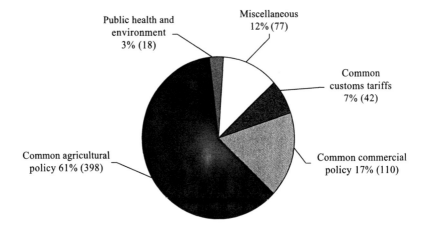

Figure 1.5 Commission Regulations 2003 (645)

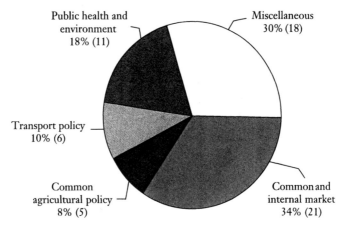

Figure 1.6 Council Directives 2003 (61)

Commission in 2003 were adopted in exercise of implementing powers conferred on it by the Council. This follows from the fact that the relevant legal basis only refers to the EC Treaty indirectly, via an earlier act adopted by the Council. Therefore, before it is possible to make a formal determination of the subject-matter involved, the legal basis of that underlying act has to be identified. Also this time the assessment has been based on data from CELEX (see Figures 1.4–1.7).

A number of observations may be made. Particularly interesting for our present purposes is the fact that there is a fairly even distribution between

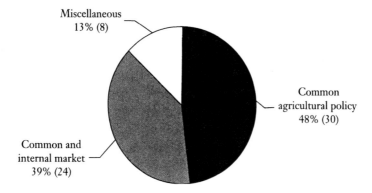

Miscellaneous
13% (8)

Common
agricultural policy
48% (30)

Common and
internal market
39% (24)

Figure 1.7   Commission Directives 2003 (62)

acts adopted by the Council and acts adopted by the Commission. This confirms the general validity of the principle of division of responsibility and the claim that the Council is expected to pass on part of its responsibility for adoption of legislation to the Commission (and that they are both active, therefore, in the same fields of co-operation). Differences relate instead to the type of legal instrument. Even if the EC Treaty, normally, leaves the choice of legal instrument open, a clear preference can be seen for regulations in some fields of co-operation and directives in others. This highlights the fact that the formal characteristics of each type of legal instrument differ and, above all, that the directive, in comparison with the regulation, is intended to 'leave to the national authorities the choice of form and methods.'[35] Apparently this is something which it is considered more important to ensure in some fields than others.[36]

---

[35] See Article 249 EC. It should be pointed out, however, that despite their formal differences, in practice, the distinction between regulations and directives has become rather blurred. That, indeed, is the result of a number of legal principles introduced by the Court of Justice which all give directives effects similar to those of regulations (cf. above Ch 1, n 9) but it is also the result of the way in which many regulations and directives are drafted. According to Antonio Tizzano, 'increasingly often nowadays the acts of the institutions do not correspond in practice to the classification laid down by the Treaty . . . the fundamental distinction itself between "regulations" and "directives" has not only become attenuated, but in certain respects has even disappeared.' See Tizzano, A., The Instruments of Community Law and the Hierarchy of Norms, in *The Treaty on European Union: Suggestions for Revision* (T.M.C. Asser Instituut 1996), at pp. 168–169. See also Winter, above Ch 1, n 32, at p. 50.

[36] Cf. Kapteyn, P. J. G. and VerLoren van Themaat, P., *Introduction to the Law of the European Communities* (Kluwer Law International 1998), at p. 189. Here it is explained that '[t]he question whether, and in what form, [the Institutions] may adopt acts will depend on the definition of the

The assessment shows that no field of co-operation has generated more legislation than the common agricultural policy. Often a link to the common agricultural policy can also be found in legislation adopted in other fields. So, for example, is it not unusual that legislation adopted in the field of the common customs tariffs concerns import quotas for tomatoes or that legislation adopted in the field of the common commercial policy concerns arrangements for trade in bananas. Certainly no less significant, in legislation adopted in the field of the common agricultural policy a link can often be found to other fields, such as consumer protection or free movement of goods. It may be noted in this respect that the Court of Justice has repeatedly explained that the choice of legal basis and, thus, the field in which formal competence to adopt legislation will be found, 'must rest on objective factors which are amenable to judicial review.'[37] But this is complicated by the fact that the 'objective factors' are not always so easy to discern. In reality the choice of legal basis entails a considerable discretion and it would seem that it is often procedural rather than substantive preconditions that are decisive for the choice of legal basis. One obvious incentive for placing legislation within the field of the common agricultural policy rather than the field of consumer protection or free movement of goods is that this makes it possible to limit the involvement of the European Parliament.[38]

powers conferred upon them in specific Articles of the Treaties. If the specific Articles in the Treaties or in regulations do not mention one or more of the three legal instruments by name, the interpretation of those Articles will be the basis for determining whether an act adopted there under may have the character of a regulation, a directive, or a decision.' It may be observed that the number of Articles in the EC Treaty which do not mention one or more of the three legal instruments by name has increased drastically, over the years and, therefore, that there is now much room for choice. See Weatherill, S. and Beaumont, P., *EU Law: the Essential Guide to the Legal Workings of the European Union* (Penguin Books 1999), at pp. 150–153 and Appendix at pp. 1065–1070.

[37] See e.g. Case C-271/94 *European Parliament v Council* [1996] ECR I-1689, paragraph 14. As explained by the Court, those 'objective factors' include in particular the aim and content of the measure. See e.g. Case C-300/89 *Commission v Council* [1991] ECR I-2867, paragraph 10; and Case C-426/93 *Germany v Council* [1995] ECR I-3723, paragraph 29.

[38] Cf. Case C-269/97 *Commission v Council* [2000] ECR I-2257 (Judgment of 4 April 2000): for a study of the logic underlying the choice of legislation in a specific field of co-operation see Snyder, above Ch 1, n 5. See, in general, Cullen, H. and Worth, A. C., Diplomacy by Other Means: the use of Legal Basis Litigation as a Political Strategy by the European Parliament and Member States (1999) 36 *CMLRev* 1243.

Even if it has not been specified in the charts, it should be made clear that the Council had to adopt 70% of the directives (43) and 17% of the regulations (33) in accordance with the so-called co-decision procedure (see below 4.3.2.3). Quite logically, these can all be referred to those fields of co-operation where that procedure had to be applied. The co-decision procedure provides the European Parliament with a rather extensive right to participation and the political importance of matters dealt with is well-reflected in many of the directives it gave rise to in 2003. Examples are Directive 03/102/EC relating to the protection of pedestrians and other vulnerable road users before and in the event of a collision with a motor vehicle; Directive 03/42/EC on occurrence reporting in civil aviation; and Directive 03/33/EC on the approximation of the laws, regulations, and administrative provisions of the Member States relating to the advertising and sponsorship of tobacco products.[39]

Furthermore, it should be made clear that the Council made quite frequent use of the possibility to exercise implementing powers itself. This, it may be recalled, is something which should only happen in 'specific cases' (see above 1.1.1). The assessment shows that 63 of the 193 Council regulations and one of the 61 Council directives had their legal basis in a provision of another regulation or directive adopted by the Council and not, directly, in a provision of the EC Treaty.

Proceeding, then, to some general observations with respect to substance, it should be made clear that several regulations and directives adopted by the Commission deal with matters of unambiguous 'legislative bearing'. Two older examples of this will be examined below (see below 1.3.1). But most typically, regulations and directives adopted by the Commission have a content which is technical and intended for application in a routine manner. One example of this can be found in a considerable number of regulations that control the sale by national authorities of agricultural stocks (the so-called mountains of beef, etc.).[40]

---

[39] See, respectively, European Parliament and Council Directive 03/102/EC of 17 November 2003 relating to the protection of pedestrians and other vulnerable road users before and in the event of a collision with a motor vehicle (OJ 2003 L 321/15), European Parliament and Council Directive 03/42/EC of 13 June 2003 on occurrence reporting in civil aviation (OJ 2003 L 167/23), and European Parliament and Council Directive 03/33/EC of 26 May 2003 on the approximation of the laws, regulations and administrative provisions of the Member States relating to the advertising and sponsorship of tobacco products (OJ 2003 L 152/16).

[40] See e.g. Commission Regulation 1034/03 of 17 June 2003 on periodical sales by tender of beef held by certain intervention agencies (OJ 2003 L 150/21), at pp. 21–23.

Another example can be found in a number of directives intended to adapt, continuously, regulations adopted by the Council to technical or scientific progress.[41]

The fact that regulations and directives adopted by the Commission have a content which is technical and intended for routine application does not necessarily mean that they do not have a 'legislative bearing'. Although refraining here from any attempt to deal with the matter in a more systematic manner, it should be pointed out that it is not unusual that the content of regulations and directives adopted by the Council is rather brief and built up around the clause by which responsibility is transferred to the Commission. An illustration can be taken from Directive 70/373/EEC on the introduction of methods of sampling and analysis for the official control of feedingstuffs (cf. below 3.3.2.2).[42] Contrary to what the title may lead one to believe this does not say so much about the methods of sampling and analysis. After having established an obligation for the Member States to comply with the methods, the responsibility for actually adopting them is transferred to the Commission. Acting in compliance with that arrangement, the Commission has on a regular basis adopted and adjusted the methods of sampling and analysis (thus exercising its powers of 'implementation'). An example from 2003 is Directive 03/126/EC.[43] Even if this type of implementing legislation has a content which is technical and intended for application in a routine manner is it really less important than the legislation it is implementing?

1.2.2   *The role of committees*

The initial assertion that the committee system has become a funda-mental feature of all fields of co-operation is manifestly confirmed by the assessment of regulations and directives adopted in 2003. Only 26 of 707 regulations and directives adopted by the Commission had come about

---

[41] See e.g. Commission Directive 03/83/EC of 24 September 2003 adapting to technical progress Annexes II, III and VI to Council Directive 76/768/EEC on the approximation of the laws of the Member States relating to cosmetic products (OJ 2003 L 238/23) at pp. 23–27.

[42] See Council Directive 70/373/EEC, below Ch 3, n 119.

[43] See Commission Directive 03/126/EC of 23 December 2003 on the analytical method for the determination of constituents of animal origin for the official control of feedingstuffs (OJ 2003 L 339/78).

without it having been required to follow a committee procedure. The assessment shows also that a total number of 78 committees were involved.[44] Thirty-nine of these operated (exclusively or mainly) in accordance with the management committee procedure and 36 (exclusively or mainly) in accordance with the regulatory committee procedure. Not more than three committees operated (exclusively) in accordance with the advisory committee procedure.[45]

Taking a brief look at the relationship between the type of committee procedure and the field of co-operation, it may be noted, first, that two of the three committees which operated (exclusively) in accordance with the advisory committee procedure were involved in the adoption of legislation relating to the field of common and internal market, and one was involved in the adoption of legislation falling within the field of economic and social cohesion. Only 12 of the 39 committees which operated (exclusively or mainly) in accordance with the management committee procedure were not involved in the adoption of legislation within the field of the common agricultural policy. Of the 36 committees which operated (exclusively or mainly) in accordance with the regulatory committee procedure only nine were involved in the adoption of legislation in the field of the common agricultural policy; 10 were involved in the adoption of legislation in the field of the common or internal market, and two were involved in the adoption of legislation relating to the field of public health and the environment. It may be noted, also, that the regulatory committee procedure was that which was prescribed by legislation in all cases where directives were adopted.[46]

Finally it should be pointed out that the overall impression with respect to the way in which the responsibility for exercise of implementing powers has been dealt with in regulations and directives adopted

---

[44] Presumably, this means that the activities of most comitology committees relate to matters which are being dealt with in other forms of legal instrument than regulations and directives (thus falling outside the scope of the current assessment). Cf. the Report from the Commission on the working of committees in 2002 (OJ 2003 C 223 E), at pp. 16–59. This lists altogether 257 comitology committees in operation that year.

[45] It should be pointed out that a fourth type of procedure, the so-called safeguard procedure (see below 4.2.2.2 and 4.4.2.2), was always used in combination with other procedures, typically the regulatory committee procedure.

[46] It should be pointed out that in at least one case the committee involved, the Standing Committee for Plant Health, operated exceptionally in accordance with the advisory committee procedure. See Council Directive 91/414/EEC of 15 July 1991 concerning the placing of plant protection products on the market (OJ 1991 L 230/1).

by the Council during 2003 is that this differs depending upon the degree of participation by the European Parliament. In those, relatively few, cases where the co-decision procedure applied, the matter was either not regulated at all (i.e. no explicit arrangement for exercise of implementing powers, presumably leaving it to national authorities)[47] or regulated very carefully, in a number of detailed provisions.[48]

1.3   The committee system: a schematic description

1.3.1   The starting point for a closer study

In order to provide some basic understanding of the way in which the committee system actually functions, two pieces of implementing legislation will be taken as the starting point for an empirical study. Following a brief explanation of the content of that legislation, the experience of the Swedish representatives involved in the underlying negotiations will be summed up and structured in the form of a schematic description. Thus representing a very typical situation, the first piece of legislation was adopted by the Commission in collaboration with a committee following the management committee procedure (see below 1.1.2). The second piece of legislation, by contrast, was the result of one of those rare situations in which the Commission failed to secure the support of a committee following the regulatory committee procedure and, therefore, it was adopted by the Council (see below 1.1.2).

The first piece of implementing legislation, Commission Regulation 494/98/EC laying down detailed rules for the application of minimum administrative sanctions in the framework of the system for identification and registration of bovine animals,[49] was adopted by the Commission on the basis of a responsibility conferred upon it in Council Regulation 820/97/EC

---

[47]   See e.g. European Parliament and Council Directive 03/54/EC of 26 June 2003 concerning common rules for the internal market in electricity (OJ 2003 L 176/37).

[48]   See e.g. European Parliament and Council Directive 03/6/EC of 28 January 2003 on insider dealing and market manipulation (market abuse) (OJ 2003 L 96/16).

[49]   See Commission Regulation 494/98/EC of 27 February 1998 laying down detailed rules for the implementation of Council Regulation 820/97/EC as regards the application of minimum administrative sanctions in the framework of the system for the identification and registration of bovine animals (OJ 1998 L 60/78).

(which, in turn, was adopted on the basis of what is now Article 37 EC: a provision relating to the common agricultural policy).[50]

The overall objective of Council Regulation 820/97/EC was to re-establish stability in the market in beef and beef products after the first wave of the so-called mad cow crisis. In the Preamble the need is emphasized to ensure rapid and efficient exchange of information and, at the same time, improve the transparency of the conditions for production and marketing. The hope expressed is that this will help to encourage consumer confidence. Structurally, Council Regulation 820/97/EC is split into two parts or titles. The first lays down rules relating to the identification and registration of bovine animals at the production stage, and the second rules relating to the labelling of beef and beef products at the marketing stage.

Essentially, the part which will be focused on here, the first part, provides that the competent national authority shall set up a computerized database which will make it possible to trace the identity and the movements of all bovine animals. For that reason each keeper of animals is required to keep an up-to-date register in an approved format and to supply the competent authority with all information concerning the origin, identification, and, where appropriate, destination of animals which he has owned, kept, transported, marketed, or slaughtered. In addition to that, in order to permit movements to be traced, each keeper is required to make sure that his animals are identified by an ear-tag applied in each ear and accompanied by a passport.

In accordance with a specific provision inserted at the end of the first part of Council Regulation 820/97/EC, 'the Commission shall adopt detailed rules for the implementation' of the rules relating to identification and registration in accordance with a management committee procedure (a similar provision is found at the end of the second part).[51] Even if the scope of the responsibility thus conferred on the Commission is phrased in wide terms, it is emphasized that the 'detailed rules' it is expected to lead to shall cover certain matters in particular, such as the application of administrative sanctions.

---

[50] See Council Regulation 820/97/EC of 21 April 1997 establishing a system for the identification and registration of bovine animals and regarding the labelling of beef and beef products (OJ 1997 L 117/1). This was later replaced by European Parliament and Council Regulation 1760/00/EC of 17 July 2000 establishing a system for the identification and registration of bovine animals and regarding the labelling of beef and beef products (OJ 2000 L 204/1).

[51] See Article 10 of Council Regulation 820/97/EC, above Ch 1, n 50.

One of a number of implementing measures this has given rise to is Commission Regulation 494/98/EC.[52] In this the need is addressed for sanctions which should be applied by the competent authorities in situations 'where non-compliance with the conditions for the identification and registration of bovine animals leads to a presumption in particular of infringements of Community veterinary legislation which may endanger human and animal health.' Structurally, Commission Regulation 494/98/EC focuses on the establishment of two types of minimum administrative sanctions. The first, providing for a possibility to impose restrictions on the movement of an animal,[53] and the second, intended for more exceptional situations, providing that an animal shall be 'destroyed ... without compensation from the competent authority.'[54]

The second piece of implementing legislation, Council Regulation 1139/98/EC, was the product of a situation in which the measure envisaged by the Commission was not given the necessary support of a committee and the matter was, therefore, placed in the hands of the Council. The formal framework is found in Council Directive 79/112/EEC on the approximation of the laws relating to the labelling, presentation, and advertising of foodstuffs for sale to the ultimate consumer (adopted on the basis of what is now Article 94 of the EC Treaty, falling within the field of the common market).[55]

Like Council Regulation 820/97/EC Council Directive 79/112/EEC was also adopted with the overall objective of protecting consumers. But in the Preamble a number of parallel concerns are addressed. Perhaps most noteworthy, in that respect, is the need to resolve a situation where

[52] For other examples, see Commission Regulation 2628/97/EC of 29 December 1997 laying down detailed rules for the implementation of Council Regulation 820/97/EC as regards transitional provisions for the start-up period of the system for the identification and registration of bovine animals (OJ 1997 L 354/17); Commission Decision 99/693/EC of 5 October 1999 recognising the fully operational character of the Swedish database for bovine animals (OJ 1999 L 273/14); and Commission Regulation 2680/99/EC of 17 December 1999 approving a system of identification for bulls intended for cultural and sporting events (OJ 1999 L 326/16).

[53] See Article 1 of Commission Regulation 494/98/EC, above Ch 1, n 49.

[54] See Articles 2–4 of Commission Regulation 494/98/EC, above Ch 1, n 49.

[55] See Council Directive 79/112/EEC of 18 December 1978 on the approximation of the laws of the Member States relating to the labelling, presentation and advertising of foodstuffs for sale to the ultimate consumer (OJ 1979 L 33/1). This was later replaced by European Parliament and Council Directive 00/13/EC of 20 March 2000 on the approximation of the laws of the Member States relating to the labelling, presentation and advertising of foodstuffs (OJ 2000 L 109/29).

the differences between national rules impede the free movement of goods. Structurally, the directive can be said to impose an obligation on each Member State to introduce a prohibition against misleading labelling of foodstuffs and to establish basic rules for correct labelling. The responsibility for adoption of implementing measures, this time, is not set out in one specific provision but in several. Of particular relevance for our present purposes is a provision in which it is explained that supplementary and more detailed rules for correct labelling shall be possible to prescribe for certain types of foodstuffs (there is no explicit reference to the Commission as such). Acting on the basis of that provision, in 1997 the Commission prepared a draft regulation intended to establish labelling rules for foodstuffs produced from genetically modified soya or maize.[56]

But as already noted, the draft regulation prepared by the Commission was not given the necessary support of a comitology committee (operating in accordance with the regulatory committee procedure) and, therefore, the matter was placed before the Council. The immediate result of this was seen a few months later with the adoption of Council Regulation 1139/98/EC concerning the compulsory indication of the labelling of certain foodstuffs produced from genetically modified organisms.[57] Here, labelling rules were laid down which were less strict than those envisaged in the draft regulation that had been prepared by the Commission.[58] In the Preamble it is emphasized, again, that differences between national rules relating to labelling of the products concerned impede the free movement of goods and that there is a need, therefore, for uniform rules. Interestingly, an implicit reference to the matter of controversy can be found in the explanation that the rules finally agreed on

[56] See Draft Commission Regulation of 25 February 1997 concerning the compulsory indication on the labelling of certain foodstuffs produced from genetically modified organisms of particulars other than those provided for in Directive 79/112/EEC (SEC(97) 2253).

[57] See Council Regulation 1139/98/EC of 26 May 1998 concerning the compulsory indication on the labelling of certain foodstuffs produced from genetically modified organisms of particulars other than those provided for in Directive 79/112/EEC (OJ 1998 L 159/4).

[58] It may be noted that at the moment of adopting Council Regulation 1139/98/EC (see above Ch 1, n 57) the Council invited the Commission to supplement the new Regulation (through the adoption of rules relating to 'the problem of adventitious contamination'). This in turn led to the adoption of Commission Regulation 49/00/EC of 10 January 2000 amending Council Regulation 1139/98/EC concerning the compulsory indication on the labelling of certain foodstuffs produced from genetically modified organisms of particulars other than those provided for in Directive 79/112/EEC (OJ 2000 L 6/13).

'are no more burdensome than necessary but sufficiently detailed to supply consumers with the information they require.'

1.3.2   *The national experience*

In spite of the fact that the two pieces of implementing legislation which are presented above relate to completely different situations, much of the information provided by the national representatives involved in their adoption point at an identical experience. This will be used to make a schematic description of the functioning of the committee system. Although limited, strictly speaking, to the work of the two committees involved in the cases presented above (this was, in the case of Commission Regulation 494/98/EC, the so-called FEOGA Committee, and, in the case of Council Regulation 1139/98/EC, the so-called Standing Committee for Foodstuffs), it is submitted that the description can claim general validity and that derogations, to the extent they occur, should primarily be seen as simplified variants, intended to secure that matters of routine are given a speedy treatment.[59]

1.3.2.1   *The initiation of the process*

In contrast to what the legal rules seem to indicate, the role of a comitology committee in the process for adoption of implementing measures is not merely *reactive*, i.e. restricted to the question whether a draft text should be approved or not, but also *indicative* and the committee constitutes the forum for an ongoing dialogue between the Commission and the national administrations. Long before it is formally required to do so, the Commission will discuss with the representatives of the national administrations if there is a need to proceed with a matter and, if so, what should be done.[60]

---

[59] It should be pointed out, in support of that submission, that the study referred to above (see above Ch 1, n 29) was subject to an official hearing in which the accuracy of the findings was confirmed by a number of high-ranking officials representing Swedish ministries and administrative agencies. The general validity of the schematic description has also been confirmed by various representatives of the Community Institutions. Furthermore, most points in the description have been identified in other studies. See e.g. Joerges and Neyer, above Ch 1, n 28; and Falke and Winter, above Ch 1, n 11. Furthermore, a follow-up study was conducted in 2004 in which the findings of the previous study were confirmed.

[60] Cf. Joerges and Neyer, above Ch 1, n 28, at p. 279. Here it is concluded, with respect to the Standing Committee for Foodstuffs that '[p]oints which are bound to arise in the foreseeable

The fact that the Commission has the formal right of initiative is of little importance and it is not likely to push a matter which is not given sufficient support in a committee, nor is it likely to stand in the way of a matter which is.[61] In practice, therefore, the process for adoption of implementing measures is often triggered by the representatives of the national administrations themselves. Put in the words of a Swedish representative: 'it is common knowledge that if one wants to influence a matter, one should write the proposal oneself and submit it to the Commission in good time.'

Within the committee, representatives of the national administrations are organized in delegations, each of which is considered to be one member. The delegations normally contain two people each: one designated as 'representative' and another as 'accompanying expert'.[62] Apparently, the main significance of this distinction is related to budgetary rules and the expenditures for the far from infrequent meetings (even if most contacts are maintained in letters or, increasingly, by e-mail[63]).[64]

future are handled at an early stage and they can still be quite openly discussed. Where serious objections against proposals are raised, decisions will be postponed. Even delegations of Member States tend to use the Standing Committee for Foodstuffs as a forum for an exchange of views on new and unsettled issues.'

[61] Cf. Joerges and Neyer, above Ch 1, n 28, at p. 279.

[62] See Article 6(1) of the Standard Rules of Procedure of 6 February 2001 for committees set up under Council Decision 99/468/EC (OJ 2001 C 38/3).

[63] Cf. Article 13 of the Standard Rules of Procedure, above Ch 1, n 62.

[64] In the case of the Standing Committee for Foodstuffs and the FEOGA Committee— which are both relatively 'busy'—meetings are organized on a regular basis, often once per week. It would seem that only costs relating to the participation of a representative are borne by the Community (the Commission). This means that costs relating to the participation of an accompanying expert have to be paid nationally. The distinction between representatives and accompanying experts may also be relevant for the organization of work within each national delegation. In this respect it may be noted that as far as the Swedish administration is concerned the 'representative' is typically an employee of a governmental ministry and the 'expert' an employee of a specialized authority or agency. The agency involved was, in the case of Commission Regulation 494/98/EC, the National Board for Agriculture (*Jordbruksverket*), and, in the case of Council Regulation 1139/98/EC, the National Food Administration (*Livsmedelsverket*). For an overview of the Swedish system for public administration, see Sterzel, F., Public Administration, in Tiberg, H. and Sterzel, F. (Eds.), *Swedish Law—a Survey* (Juristförlaget 1994), at pp. 74–77; and Ragnemalm, H., Administrative Justice in Sweden, in Wade, W., Ragnemalm, H., and Strauss, P. L., *Administrative Law: the Problem of Justice Volume I* (Giuffrè 1991), at pp. 252–253. For an overview of the relationship between the Swedish system for public administration and Community law, see Bernitz, U., Sweden and the European Union: on Sweden's implementation and application of European law (2001) 38 *CMLRev* 903.

All formal contacts with and within the committee pass through its Chairman. The Chairman is a person appointed by the Commission, typically a Head of Division or Unit in the relevant Directorate-General, backed up by two or more assistants. Unlike the full members of the committee—the national delegations—the Chairman has no voting rights[65] and his or her responsibility relates to a set of administrative tasks: to prepare and host meetings, to send invitations and distribute documentation, to keep protocols, to communicate with the European Parliament, and reply to requests for access to information.[66] The fact that the Chairman, and thus the Commission, has no formal power to control the actual deliberations was emphasized by the representatives interviewed, all of which shared the view that the 'negotiations are run by the delegations themselves.' But at the same time it was admitted that the Chairman still has a certain scope to influence the result of the deliberations through, for example, agenda-setting, mediating, and summing-up.

With respect to the routines of the representatives of the national administrations, which of course may vary, some important information can be obtained from the Swedish Government's Guidelines for the Administration of EU-matters. Here the need is addressed for the Member States to defend their national interests in all situations and it is stressed, therefore, how important it is that all Swedish representatives are given adequate and precise instructions (no distinction being made between 'representatives' in the more narrow sense and 'accompanying experts').[67] As follows from this rather detailed document, the responsibility for appointment of representatives and for issuing their instructions lies with the Ministry in charge of a particular field of co-operation. Furthermore, in order to ensure that the Government is well-informed about matters being dealt with in committees, the Ministry shall also make sure that it has received a written report within 24 hours after a meeting has ended.

1.3.2.2   *The preparation of a draft text*

If the Commission and a committee agree to proceed with a specific matter and initiate the process for adoption of implementing measures,

---

[65] See Article 2 of Council Decision 87/373/EEC, below Ch 4, n 48; and Articles 3 to 5 of Council Decision 99/468/EC, below Ch 4, n 275.

[66] See the Standard Rules of Procedure, above Ch 1, n 62. Cf. the statement made by the Commission in Case T-188/97, below Ch 4, n 310.

[67] See the Guidelines for the Administration of EU-matters, above Ch 1, n 23, at pp. 4–5.

the task of preparing a draft text is entrusted to a so-called working group (this was, in the case of Commission Regulation 494/98/EC, the Working Group for Veterinary Controls and, in the case of Council Regulation 1139/98/EC, the Working Group for Novel Foods). Unfortunately, the formal status of a working group is far from clear. In the view of the Swedish representatives, it is an integral part of the Commission (as opposed to the committee which they perceive as free-standing). The Commission, by contrast, seems to see the working group as being placed under the auspices of the committee (which the Commission also perceives as free-standing).[68] Quite clearly, the reason for this is that also the members of a working group—formally designated 'experts'—are representatives of the national administrations and that the Commission is far from happy to be functionally associated with and, indeed, legally accountable for their work.[69]

Importantly, the experts of a working group, typically two representatives from each Member State, are not appointed *ad personam* but as exchangeable emissaries: the decisive factor is not their personal knowledge but the assistance one can count on from the national authorities to which the experts belong. This means that the composition of a working group can vary depending on the matter dealt with. It would appear that most Governments pick their representatives in a working group from the authority or agency which is considered to have specialized knowledge of the field involved.[70] This was confirmed in the case of Commission Regulation 494/98/EC (where the Swedish experts in the Working Group for Veterinary Controls came from the National Board for Agriculture). But in the case of Council Regulation 1139/98/EC one of the two Swedish experts came from the Ministry of Agriculture and the other from the National Food Administration. The main reason for this was that matters dealt with were considered to have political

[68] See Article 7 of the Standard Rules of Procedure, above Ch 1, n 62. Cf. also Falke and Winter, above Ch 1, n 11, at p. 566.

[69] In practical terms, when a so-called meeting of experts shall be convened, the Chairman sends an invitation to the Governments' Permanent Representations which is then passed on to the relevant national authority.

[70] See, for an identical conclusion, Falke and Winter, above Ch 1, n 11, at p. 566. Cf. also Peter Van der Knaap who claims that Commission expert groups consist primarily (but not exclusively) of national officials. See Van der Knaap, P., Government by Committee: Legal Typology, Quantitative Assessment and Institutional Repercussions of Committees in the European Union, in Pedler, R. H. and Schaefer, G. F. (Eds.), *Shaping European Law and Policy: the Role of Committees and Comitology in the Political Process* (European Institute of Public Administration 1996), at p. 86.

consequences which 'required different considerations than those the technical agencies are best suited to deal with.'

On the basis of the information a working group accumulates through its experts a draft text is formulated. Discussions continue until agreement has been reached on a text which is supported by everyone and it is not unusual that a test-vote is made to get a 'clear picture' of the situation. It is considered extremely important to find solutions that all members, from all Member States, can be satisfied with. Apparently, the spirit is not only characterized by continuity—that any problem will have to be dealt with sooner or later—but also by professional pride, mutual respect, and even friendship. The Chairman, here also a representative from the Commission, is not excluded: in contrast to his or her colleague in the committee the Chairman of a working group is actively involved in the deliberations. Here, the lack of formal voting rights makes less difference and his or her ability to influence the content of the text is not insignificant.

1.3.2.3   *The approval of implementing legislation*

Once adopted in a working group, the draft text is passed on to the Chairman of the committee who will then distribute it to the national delegations (together with an invitation to the meeting in which they shall give their opinion).[71] The time before the meeting is used by the national representatives in the committee to double-check with their colleagues in the working group that the draft text has not been 'enriched' with new substantive elements on its way from the working group to the committee (i.e. elements introduced by the Chairman, by mistake or, worse, deliberately, as the result of undue pressure from one or a few national delegations or, indeed, his or her principal, the Commission).[72]

---

[71] According to Article 3(1) of the Standard Rules of Procedure (see above Ch 1, n 62), the Chairman of the committee shall send its members the draft text no later than 14 calendar days before the date of the meeting. A shorter period may however be set in urgent cases and where the implementing legislation must be applied immediately, i.e. in cases dealt with under the management committee procedure.

[72] It may be noted, in this context, that the Commission will consult its Legal Service before a draft text is finally presented to the committee and that this may cause changes of a less objectionable nature. If so, the text may be referred back to the working group. In order to avoid such delays, when legal problems are anticipated, the Legal Service may be asked to give its view at the preparatory stage.

Since the text has already been thoroughly dealt with in the working group it is not likely that any questions of controversy are still open when the committee meets to give its opinion. Therefore, the text is normally given consensual support and there is no need to enforce the vote. This explains the statistical fact that the situations in which the committee is unable to give the draft text presented by the Commission its support are 'virtually non-existent' (see above 1.1.3).

If, exceptionally, there would not be sufficient support in the committee for a draft text, the matter will most likely be referred back to the working group for further discussion. The vote is only used if progress is blocked by one or a few delegations or if the preconditions for action have changed (and there is a widespread feeling, therefore, that a matter ought to be dealt with at a higher political level).

1.3.3   The consultation of external parties

It follows from the description above that the functional core of the committee system is found in the activities of a working group. The working group provides a forum for colleagues of different nationalities, representing different administrative traditions, to meet in a spirit of mutual respect. From this it follows that it would not be opportune for the experts from one delegation to interfere with the habits of those from another and question the way in which they reach their opinion. The spirit of mutual respect extends to the question whether there is a need to take the views of 'outside' interests into consideration and, linked to this, the routines for consultation of external parties. If such consultation is made at all, its result and the evaluation thereof will only reach the working group as an integral part of the position taken by a delegation in the deliberations.

Against the background of the observation that, in principle, the committee system rests on the idea that the responsibility for consultation is left at the national level, it is noteworthy that an increasing number of arrangements have been made for consultation at the Community level. Today, these are often manifested in the procedural requirements that regulate activities in a specific field.[73] The exact nature

[73] Typically, such procedural requirements are laid down in legislation. See e.g. Council Directive 89/107/EEC of 21 December 1988 on food additives in foodstuffs intended for human consumption (OJ 1989 L 40/27). This confers upon the Commission a responsibility for exercise

of such requirements is far from clear and no real attempt will be made to explain it. This, indeed, is something which would require a book of its own.

Typically, the consultation of external parties at the Community level takes place within special 'consultative' or 'scientific' committees.[74] Thereby distinguishing themselves from the regular committees and working groups, these committees are set up by the Commission itself and it is also the Commission which appoints their members. Even if these committees 'provide an excellent source of expertise and knowledge from a wide range of national and sectorial specialists upon which the Commission can draw'[75] they cannot, by their very nature, claim any *right* to participate in the decision-making process.[76] The first

of implementing powers in co-operation with the so-called Standing Committee for Foodstuffs (in accordance with a regulatory committee procedure). Article 6 of the Directive provides that provisions 'that may have an effect on public health shall be adopted after consultation with the Scientific Committee for Food'. It should be noted also that the significance of consultation has been underlined by the Court of Justice. Perhaps most noteworthy in that respect is Case C-212/91 (see below Ch 1, n 76).

[74]   Cf. Article 8(1) of the Standard Rules of Procedure, above Ch 1, n 62. Here the possibility is envisaged for the Chairman of a committee and, presumably, also the Chairman of a Working Group 'to invite experts to talk on particular matters, at the request of a member or on his or her own initiative.' Most Commission consultative committees and expert groups can be found in fields where the dependence on technical knowledge and technical expertise is greatest (e.g. agriculture, nuclear safety and telecommunications). See Van der Knaap, above Ch 1, n 70, at p. 86.   [75]   See Van der Knaap, above Ch 1, n 70, at p. 86.

[76]   This, indeed, is underlined in the General Budget of the European Union where these committees are lumped together under the heading 'committees whose consultation is not compulsory for the Commission' (see e.g. above Ch 1, n 21). Cf. however Case C-212/91, *Angelopharm v Hamburg* [1994] ECR I-171, at paragraph 33. Here the Court stated that a comitology committee, the so-called Cosmetics Adaptation Committee, 'must, in the nature of things and apart from any provision laid down to that effect, be assisted by experts on scientific and technical issues delegated by the Member States.' The Court's statement has been hailed by some commentators as a new dawn in the integration of scientific expertise in social regulation 'designed to promote the adequacy of regulatory policies by ensuring that they take "the latest international research" into account.' See Joerges, C., Scientific Expertise in Social Regulation and the European Court of Justice: Legal Frameworks for Denationalized Governance Structures, in Joerges, C., Ladeur, K.-H., and Vos, E. (Eds.), *Integrating Scientific Expertise into Regulatory Decision-Making: National Traditions and European Innovations* (Nomos 1997), at p. 314. Cf. also Falke, J., Comitology and Other Committees: a Preliminary Empirical Assessment, in Pedler, R. H. and Schaefer, G. F. (Eds.), *Shaping European Law and Policy: the Role of Committees and Comitology in the Political Process* (European Institute of Public Administration 1996), at pp. 150–151; Vos, E., The Rise of Committees (1997) 3 *ELJ* 210, at p. 212; and Lenaerts, K. and Nuffel, P. van, *Constitutional*

type, the consultative committees, were used by the Commission in the early 1960s as a means to involve various interest groups in the integration of national agriculture policies (see below 2.2.2.1).[77] Presumably, the second type also, the scientific committees, has a long history. Support for that is found in a ruling from 1977 in which the Court observed that the Commission had established the so-called Scientific Committee for Animal Nutrition: a consultative body of 'highly qualified scientists' not to be instructed by any government (see below 3.3.2.3).[78]

1.4 Striking the balance of powers

1.4.1 The development of the committee system: how and why?

It is submitted that the most important conclusion which can be drawn from the description above is that the role of comitology in the exercise of

---

Law of the European Union (Sweet & Maxwell 1999), at p. 466. But there are many reasons to be sceptical about this interpretation. A more balanced assessment is offered by Kieran Bradley, who argues that the Council (and the European Parliament) have accepted the authority of various consultation bodies but emphasizes that to the extent that such bodies must be involved in the process for adoption of implementing measures this is only 'because the Council has so determined, rather than because such a requirement is imposed by some revolutionary new principle of Community law against which the validity of such rules could be judged.' See Bradley, K., Institutional Aspects of Comitology: Scenes from the Cutting Room Floor, in Joerges, C. and Vos, E. (Eds.), *EU Committees: Social Regulation, Law and Politics* (Hart Publishing 1999), at pp. 81–83 and 86. For a similar conclusion, see Türk, A., The Role of the Court of Justice, in Andenaes, M. and Türk, A. (Eds.), *Delegated Legislation and the Role of Committees in the EC* (Kluwer Law International 2000), at pp. 240–245. Cf. also Case T-13/99 *Pfizer Animal Health SA v Council of the European Union* [2002] ECR II-3305 (Judgment of 11 September 2002), in particular paragraphs 262 and 270.

[77] On 18 July 1962 the Commission decided to set up consultation committees for all groups of agricultural products. See *Bulletin EEC* No 9/10-1962, at p. 62. Cf. below Ch 2, n 222. See also Lindberg, L., *The Political Dynamics of European Integration* (Oxford University Press 1963), at p. 237; *Bulletin EEC* 2-1959, at pp. 44–45 and *Bulletin EEC* 3-1959, at p. 59.

[78] More recent examples of these types of committees can be found in Commission Decision 98/235/EC of 11 March 1998 on the advisory committees dealing with matters covered by the common agricultural policy (OJ 1998 L 88/59); Commission Decision 95/260/EC of 13 June 1995 setting up a Consumer Committee (OJ 1995 L 162/37) and Commission Decision 97/579/EC of 23 July 1997 setting up Scientific Committees in the field of consumer health and food safety (OJ 1997 L 237/18).

implementing powers should not, in the first place, be thought of for voting requirements and mechanisms of political control but for the fact that it places the responsibility for deliberations in the hands of the national administrations. The functional core is found in the activities of a working group (which, in matters of routine management, may be performed by the committee itself). Here colleagues of different nationalities, representing different administrative traditions, meet in a spirit of mutual respect to agree on common solutions to their problems. The role of the Commission, within a working group but also within a committee, is rather that of a co-ordinator or mediator than a decision-maker.

Judging from the statistics, it is not only co-operation between the various national representatives that is functioning well but also that between the national representatives and the Commission. This, indeed, is confirmed by the low rate of cases where the draft text presented to a committee was not supported by a positive opinion (see above 1.1.3) and also by the general tendency that an ever growing proportion of legislation is being adopted by the Commission (see above 1.2.1). The conclusion is remarkable, since the legal rules which regulate their relationship are based on the assumption that there is a fundamental conflict of interests (see above 1.1.3).

In the light of the observation that the co-operation which takes place within the committee system is functioning well and, at the same time, rests on a legal ground built by people who fear a conflict of interests, this book will attempt to explain how the system has developed and why. The hope is that this, in turn, will make it possible to provide an adequate answer to the question of what comitology really is and, in particular, what place it has in the legal order established by the EC Treaty.

1.4.2   A contextual approach

Even though the book will end with a discussion on the future of comitology, its scientific ambition is strictly analytical. That this is a sufficient challenge has already been acknowledged by a number of legal scholars. Perhaps most forcefully, in that respect, Christian Joerges has argued that both law and political science appear to have difficulties in tackling comitology and Joseph Weiler has described it as 'a phenomenon which requires its very own science which no single person has mastered.'[79] Even if much has been written, in law as well as political science, about comitology, there is still a gap. To quite some extent, this is a result of the fact that the methodological tools and sources traditionally employed by these disciplines lead their masters to focus on *either* functional *or* formal aspects.

For most lawyers, a natural starting point is found in the legal rules underpinning the committee system and the formal preconditions for exercise of implementing powers. The idea of an institutional balance of powers is central. Starting with its early rulings, the Court of Justice has insisted that the Community legal order is characterized by a balance of powers: between the Community and the Member States but also within the Community, between its institutions.[80] As explained by the Court in Case C-70/88 *European Parliament v Council*, the EC Treaty has set up 'a system for distributing powers among the different Community institutions, assigning to each institution its own role in the institutional structure of the Community and the accomplishment of the tasks entrusted to the Community.'[81]

The idea of an institutional balance rests on the submission that each institution represents a particular aspect of the wider interest.[82] So, for example, the Court of Justice has explained that the power reflected by the European Parliament's right to be consulted before legislation is adopted 'represents an essential factor in the institutional balance intended by the Treaty. Although limited, it reflects at Community level the fundamental democratic principle that the peoples should take part in the exercise of powers through the intermediary of a representative assembly.'[83] Against the background of that submission, the Court has developed the idea of an institutional balance into a tool for constitutional control. According to the Court, '[o]bservance of the institutional balance means that each of the institutions must exercise its powers with due

---

[79] See Joerges and Neyer, above Ch 1, n 28, at p. 282; and Weiler, J. H. H., *European Democracy and Its Critics: Five Uneasy Pieces*, Harvard Jean Monnet Working Paper 1/95, at p. 6 (at internet http://www.jeanmonnetprogram.org/papers). See also Bradley, K., above Ch 1, n 76, at p. 76.

[80] See e.g. Case 9/56, below Ch 2, n 57, at p. 152.

[81] Case C-70/88 *European Parliament v Council* [1990] ECR I-2041, at p. 2072 (paragraph 21).

[82] See e.g. Case C-70/88, above Ch 1, n 81, p. 2073 (paragraph 26). See also Lenaerts and Nuffel, above Ch 1, n 76, at p. 42; Lenaerts, K., Constitutionalism and the Many Facets of Federalism (1990) 38 *AJCL* 205; and Craig, P., Democracy and Rule-making within the EC: an Empirical and Normative Assessment, in Craig, P. and Harlow, C. (Eds.), *Lawmaking in the European Union* (Kluwer Law International 1998).

[83] Case 138/79 (see below Ch 4, n 162), at p. 3360 (paragraph 33).

regard for the powers of the other institutions. It also requires that it should be possible to penalise any breach of that rule which may occur.'[84]

But as clear as this may seem, since the words in which the role of each institution has been laid down in the EC Treaty are not always precise, the exact point where the powers of one institution end and those of another begin is often difficult to ascertain. This, indeed, is underlined by the fact that the parties involved in cases of conflict tend to be equally firm believers in interpretations which are impossible to reconcile. To mention but one example here, in the debate which took place after the birth of the committee system, the idea of an institutional balance was used both to sustain and resist the demand that implementing powers conferred upon the Commission should be precisely circumscribed and leave no room for autonomous responsibility (see below 2.3.3.1 and 2.3.3.2).[85]

In the light of the above, the approach taken in this book is a contextual one. Although focusing on legal rules in the strict sense—legislation and judicial rulings—care will be taken to make it clear that legislation is a result of political negotiations and that the content of judicial rulings, sometimes, can only be fully understood in the light of those negotiations. Put more concretely, the question of how and why will be dealt with by trying to identify the positions taken by the major actors in the development of the committee system: the Governments, the Council, the European Parliament, the Commission, and the Court of Justice. The research is based on traditional sources of law—treaty texts, legislation, preparatory works (political initiatives and programmes, preparatory studies, proposals for legislation, etc),[86] and judicial rulings—but, in a somewhat unorthodox manner, the sources will be presented in a

---

[84] See Case C-70/88, above Ch 1, n 81, at p. 2072 (paragraph 22).

[85] According to the French Government, if this was not done 'the balance of powers, which is a feature of the institutional structure of the Community and a basic guarantee provided by the Treaty, would not be respected' (see below 2.3.3.2). At the same time Commission President Hallstein voiced his fear for what the consequences might be if the 'carefully arranged balance of powers ... were shifted' (see below 2.3.3.1). Cf. also the Commission's claim that 'the regulatory committee procedure would mean a modification of the institutional balance, and that the management of the veterinary policy will be rendered more difficult.' See *Europe* (bulletin quotidien) 28 February 1968.

[86] The question of the extent to which preparatory works are—and should be—used as a source of Community law has been given increasing attention by legal scholars the last few years. See e.g. Schønberg, S. and Frick, K., Finishing, Refining, Polishing: on the Use of *travaux préparatoires* as an Aid to the Interpretation of Community Legislation (2003) 28 *ELRev* 149.

chronological order, so as to make it possible to re-construct the process underlying the legal development. The general assessment covers the development of the committee system currently in force (1958–2000) and the most important events which have taken place since then, which may shape the future system, are only discussed in the final part on prospects.

The aim is to present all aspects which have been decisive for the development of the committee system. Much time and care have been spent to get the most relevant facts and to get them right. But the aim to present all aspects which have been decisive for development is only realistic if one permits oneself to make a number of simplifications with respect to the selection of facts. So, for example, it is not possible to give a full account of all events and insights which have driven the Community, at the various stages of its existence, to self-reflection and institutional reform. For this reason, it is not claimed that the story to be told is the entire story but that it is a credible story which can provide an adequate answer to the question of what comitology really is and, in particular, what place it has in the legal order established by the EC Treaty.

The skeleton around which the book has been built up is chronological or historical. This means that the facts on which it is based have not, in the first place, been sorted into categories but that they are presented together with other facts relating to the same stage of development. This goes for treaty texts, legislation, and preparatory works and also for judicial rulings: it has been considered highly appropriate to place the Court of Justice alongside all others actors involved in the development of the committee system. Only a relatively small number of all rulings involving comitology have been selected for study. The basic submission is that these rulings are the most important ones from an inter-institutional or constitutional point of view: that they involve matters of high principal significance and were given at a crucial stage of the development.

1.4.3   Outline

The book is divided into two main parts: a first part where the general development of the committee system is outlined and those aspects identified which must be considered to have been decisive (Chapters 2–4); and a second part where the conclusions are drawn that shall answer the question how and why (Chapter 5). Even if the first part is rather descriptive in character, it is based on a careful analysis. This is manifested in the selection and presentation of facts but also in the choice of direction: the problems, arguments, ideas, and sources which were reflected upon before the decision was taken where to proceed. Therefore, whether the reader feels that the analysis is clearly stated or not, the judgment over its quality follows from the judgment over the story-line.

Chapter 2 gives an account of the development of the committee system during the period which stretches from 1958 to 1970. This 'transitional period' contains the passage of the Community from a political dream to an institutional machinery that could run a common market. In those parts of the Chapter where more general aspects are addressed, the focus will be on the efforts made to accommodate national expectations and a rapidly growing awareness that co-operation would only be successful if terms could be found which were acceptable to all Governments. Parallel to this, the committee system was born. The direct reasons for this are examined in the context of the common agricultural policy: the field of co-operation which was immediately felt to be the touchstone for progress. Once it had been born the committee system rapidly grew in importance and spread to more and more fields of co-operation. In this respect, special attention will be given to 'the crisis of the empty chair' and the discussions which led to the Luxembourg Compromise and, then, the efforts that were made towards the end of the transitional period to intensify the existing co-operation.

Chapter 3 deals with the development of the committee system during the notorious years that started after the completion of the transitional period and ended with the first major reform: 1970 to 1985. For reasons which are not so easy to comprehend, this was widely conceived as the years of paralysis or even the Dark Ages. Even if no attempt will be made to provide a full explanation of the problems with which the Community was beset, some of the more important reasons will be identified. The focus will be on the Community's failure to deal with two new challenges: the project for establishment of an economic and monetary union and enlargement. The immediate relevance of this failure for the development of the committee system is that it forced the Community and its Member States to admit the need for refined procedures. As will be seen in this Chapter, this was a slow and painful process which was started cautiously with informal agreements but led to a full scale reform of the Treaty. Throughout the process, the use and abuse of the committee system was considered to be a key issue.

Chapter 4 covers the period 1985 to 2000 and the development of the committee system during the years that saw the old Community transform into a European Union. As will be seen in this Chapter, the exact nature of the new Union was far from clear but was something which had to be discussed and specified after it had come into existence. This fed the hopes of those who were not yet satisfied and made them fight even harder than before. No one fought harder than the European Parliament. Once it was given what it had always asked for—a real right to participate in the legislative process—it immediately used that right to get more and soon the European Union was ravaged by an inter-institutional battle. A breeding ground for this battle was found in the so-called Comitology Decision and the 'constitutional' arrangement for exercise of implementing powers as that had resulted from the 1985 reform of the Treaty. Quite naturally, this will be discussed in great detail. In particular, time will be spent to understand what positions were taken by each actor and why. It was not until 1999 that the much contested Comitology Decision was replaced by a new one which seemed to satisfy the European Parliament. This will be dealt with thoroughly.

Chapter 5 starts with a rather extensive summary. This, it is hoped, will make it possible to see a pattern with respect to the development of the committee system: the rather surprising consistency with which the actors involved have taken their positions. Importantly, it will also make it possible to see which actors and positions have dominated the development and, indeed, the crucial moments of change, when prior positions have been reconsidered or even abandoned. Even if some conclusions will be presented which concern more general aspects of the development of the committee system, the focus will be on the actors and their positions. Finally, the overall conclusions will be discussed in the context of some recent events which are likely to have implications for the future of comitology and, indeed, the legal order which it is a part of.

The Transitional Period

'There are no victors and vanquished: we can therefore rejoice'[1]

2.1 Introduction

2.1.1 The preconditions for establishment of a common market

The European Community came into being through the signing, in 1951, of the European Coal and Steel Community (ECSC) Treaty and, in 1957, of the European Economic Community (EEC) Treaty and the European Atomic Energy Community (EAEC) Treaty. In all these treaties, provision had been made for 'the creation of autonomous institutions possessing the power to develop the new structure independently of the participant states.'[2] But the important difference was that, in comparison with the rather limited range of activities covered by the ECSC Treaty and the EAEC Treaty, the EEC Treaty had a broader scope. Over wide areas it did no more than formulate guiding principles to serve as the basis for common policies which had to be worked out and then implemented with constant adjustment to day-to-day problems.

According to the EEC Treaty, its overall objectives were 'to promote throughout the Community a harmonious development of economic activities, a continuous and balanced expansion, an increase in stability, an accelerated raising of the standard of living and closer relations

---

[1] The Dutch Minister of Foreign Affairs, Joseph Luns, at the end of the Council's special session on 30 January 1966 (see below 2.3.4), quote in *Europe* (*bulletin quotidien*) 31 January 1966.

[2] Weatherill and Beaumont, above Ch 1, n 36, at p. 4.

between the States belonging to it.'[3] This was to be achieved progressively, by establishing a common market and by approximating national economic policies.[4] During the period which followed upon the entry into force of the EEC Treaty most efforts were directed towards establishing a common market.

However clear it may seem to some people exactly what constitutes a common market, this was not so clear in the case of the common market envisaged by the EEC Treaty. Politically, as well as legally, its most important aspect was not its substantive but rather its procedural meaning. The common market was to be established in three stages, each of four years.[5] Only after the completion of this so-called transitional period was the Community to be regarded as fully operational. Whatever the prior expectations had been—and, as will be seen, they certainly had not been the same in all camps—by the end of the transitional period, on 1 January 1970, the substantive meaning of the common market was only going to be the sum of achievements which had been made up to that date.[6] Numerous provisions of the EEC Treaty required more or less clearly defined measures to be adopted during the transitional period. Most of these were explicitly linked to the establishment and operation of the common market. There cannot be much doubt that the precision, or more often lack of precision, with which these provisions had been drafted was a result of the level of agreement which was reached at the time when they were negotiated.

One of the areas in which provisions had been most clearly defined was that concerning the establishment of a customs union.[7] In essence this meant that customs duties and other charges on trade between the Member States would have to be eliminated and that a common customs tariff should be applied to trade with non-Member States. Of the areas in which the provisions were less clear, those concerning the adoption of a common agricultural policy, a common commercial policy, and a common transport policy stand out.[8] While it was clearly stated that these policies had to be brought into force at the latest by the end of the

[3] See Article 2 EEC (1958).   [4] See Article 2 EEC (1958).

[5] See Article 8 EEC (1958).

[6] See, in general, Rambow, G., The End of the Transitional Period (1968–69) 6 *CMLRev* 434.

[7] See Articles 12–29 EEC (1958).

[8] See Articles 38–47 EEC (1958) in respect of the common agricultural policy; Articles 110–119 EEC (1958) in respect of the common commercial policy; and Articles 74–84 EEC (1958) in respect of the common transport policy.

transitional period, their actual substance had been left to be developed in legislation adopted by three Community Institutions: the Council of Ministers, the Commission, and the European Parliament.[9]

While the Council was the Institution in which the interests of each Member State were to be represented by its Government,[10] the Commission was designed to act in the general interest of the Community as such and its members, the Commissioners, were therefore expressly forbidden to seek or take any instructions from any Government or from any other body.[11] The European Parliament was to provide a direct link with 'the peoples of the States' as at the time, the MEPs were not directly elected but selected by the national parliaments.[12] In addition to the three Community Institutions assigned with the adoption of legislation a fourth Community Institution, the Court of Justice, was charged with the task of ensuring that the law was observed.[13]

In essence, the procedure for adoption of legislation reserved for the Commission the right to make proposals which the European Parliament was then entitled to discuss and comment upon.[14] Besides that rather humble task the European Parliament was entrusted with a responsibility for supervision of the Commission, for example by calling upon its members to account for their performance. The dominant Institution in the procedure for adoption of legislation was the Council, for in the majority of cases it alone was responsible for the final decision. Initially compelled to act by unanimity, at the start of the third stage of the transitional period the general rule for voting in the Council was supposed to shift to qualified majority. In the words of the 1961 General Report on the Activities of the European Communities:

... this institutional order rests—and this is its first main feature—on permanent co-operation between the Council, in which the six Governments are represented, and the Commission, which is an independent Community organ. The important economic policy decisions lie with Council, but as a rule it cannot act without a proposal from the Commission, that is to say without

---

[9] The term legislation is to be used in the rather wide sense in which it has come to be used by the Community Institutions themselves: to denote the binding measures listed in Article 249 EC (2003), i.e. regulations, directives, and decisions. Cf. above 1.2.1.

[10] See Article 146 EEC (1958).   [11] See Article 157 EEC (1958).

[12] See Article 137 EEC (1958).   [13] See Article 164 EEC (1958).

[14] For a detailed explanation of the so-called consultation procedure, see Kapteyn and VerLoren van Themaat, above Ch 1, n 36, at pp. 419–424.

Community initiative. More and more the decisions of the Council will have to be taken by majority vote, and this will increase its effectiveness. However, it will be able to take such decisions only on a proposal put forward by the Commission, so that its vote will not express a coalition of national interests, but the approval of the Community interest. Despite the pre-eminent position of the Council, the Commission itself—and this is a second main feature of the system—is not subordinated to the Council. It is to the Parliament, representing the peoples of the Community, that it is responsible. It is the Parliament alone that can oblige it to resign. The exclusive control of the Parliament guarantees the independence of the Commission and also ensures that there shall be no arbitrary decisions or lack of impartiality on its part.[15]

Since the establishment and, indeed, operation of a common market was thought to include the adoption of a common agricultural policy, a common commercial policy, and a common transport policy, the negotiations required to give these policies concrete meaning was at the top of the agenda from the very start. In part, this was because some of the most important problems which it had not been possible to solve before 1957 could no longer be avoided. It was not long before some progress was noted. As reported by the Commission, the year 1960–61 was 'the year of the common policies.'[16] The Commission had devoted a great part of its activity to the preparation or finalizing of proposals on the means to be used in the field of common policies and the concrete measures to be undertaken.

2.1.2 The national expectations

Even before the EEC Treaty entered into force in 1958 several attempts had been made to liberalize international trade. Most importantly, the International Monetary Fund (IMF) had been established in 1944, the General Agreement on Tariffs and Trade (GATT) in 1947 and the Organisation for Economic Co-operation and Development (OECD) in 1948. There was no doubt that these efforts were all going to be considerably affected when some of the largest and oldest industrialized countries in the world got together to form a common market. The

---

[15] Fourth General Report on the Activities of the European Economic Community 1961 (Office for Official Publications 1962), at pp. 18–19.

[16] General Report 1961, above Ch 2, n 15, at p. 12.

preferential treatment which the Member States of the Community were
to grant each other would inevitably lead to diversions of trade and much
trade would increasingly shift to other Member States. But this 'seclu-
sionist' effect was mitigated by a 'growth' effect: since the common
market was expected to stimulate economic activity in general, it was
hoped that in the long run it would also improve trade with non-Member
States.[17] Which of the two conflicting effects would be the stronger
depended on what type of commercial policy the Community pursued.

Against the background of the international efforts for trade liberalization, the Governments, when signing the EEC Treaty, had declared
their intention 'to contribute, by means of a common commercial policy,
to the progressive abolition of restrictions on international trade.'[18] In
spite of this, the Community was subject to severe attacks from its
Member States' international trading partners—in particular the United
States—and constantly had to defend itself against charges of protectionism.[19] Whether such criticism was justified or not, there can be no
doubt that it was very difficult for the Member States to rally round the
type of common commercial policy which their partners expected. The
reasons were manifold. Perhaps most importantly, there were great differences in their own expectations, differences which they had not yet
discovered how to reconcile.

Germany and the Benelux Countries were all poor in raw materials
and had traditionally been dependent on foreign trade.[20] Germany was
also the Community's largest food importer and much of its imports, for
example grain purchased from Argentina, were tied to agreements for
exports of manufactured products. As a consequence the general level of
tariff protection was very low in both Germany and the Benelux
Countries. France and Italy, by contrast, were comparatively self-
sufficient and had maintained high tariffs and rigid import quotas. While
Germany and the Benelux Countries expected that the introduction of
customs union would increase trade with the other Member States and at
the same time make them stronger in the international market, France
and Italy were anxious to 'cushion the shock of adjustment.'[21] They

[17] See Everling, U., Legal Problems of the Common Commercial Policy in the European
Economic Community (1966–67) 4 *CMLRev* 141, at pp. 144–146.
[18] The Preamble of the EEC Treaty (1958). See also Articles 18 and 110 EEC (1958).
[19] See Lindberg, above Ch 1, n 77, at p. 207.
[20] See Lindberg, above Ch 1, n 77, at pp. 111–116 and 267.
[21] Lindberg, above Ch 1, n 77, at pp. 167, 187 and 268.

hoped instead that the establishment of a common market could secure outlets for their agricultural surpluses and facilitate structural reforms.

Under heavy pressure from farmers' organizations, France in particular refused to take any steps towards completion of customs union if agreement could not first be reached on the adoption of a common agricultural policy.[22] It was soon realized therefore that the successful resolution of problems relating to the common agricultural policy was a touchstone for progress in other areas. As emphasized by the Commission,

[a]ny faltering in this field would risk compromising achievements elsewhere, just as it might also jeopardise that balanced expansion of the Community economy which implementation of the Treaty is intended to bring about.[23]

2.2 The birth of the committee system

2.2.1 *The common agricultural policy: a touchstone for progress*

The EEC Treaty clearly stated that trade in agricultural products should be subject to the same provisions relating to the establishment and operation of the common market that applied to any other type of product.[24] At the same time, trade in agricultural products had been singled out so as to permit additional considerations of a predominantly social nature.[25] Thus the EEC Treaty required the adoption of a common agricultural policy including the establishment of a common organization of agricultural markets.[26] The actual contents of that policy had been left to be discussed in an Intergovernmental Conference to be held immediately after the EEC Treaty's entry into force.[27]

The Conference was held in the Italian town of Stresa between 3 and 11 July 1958 and resulted in the drawing up of a number of general principles.[28] Against the background of these the Commission was then asked to submit proposals for legislation to be adopted by the Council

---

[22] See Lindberg, Ch 1, n 77, at p. 193.

[23] General Report 1961, above Ch 2, n 15, at p. 12.   [24] See Article 38 EEC (1958).

[25] See Article 39 EEC (1958).   [26] See Article 40 EEC (1958).

[27] See Article 43 EEC (1958).

[28] See First General Report on the Activities of the European Economic Community 1958 (Office for Official Publications 1959), at pp. 76–83.

in the form of regulations, directives, or decisions. But when the Commission presented a first draft on 11 December 1959, it became clear that there were several aspects on which the Council was far from ready to agree.[29] This in turn led to a deadlock which could only be resolved after a decision had been taken to accelerate the reduction of customs duties.[30] On the basis of fresh indications the Commission submitted its definite proposals on 30 June 1960.[31] Some of the more obvious changes concerned its own role in the future management of the common agricultural policy. The meaning and implications of this will be returned to below.

When the Council met again, this time to discuss the revised proposals, fundamental differences of opinion persisted. In order to avoid any new deadlock a decision was therefore taken to set up a Special Committee on Agriculture and to entrust it with further negotiations.[32] The initiative was still to lie with the Commission which would continue to present the dossier. As a result of this, a conclusion was reached on 20 December 1960 that the common agricultural policy should be based on a system of levies and that the Commission could go ahead with the drafting of regulations specifying the products to which the system would apply.[33] Although the Commission completed its work by the summer of 1961, agreement could only be reached in the Council on 14 January 1962.[34] On the same day a decision was taken to pass to the second stage of the transitional period.[35] This was a major achievement. As noted in the *Financial Times*, '[t]he fact that the six governments were able to reach a compromise shows that in the last

[29] For a summary of the Commission's initial proposal, see *Bulletin EEC* 5-1959, at pp. 17–28.

[30] See Decision 60/912/EEC of the Representatives of the Government of the Member States, meeting within the Council, of 12 May 1960 on speeding up the pace at which the objectives of the Treaty are achieved (OJ 1960 58/1217). See Lindberg, Ch 1, n 77, at pp. 167–205 and 237.   [31] See *Bulletin EEC* 5-1960, at p. 39.

[32] See *Europe (bulletin quotidien)* 29 July 1960; and *Europe (bulletin quotidien)* 12–13 September 1960.   [33] See *Europe* (documents) 31 December 1960.

[34] See *Europe (bulletin quotidien)* 14 and 15 January 1962.

[35] See Council Decision 62/101/EEC of 14 January 1962 concerning the passage to the second stage of the transitional period (OJ 1962 10/164). It is noteworthy that an agreement was also reached to accelerate again the speed for reduction of customs duties. See Decision 62/528/EEC of the Representatives of the Government of the Member States meeting within the Council of 15 February 1962 on additional measures to speed up the pace at which the objectives of the Treaty are achieved (OJ 1962 41/1284).

resort they were willing to gamble with votes at home rather than stand accused of blocking the advance towards closer unity.'[36]

According to Council Regulations 19–24/62/EEC, common organizations were to be gradually established for the markets in cereals, pork, eggs, poultry, fruit and vegetables, and wine.[37] The solution chosen in the case of the first four products was based on the idea that a system of levies for imports and of refunds for exports would make it possible to guarantee stability of prices and finance structural reforms. This was to be developed progressively so that, at the end of the transitional period, it would only apply in respect of international trade. The solution chosen in respect of the market in fruit and vegetables and the market in wine was one characterized by common rules on competition, most notably in respect of standards of quality.[38]

In addition to the above-mentioned regulations a number of related measures were adopted. Most important of these was Council Regulation 25/62/EEC on the financing of the common agricultural policy.[39] This was based on the idea that the Community should take over financial responsibility from the Member States so that, by the end of the transitional period, all incomes from the common agricultural policy would go directly to the Community which would then bear all the costs. But it was only possible to agree on how this should be done during the first three years and a provision was therefore inserted according to which the matter would be settled before 1 July 1965. This device would later trigger off the crisis which led to the so-called Luxembourg Compromise (see below 2.3.2).

---

[36] *Financial Times* 15 January 1962. Reference in Lindberg, above Ch 1, n 77, at p. 273.

[37] See Council Regulation 19/62/EEC of 4 April 1962 on the progressive establishment of a common organisation of the market in cereals (OJ 1962 30/933); Council Regulation 20/62/EEC of 4 April 1962 on the progressive establishment of a common organisation of the market in pork (OJ 1962 30/945); Council Regulation 21/62/EEC of 4 April 1962 on the progressive establishment of a common organisation of the market in eggs (OJ 1962 30/953); Council Regulation 22/62/EEC of 4 April 1962 on the progressive establishment of a common organisation of the market in poultry (OJ 1962 30/959); Council Regulation 23/62/EEC of 4 April 1962 on the progressive establishment of a common organisation of the market in fruit and vegetables (OJ 1962 B 30/965); and Council Regulation 24/62/EEC of 4 April 1962 on the progressive establishment of a common organisation of the market in wine (OJ 1962 30/989).

[38] For a detailed analysis of the above regulations, see Olmi, G., La mise en œuvre par la C.E.E. de l'organisation commune des marchés agricoles (1963) 6 *RMC* 420.

[39] Council Regulation 25/62/EEC of 4 April 1962 on the financing of the common agricultural policy (OJ 1962 B 30/991). For a detailed analysis, see Weber, J. H., The Financing of the Common Agricultural Policy (1966–67) 4 *CMLRev* 263.

One of the questions which provoked the most difficulty when the first Regulations relating to the common agricultural policy were negotiated concerned the Commission's role in their management. Disagreements on this arose at all stages of the discussions and the divergent views could only be reconciled after the question had been given highest priority in the Council's 'long session' between 20 and 22 December 1961.[40] The controversy surrounding the question was undoubtedly a result of some Governments' unwillingness to concede powers in an area which had not been more closely defined in the EEC Treaty. But it was also an expression of the feeling that the question involved a discussion of principle and that the solution finally chosen would set a precedent to be used in other fields of activity.[41] Since this is the point in the development of the Community at which we find the birth of the committee system, a more detailed examination of this question is appropriate.

2.2.2   A need for co-operation with the national administrations

2.2.2.1   Insistence on a mechanism for supervision

In its first set of proposals the Commission had planned a solution which would not only give itself a central role in the continuous management of the common agricultural policy but also considerable powers to decide exactly what measures this required. Support for this proposition could be found in Article 155 EEC (1958) which stated that, '[i]n order to ensure the proper functioning and development of the common market, the Commission shall . . . exercise the powers conferred on it by the Council for the implementation of the rules laid down by the latter.' As part of its responsibility for management, the Commission suggested that it should be permitted to run a number of so-called European Offices.[42] Acting on the Commission's orders these would calculate intervention prices, make support purchases, and issue import certificates. Acknowledging a certain need for external stimulus, the Commission also envisaged the setting up of 'consultative committees'. These would above all enable it continuously to pursue a dialogue with representatives of both

---

[40] See *Europe (bulletin quotidien)* 22 December 1961.
[41] See *Europe (bulletin quotidien)* 28 November 1961.
[42] See *Bulletin EEC* 5-1959, at pp. 17–28; and *Bulletin EEC* 5-1960, at p. 40.

governmental and non-governmental interests affected by the common agricultural policy.[43]

Nevertheless, when the proposals were placed before the Council it soon became clear that the Commission asked for more than some Governments were willing to give it. One result of this was that the Commission's European Offices were replaced by so-called Intervention Agencies run by the Member States themselves.[44] But most importantly, the idea emerged that representatives of governmental interests should be given greater opportunity to influence decision-making beyond that offered by participation in the consultative committees. In a first attempt to accommodate this wish, in its proposals of 30 June 1960 the Commission suggested that the composition of the consultative committees should be reduced so as to exclude governmental representatives who would meet, instead, in a new type of body—the 'directors' committees'—with which the Commission would be obliged to consult before taking any decisions.[45]

The Governments were prepared to accept this solution in other fields of activity: in negotiations relating to the field of competition, agreement was being finalized on the setting up of the so-called Advisory Committee on Restrictive Practices and Dominant Positions.[46] But in the field of common agricultural policy, it proved to be unacceptable. The French Government argued that it would not provide sufficient opportunity to 'assure the effective direction' and the German Government insisted that in all cases the final decisions must be taken by the Council.[47] In the end, therefore, it was concluded that 'some more supple institutional form should be found for co-operation between the Commission and the national authorities responsible for the execution of agricultural policy measures.'[48]

---

[43] See *Bulletin EEC* 5-1959, at pp. 17–28.

[44] In some Member States existing bodies were pressed into service when new responsibilities arose, in others new bodies were set up especially to carry out the tasks. See Fennell, R., *The Common Agricultural Policy of the European Community* (Granada 1979), at p. 55.

[45] See *Bulletin EEC* 5-1960, at p. 40; and General Report 1961, above Ch 2, n 15, at p. 127.

[46] See Council Regulation 17/62/EEC of 6 February 1962 implementing Articles 85 and 86 of the EEC Treaty (OJ 1962 P 13/204). Cf. also the Advisory Committee for Consultation on Trade Agreements established by Council Decision 61/1104/EEC of 9 October 1961 concerning a consultation procedure in respect of the negotiation of agreements concerning commercial relations between Member States and third countries (OJ 1961 71/1273); and the Advisory Committee on the Euratom Supply Agency established by the Statutes of the Euratom Supply Agency of 6 November 1958 (OJ 1958 B 27/534).

[47] See *Europe (bulletin quotidien)* 10 October 1960. See, in general, Lindberg, above Ch 1, n 77, at p. 277.   [48] See *Bulletin EEC* 10-1960, at p. 47.

2.2.2.2   Objections to the idea of independent agencies

Various solutions were subsequently presented in an attempt to agree terms for the institutional arrangement.[49] Most notably the French Government proposed that the power to take certain management-related decisions should be entrusted to *comités de gestion* or 'management committees' composed of representatives of both the national administrations and the Commission.[50] The power to take more important decisions would remain within the competence of the Council. While the objective of the French proposal was said to be 'to facilitate the work of the Commission and to render its relationship with the national administrations more efficient', in effect it left the Commission without its own powers of decision.[51] Clearly, the management committees proposed by the French Government were conceived of not as subordinate to the Commission but as free-standing organs.[52] For this reason, they were also supposed to have their own secretariats.

As observed by one commentator,[53] this was in fact a solution similar to that which had been chosen in 1959 when the so-called Administrative Commission for the Social Security of Migrant Workers was set up as a 'specialised organ' operating within the field of free movement of workers.[54] But this time a number of objections were raised. Perhaps most importantly, several Governments reacted strongly against 'the idea of seeing the Commission de-possessed of a part of its responsibilities to the benefit of intergovernmental organs, a precedent which could become unfortunate for the general development of common policies in all of the Community's fields.'[55] In addition the argument was put forward that the decisions which the proposed management committees should take would not be amenable to judicial review and that there was a risk therefore that they could come to be declared illegal.[56] An indication of

---

[49] See Olmi, above Ch 2, n 38, at p. 437.

[50] See *Europe (bulletin quotidien)* 28 and 30 November 1961.

[51] See *Europe (bulletin quotidien)* 30 November 1961.

[52] See *Europe (bulletin quotidien)* 30 November 1961.

[53] See Maas, H. H., The Administrative Commission for the Social Security of Migrant Workers: an Institutional Curiosity (1966-67) 4 *CMLRev* 51, at p. 62.

[54] See, in particular, Articles 43, 44, and 49 of Council Regulation 3/58/EEC of 25 September 1958 regarding the social security of migrant workers (OJ 1958 B 30/561).

[55] See *Europe (bulletin quotidien)* 30 November 1961.

[56] See *Europe (bulletin quotidien)* 30 November 1961. That this risk was real was later to be confirmed by the Court in its ruling concerning the Administrative Commission for the Social Security of Migrant Workers in Case 98/80 (see below Ch 2, n 151).

this could be found in the recent ruling in Case 9/56 *Meroni & Co. S.p.A. v High Authority of the ECSC.*[57] Here the Court of Justice had shown itself prepared to accept 'a delegation of powers' to organs other than the Community Institutions only if very strict requirements were satisfied.

The background to that case, which fell within the context of the ECSC Treaty, was that a compulsory arrangement had been created for undertakings using ferrous scrap.[58] Implementation of the arrangement had been entrusted to two Brussels-based bodies established under private law. Most significantly, one of them, the Imported Ferrous Scrap Equalisation Fund, had been given the power to fix the rates of contributions payable and to notify individual undertakings of the amount of the contributions to be paid. But should there be any failure to pay, an 'enforceable decision' to that end was to be taken by the forerunner to the Commission, the High Authority. Eventually such a decision was taken against the Italian company Meroni & Co. S.p.A. But considering that its own role was limited to 'the mere adoption of data furnished by an independent body' the High Authority had seen no reason to state the grounds on which the decision was based.[59]

In the subsequent legal challenge brought by Meroni & Co. S.p.A., the Court found that the fact that the decision had not been accompanied by an explanation was sufficient grounds upon which to annul it.[60] But the Court went on also to discuss the more general question whether a delegation of powers could be permitted without interfering with the institutional balance. Two findings are of particular relevance for present purposes. The first was the meaning given to the notion of delegation. In this respect the Court indicated very clearly that if the arrangement had been such that the High Authority had 'taken over' the deliberations of the Imported Ferrous Scrap Equalisation Fund, this would not constitute a delegation in the strict sense but merely 'the granting of a power to

[57] Case 9/56 *Meroni & Co. S.p.A. v High Authority of the ECSC* [1957–58] ECR 133.

[58] The relevance of this ruling, not only within the context of the ECSC Treaty, but for the EC as a whole, has since been extensively explored and, most often, confirmed in the legal literature. See, for example, Kapteyn and VerLoren van Themaat, above Ch 1, n 36, at p. 245; Hartley, T. C., *The Foundations of European Community Law* (Clarendon Press 1994), at pp. 122–125; Lenaerts, K., Regulating the Regulatory Process: 'Delegation of Powers' in the European Community (1993) 18 *ELRev* 23, at pp. 41–42; Bradley, K., Comitology and the Law: Through a Glass Darkly (1992) 29 *CMLRev* 693, at p. 697; Schwarze, J., *European Administrative Law* (Sweet & Maxwell 1992), at pp. 1205–1206; and Türk, above Ch 1, n 11, at p. 186.

[59] At p. 148 of the Judgment, above Ch 2, n 57.

[60] At pp. 141–143 of the Judgment, above Ch 2, n 57.

draw up resolutions the application of which belongs to the High Authority, the latter retaining full responsibility for the same.'[61] The second finding was reached after the Court had established that a delegation had effectively taken place.

Through a rather wide interpretation of the provision of the ECSC Treaty which provided a legal basis for the contested arrangement, it was acknowledged that a delegation of certain tasks was possible to 'bodies established under private law, having a distinct legal personality and possessing powers of their own'.[62] But that was strictly limited, with respect both to the manner in which the delegation had to be made and the scope of the powers it could involve. This meant, first, that the delegation had to be made in a way which could ensure that all legal restrictions on the exercise of powers would continue to apply. The duty to state reasons and the rules relating to judicial review were specifically emphasized.[63] Then, as to the scope of the powers, the Court explained that it could only permit a delegation if it involved 'clearly defined executive powers' the exercise of which would be open to review 'in the light of objective criteria' laid down by the delegating Institution.[64] According to the Court, to go further than that and accept a delegation which entailed the exercise of 'a discretionary power' would undermine the fundamental guarantee for effectiveness and accountability stemming from the institutional balance of powers.[65]

2.2.2.3   *The establishment of management committees: a balanced solution*

The initial step towards resolution of the question relating to the institutional arrangement was taken on 28 November 1961. In accordance with a compromise negotiated within the Special Committee on

---

[61]   At p. 147 of the Judgment, above Ch 2, n 57.

[62]   At p. 151 of the Judgment, above Ch 2, n 57. Cf. Article 53 ECSC (1952).

[63]   At p. 149 of the Judgment, above Ch 2, n 57.

[64]   At pp. 149–154 of the Judgment, above Ch 2, n 57.

[65]   At p. 152 of the Judgment, above Ch 2, n 57. It should be noted that an even more restrictive approach to the delegation of powers to organs other than Community Institutions was taken in Case 98/80 *Romano v Institut National d'Assurance Maladie-Invalidité*. This concerned the arrangement established by Council Regulation 3/58/EEC (see above Ch 2, n 54) regarding the social security of migrant workers and, in particular, the power of the Administrative Commission for the Social Security of Migrant Workers to lay down certain criteria which national authorities should take into account when applying EEC legislation on invalidity pensions. In its

Agriculture, the suggestion was made that the responsibility for adoption of measures of a 'practical nature' should be entrusted to the Commission and management committees jointly.[66] In particular, management committees should be permitted to exercise a control-function—an opportunity to prevent the adoption of measures which they did not support—something which had not been envisaged in the case of the directors' committees or, indeed, in the case of the Advisory Committee on Restrictive Practices and Dominant Positions (see above 2.2.2.1). If measures favoured by the Commission were supported by a committee, it would be left with a simple choice: either it would adjust to the opinion of the committee or it would have to pass everything over to the Council in the form of a proposal for legislation.

Apparently, the compromise negotiated within the Special Committee on Agriculture was acceptable to most Governments. But a few of them were still resistant. Most notably the Dutch refused to agree to a solution which would place the Commission 'under the tutelage of intergovernmental organs.'[67] But this was not reason enough to seek an entirely different solution. Instead a further step along the same path was taken a few weeks later when the Commission presented a number of adjustments which would let some of the formal powers slip back into its own hands. The changes stressed the sole right of the Commission to take the actual decision on the adoption of the measures in question but did not

rather straightforward ruling the Court of Justice read Article 155 EEC (1958) and the opportunity for the Council to confer implementing powers on the Commission as exclusive, thus giving rise to a complete prohibition on the Council to empower an organ which was not an institution 'to adopt acts having the force of law.' Support for that conclusion was found in a strict interpretation of the rules of the EEC Treaty relating to judicial review: Articles 173 and 177 EEC (1958). Without considering its ruling in Case 9/56 (see above Ch 2, n 57) and the possibility envisaged therein that a delegation could be made in such a manner as to ensure that the rules relating to judicial review would continue to apply the Court stated that its jurisdiction was limited to acts of Community Institutions. See Case 98/80 *Romano v Institut National d'Assurance Maladie-Invalidité* [1981] ECR 1241 (Judgment of 14 May 1981), in particular at p. 1256 (paragraph 20). Cf. the Opinion of Advocate General Warner, at p. 1265. The significance of the ruling in Case 98/80 is difficult to appreciate. This is even more so in the light of the recent ruling in Case C-164/98 *DIR International Film et al. v Commission* where the Court seemed to accept that its ruling in Case 9/56 was restated as a prohibition against 'a delegation of powers coupled with a freedom to make assessments implying a *wide* discretionary power' (emphasis added). See Case C-164/98 *DIR International Film et al. v Commission* [2000] ECR I-447 (Judgment of 27 January 2000), paragraph 6.

[66] See *Europe (bulletin quotidien)* 30 November 1961.

[67] See *Europe (bulletin quotidien)* 13 December 1961.

change the essential fact that management committees should be intimately involved in the underlying deliberations and also be permitted to exercise a control-function. The important difference was that the control-function should only enter into force after the Commission had taken its decision: if a measure had been objected to by a committee, in a negative opinion (given by a qualified majority of the votes), the Council would be enabled to replace it by another. The Council would no longer deal with the matter in the form of a proposal for legislation but rather as a sort of 'appeal' against the measure resulting from a decision for which the Commission, alone, was responsible.

Somewhat surprisingly, the adjustments presented by the Commission were accepted by the Council on 21 December 1961.[68] It may be suspected that this rather rapid conclusion of the matter was due to the fact that the European Parliament had just found out about the plans for 'creation of new organs' and had immediately telegraphed a resolution in which it demanded that no decisions should be taken before it had been permitted to give its opinion.[69] This, indeed, was reason enough for the Governments to end their quarrels. It had already proven difficult enough to find a solution which was acceptable within the Council: if the European Parliament were also to have a say, then the end would be miles away. Therefore, when the first Council Regulations relating to the common agricultural policy were eventually adopted on 4 April 1962 they all included, in identical words, a procedure which enabled the Commission to adopt 'measures for their application' in close co-operation with a management committee. An example can be taken from Council Regulation 19/62 on the progressive establishment of a common organization of the market in cereals:

Article 25

1   A Management Committee for Cereals (hereinafter called the 'Committee') shall be established, consisting of representatives of Member States and with a representative of the Commission as Chairman.

---

[68] See *Europe (bulletin quotidien)* 22 December 1961. It may be pointed out that the Dutch Government reserved itself (confirming its preference for purely advisory organs).

[69] See Résolution (Parlement européen) du 20 décembre 1961 sur les attributions de la Commission européenne dans la mise en œuvre de la politique agricole commune (Annuaire-Manuel 1961–62, pp. 468–469). Based on Rapport du 20 décembre 1961 fait au nom de la commission de l'agriculture sur les attributions de la Commission dans la mise en œuvre de la politique agricole commune (rapporteur: Käthe Strobel), PE Doc 119-61. Cf. also the Deringer Report, below Ch 2, n 73, at p. 42 (paragraph 141).

2   Within the Committee, the votes of Member States shall be weighted in accordance with Article 148 (2) of the Treaty. The Chairman shall not vote.

Article 26

1   Where the provisions of this Regulation expressly call for the procedure defined in this Article to be applied, the Chairman shall refer the matter to the Committee, either on his own initiative or at the request of the representative of a member state.

2   The representative of the Commission shall submit a draft of the measures to be taken. The Committee shall deliver its opinion on such measures within a time limit to be set by the Chairman according to the urgency of the questions under consideration. An opinion shall be adopted by a majority of twelve votes.

3   The Commission shall adopt measures which shall apply immediately. However, if these measures are not in accordance with the opinion of the Committee, they shall forthwith be communicated by the Commission to the Council. In that event the Commission may defer application of the measures which it has adopted for not more than one month from the date of such communication.

The Council may, by a qualified majority, take a different decision within one month.

As has just been noted, the solution finally adopted resulted from a rather precipitous conclusion of a discussion which had been going on for more than two years. Far from all disagreements on matters of principle had been overcome and several Governments felt that the last word had not yet been said. Therefore, when the above Regulations were adopted, in specific provisions placed after those in which the procedure for co-operation between the Commission and the management committees had been laid down, the statement was made that at the end of the transitional period, the Council would have to decide 'in the light of experience' whether the procedure should be retained or amended.[70] This would prove to be a triumph for pragmatism over ideologies: when the time did come to decide, the procedure was no longer controversial (see above 2.4.5.2).

---

[70] See e.g. Article 28 of Council Regulation 19/62/EEC, above Ch 2, n 37. Cf. Council Regulation 2602/69/EEC, below Ch 2, n 265.

2.2.3   *The European Parliament demands a* droit de regard

Without the opportunities that the management committees offered the Governments of continuous control and influence the responsibility entrusted to the Commission would not have been the same. It would appear, indeed, that in this way their readiness to leave powers to the Commission was even increased.[71] Another aspect which must not be underestimated is the opportunity the Commission was now given to develop its relationship with the national administrations. As noted after their first year of operation, the management committees 'ensured a useful collaboration between the Governments of the Member States and the Commission which has permitted the resolution of divergent opinions on technical matters, without the need of involving an inter-change between the Council and the Commission, and to accomplish speedily a considerable volume of work.'[72] But irrespective of such advantages, the fact remained that the management committees were institutional innovations, the establishment and operation of which gave raise to a number of questions.

Nowhere was the preoccupation with the management committees more profound than in the European Parliament. Even if the solution finally opted for was less drastic than first feared (see above 2.2.2), the fact that they themselves had not been given a chance to express an opinion was enough for the MEPs to look upon the management committees with suspicion. This suspicion they would never be able to overcome. Instead, it was to be added to by an increasing awareness that matters which they felt ought be dealt with under normal legislative procedures were placed in the hands of a 'mixed' administration in which the Commission and the Council were both involved but the European Parliament excluded. An initial sign of this can be seen in the so-called Deringer Report of 5 October 1962.[73] In this rather complex document, the chairmen of 12 parliamentary committees express their common views on the experience which had been gained in the Community during the previous year of activity.

Perhaps the most important finding of the Deringer Report was that many of the difficulties encountered were due to the fact that

---

[71]   See Bertram, above Ch 1, n 24, at p. 262.

[72]   See Olmi, G., The Agricultural Policy of the Community (1963–64) 1 *CMLRev* 118, at p. 147.

[73]   See Rapport du 5 octobre 1962 fait au nom du comité des présidents sur le cinquième Rapport général sur l'activité de la CEE (rapporteur: Arved Deringer), PE Doc 74-1962.

the relationship between the Community administration—the Commission—and the national administrations was characterized by rivalry. In order to come to terms with this *problème épineux*, the Report judged it indispensable to improve the preconditions for co-operation, in particular, through the creation of organs which would bring the Commission and the national administrations closer together.[74] This was one of the lessons that could be learned from the field of common agricultural policy. Here the new management committees had introduced the possibility for the national administration to participate in the work of the Commission. The positive result was twofold: not only had the Governments or, more precisely, the Council, shown a readiness to entrust the Commission with powers to adopt binding decisions of an unambiguous legal status, but an incentive had also been created for the national administrations to apply those decisions in a uniform manner.[75]

But having approved, in principle, the continuous establishment of organs such as the management committees, the Deringer Report emphasized that there were reasons to be cautious so that the co-operation between the Commission and the national administration would not lead to disorder.[76] At the centre of the concern was a fear that it would become difficult, or even impossible, for the European Parliament to perform its duties: to exercise political supervision over the Commission and participate in the adoption of legislation by means of consultation (see above 2.1.1). In order to avoid such an eventuality, two conditions were advanced with which the Council and the Commission were asked to comply. First, with respect to supervision, the Commission had to be able, but also willing, to assume political responsibility for the new organs for co-operation.[77] Then, with respect to consultation, the success or effectiveness of the co-operation must not lead to a situation in which an increasing number of matters of political significance were dealt with in accordance with procedures that did not permit the European Parliament to discuss its position publicly and promote it. More specifically:

... the powers given by the Council to the Commission must be defined in a manner which is sufficiently precise and concrete for the Court of Justice

---

[74] At p. 33 (paragraph 113) of the Deringer Report, above Ch 2, n 73.

[75] At pp. 32–33 (paragraphs 111–113) of the Deringer Report, above Ch 2, n 73.

[76] At p. 33 (paragraph 113) of the Deringer Report, above Ch 2, n 73.

[77] At pp. 33 and 36 (paragraphs 111 and 123) of the Deringer Report, above Ch 2, n 73.

always to be able to verify if the Commission has kept itself within the limits of those powers and, to the extent that fundamental political questions are involved, the Parliament must not be excluded. Even if the involvement of the Parliament in the drafting of legislation is not envisaged and if the Com- mission does not consult it, the Parliament has the right and the duty, by virtue of its great supervisory power and in the interest of the Community and its peoples, to discuss its position publicly and promote it.[78]

Only a few days after the presentation of the Deringer Report, the President of the EEC Commission, the German Professor of Constitu tional Law, Walter Hallstein, was invited to the European Parliament to give his comments. This gave him the opportunity to confirm that many of the difficulties encountered were indeed due to the fact that the rela tionship between the Commission and the national administrations was characterized by rivalry and to emphasize that this was not only a *problème épineux* but a 'constitutional' challenge.[79] Trying to meet this challenge, he said, one has to remember that the application of the EEC Treaty is not a matter for the Community Institutions alone but calls also for action by the Member States. Therefore, to enable all those involved to perform a useful result, a certain pragmatism was called for: 'the experience gained by other federations and the various solutions they have produced provide us with material for study and the necessary tips.'[80] Proceeding to the question whether such pragmatism would accord with the intention of the EEC Treaty, Professor Hallstein explained that two extreme interpretations could be thought of: one would give strict priority to 'a sort of principle of separation of powers'; the other, that of the 'mixed' administration indicated in the Deringer Report, would produce a result that could not be imputed to one party or another but only to the whole. In his view, neither of the interpretations was correct:

It would be more correct to say that the division of responsibilities laid down in the Treaty and the principle of co-operation are complementary. Indeed they must fit in with each other—the force of logic may even force them to fit in. A clear allocation of responsibilities to various institutions in an action intended to produce a homogeneous result is only conceivable with

---

[78] See p. 44 (paragraph 151) of the Deringer Report, above Ch 2, n 73.

[79] See Introduction to the debate in the European Parliament of 17 October 1962 on the Fifth General Report 1962 on the Activities of the EEC, in *Bulletin EEC* 11-1962, at p. 6.

[80] Introduction to the debate in the European Parliament, above Ch 2, n 79, at pp. 6–7 and 14.

co-operation as an essential corollary. This means refusing to let the assertion of exclusive competence be pressed to the point of dogma—*fiat justitia pereat communitas*—as well as refusal to accept a free-for-all in which no one can tell who made what contribution to the final result ... The most instructive example of the need for such co-operation can be found in the Management Committees set up under our agricultural policy.[81]

Having stated his 'balanced' view on the right way forward, Professor Hallstein set out to deal with the fear that the co-operation between the Commission and the national administrations would interfere with the prerogatives of the European Parliament. The answer was a strikingly clear expression of a position the Commission would stick to over the years to come. Although admitting that the worries were fully understandable, Professor Hallstein found little reason to promise the European Parliament that the conditions advanced in the Deringer Report would be complied with.[82] Not only was he unwilling to declare that the Commission was prepared to assume a political responsibility for the new organs for co-operation, but he categorically refused to accept the idea that any limitations should be set on the scope of matters dealt with or that the European Parliament should be entitled to some form of consultation. Apparently there was now less room for pragmatism. Therefore, '[t]ill such time as the present rules are altered, this strengthening of its position can only be attained by more effective application of the existing possibilities.'[83]

2.3 The Luxembourg Compromise

2.3.1 A formula of synchronization

Following the adoption of the first Regulations relating to the common agricultural policy the expectations were high that it should be possible to make an advance also in other areas of co-operation. In particular,

[81] Introduction to the debate in the European Parliament, above Ch 2, n 79, at pp. 10–11.

[82] But he assured 'that the Commission will never in defence to anyone be ready to take a decision in which the interest of the Community is subordinated to its own convenience.' See Introduction to the debate in the European Parliament, above Ch 2, n 79, at p. 12.

[83] Introduction to the debate in the European Parliament, above Ch 2, n 79, at pp. 12–13. As noted by Hallstein, '[t]he Parliamentary Report raises a further legal question, namely, whether

Germany and the Benelux Countries insisted that negotiations for further liberalization of international trade should now be initiated within GATT. They further believed that the time was ripe for an enlargement of the Community so as to include the United Kingdom. One reason for this was that they preferred to have the United Kingdom on their side rather than as a competitor in the international market (see below 3.1.1).

Nevertheless, after more than one year of negotiations between the Community and the United Kingdom the French President, General Charles de Gaulle, suddenly announced on 14 January 1963 that he considered the enlargement premature and saw no purpose in continuing the negotiations.[84] In reaction to this, other Governments decided to block action in the field of the common agricultural policy. This in turn led to a major crisis which was only resolved after the Council resorted to a 'formula of synchronisation' which made it possible to approach the differing interests along parallel lines.[85] In more specific terms, an agreement was reached to adopt new regulations relating to the common agricultural policy, to arrange for co-operation with the United Kingdom, and to begin negotiations within GATT.[86] The resolution of the crisis was followed by 'a period of rapid advance in the building of Europe.'[87] In addition to a substantial cut in customs duties, a series of regulations were adopted on the common organization of new agricultural markets.[88] But most spectacularly the so-called Kennedy Round of the negotiations in GATT was opened on 4 May 1964.

All the Member States of the Community were already parties to GATT before the Community was established. For this reason the EEC Treaty made it clear that the commitments which each Member State

and how far the Commission may be authorized to reach decisions or to issue regulations without being required to consult Parliament. In practice, however, the Report supplies the answer itself: where it is the implementation of a basic regulation that is concerned, the Treaty only requires that Parliament shall have been consulted when the regulation itself was issued. The importance of the implementing act makes no difference.'

[84] See *Le Monde* 15 January 1963. Reference in Kapteyn and VerLoren van Themaat, above Ch 1, n 36, at p. 19.

[85] See Sixth General Report on the Activities of the European Economic Community 1963 (Office for Official Publication 1964), at pp. 11–19.

[86] See General Report 1963, above Ch 2, n 85, at p. 16.

[87] See Seventh General Report on the Activities of the European Economic Community 1964 (Office for Official Publication 1965), at p. 13.

[88] See Council Regulation 13/64/EEC of 5 February 1964 on the progressive establishment of a common organisation of the market in milk and milk products (OJ 1964 34/549); Council

had made to other parties of GATT would still have to be respected in the future.[89] At the same time, the intention had been stated clearly that these commitments ought to be re-negotiated—both between the Member States and within GATT—so as to allow them eventually to be taken over by the Community itself. According to the EEC Treaty, this 'streamlining' was to be guided by a liberal approach. So it was explicitly envisaged that the Member States should seek to 'contribute to the development of international trade and the lowering of barriers to trade by entering into agreements designed, on the basis of reciprocity and mutual advantage, to reduce customs duties below the general level of which they could avail themselves as a result of the establishment of a customs union between them.'[90] As explained by the Commissioner responsible for external trade, Jean Rey, at the inaugural session of the Kennedy Round, this meant that the most preferential aspects of the trade arrangement between the Member States should be extended as far as possible so as to include also their partners in GATT.[91]

Clearly a lot was at stake. Not only were Germany and the Benelux Countries supposed to get what they had been waiting for, but for the first time all Member States would negotiate as one, represented by the Commission. As enthusiastically reported back, the initial discussions had shown 'the weight the Community carries at the conference table, the authority attaching to its view, and at the same time its determination to make an effective contribution to the success of the negotiations.'[92]

2.3.2   The crisis of the empty chair

2.3.2.1   The Commission makes a miscalculation

During the period between 1 January and 30 June 1965 the Presidency of the Council was held by France. One of the more important matters on

Regulation 14/64/EEC of 5 February 1964 on the progressive establishment of a common organisation of the market in beef and veal (OJ 1964 34/562); and Council Regulation 16/64/EEC of 5 February on the progressive establishment of a common organisation of the market in rice (OJ 1964 34/574). Cf. also Council Regulation 17/64/EEC of 5 February 1964 on the conditions for granting aid from the European Agricultural Guidance and Guarantee Fund (OJ 1964 P 34/586).

[89]   See Article 234 EEC (1958).

[90]   See Article 18 EEC (1958). Cf. Article 110 EEC (1958).

[91]   See the statement by Commissioner Jean Rey in *Bulletin EEC* 6-1964, at p. 5. See in general Everling, above Ch 2, n 17.   [92]   See General Report 1964, above Ch 2, n 87, at p. 15.

the agenda was that of the financing of the common agricultural policy, or, as the French Government preferred to call it, 'the final definition of the financial regulation.'[93] It may be recalled that this was a matter which had to be settled before 1 July 1965 and that a solution had already been adopted which envisaged the gradual take over by the Community of the financial responsibility from the Member States (see above 2.2.1). Another matter of priority was the merger of the executives of the ECSC, EEC, and EAEC into a single Council and a single Commission.

In respect of the last of these issues, an important success was noted on 3 March 1965 when the so-called Merger Treaty was agreed.[94] It was expected that ratification would proceed smoothly and that the new organization could enter into operation as early as at the beginning of 1966. But in respect of the financing of the common agricultural policy, things did not develop the way the French had hoped. An initial sign of this could be seen already during the first weeks of the Presidency, when the Dutch, Italian, and German Governments made it clear that they were not prepared to let the Community dispense of large sums of money without getting in exchange some kind of supranational *préalable* in the form of an independent source of revenue for the Commission and a commitment to increase the supervisory authority of the European Parliament.[95] The French had long since rejected such an idea.

The existing tensions were transformed into open antagonism when the Commission presented its proposals for the financing of the common agricultural policy on 31 March 1965.[96] Instead of opting for compromise and a solution which would be less difficult for all Governments to agree to, the Commission chose to take a stand, the boldness of which surprised even the most optimistic Europeans.[97] To its proposals for

---

[93]   See the statement by Charles de Gaulle on 9 September 1965, below Ch 2, n 106.

[94]   See below Ch 2, n 154.

[95]   See Lambert, J., The Constitutional Crisis 1965–1966 (1966) 4 *JCMS* 195, at pp. 197 and 208; and Lindberg, L., Integration as a Source of Stress on the European Community System (1966) 10 *IO* 233, at p. 246.

[96]   It may be noted that Commission President Hallstein had presented the 'general orientation' of the proposals to the European Parliament a few days before they were submitted to the Council. As explained by Lambert this was a breach with established practice under which the Council was the first to be informed. See Lambert, above Ch 2, n 95, at p. 198. Cf. *Europe (bulletin quotidien)* 23 and 24 March 1965.

[97]   See Lindberg, above Ch 2, n 95, at p. 248. It may be noted, however, that the European Parliament, when it came to debate the proposals, was to manifest its disappointment and dissatisfaction, holding that the proposals did not go far enough. See Lambert, above Ch 2, n 95, at p. 205.

the financing of the agricultural policy, the Commission had tied the proposals that not only agricultural levies but also customs duties should be designated as the Community's 'own resources' and that the European Parliament should be given an enhanced power of budgetary control.[98]

The French Government protested energetically against the proposals presented by the Commission, insisting that the Council 'had not been convened to examine suggestions about the future development of the Communities, but to resolve a very practical and pedestrian question, the financing of the agricultural policy for the next five years.'[99] The reaction had not been difficult to predict. Therefore, in order to make the proposals less unattractive, France was offered an extremely favourable financial arrangement.[100] But contrary to the expectations of the Commission, the French President, General Charles de Gaulle, 'exploded' when the terms of the proposals were explained to him and exclaimed: 'Do they think they can buy off de Gaulle with such a piece of cheese?'[101]

2.3.2.2   The French Government abandons the Council

The full set of proposals was not discussed in the Council until the last few days of the French Presidency and, not surprisingly, the session ended in deadlock.[102] As explained by the French Minister of Foreign Affairs, Maurice Couve de Murville, the Council had not been able to reach a common position on the vital question whether the arrangement should extend over the whole transitional period or only over one or two years.[103] The next morning, the French Government issued a communiqué in which it said that nothing more could be done in Brussels until it had 'drawn the obvious political, economic and legal conclusions from the situation thus created.'[104] Only a few days later, the Secretary-General of the Council was informed that for the time being the French Government

---

[98] For a detailed analysis, see Lambert, above Ch 2, n 95, at pp. 198–205.

[99] See Editorial Comments (1965–66) 3 *CMLRev* 1, at p. 3.

[100] According to one estimate, France would have paid 18% against Germany's 39%. At the same time, French farmers would have received at least 50% of the total expenditures. See Lindberg, above Ch 2, n 95, at p. 248.   [101] See Lindberg, above Ch 2, n 95, at p. 249.

[102] See Ninth General Report on the Activities of the European Economic Community 1966 (Office for Official Publications 1967), at pp. 24–25.

[103] See *Bulletin EEC* 8-1965, at pp. 44–45.

[104] See *Bulletin EEC* 8-1965, at p. 45; and General Report 1966, above Ch 2, n 102, at pp. 24–25.

would not be represented at Council sessions, nor at meetings of the Committee of Permanent Representatives.[105]

Although initially unclear exactly what the French Government was hoping to obtain as a result of its *politique de la chaise vide*, it soon became evident that its grievances did not in the first place relate to the financing of the common agricultural policy but to the role played by the Commission. The tenor of the French position was made clear in a press conference held by General de Gaulle on 9 September 1965. His statement deserves to be restated at some length:

What we wanted yesterday, and what we want today, is a Community which is both equitable and reasonable. Equitable: that means that, taking account of their particular circumstances, agricultural products should be subject to the Common Market at the same time as industrial products. Reasonable: that means that nothing of any importance, either in the initial planning or the later operation of the Common Market, should be decided, and certainly not applied, except by the responsible authorities in the six countries, that is to say, the national governments subject to parliamentary control. But we know—and heaven knows how well we know it—that there is a different conception of a European federation in which, according to the dreams of those who have conceived it, the member countries would lose their national identities, and which, moreover, in the absence of a federator such as Caesar and his successors, Charlemagne, the Emperor Otto and Charles V, Napoleon and Hitler each tried to become in the west— in his own fashion—and such as Stalin tried to become in the East, would be ruled by some sort of technocratic body of elders, stateless and irresponsible.

One knows also that, in opposition to this project devoid of all realism, France proposed a plan for organised co-operation between the states, evolving no doubt towards a confederation. This plan alone appears to her to correspond to what the nations of our Continent really are. This plan alone would one day permit other countries like England or Spain to join in, because these countries, like ourselves, do not wish to lose their sovereignty. It alone would make an *entente* of the whole of Europe conceivable one day.

However, and whatever the reservations about the political theories involved, it looks as if the very long and detailed negotiations at Brussels

---

[105] The Council agreed on 26–27 July 1965 that the most urgent decisions should be taken by the written procedure, and this was accepted by France. It is noteworthy that the French Government did not withdraw its representatives in the various management committees. See further, Kaiser, J. K., Das Europarecht in der Krise der Gemeinschaften (1966) 1 *EuR* 14.

were on the point of being concluded. Certainly, we had had the greatest difficulty in getting our partners—in practice—to admit that farm produce should form an integral part of the Community. Well, as everyone is aware, this is for us a *sine qua non* condition, for, if it were not fulfilled, we should remain burdened with the very heavy cost—much greater than that of our neighbours—of supporting our agricultural, and we should consequently be handicapped in industrial competition, too. That is why we were only able to agree, in January 1962, that the Community pass into the second phase of the Treaty, which involved reduction in customs duties, on the condition of a formal commitment to settle the agricultural problem, particularly from the financial point of view, by 30 June of this year at the latest, and under conditions and following a timetable precisely laid down. Although at the time there were some tears and grinding of teeth, we were able at the last moment to gain the agreement of our partners, and we had the right to believe that they would meet their commitments by the agreed deadline.

Whilst observing that the cumbersome international machinery built at great cost around the Commission frequently duplicated the qualified services of the six governments, we noted the competence of these officials on the basis of their work and observed that they refrained from excessive encroachment upon the only valid powers, which are the individual states.

It was too good to last! In Brussels, on 30 June, our delegation came up against a serious stumbling-block concerning the final definition of the financial regulation, as previously agreed on. Shortly before, the Commission had suddenly abandoned its political discretion and formulated terms in connection with this financial regulation whereby it would have a budget of its own, possibly of up to 20,000 million new francs ($4,000 million), the states having made over into its hands the levies and customs receipts which would literally have made it a great independent financial power. And then those very states, having fed these enormous amounts to it at the expense of their tax-payers, would have no way of supervising it.

It is true that the authors of the plan alleged that the budget would be submitted to the Assembly for consideration. But intervention by this Assembly, which is essentially an advisory body, the members of which were in no way elected for this purpose, would merely aggravate the nature of the usurpation of powers which was being demanded. Finally, regardless of whether or not there was premeditated collusion with the Commission's supranational claims, the attitude adopted by certain delegations (who stated their readiness to approve and support these claims), and finally the fact that some of our partners at the last moment went back on their undertakings, we had no alternative, in the circumstances, but to break off the Brussels negotiations.

I must add that in the light of this event we have been more clearly able to assess in what position our country risks finding itself if some of the provisions initially laid down in the Rome Treaty were actually enforced. It is on the basis of this text that from 1 January next the decisions in the Council of Ministers would be decided by majority vote; in other words, France would be exposed to the possibility of being overruled in any economic matter, whatsoever, and therefore in social and sometimes political matters, and that, in particular, all that has been achieved by French agriculture could be threatened at any moment, without France's let or leave. Moreover, after this same date, the proposals made by the Commission in Brussels would have to be accepted or rejected in their entirety by the Council of Ministers without the States being able to change anything, unless by some extraordinary chance, the Six States were unanimous in formulating an amendment. We know that the members of the Commission, although appointed by agreement among the governments, are no longer responsible to them, and that, even on the conclusion of their terms of office, they can only be replaced by the unanimous agreement of the Six, which, in effect, renders them immovable. One can see where such a subordinate position could lead us, if we allowed ourselves to deny, at one and the same time, our freedom of action and our Constitution, which lays down that 'French sovereignty resides in the French people, which exercises it through its representatives and by means of referenda' without making any sort of exception at all.[106]

There can be no doubt that the French Government sought to emphasize the fundamental nature of the crisis as clearly as possible.[107] Even if a solution could have been found to the problem of financing the common agricultural policy, more fundamental divergences of opinion would have stayed on the agenda only to reappear at some later date. While it is more than likely that the Commission's proposals had been deliberately designed to provoke a discussion on 'constitutional' problems, the French Government appeared to have its mind set on getting a decision—once and for all—that the Commission should have no political role to play and that the Community must not develop beyond the control of its members.

[106] See *Le Monde* 10 September 1965. Reference (translated) in Lambert, above Ch 2, n 95.

[107] It may be noted in this context that the French boycott conveniently coincided with the French elections, in which de Gaulle was re-elected on 5 December 1965 with a narrow margin of victory against pro-European Jean Lecanuet and François Mitterand. See further Teasdale, A. L., The Life and Death of the Luxembourg Compromise (1993) 31 *JCMS* 567, at p. 568.

2.3.3 A clarification of the positions

2.3.3.1 The Commission defends its integrity

Not surprisingly, the reactions of the other Member States to the position taken by the French Government were anything but reserved, especially after the press conference of 9 September 1965. General de Gaulle was severely criticized and there was a massive outpouring of support for a continuation of the integration process and, no less significant, for the Commission itself.[108] At the same time, various efforts were made to persuade the French Government to resume its seat.[109] Most importantly, on the basis of suggestions put forward by the Belgian Minister of Foreign Affairs, Paul-Henri Spaak, a Council Declaration was adopted on 26 October 1965. While inviting the French Government to attend an extraordinary session, the other Governments solemnly reaffirmed that the solution of the problems would have to be found 'within the framework of the Treaties and of their institutions.' One of the features which made the proposed session extraordinary was that no representative of the Commission should be present. The invitation was finally accepted on 23 December 1965 and then scheduled for 17 and 18 January 1966.[110]

For the parties involved it was clear that the French Government's concerns did not only relate to the Commission as such, but also to the role played by its President, Professor Hallstein. As German Minister of Foreign Affairs and, indeed, Konrad Adenauer's closest comrade, Walter Hallstein had been deeply involved in the framing of the EEC Treaty and it was no secret that he had high expectations on the Commission's place in a future Europe.[111] To the perplexity of some, Professor Hallstein had told American journalists that he should be regarded 'as a kind of Prime Minister of Europe' and started to receive the increasing number of international representatives that came to see him with similar ceremony to that used by states.[112] Although not invited to the extraordinary session, Professor Hallstein lost no time in defending the integrity and

---

[108] See e.g. Lindberg, above Ch 2, n 95, at p. 243.

[109] For an outline of the various efforts made to convince France to resume its place in the Council, see General Report 1966, above Ch 2, n 102, at pp. 24–30.

[110] See General Report 1966, above Ch 2, n 102, at pp. 28–30.

[111] See, in general, Loth, W., Wallance, W., and Wessels, W. (Eds.), *Walter Hallstein: the Forgotten European?* (Macmillan Press 1998).

[112] See Editorial Comments (1965–66) 3 *CMLRev* 189, at p. 190; and point 5 of the French Government's memorandum, below Ch 2, n 122.

aspirations of his Commission. In a broadcast from the *Bayerischer Rundfunk* on 5 November 1965 he rhetorically posed the question of what type of public authority there should be to establish order in the Community:

An independent Commission entrusted with certain powers of current administration and with the exclusive right of initiating legislation, plus a federative organ—the Council—consisting of representatives of the Governments and entrusted with the task of deciding the general lines of Community policy and passing Community law: this is the balanced, cautious arrangement set up by the Treaty of Rome. These institutions naturally deal with politics. They make agricultural policy, customs and commercial policy, transport policy, economic and monetary policy; in short, all kinds of economic and social policy. Wherever it is economically necessary they establish a legal order that applies in all six Member States. Without actually constituting a government, they exercise functions that are indispensable to the modern economy and that are exercised in the Member States by the Governments. These institutions cannot be set aside or stripped of their powers without halting progress towards a unified economic area embracing the Member States and without the order established in this area collapsing.

But the organs of the Community can be rendered ineffective in other ways than just eliminating them; they could be hamstrung if the carefully arranged balance of powers between them were shifted. What, for instance, would be the consequence if the Commission, instead of being an independent organ, designed and able to work alongside the Council, were to become a secretariat dependent on the Governments, an administrative agency of subsidiary importance—and for the moment I am ignoring the problem that arises from the fact that the Council already has a Secretariat, and that the constant presence of the Member States is assured by their Permanent Representatives, the Member States' Ambassadors to the Community.

Let me give you just one example to illustrate the significance of this problem. The Treaty of Rome itself recognises that the substantive content of the various common policies cannot be worked out in governmental negotiations alone. Such a method was not expected to produce results. The Treaty of Rome therefore entrusted the job to the Community institutions. And experience with agricultural policy has shown that, if a unified policy for a given sphere is to be worked out and implemented, the Commission—the Community organ *par excellence*—must dispose of a measure of political momentum. As the common agricultural policy is the indispensable complement to free movement of industrial products, the Commission has been very active in this sphere. Agricultural policy is, as a result, considerably further advanced than common policy in other fields. With commercial policy, tax policy, economic policy, for instance, we are far behind the stage reached in agricultural policy. Were the Commission to undergo essential changes in its importance and functions today, the chances of making further progress with these other common policies would be drastically reduced.[113]

Proceeding to the part of his answer which concerned the choices which would have to be made as to the future form of the Community, he explained:

Some people ask whether, given the connection with overall political developments in Europe, it is not inevitable that the overall political problem should be one of the factors shaping the order established in the European Community for the economic and social sector. In other words, must we not first put the basic question which arises in relation to the overall political unity of Europe—i.e. the question of what form this 'political unity of Europe' shall take, and only afterwards, in the light of the answers to this question, settle the final form of 'economic' integration? The French approach to this basic question is that we must decide between a 'Europe of the States' and an integrated, a supranational Europe. The German version is that the choice must be made between federation and confederation—not a very happy version, if only because these two concepts do not express any genuine alternatives but only differing degrees of unification.

This is what some say. Others (and not only the faint-hearted, who are inclined by nature to dodge difficult questions) ask whether all this has to be decided today. Is it really impossible to detach that part of the 'dossier' which is being discussed at the present time? Can we not at least ease the pressure, can we not to some extent 'take the politics out of' the question surrounding the European Community, inasmuch as these general political controversies need not be fought out today?[114]

But, insisted Professor Hallstein, that question had already been settled:

The formula chosen is the Community: Coal and Steel Community, Atomic Community, Economic Community. This solution—we have had a look at its main features—is in itself a compromise between the unitary concept (the

---

[113] See *Bulletin EEC* 12-1965, at pp. 5–13. [114] See *Bulletin EEC* 12-1965, at pp. 5–13.

'supranational', if we wish to understand the word in this sense) and the concept of alliance, co-operation, confederation or whatever we prefer to call the loose forms of collaboration. This Community solution is valid by virtue of law, for 'pacta observanda sunt'—and that is one of the most basic principles of what we know as Western civilisation.[115]

2.3.3.2   The French Government states its demands

The extraordinary session was initiated as planned on 17 January 1966 under the Presidency of Luxembourg. This was the first time since the outbreak of the crisis that all Governments were present and 'the atmosphere was good, frank and constructive, everyone came with a wish to search for solutions enabling the Community to reassume its progress.'[116] The discussions were started by Couve de Murville setting out the demands of the French Government. This he did by first confirming that the major cause of the crisis was the attitude of the Commission. According to him, the French Government considered that the Commission had 'placed before the Council unexpected proposals, going beyond what has been asked from it, posing serious—controversial—problems which are not possible to solve under present circumstances.'[117] In order to overcome the crisis and prevent new difficulties of this nature from reappearing an agreement had to be reached on, first, the procedure used by the Council for voting on the Commission's proposals and, secondly, the Council's relationship with the Commission.

Dealing first with the issue of voting, Couve de Murville argued that the automatic shift to qualified majority voting provided for in the EEC Treaty had to be considered in the light of the fact that the Community had not yet reached the envisaged level of political integration.[118] While stressing that the French Government did not object to the use of qualified majority voting in principle, he therefore demanded some sort of guarantees that it would not be used in questions of national and political interests.[119] As General de Gaulle had already pointed out, it

---

[115] See *Bulletin EEC* 12-1965, at pp. 5–13.

[116] Representation permanente de la Belgique auprès des Communautes europeennes, No C/QC/130A/15.259 (Conseil extraordinaire CEE; Luxembourg 17–18 janvier 1966), at p. 1.

[117] Representation permanente de la Belgique, above Ch 2, n 116, at p. 2.

[118] Representation permanente de la Belgique, above Ch 2, n 116, at p. 2.

[119] Process-verbal de la session extraordinaire du Conseil de la Communauté Economique Européenne tenue à Luxembourg, 17–18 et 27–28 janvier 1966, Conseil of the CEE, no C/12 f/66 (AE 1) final, at p. 17.

was a sufficient denial of sovereignty to accept that proposals presented by the Commission could be adopted by qualified majority at all; to apply the new procedure without 'any sort of exception' was unacceptable (see above 2.3.2.2).

Proceeding then to the second issue, Couve de Murville asked for confirmation that co-operation between the Council and the Commission was the driving force of the Community which should therefore be manifest at every stage.[120] This he said was not a question of modifying the role of the Commission as that had been established in the EEC Treaty but of assuring that it would 'stick to its role and not try to give itself powers which the Treaty does not confer on it.'[121] As a basis for such a clarification, Couve de Murville submitted a memorandum in ten points, indicating the fields in which the French Government felt that changes needed to be made.[122] This was immediately dubbed 'the ten capital sins that the Commission must no longer commit.'[123]

One of the things which came most strongly under attack was the tactics which were no doubt used by the Commission to put pressure on the Governments to accept its proposals by dealing directly with politicians and high officials, appearing before interest groups and party conventions, and participating in television and radio debates.[124] In order to come to terms with this the French Government requested that the Commission should consult the Governments before presenting its proposals and that there should be 'a rule that in no case may the Commission reveal the tenor of its proposals to the Parliament or to the public before they have been officially referred to the Council.' Another thing was that the Commission—according to the French Government—had lost sight of the procedures for relations with other international organizations (this was a clear reference to the negotiations in the Kennedy Round). It was required therefore that 'the Council should judge, case by case, and purely in the light of Community interests, the form and nature of the links to be established.'

Of greatest significance for present purposes was the French Government's discontent with the Commission's habit of making

---

[120] Representation permanente de la Belgique, above Ch 2, n 116, at p. 4. Cf. point 1 of the French Government's Memorandum, below Ch 2, n 122.

[121] Process-verbal de la session extraordinaire, above Ch 2, n 119, at p. 6.

[122] See the French Government's Memorandum, in *Bulletin EEC* 3-1966, at pp. 6–7.

[123] See *Le Monde* 19 January 1966. Reference in Lindberg, above Ch 2, n 95, at p. 250.

[124] See Lindberg, above Ch 2, n 95, at p. 251.

proposals in which it reserved extensive powers for itself. The problem was spelt out in the third point of the memorandum:

a) The Commission often proposes to the Council decisions which, instead of dealing with the substance of the problems posed, merely give the Commission powers to act later but without specifying the measures which it will take if such powers are conferred upon it (1963 proposal of trade; certain commercial policy proposals).

b) In certain cases the Commission can obtain authority from the Council to put into effect the rules which the latter lays down. This delegation of powers must not imply that the tasks entrusted to the Commission will then be outside the purview of the Council. True, in certain sectors such as agriculture, the Council can intervene at executive level through its representatives on the Management Committees. However, it must be noted that far from being content with this system the Commission is endeavouring to replace the Management Committees by simple Advisory Committees which have no hold over it (the case of Regulation 19/65 on cartels; Commission proposal of 1965 on transport).

Therefore, as reasoned by the French Government:

c) It is important that the executive powers thus vested in the Commission should be precisely circumscribed and leave no room for discretion or autonomous responsibility, failing which the balance of powers, which is a feature of the institutional structure of the Community and a basic guarantee provided by the Treaty, would not be respected.

As had already been acknowledged by General de Gaulle there was a direct link between the French Government's concern over the way in which the Commission drafted its proposals and the voting procedure in the Council. In spite of the passage to qualified majority voting it was still only going to be possible for the Council to amend the Commission's proposals by unanimous decision.[125] Therefore, in practice it would not be possible to have the proposal reformulated so as to specify more clearly what powers should be left to the Commission and under what conditions if the proposal enjoyed the support of only one of the Governments. Obviously, for the French Government there was a great risk that such an 'unspecified' proposal would still be approved by a qualified majority. As clearly admitted, this type of coalition-building was something which it feared the Commission mastered far too skilfully.

---

[125] See Article 149 EEC (1958).

2.3.4 A compromise with several components

The other Governments admitted that the issues raised by the French had to be taken seriously. Following two days of intense and relatively fruitful negotiations in the Council the decision was therefore taken to leave the preparation of a final text to the Committee of Permanent Representatives (Coreper) and to suspend the extraordinary session until 27 and 28 January 1966.[126] The Council finally reached a compromise when the session resumed.

As a reflection of the multitude of considerations which lay behind the crisis, the compromise through which it was resolved had several components. Most clearly spelt out was a public statement concerning the use of qualified majority voting and the relations between the Council and the Commission.[127] But no less important was an agreement to settle 'as a matter of priority' the problem of financing the common agricultural policy, to renew the mandate for negotiations in GATT (the Kennedy Round), and to begin discussions on the composition of a new single Commission.[128]

According to the part of the public statement which related to the use of qualified majority voting, all Governments except the French were willing to accept that, whenever 'very important interests of one or more partners [were] at stake, the Members of the Council [would] endeavour, within a reasonable time, to reach solutions which [could] be adopted by all the Members of the Council while respecting their mutual interests and those of the Community'. The French Government went further, requiring that in the same situation 'the discussion must be continued until unanimous agreement is reached.' It is clear from the statement that the French Government's view was not accepted by the others. Instead it was noted that there was a difference of opinion on what precisely would happen when a complete resolution of a dispute within the Council was not achieved. For that reason, this part of the compromise has often been referred to as an 'agreement to disagree'.[129] However significant that may seem there can be no doubt that the matter was considered to be a *question d'école* rather than an *eventualité concrète*.[130] Already at an early stage of the

---

[126] See *Bulletin EEC* 3-1966, at p. 7.   [127] See *Bulletin EEC* 3-1966, at pp. 8–9.

[128] See *Bulletin EEC* 3-1966, at p. 10.   [129] See e.g. *Bulletin EC* Supplement 2/78, at p. 12.

[130] See Representation permanente de la Belgique auprès des Communautes europeennes, no C/QC/130/15.369 (Conseil extraordinaire CEE; Luxembourg 28–29 janvier 1966), at p. 13.

negotiations the conclusion had been reached that the Community should only function if solutions could be found which were acceptable to everyone.[131] As concluded, therefore, it was unlikely that the Council would ever find it necessary to vote on any matter of greater importance.[132]

Although the section of the statement dealing with qualified majority voting is the component most commonly thought of in the context of the so-called Luxembourg Compromise, the section which concerned relations between the Commission and the Council was certainly of no less significance. In contrast to the rather lengthy discussion which the first matter gave rise to, the second was more easy for the Governments to deal with. On the basis of the French Government's memorandum, a series of 'methods of co-operation' were formulated. As clearly stated, these were only to be adopted after 'a *future* exchange of views' with the Commission (emphasis added).

This was indeed an expression of the wish to respect the letter of the EEC Treaty,[133] but it also reflected the French Government's insistence on the rapid putting in place of the new single Commission. According to Couve de Murville, it would be both 'unnecessary and unpleasant' to initiate any discussions with the current Commission;[134] apparently, the French Government even had the intention not to return as long as it remained in office.[135] This attitude was based on the opinion that the methods of co-operation which had been agreed on would not be sufficient if certain key positions in the Commission were not at the same time subject to a principle of rotation.[136] It had become obvious to everyone that the French Government's overriding priority was to get rid of Commission President Hallstein.

The methods of co-operation listed by the Council followed closely the memorandum presented by Couve de Murville. One of the few points of the memorandum which had not been retained by the Council

---

[131] See Process-verbal de la session extraordinaire, above Ch 2, n 119, at p. 20. Cf. Representation permanente de la Belgique, above Ch 2, n 130, at pp. 2–4.

[132] See Representation permanente de la Belgique, above Ch 2, n 130, at pp. 3 and 7. Cf. Process-verbal de la session extraordinaire, above Ch 2, n 119, at pp. 20–21.

[133] Cf. Article 162 EEC (1958) according to which '[t]he Council and the Commission shall consult each other and shall settle by common accord their methods of co-operation.'

[134] See *Europe* (*la journée politique européenne*) 18 January 1966.

[135] See *Europe* (*la journée politique européenne*) 18 January 1966.

[136] See Process-verbal de la session extraordinaire, above Ch 2, n 119, at p. 37.

was that relating to the exercise of implementing powers. But this should not be taken to mean that the matter was not considered. In the text prepared by the Committee of Permanent Representatives, a 'method' was envisaged according to which the Council and the Commission would specify—together—what type of implementing powers were to be entrusted to the Commission and what role was to be given to management committees.[137] But, as noted by a number of Governments, both these questions fell within the exclusive competence of the Council.[138] Since this meant that the necessary improvements could be made without the need to involve the Commission it was deleted.

2.3.5   The immediate result

2.3.5.1   A reason for institutional concern

Following resolution of the crisis, the Commission issued a communiqué saying that it was 'pleased that the Community could now resume its normal activities'.[139] It also explained that it was ready to hold the requested consultations 'in order to make even closer collaboration possible between itself and the Council.' It is not clear whether this was ever done. Seemingly, no consultations were held by the existing Commission during its remaining time in office and the new Commission—as every subsequent Commission—officially refused to recognize the Compromise.[140] In spite of that, the result was undoubtedly such as to chill off the Commission's political aspirations and tie it closer to the Governments.

Unlike the Commission, the European Parliament took an active stance against the Compromise. As clarified in a resolution adopted on 9 March 1966, the European Parliament regarded the 'new procedures' as a threat to its own status as the Institution which exercises political control over the Commission.[141] The dissatisfaction of the European Parliament

---

[137] See Process-verbal de la session extraordinaire, above Ch 2, n 119, at p. 71.

[138] See Process-verbal de la session extraordinaire, above Ch 2, n 119, at pp. 28 and 71.

[139] See General Report 1966, above Ch 2, n 102, at p. 33.

[140] See *Europe* (*bulletin quotidien*) 4 July 1968 and Vasey, M., Decision Making in the Agriculture Council and the Luxembourg Compromise (1988) 25 *CMLRev* 725, at p. 726.

[141] See European Parliament Resolution of 9 March 1966 concerning the present situation of the European Community adopted by the European Parliament (OJ 1966 769/66).

was re-affirmed two years later when its activist member Henk Vredling claimed that the new Commission—in spite of its official attitude—had actually accepted the Compromise and that this in turn had caused an 'institutional impasse' (see below 2.4.4).[142]

As will be seen in the next chapter, the crisis of the empty chair was to cast its shadow over both Member States and Community Institutions for many years to come. Arguably, it remains a factor which must be taken into consideration in discussions on the institutional and constitutional form of the Community (cf. below 4.1.1). But in a more limited perspective, a number of immediate reactions can be identified. These relate to the problem which triggered off the crisis, that of the financing of the common agricultural policy, but also to the negotiations in GATT, the composition of the new Commission, and the future use of management committees.

2.3.5.2   *The financing of the common agricultural policy and the GATT negotiations*

The negotiations in the Kennedy Round had been more or less paralysed during the crisis.[143] Following the Compromise and the agreement to renew the Commission's mandate, it was expected that they could now be resumed. But it soon became clear that there were a number of problems which had first to be overcome. Most importantly, the Council was still 'dragging about with the unfortunate financial regulation like a saucepan with its handle.'[144] For a long time therefore the French Government refused to consent to any new instructions for the Kennedy Round. The German Government reacted vigorously. Although not contesting the priority of the financial regulation as such, it considered that the 'formula of synchronisation' required simultaneous progress, notably by enabling the Commission at least to resume its seat at the conference table. Therefore turning the French thesis against its authors, the German Government explained that should there not be any progress in respect of the Kennedy Round, this would complicate the discussions on the financial regulation.[145]

Fears that the crisis was about to re-erupt were expelled on 6 April 1966 when it was reported that the French Government had proven

---

[142]   See *Europe (bulletin quotidien)* 4 July 1968.

[143]   See *Europe (bulletin quotidien)* 10 November and 21 December 1965.

[144]   Quote from Couve de Murville, in *Europe (bulletin quotidien)* 4 April 1966.

[145]   See *Europe (bulletin quotidien)* 2 April 1966.

willing to relax its approach and that the German Government had noted this gesture with gratitude.[146] The negotiations in the Kennedy Round were re-opened on 3 May 1966 and on 11 May 1966 agreement was reached on Council Regulation 130/66/EEC on the financing of the common agricultural policy.[147] In order to circumvent political differences of opinion, it was decided that this would only be valid until the end of the transitional period and the idea of designating agricultural levies as a basis for the Community's own resources before that date was dropped.[148] Further progress was noted on 26 July 1966 when agreement was reached on a series of new Regulations relating to the common agricultural policy.[149] Since 'the most difficult chapters of the common agricultural policy' had now been passed, the decision was taken to set the definite date for completion of customs union as 1 July 1968.[150]

Following renewal of the Commission's mandate, the negotiations in the Kennedy Round were given a fresh impetus and the final act was signed in Geneva on 30 June 1967.[151] According to the Director-General of GATT, Wyndham White, this meant 'that the results of the most far-reaching international trade negotiation of all times had been given formal approval.'[152] For the Community, the implications were far-reaching. Its Member States were not only going to get better access to the world market but they would become exposed to more international competition than they had ever been before.[153]

[146] See *Europe* (*bulletin quotidien*) 6 April 1966.

[147] See *Europe* (*bulletin quotidien*) 4 May and 10 June 1966. See Council Regulation 130/66/EEC of 26 July 1966 on the financing of the common agricultural policy (OJ 1966 B 165/2965).

[148] See further Weber, above Ch 2, n 39, at p. 276.

[149] See, in particular, Council Regulation 136/66/EEC of 22 September 1966 on the establishment of a common organisation of the market in oils and fats (OJ 1966 P 172/3025); Council Regulation 159/66/EEC of 25 October 1966 on supplementary dispositions for the common organisation of the markets in fruit and vegetables (OJ 1966 192/3286); and Council Regulation 1009/67/EEC of 18 December 1967 on the common organisation of the market in sugar (OJ 1967 B 308/1). For a detailed analysis, see Olmi, G., Common Organisation of Agricultural Markets at the Stage of the Single Market (1967–69) 5 *CMLRev* 359.

[150] See Council Decision 66/532/EEC of 26 July 1966 concerning the abolition of customs duties and the prohibition of quantitative restrictions between the Member States and the entering into force of the rules of the common customs tariff (OJ 1966 165/2971). See *Europe* (*bulletin quotidien*) 10 June and 25 and 27 July 1966.

[151] The Council approved the Commission's report on the results on 27 November 1967 thus endorsing the commitments entered into on behalf of the Community.

[152] See *Bulletin EEC* 8-1967, at p. 17.

[153] See General Report 1966, above Ch 2, n 102, at pp. 18–19.

2.3.5.3   *The new Commission*

In spite of the French Government's insistence on the rapid putting in place of the new single Commission (see above 2.3.4), the Merger Treaty only entered into effect on 1 July 1967.[154] On the same day, Walter Hallstein was replaced by Jean Rey, the Belgian Commissioner who had been responsible for the negotiations in the Kennedy Round. One of the new incoming members was General de Gaulle's personal adviser Raymond Barre, now Commissioner responsible for economic and financial affairs. Recalling the old Commission's attempt to 'buy off de Gaulle with a piece of cheese' the safeguards which came to surround the appointment of the new come close to poetic justice—at least from a French perspective.[155] Apparently consultations between the French and the German Governments had resulted in an agreement that Walter Hallstein would be appointed as President of the single Commission but that he would remain in this office for only a few months and would then submit his resignation.[156] But this was refused by Hallstein, who informed the German Chancellor, Kurt Georg Kiesinger, that he was not interested. Instead, he was to become leader of the so-called European Movement.[157]

The Governments had decided that the candidate to be considered as President would have to enter into a 'personal agreement' according to which the term of office should only be renewed on an annual basis.[158] Evidently, this was something which Jean Rey was prepared to accept. As he clarified in one of his first public appearances, his Commission was to do its best to ensure 'more personal and more constant co-operation with the Governments of the Member States, not only with the Council of

---

[154] See Treaty of 8 April 1965 establishing a single Council and a single Commission of the European Communities (OJ 1967 152/1). Cf. Decision 67/447/EEC, 67/31/EAEC of 1 July 1967 on the nomination of the members of the Commission of the European Communities as well as the President and the Vice-President of this Commission (OJ 1967 152/21).

[155] See above Ch 2, n 101.

[156] See Editorial Comments (1966–67) 4 *CMLRev* 373, at p. 375; and First General Report on the Activities of the European Communities 1967 (Office for Official Publications 1968), at p. 26. Cf. also the remarks made by the President of the Economic and Social Committee in his speech on 29 June 1967, published in *Bulletin EEC* 8-1967, at p. 19. See, in general, Loth *et al.*, above Ch 2, n 111.   [157] See *Europe (bulletin quotidien)* 22 January 1968.

[158] See General Report 1967, above Ch 2, n 156, at p. 26. Cf. Article 33 of the Merger Treaty, above Ch 2, n 154.

course, with which we meet regularly, but—I wish to repeat this—with the Governments themselves.'[159]

2.3.5.4   The future use of management committees

As will be seen in the next chapter, the Luxembourg Compromise came to be most commonly considered for its inhibitory effects on decision-making in the Council. This was the result of a development over time for which additional factors—such as the accession of the United Kingdom—were decisive. But at the time when the Compromise was entered into, the agreement and, indeed, disagreement on voting in the Council was but one component of several. As has been seen above, the French Government's agenda had been centred on its fear that the Community 'would be ruled by some sort of technocratic body of elders, stateless and irresponsible' (see above 2.3.2.2). This fear was by no means new. So, for example, in 1962 it had been at the core of the discussions on a common agricultural policy—reflected most clearly in the French proposal for creation of management committees.[160] In this perspective, the demands made by the French Government during the crisis, and the Compromise finally agreed on, should rather be seen as a series of measures intended not to obstruct co-operation but to make sure that it would continue in a way which was acceptable to all Member States.

At the same time reminding and requiring the Commission to manifest a certain loyalty to the Council, mechanisms were introduced with the purpose of guaranteeing the Governments a continuous input and control. While it is true that the most far-reaching of these mechanisms was that relating to voting in the Council, it is mistaken to believe that this was intended to call off the planned shift to qualified-majority voting. As General de Gaulle himself emphasized, the French asked only for an 'exception'.[161] Whatever the divergence of views as to its absolute meaning, it was also an exception which was agreed on.[162] Of greater practical use was the mechanism offered by a more systematic use of management committees.

---

[159] Address by Commission President Jean Rey to the European Parliament on 20 September 1967. See *Bulletin EEC* 9/10-1967, at p. 7. It may be noted that in 1970, also Jean Rey was forced to resign. See Editorial Comments (1970) 7 *CMLRev* 254, at p. 257.

[160] See above Ch 2, n 50.   [161] See above Ch 2, n 106.   [162] See above 2.3.4.

Nearly all regulations adopted by the Council in the field of the common agricultural policy after the crisis entailed delegation of powers to the Commission subject to the requirement that it would co-operate with management committees.[163] More importantly, during the period which followed the Luxembourg Compromise, the use of management committees spread beyond the field of the common agricultural policy. As a doctoral thesis concluded in 1967:

...the management committee procedure, introduced into Community practice as a compromise in the limited area of agricultural market organisations, may thus develop into the normal procedure of decision-making by the Commission, as far as powers delegated by the Council are concerned. Whenever close co-operation between Commission and Member States seems desirable—and there is no field in which it does not—the Governments are often no longer content with participating in the formulation of Commission decisions through merely consultative committees, but press for more effective channels for influence, and insist, above all, that the Council, in spite of transference of powers to the Commission, should retain a right of control.[164]

But it should be noted that this venture into new fields of co-operation was paralleled by and, indeed, conditioned upon the introduction of new and more sophisticated instruments for influence.

2.4   The spread of the committee system

2.4.1   *Progress towards a common commercial policy*

2.4.1.1   *A threat to the achievements in GATT*

In accordance with the decision taken by the Council in 1966, customs union was to be completed on 1 July 1968.[165] This indeed was going to be 'a major economic, psychological and political event.'[166] From that

---

[163] See e.g. the Jozeau-Marigné Report, below Ch 2, n 220.

[164] See Bertram, C., *Das Verwaltingsausschussverfahren: Ein neuartiges Recht-setzungsverfahren der Europäischen Wirtschaftgemeinschaft* (Rheinischen Friedrich-Willhelms-Universität zu Bonn 1967). Quote from Bertram, above Ch 1, n 24, at p. 249.   [165] See above Ch 2, n 150.

[166] See the statement by Commission President Jean Rey on 1 July 1968, in *Bulletin EC* 8-1968, at p. 5.

date onward all customs duties on trade between Member States would be prohibited and a common customs tariff applied to trade with the rest of the world. The economic advantages for the Member States were expected to be considerable.[167] As had been concluded after the Kennedy Round of the negotiations in GATT, the Member States would also become more exposed to international competition than they had ever been before.[168] For this reason in particular, the EEC Treaty required the gradual introduction of a common commercial policy based on 'uniform principles, particularly in regard to changes in tariff rates, the conclusion of tariff and trade agreements, the achievement of uniformity in measures of liberalisation, export policy and measures to protect trade such as those to be taken in case of dumping and subsidies.'[169]

The Commission had submitted its first set of proposals relating to a common commercial policy in 1961 and in 1962 the Council had established an action programme for the transitional period.[170] In spite of this, progress had been disappointing.[171] Clearly the Governments were far from willing to 'concede powers whose exercise has so far-reaching political and economic consequences for their nations.'[172] But as the date for completion of customs union came closer the matter became increasingly difficult to avoid and in 1968 with a delay of several years, progress was finally made towards a common commercial policy. This can be explained by looking at the simultaneous development in the Community's relations with its most important trading partner: the United States.

Since the conclusion of the Kennedy Round difficulties with its balance of payments had led the United States Government to adopt a number of protective measures designed to strengthen the dollar. Most significantly laws on countervailing duties and import quotas which had been passed prior to the establishment of GATT were enforced. Although not in conformity with the general rules of GATT these laws remained valid by virtue of exemptions which the United States had

[167] For an extensive discussion, see Everling above Ch 2, n 17.

[168] See General Report 1966, above Ch 2, n 22, at pp. 18–19.

[169] See Articles 111 and 113 EEC (1958).

[170] See Council Decision 62/1005/EEC of 25 September 1962 concerning an Action Programme on Commercial Policy (OJ 1962 B 90/2353).

[171] See, in general, Everling, above Ch 2, n 17.

[172] See Everling, above Ch 2, n 17, at p. 162.

obtained at its accession.[173] In the Commission's view this was 'a regrettable element of uncertainty in the development of a climate of co-operation and mutual trust in trade relations with the United States' and gave it reasons to fear that the United States would not be able to keep up with the speed for reduction of customs duties agreed at the Kennedy Round.[174]

The situation did not improve after the United States President Lyndon B. Johnson presented a stringent plan which envisaged, among other things, the introduction of an import charge and an export subsidy.[175] Reactions on behalf of the Community were anything but reserved. As the new French Commissioner, Raymond Barre, warned on 23 January 1968, this would not only mean that the achievements of the Kennedy Round would be seriously threatened but could also lead to 'reactions which could inhibit the freedom of international trade and international economic co-operation.'[176] In spite of numerous consultations between the Commission and the United States Government, the situation was aggravated and the Community soon found itself faced with two alternative lines of action: one favoured by the German and the Dutch Governments, to proceed with the reduction of customs duties as planned irrespectively of the United States; and another favoured by the French Government, to respond by analogous means.[177]

2.4.1.2   The Governments forced into rapprochement

Following heated discussions under the French Presidency, on 9 April 1968 the Council opted for what was referred to as *la petite acceleration*.[178] In essence, this meant that a certain delay on behalf of the United States would be accepted and that all other parties to GATT—including the Community—should go ahead with the reductions as planned if by the end of the year, a number of conditions had been satisfied. Most significantly the United States was required to refrain from introducing any import charge or export subsidy. The solution was bound to fail. During

---

[173] See Second General Report on the Activities of the European Community 1968 (Office for Official Publications 1969), at p. 377.

[174] See General Report 1968, above Ch 2, n 173, at p. 378.

[175] See the first speech by Commissioner Raymond Barre to the European Parliament on 23 January 1968, in *Bulletin EC* 2-1968, at p. 19.

[176] Speech by Raymond Barre, above Ch 2, n 175, at p. 19.

[177] See *Europe (bulletin quotidien)* 7 February, 1, 4, and 6 March and 16 April 1968.

[178] See *Europe (bulletin quotidien)* 9 April 1968.

the period which followed, export subsidies introduced by a troubled French Government (see below 2.5.1) gave the United States Government reason to place a supplementary duty on imports of French products.[179] This in turn led to further escalation and the outbreak of an outright 'dispute' between the Community and the United States.[180] By the time the Council came to examine the Commission's account of the situation at the end of 1968 everyone knew that *la petite acceleration* had failed.

However great the difference between the Governments' notions of a common commercial policy, the conflict with the United States forced them to seek a *rapprochement*. The first result of this was the adoption of a series of shelved proposals for regulations intended to ensure a uniform protection should the markets be 'threatened with disturbance.'[181] In principle, this meant that inadequate and sometimes conflicting rules on the national level were replaced by common rules providing for close co-operation between the Commission and the national administrations. In order to avoid new conflicts, the Commission had already up-dated its proposals so that use could be made of the same type of management committee procedures that were now tried and tested in the field of the common agricultural policy.[182] But it soon turned out that this was not enough to satisfy some Governments' demands. Torn between the wish for national control and the need for concessions, they insisted instead that 'a more restrictive formula' had to be found.[183] Following heated discussions in the Council, the Regulations which were finally adopted therefore gave life to a new type of committee procedure.

2.4.2 The establishment of regulatory committees

The first important step towards a common commercial policy was taken with the adoption on 5 April 1968 of Council Regulation 459/68/EEC on protection against dumping.[184] This made it possible to charge a duty on

---

[179] See *Europe (bulletin quotidien)* 2 July 1968 and 30 August 1968.

[180] See *Europe (bulletin quotidien)* 19 December 1968.

[181] See *Europe (bulletin quotidien)* 8 April 1968.   [182] See e.g. *Bulletin EC* 8-1968, at p. 5.

[183] See *Europe (bulletin quotidien)* 28 February 1968.

[184] See Council Regulation 459/68/EEC of 5 April 1968 on protection against dumping or the granting of bounties or subsidies by countries which are not members of the Community (OJ 1968 L 93/1).

any imported product which had been subject to dumping or which had been given a subsidy in its country of origin. A procedure was set out at some considerable length for 'close and constant co-operation' between the Commission and governmental representatives within the so-called Committee on Protection against Dumping.[185] At the same time as a presumption had been created in favour of the introduction of an anti-dumping duty, a clear signal was sent to the Commission that it would only be permitted to play an active role to the extent it could mediate effectively between the interests of all Governments.

In essence, Council Regulation 459/68/EEC entrusted the Commission with an examination of facts submitted to it by a Member State. On the basis of its examination, the Commission could then make a proposal to the Council that an anti-dumping duty should be introduced. But the Commission could only choose not to propose the introduction of a duty if none of the governmental representatives in the Committee objected. If objections were made, the Commission was compelled to submit the matter to the Council which could then order it to re-open the examination. The Commission was also given the opportunity to introduce a provisional anti-dumping duty for the period before the facts in a specific case had been finally established. This it could do on its own initiative or after having been requested to do so by a representative in the Committee. Nevertheless, should the Commission decide not to act upon such a request, it was obliged to communicate its decision to the Council, which could then take a different decision.

Further advance was made with the adoption on 27 June 1968 of Council Regulation 802/68/EEC on the common definition of the concept of origin of goods.[186] This provided a framework for the establishment of rules which made it possible to differentiate between products on the basis of their country of origin. One of the situations which were mentioned as an example of when this could be required was when it had to be established whether textiles of synthetic fibres originated from the United States since, in that case, an especially high tariff would have to be applied.[187] On the same date, Council Regulation 803/68/EEC was adopted in which uniform rules were established for the

---

[185] See, in particular, Articles 12–14 of Council Regulation 459/68/EEC, above Ch 2, n 184.

[186] See Council Regulation 802/68/EEC of 27 June 1968 on the common definition of the concept of the origin of goods (OJ 1968 L 148/1).

[187] See *Europe (bulletin quotidien)* 28 June 1968.

valuation of goods for customs purposes.[188] Characteristic of both these Regulations was the fact that they left a far-reaching responsibility for adoption of rules relating to their application to the Commission in 'close and effective co-operation' with governmental representatives within, in the first case, the so-called Committee on Origin of Goods, and, in the second case, the so-called Customs Valuation Committee.[189] These could be rules defining the concept of origin, specifying the conditions with which certificates of origin should comply, or determining the price which should be taken as a basis for a valuation.

In principle, the procedure which had been laid down in Council Regulation 459/68/EEC on protection against dumping was only a more cautious version of that already in use in the field of the common agricultural policy. In both cases, the Committee's formal right of influence had been based on its ability to manifest its discontent with the Commission's planned line of action. But with the adoption of Council Regulation 802/68/EEC and Council Regulation 803/68/EEC a new philosophy was introduced. According to the procedures for co-operation with the Committee on Origin of Goods and the Customs Valuation Committee, the Commission was only permitted to adopt the rules it envisaged if they had first been approved in a positive opinion. Should the Committee disprove, by means of a negative opinion, or more importantly not be able to agree on any opinion at all (by qualified majority), the Commission had to hand the matter over to the Council in a proposal for legislation. But if the Council were unable to act within a certain period, the Commission could proceed as intended. This latter mechanism was referred to as a *filet* or 'safety net' intended to secure that some sort of action should always be taken. Below follow the provisions by which the procedure was laid down in Council Regulation 802/68/EEC:[190]

Article 12

1   A Committee on Origin (hereinafter called the 'Committee') shall be set up and shall consist of representatives of the Member States, with a representative of the Commission acting as Chairman.

2   The Committee shall draw up its own rules of procedure.

[188] See Council Regulation 803/68/EEC of 27 June 1968 on the valuation of goods for customs purposes (OJ 1968 L 148/6).

[189] See, in particular, Articles 12–14 of Council Regulation 802/68/EEC, above Ch 2, n 186.

[190] Cf. Articles 15–17 of Council Regulation 803/68/EEC, above Ch 2, n 188.

Article 13

The committee may examine all questions relating to the application of this regulation referred to it by its Chairman, either on his own initiative or at the request of a representative of a member state.

Article 14

1   The provisions required for applying Articles 4 to 7, 9 and 10 shall be adopted in accordance with the procedure laid down in paragraphs 2 and 3 of this Article.

2   The representative of the Commission shall submit to the Committee a draft of the provisions to be adopted. The Committee shall deliver an opinion on the draft within a time limit set by the Chairman having regard to the urgency of the matter. Decisions shall be taken by a majority of twelve votes, the votes of the Member States being weighted as provided in Article 148(2) of the Treaty. The Chairman shall not vote.

3   (a) The Commission shall adopt the envisaged provisions if they are in accordance with the opinion of the Committee.

   (b) If the envisaged provisions are not in accordance with the opinion of the Committee, or if no opinion is delivered, the Commission shall without delay submit to the Council a proposal with regard to the provisions to be adopted. The Council shall act by a qualified majority.

   (c) If, within three months of the proposal being submitted to it, the Council has not acted, the proposed provisions shall be adopted by the Commission.

As had been agreed in the Council, the uniform system of protection would also include a series of regulations regarding the power to use quantitative quotas. Above all this should enable the Commission to increase or adjust quantitative quotas for products from countries which were parties to GATT but which had not achieved the agreed reduction of customs duties. But contrary to the previous regulations—which all entered into effect on 1 July 1968—these were thought to require 'a more careful analysis.'[191] The most problematic question was that of the Commission's discretion and the type of procedure which should be used to guarantee that it would co-operate with governmental representatives.[192] After long-lasting disagreement in the Council, the question was only resolved once it had become clear that the United States was not going to comply with the conditions for *la petite acceleration* (see above 2.4.1.2). This time the result was also more restrictive than that which had

---

[191] See *Europe (bulletin quotidien)* 28 June 1968.
[192] See *Europe (bulletin quotidien)* 10 June 1968.

been proposed by the Commission. As manifested in Council Regulation 2043/68/EEC, the Commission would have to work together with the so-called Committee for Administration of Quotas on terms identical to those laid down in the case of the Committee on Origin of Goods and the Customs Valuation Committee.[193]

Initially the committees which had been introduced by Council Regulation 802/68/EEC, Council Regulation 803/68/EEC, and Council Regulation 2043/68/EEC were only conceived of as another form of management committee.[194] But it was soon concluded that the new committees were used in situations where the Commission was empowered to adopt implementing rules of a general and, indeed, permanent nature.[195] For this reason the Commission begun to refer to them as 'legislative committees'.[196] But the label which soon became commonly accepted was 'regulatory committees' (see below 2.4.4).

2.4.3   Early efforts for harmonization of the conditions for trade

2.4.3.1   A programme for action in the veterinary sector

In spite of the fact that all customs duties had been abolished as from 1 July 1968, there were still many obstacles which had to be overcome in

[193] See Council Regulation 2043/68/EEC of 10 December 1968 on the progressive establishment of a common procedure for managing quantitative quotas for imports into the Community (OJ 1968 L 303/39). See also Council Regulation 2041/68/EEC of 10 December 1968 concerning the drawing up of a common liberalisation list for imports into the Community from non-member countries (OJ 1968 L 303/1); and Council Regulation 2045/68/EEC of 10 December 1968 establishing a special import procedure for certain products from certain non-member countries (OJ 1968 L 303/43).

[194] See e.g. Bertram, above Ch 1, n 24; and Schindler, P., The Problems of Decision Making by Way of the Management Committee Procedure in the EEC (1971) 8 *CMLRev* 184. It should be noted that a procedure similar to that used in the case of the new regulatory committees was already in use for decisions concerning the financing of development projects under the so-called Yaoundé Convention on the Association of African States. See Article 11 of the Internal Agreement EEC/64/354 on the measures to take and procedures to follow in the application of the Convention of association between the European Economic Community and the Associated African States and Madagascar (OJ 1964 93/1490).

[195] See the Jozeau-Marigné Report, below Ch 2, n 216. See also Olivier, M. G., Les pouvoirs de gestion de la Commission, in *La Commission des Communautés européennes et l'élargissement de l'Europe*, Colloque organise les 23–24–25 novembre 1972 par l'Institut d'études européennes (Editions de l'Université de Bruxelles 1974), at p. 159.

[196] See e.g. General Report 1968, above Ch 2, n 173, point 484.

order for there to be a common market. So, for example, little had been done to come to terms with the differences between the Member States as to the conditions which had to be met before products could be sold.[197] Therefore, parallel to the progress towards a common commercial policy, there was a call for harmonization of national legislation 'to the extent required for the proper functioning of the common market.'[198]

Most forcefully, the French Government, but also the Dutch, demanded a strict harmonization of legislation relating to foodstuffs so that national rules relating to public health and consumer protection would not be used for political and protectionist reasons.[199] As explained by the French Minister of Foreign Affairs, Michel Debré, '[t]he varied nature of the rules to which the manufacture and marketing of many products, notably foodstuffs, are subject in each of the Member States can inhibit the internal expansion of trade and the formation of a homogeneous market, just as the existence of technical obstacles does.'[200] One of the related events which had caused much stir was that resulting from a finding that feedingstuffs for Dutch veal contained hormones. In spite of the fact that this had only happened in a few cases which had been identified immediately, some Member States placed a ban on all imports of Dutch veal.[201] Similarly, a ban which had been placed on imports of Italian pork after an outbreak of the so-called African Plague included ham and sausages which had been produced well before the appearance of the disease.[202]

In an early effort to come to terms with this type of problem, on 12 March 1968 the Council adopted a programme for action in the veterinary sector.[203] The programme insisted, on the one hand, that each Member State should have a right to take safeguard measures, and on the other, addressed the need for harmonization of national legislation in order 'to render impossible abuses or temptations for the national authorities to use veterinary measures for protectionist reasons.'[204] The

---

[197]   See further Eckert, D., annotation (1967) 11 *NJurW* 1967, at pp. 473–480.

[198]   See Article 3(h) EEC (1958). Cf. Article 100 EEC (1958).

[199]   See e.g. *Europe* (*bulletin quotidien*) 17 and 19 July 1968. Cf. Lindberg, above Ch 1, n 77, at p. 268.

[200]   Programme for strengthening the EEC: Memorandum of the French delegation presented by the Minister of Foreign Affairs, Michel Debré, at the Council meeting on 4–5 November 1968, in *Bulletin EC* 12-1968, at p. 16.   [201]   See *Europe* (*bulletin quotidien*) 27 February 1968.

[202]   See *Europe* (*bulletin quotidien*) 27 February 1968.

[203]   See Council Resolution of 12 March 1968 on Community measures to be taken in the veterinary sector (OJ 1968 C 22/18).   [204]   See *Europe* (*bulletin quotidien*) 27 February 1968.

programme was based on the idea that a procedural framework needed to be established which enabled the Commission to confirm or reject the protective measures in 'close and practical collaboration' with the Member States within the so-called Standing Veterinary Committee.[205]

2.4.3.2   *The introduction of a double safety net*

When the Commission presented the proposals called for in the programme for action in the veterinary sector—more or less parallel to those relating to protection in the field of the common commercial policy— these envisaged that the Standing Veterinary Committee should operate in accordance with the management committee procedure. But it soon became clear that several Governments were insisting on a solution which would enable them to exercise a stronger control. This time the choice of procedure also gave rise to heated discussions within the Council.[206] Some of the problems relating to the setting up of the Standing Veterinary Committee were linked to the multitude of considerations inherited in the actual subject-matter. Thus, for example, the representatives of the Italian Government, who came from the Ministry of Agriculture, repeatedly refused to commit themselves, claiming that the matter fell within the competence of the Ministry of Health.[207] But more importantly, there were different views on what should happen when a matter, which had not been approved by the Committee, was referred to the Council but the Council could not reach an agreement within the specified period of time.[208] After several months, the problem finally made the top of the agenda and on 15 October 1968 the Council adopted Decision 68/361/EEC setting up a Standing Veterinary Committee and also approved the rules which should govern its method of work for a transitional period of 18 months.[209]

For the first time a construction was adopted which gave the committee an autonomous legal basis. The idea was that the Standing Veterinary Committee should come to be used within the framework of much future legislation and that it would be sufficient then

---

[205] See *Europe (bulletin quotidien)* 27 February 1968.

[206] See *Europe (bulletin quotidien)* 28 February, 6 March, 26 June and 12, 17, 19, 22, and 23 July 1968.   [207] See *Europe (bulletin quotidien)* 17 June 1968.

[208] See *Europe (bulletin quotidien)* 28 February, and 12 July 1968.

[209] See Council Decision 68/361/EEC of 15 October 1968 setting up a Standing Veterinary Committee (OJ 1968 L 255/23). See *Europe (bulletin quotidien)* 17, 19, 22, and 23 July 1968; and *Bulletin* EC 12-1968, at p. 52.

to include a reference to the founding Decision. As explained in Council Decision 68/361/EEC, '[t]he Committee shall, in the cases and under the conditions provided for therein, carry out the duties devolving upon it under the instruments adopted by the Council in the veterinary field.'[210] The exact meaning of this was clarified in the rules of procedure, later to be incorporated in legislation adopted by the Council in the veterinary field.[211] Here it was explained that the Standing Veterinary Committee was to operate in accordance with a regulatory committee procedure similar to that which had been established in the field of the common commercial policy.[212] But this time an even more restrictive formula had been chosen for the situation in which a matter was referred to the Council. According to the procedure used in the field of the common commercial policy, the so-called safety net would ensure that the Commission could proceed as planned if the Council could not decide (by a qualified majority) what other measures should be taken within a certain period. But in the case of the Standing Veterinary Committee, a new *contre-filet* or 'double safety net' was introduced. This meant that the Council could (by a simple majority) prevent the Commission from acting after the expiry of the period even if it had not been able to decide what other measure should be taken (cf. below 3.3.2.2).

2.4.4 The European Parliament agrees on the need for delegation of powers

The development outlined above did not pass by the European Parliament unnoticed. In fact much of its work during 1968 was focused on the question of the Commission's responsibility for implementation and the role of committees. Already on 19 October 1967, the European Parliament had adopted a resolution which urged the Commission and the

---

[210] See Article 2 of Council Decision 68/361/EEC, above Ch 2, n 209.

[211] For some early examples, see Council Directive 69/349/EEC of 6 October 1969 amending the Directive of 26 June 1964 on health problems affecting intra-community trade in fresh meat (OJ 1969 L 256/5); Council Directive 71/285/EEC of 19 July 1971 amending the Directive of 26 June 1964 on animal health problems affecting intra-Community trade in bovine animals and swine (OJ 1971 L 179/1); and Council Directive 72/461/EEC of 12 December 1972 on health problems affecting intra-Community trade in fresh meat (OJ 1972 L 302/1).

[212] See *Europe (bulletin quotidien)* 23 July 1968. When agreed, the solution was not thought to be permanent. As required by the Italian Government, after 18 months a decision had to be taken whether any changes were required.

Council to 'exercise extreme caution in the matter of establishing new committees' and instructed its own committees to keep a close watch on the matter.[213] Over the months that followed a number of reports were adopted in which the development was analysed and discussed.[214] These in turn gave rise to heated debates in the European Parliament. One such debate was started after an MEP, Henk Vredeling, had questioned the Commission's independence and expressed profound concern with the developments that were taking place.[215] This, he said, was not only characterized by the institution of new committees but, in particular, by a tendency that an increasing number of legislative matters were being dealt with in the form of implementing measures adopted by the Commission.

None of the reports was more important than the so-called Jozeau-Marigné Report, presented by the European Parliament's Legal Committee on 30 September 1968.[216] This confirmed Vredeling's claim

---

[213] See Résolution (Parlement européen) du 19 octobre 1967 sur la proposition relative à une directive concernant l'introduction de modes de prélèvement d'échantillons et de méthodes d'analyse communautaires por le contrôle officiel des aliments des animaux, complété par le noveau projet de décision concernant l'institution d'un Comité permanent des aliments des animaux (OJ 1967 268/20). Based on Rapport du 17 octobre 1967 fait au nom de la commission de l'agriculture sur la proposition de la Commission de la C.E.E. au Conseil relative à une directive concernant l'introduction de modes de prélèvement d'échantillons et de méthodes d'analyse communautaires pour le contrôle officiel des aliments des animaus, complété par le nouveau projet de décision concernant l'intstitution d'un Comité permanent des aliments des animaux (rapporteur: Astrid Lulling) PE Doc 129/67. See also *Bulletin EC* 12-1968, at p. 64.

[214] See, most notably, Rapport du 19 juin 1968 fait au nom de la commission des affaires sociales et de la santé publique sur la proposition de la Commission des Communautés européennes au Conseil relative à un règlement concernant le traitement du saccharose destiné à la consommation humaine (rapporteur: Josef Müller) EP Doc 76/68 (subsequent Resolution in OJ 1968 C 66/42); and Rapport du 24 juin 1968 fait au nom du comité de rédaction institué par la résolution du 12 mars 1968 sur le premier rapport général de la Commission des Communautés européennes sur l'activité des Communautés (rapporteur: Hans August Lücker) PE Doc 58/68 (subsequent Resolution in OJ 1968 C 72/37).

[215] See *Europe* (*bulletin quotidien*) 4 July 1968.

[216] See Rapport du 30 septembre 1968 fait au nom de la commission juridique sur les procédures communautaires d'exécution du droit communautaire dérivé (rapporteur: Léon Jozeau-Marigné) PE Doc 115/68. See Bradley, K., The European Parliament and Comitology: On the Road to Nowhere? (1997) 3 *ELJ* 230, at p. 232; and Demmke, C. *et al.*, The History of Comitology, in Pedler, R. H. and Schaefer, G. F. (Eds.), *Shaping European Law and Policy: the Role of Committees and Comitology in the Political Process* (European Institute of Public Administration 1996), at pp. 63–64.

that the role of committees involved in the adoption of implementing measures should not be examined in isolation but had to be seen as one facet in a general trend:

The growth of the Community and the gradual development of 'derived' Community law, which includes regulations, decisions and directives implementing the Treaties, as distinct from 'primary' Community law (constituted by the Treaties) has been matched by a corresponding increase in the tasks facing the Commission and this has given rise to a problem which is at once legal, technical and political. The legal aspect is the devolution of Community powers and the powers vested in the Commission to administer common policies. The technical aspect is that the Commission is obliged to have recourse to representatives of the Member States or national experts who help to guide its work in the spheres it is called upon to regulate or administer. The political aspect is the freedom of decision left to the Commission and, in particular, the limits to this freedom.[217]

In the light of this finding, the Jozeau-Marigné Report ambitiously set out to 'establish an inventory' of the various types of procedure for the adoption of implementing measures and to determine the considerations underlying the choice between them in a specific case. This would then make it possible to conclude what the legal and political consequences of the development were and, above all, clarify the causes of unrest in the European Parliament.

The most basic observation deriving from the inventory was that not all implementing measures were adopted by the Commission in accordance with procedures for co-operation with committees. A number of examples were given of situations where the Council had granted the Commission a power to act alone as well as situations where the implementing measures had been adopted by the Council. In particular, this latter finding led the author of the Report to enter into a rather extensive discussion on the interpretation of 'delegation of powers' as provided for in Article 155 EEC (1958). Here it was noted that the ability of the Council to exercise the implementing powers, although not expressly envisaged, followed *a contrario* from the fact that the Council was not legally obliged, but simply permitted, to confer those powers on the Commission. For this reason the Council could choose to

---

[217] See the Jozeau-Marigné Report, above Ch 2, n 216, at p. 5 (paragraphs 2 and 4); or *Bulletin EC* 12-1968, at p. 64.

'reserve' the implementing powers for itself.[218] The consequences of that interpretation—for the understanding of delegation of powers but also, as will be seen in a while, for the role of committees—was far-reaching.

In one of the previous reports that had been presented, the claim had been made that Article 155 EEC (1958) was a provision of a general nature, the applicability of which was limited by other more specific provisions in the EEC Treaty which stated that legislation should be adopted by the Council (cf. the legal principle of *lex specialis legi generali derogat*).[219] This had then been used to support an argument that the requirement to consult the European Parliament could not be derogated from when implementing measures were adopted. Openly refuting that logic, the Jozeau-Marigné Report explained that the only legal distinction that one could make was between 'the texts for direct application of the Treaty' and 'the texts for their implementation' and stressed that Article 155 EEC (1958) only concerned the latter. The wording of that provision was clear and did not leave any room for reading into it a requirement for consultation of the European Parliament. Indeed, any other solution would be impracticable. But importantly, a rather strict view was taken on the meaning of implementation: if a measure was such that it went beyond the limits of 'simple technical' implementation—which was sometimes the case—then the normal procedure for legislation should be applied.[220]

Focusing then on implementing measures adopted by the Commission in accordance with procedures for co-operation with committees, a threefold classification was introduced, for the first time, of advisory, management, and regulatory committees.[221] The meaning of management and regulatory committees corresponded to that which has been outlined above (see above 2.2.2.3, 2.4.2, and 2.4.3.2). But with respect to advisory committees, a definition was used which included not only committees involved in the adoption of implementing measures, most notably the Advisory Committee on Restrictive Practices and Monopolies (see above 2.2.2.1), but also a number of bodies that enabled the Commission to consult representatives of professional and societal

---

[218] See the Jozeau-Marigné Report, above Ch 2, n 216, at p. 10 (paragraphs 7 to 9).

[219] See the Lulling Report, above Ch 2, n 213.

[220] See the Jozeau-Marigné Report, above Ch 2, n 216, at p. 13 (paragraph 19). For examples of cases in which the measure was such that it went beyond the confines of 'simple technical' implementation, see p. 14 of the Report (paragraph 21).

[221] See the Jozeau-Marigné Report, above Ch 2, n 216.

interests.[222] Somewhat unexpectedly, not only the advisory committees but also the management and regulatory committees were considered to be compatible with the EEC Treaty.[223] The most fundamental reason for this was found in the earlier conclusion that Article 155 EEC (1958) did not oblige but only permitted the Council to confer implementing powers on the Commission:

> ... it must be considered that the Council, when it confers implementing competencies on the Commission under Article 155 for the implementation of rules it establishes, is entitled to combine the attribution of these implementing competencies with certain conditions in respect of the modalities of their exercise. The Council will only transgress the restrictions placed upon it by the Treaty if it will confer on the committees a genuine power of decision. A procedure which reserves for the Council itself the right to decide at last resort, must, by contrast, be considered as compatible with the Treaty.[224]

Having thus reached the conclusion that no objections could be made on legal grounds, neither against the delegation of powers as such nor against the use of committees, the Report explained that the anxieties which had been expressed by a number of MEPs were still understandable. In contrast to the idea underlying the EEC Treaty, that the Commission alone should be the Community's executive authority, it was clear that a completely different direction had been taken. Only very rarely was the Commission acting alone and an increasing number of management and regulatory committees had been established. For that reason, the author of the Report, the Legal Committee, expressed its 'legitimate concern with an institutional evolution which it could not criticise on legal grounds but which could very well be dangerous on the political plane.'[225] In the light of that concern there was every justification for granting the European Parliament a *droit de regard* (cf. above 2.2.3): to keep it informed about matters dealt with in management and regulatory committees and to provide it with an opportunity to render an opinion

---

[222] See the Jozeau-Marigné Report, above Ch 2, n 216, at p. 25 (paragraph 41). Examples of such bodies can be found in Commission Decision 62/708/EEC of 18 July 1962 setting up an Advisory Committee on Cereals (OJ 1962 B 72/2026); and Commission Decision 65/362/EEC of 5 July 1965 setting up a Joint Advisory Committee on Social Questions arising in Road Transport (OJ 1965 130/2184).   [223] See *Bulletin EC* 12-1968, at p. 65.

[224] See the Jozeau-Marigné Report, above Ch 2, n 216, at p. 27 (paragraph 44). Cf. also p. 24 of the Report (paragraph 37).

[225] See the Jozeau-Marigné Report, above Ch 2, n 216, at p. 27 (paragraph 45); or *Bulletin EC* 12-1968, at p. 65.

whenever a problem arose, the significance of which went beyond the limits of 'simple technical' implementation.[226]

Not surprisingly, the presentation of the Jozeau-Marigné Report led to an urgent debate in the European Parliament and numerous MEPs took the opportunity to emphasize that they found the development worrying.[227] At the end of the day, the basic propositions in the Report, as well as some more critical points from other reports, were brought together in the form of a resolution.[228] This stated that the Council could exercise implementing powers itself or confer them on the Commission and that both of them should be obliged to consult the European Parliament when matters of 'notable importance' were being addressed. It was also demanded that committee procedures should only be applied with political caution and without endangering the institutional balance. This meant, in particular, that the committees ought only to be accorded a consultative role—intended to help the Commission to act in full knowledge of the facts—and that they ought under no circumstances to entail any limitations of the Commission's powers or responsibility.[229]

In the subsequent chapters it will be seen that much time would pass before any concessions were made to the European Parliament's demands. One reason for this was that the Commission had as much to win on an increasing use of implementing measures as the European Parliament had to lose. Invited to comment on the criticism, the President of the Commission, Jean Rey, explained that:

The powers of the Commission are increasing for a very simple reason which was not foreseen from the start: we have left the period of construction to enter the period of management of common policies. However normal it may be for decisions relating to construction to be taken by the Governments in the Council by unanimity, the daily administration of politics relating to tariffs,

[226] See the Jozeau-Marigné Report, above Ch 2, n 216, at p. 27 (paragraph 45); or *Bulletin EC* 12-1968, at p. 65. Cf. European Parliament Resolution of 17 October 1967 on the legal problems connected with the consultation of the European Parliament in *Bulletin EC* 12-1967/51. Accordingly, '[t]he Parliament shall be heard on all texts deriving from basic regulations and which consequently have a considerable influence on the political, economic or legal effects of these regulations'.

[227] See *Europe (bulletin quotidien)* 3 October 1968; and *Bulletin EC* 12-1968, at p. 65.

[228] See *Europe (bulletin quotidien)* 3 October 1968 (Resolution in OJ 1968 C 108/37).

[229] It may be noted that apparently the proposal that the functioning of all committees should be harmonized had been put forward in the European Parliament a few months earlier (in the so-called Bading Report). See *Europe (bulletin quotidien)* 17 May 1968.

trade, agriculture, evidently requires an organ with sufficient powers. In agricultural matters one has already had to delegate powers to us which were not written into the Treaty. This is a growing necessity. I do not believe that we can step back since the obvious necessity, by contrast, is to reinforce these powers with reasonable precautions.[230]

Most of his following remarks were confined to the question of the introduction of regulatory committees. According to Rey, the Commission felt that it was safe to retain the type of procedure which was used in the field of common commercial policy 'because it seems reasonable to make a distinction between management committees, which are not really institutions in themselves but rather Community machinery for routine administration, and committees which are regulatory and more concerned with laying down rules than with day-to-day administration.'[231] Nevertheless, attempting to give the European Parliament some comfort, he assured that 'the Commission will not go further and accept or resign itself to proposing procedures like those advocated by the Council for the veterinary field or other similar ones which might be adopted subsequently.'[232] The reason for this he said was that the 'double safety-net' enabled the Council to retain competence indefinitely.[233] But in spite of that it was not long before the Commission itself submitted proposals which envisaged that the type of procedure which was used in the case of the Standing Veterinary Committee should in fact be used again (cf. below 3.3.2.2).[234] This in turn led commentators to conclude 'that the Commission only voiced verbal objections and then proceeded to the order of the day.'[235]

2.4.5   *The Court of Justice gives its approval*

2.4.5.1   *A wide interpretation of Article 155 EEC*

The Jozeau-Marigné Report had emphasized that the creation of committees was only one aspect of a greater phenomenon, characterized, above all, by the fact that an increasing number of matters was being dealt

---

[230] Commission President Jean Rey, quote from *Europe (bulletin quotidien)* 3 October 1968.

[231] See *Bulletin EC* 12-1968, at p. 65.   [232] See *Bulletin EC* 12-1968, at p. 65.

[233] See *Bulletin EC* 12-1968, at p. 52.   [234] See e.g. OJ 1968 C 139/19.

[235] See Editorial Comments (1970) 7 *CMLRev* 103, at p. 105.

with in implementing measures adopted by the Commission on the basis of powers delegated from the Council (see above 2.4.4). Not surprisingly, this in turn was a tendency which gave many MEPs cause for concern. Even if they agreed on the need for delegation of powers, they were worried by the risk of a sliding in powers: that an increasing number of matters of political significance would be dealt with outside the normal legislative process in accordance with procedures from which the European Parliament itself was excluded. This was not eased by the fact that the European Parliament had no right to be kept informed about matters dealt with in management and regulatory committees or to give its opinion when problems arose.[236] The Commission's rather insensitive reply to the MEPs was that they should not worry. Even if it had not been envisaged at the start, the development was normal: the Community had left the period of construction to enter the period of management and there was a growing need, therefore, to provide the Commission with 'sufficient' powers (see above 2.4.4).

Within less than one year after the European Parliament had clarified its position, the new tendency was confirmed in the legal challenge brought before the Court of Justice in Case 41/69 *Chemiefarma NV v Commission.*[237] For the first time ever, the annulment was sought of an implementing measure on the ground that the scope of the powers delegated by the Council to the Commission was not only wider than foreseen in the EEC Treaty but illegal. It is submitted that this case represents one of the most crucial points in the history of Community law: it was here that the Court made up its mind not to interfere with the development under way. Even if the Court was to be given plenty of opportunity in the future to change its mind, it would prove itself faithful to its original decision and, indeed, show that it was prepared to accept the consequences of that decision. An important example of that will be examined later. But first, the arguments presented in Case 41/69 and the ruling need to be elaborated.

---

[236] See above Ch 2, n 226.

[237] See Case 41/69 *ACF Chemiefarma NV v Commission* [1970] ECR 661 (Judgment of 15 July 1970). For comments, see Bradley, K., Maintaining the Balance: the role of the Court of Justice in defining the institutional position of the European Parliament (1987) 24 *CMLRev* 41, at p. 54; and Bradley, above Ch 2, n 58, at p. 699; and, more generally, Baardman, B., annotation (1971) 8 *CMLRev* 89; Tizzano, A., annotation (1971) 4 *Forolt* 33; and Markert, K., annotation (1971) 6 *EuR* 54.

The background to the challenge brought before the Court of Justice is found in 'a gentlemen's agreement' between the Dutch company, Chemiefarma NV, a producer of pharmaceuticals, and some of its competitors in other Member States to establish a cartel which would make it possible for them to retain their respective shares of the market. When it was informed about that agreement, the Commission initiated an investigation which found that the agreement entailed illegal restrictions on trade. Therefore, after consultation of the Advisory Committee on Restrictive Practices and Monopolies (see above 2.2.2.1), a decision was adopted imposing a fine.[238] The response of Chemiefarma NV was to initiate legal proceedings, under Article 173 EEC (1958), seeking to have the Decision annulled. In support of that several complaints were advanced. Of particular significance for present purposes is the claim that the procedural rules followed by the Commission when making its investigation, rules which Chemiefarma NV felt were not providing it with an adequate opportunity of being heard, were the result of a delegation of powers that went beyond the scope permitted by the EEC Treaty.

According to the basic legislation in the field of competition, Council Regulation 17/62/EEC, a company under investigation should be given an opportunity to be heard.[239] The exact meaning of this was not specified in the Regulation. Instead a provision had been inserted in which the Commission was empowered to adopt 'implementing provisions concerning the form, content and other details of applications.' This provided the basis for Commission Regulation 99/63/EEC, the text in which the procedural rules were laid down.[240] Here it was explained, among other things, that the Commission should inform the company under investigation of the objections raised against it and that a decision should only deal with those objections in respect of which the company had been afforded the opportunity of making known its views. According to the argument presented by Chemiefarma NV, irrespective of the question whether they provided an adequate opportunity of being heard or not, these rules were so important that their adoption had to be characterized as 'a legislative activity', something which the Council was

---

[238] See Commission Decision 240/69/EEC of 16 July 1969 relating to proceedings under Article 85 of the EEC Treaty (OJ 1969 L 192/5).

[239] See Article 19(1) of Council Regulation 17/62/EEC, above Ch 2, n 46.

[240] See Commission Regulation 99/63/EEC of 25 July 1963 on the hearings provided for in Article 19 (1) and (2) of Council Regulation No 17 (OJ 1963 P 127/2268).

not permitted to entrust to the Commission, the Institution responsible for the executive activity of applying them.[241]

However reasonable this argument may have seemed, the Court of Justice was far from convinced. In rejecting the view advocated by Chemiefarma NV, the Court chose to read the EEC Treaty so as to promote a further transfer of powers to the Commission. Basing itself on a wide interpretation of Article 155 EEC (1958)—which, as the Court noted, said that 'the Council *shall* confer powers on the Commission' (emphasis added)—the conclusion was reached that there was no prohibition against those powers being used to adopt implementing measures of a general nature.[242] Applying that to the case before it, the Court emphasized that the essential element, the principle that the company under investigation should be given an opportunity of being heard, had been adopted by the Council in accordance with the normal legislative procedure and that powers to adopt implementing measures had been explicitly conferred on the Commission. Thus, 'the rules laying down the procedure to be followed in this connection, however important they may be, constitute implementing provisions within the meaning of the above-mentioned Article 155' and, consequently, the powers to adopt them had been lawfully delegated.[243]

2.4.5.2 *A right to set conditions:* qui peut le plus, peut le moins

Only a few weeks after the ruling in Case 41/69, the Court of Justice found itself faced with a new challenge to the legality of implementing measures in Case 25/70 *Einfuhr- und Vorratsstelle für Getreide und Futtermittel v Köster, Berodt & Co.*[244] This offered the Court an opportunity both to confirm its earlier choice and to demonstrate that it was prepared to accept the consequences. In contrast to the previous case, which involved implementing measures adopted in a field where all Governments had

[241] See Case 41/69, above Ch 2, n 237, paragraph 59.

[242] See Case 41/69, above Ch 2, n 237, paragraph 62. Cf. the text of Article 155 EEC (1958) according to which 'the Commission shall . . . exercise the powers conferred on it by the Council for the implementation of the rules laid down by the latter.'

[243] See Case 41/69, above Ch 2, n 237, paragraphs 64 to 66.

[244] See Case 25/70 *Einfuhr- und Vorratsstelle für Getreide und Futtermittel v Köster, Berodt & Co.* [1970] 2 ECR 1161 (Judgment of 17 December 1970). For comments, see Ehlermann, C.-D., annotation (1971) 6 *EuR* 250; Bradley, above Ch 2, n 58, at p. 700; Bradley, above Ch 2, n 216; Türk, above Ch 1, n 11, at p. 169. See also Case 30/70 *Otto Scheer v Einfuhr- und Vorratstelle für Getreide und Futtermittel* [1970] ECR 1197 (Judgment of 17 December 1970).

been less hesitant to entrust the Commission with discretionary powers, the new case concerned implementing measures adopted in a field where co-operation had proved much more problematic: the common agricultural policy. Here, the exercise of powers delegated to the Commission had been carefully circumscribed by the requirement that it should co-operate with management committees (see above 2.2.2).

It has been seen above that, in the discussions which led to the adoption of Council Regulations 19–24/62/EEC, care was taken to find a solution which could combine the continuous need for implementing measures with the demand of some Governments for control and, at the same time, did not run the risk of being declared illegal by the Court of Justice (see above 2.2.2.2). The initial impression was that the Council had been successful and that the solution finally adopted was legally correct: the Commission was given the responsibility for the actual decision and the management committees were only granted powers to formulate an opinion.[245] In spite of that, it was not long before an application was made under Article 173 EEC (1958) for the annulment of some regulations adopted by the Commission in co-operation with a management committee.[246] If this case had been allowed to proceed much controversy might have been avoided at later stages of development. But unfortunately the application was declared inadmissible by the Court in a ruling on 1 April 1965.[247] The immediate reason for this was that the applicants, not surprisingly to anyone familiar with Community law, had failed to satisfy the strict criteria for *locus standi*. In this respect, the Court said, it mattered little whether the contested Regulations were

---

[245] See Olmi, above Ch 2, n 72, at p. 146. Here it is emphasized that the new management committees, in compliance with the ruling in Case 9/56 (above Ch 2, n 57), had not been granted powers to take their own decisions but only to formulate opinions to the Commission which then takes decisions. Cf. Schindler (1971) who argues that the management committee procedure (in both the wider and the more narrow sense) is illegal as it is contrary to fundamental principles of constitutional law. See Schindler, above Ch 2, n 194.

[246] See Commission Regulation 65/64/EEC of 16 June 1964 fixing the reference prices for lemons (OJ 1964 100/1); Commission Regulation 66/64/EEC of 16 June 1964 fixing the reference prices for mandarins and clementines (OJ 1964 100/4); and Commission Regulation 74/64/EEC of 26 June 1964 fixing the reference prices for sweet oranges (OJ 1964 102/1). These were all adopted on the basis of power conferred on the Commission in Article 11 of Council Regulation 23/62/EEC, above Ch 2, n 37.

[247] See Case 40/64 *Marcello Sgarlata et al. v Commission of the EEC* [1965] ECR 215 (Judgment of 1 April 1965). Cf. also Case 1/64 *Glucoseries réunies v Commission of the EEC* [1964] ECR 413 (Judgment of 2 July 1964).

attributable to 'a direct power' or only to 'a derived or delegated power.'[248] Since most implementing measures relating to Council Regulations 19–24/62/EEC were adopted in the form of regulations, the result of this ruling was that in practice the co-operation between the Commission and the management committees had become immune from the risks of a direct challenge brought before the Court by anyone except those involved: the Council, the Commission, and the Governments.[249]

Against this background, it was clearly not a coincidence that the challenge which eventually reached the Court in Case 25/70 was not an application for annulment but a reference for a preliminary ruling under Article 177 EEC (1958), submitted by a German administrative court. That court, the *Hessischer Verwaltungsgerichtshof*, had received the case on appeal against a judgment annulling the decision of a customs authority to declare forfeit a deposit furnished by Köster, Berodt & Co, a company trading in cereals. Importantly, this decision had been taken in compliance with a rule laid down in Commission Regulation 102/64/EEC on import and export licences for cereals and processed cereal products, rice, broken rice, and processed rice products.[250] In the judgment on appeal, the rule in question had been found to be disproportionate under German constitutional law, and, therefore, was disregarded. The result was not only that Köster, Berodt & Co was entitled to reclaim its deposit but also that the effects of Commission Regulation 102/64/EEC had been nullified and, therefore, 'the legal basis of the Community itself' had been called into question.[251]

---

[248] Case 40/64, above Ch 2, n 247, at p. 227. It may be noted that the applicants objected that 'if recourse to Article 173 were to be refused by reason of a restrictive interpretation of its wording, individuals would thus be deprived of all protection by the courts both under Community law and under national law, which would be contrary to the fundamental principles governing all the Member States.' But according to the Court 'these considerations, which will not be discussed here, cannot be allowed to override the clearly restrictive wording of Article 173, which it is the Court's task to apply.'

[249] See Article 173(1) and (2) EEC (1958), which qualify the Council, the Commission, and the Governments as privileged applicants for annulment who do not have to satisfy any criteria for *locus standi*.

[250] See Commission Regulation 102/64/EEC of 28 July 1964 on import and export licences for cereals and processed cereal products, rice, broken rice and processed rice products (OJ 1964 126/2125).

[251] See the Opinion of Advocate General Dutheillet de Lamothe in Case 25/70, above Ch 2, n 244, at p. 1146. Cf. Case 6/64 *Costa v ENEL* [1964] ECR 585 (Judgment of 15 July 1964), at p. 594.

According to the contested rule, it was only possible to obtain a licence for import or export of cereals after a deposit had been paid; if no use was made of the licence within a stipulated period, the deposit would be forfeited. The legal basis for this had been found in Article 16 of Council Regulation 19/62/EEC on the progressive establishment of a common organization of the market in cereals. Here, it was clearly stated that import and export of cereals was conditional on the presentation of a licence.[252] But not much was said about the practical operation of this requirement. Instead an explanation had been inserted that 'the detailed rules for the application' of the arrangement should be adopted by the Commission in co-operation with a management committee (the Management Committee for Cereals).

Since it was not possible for the *Hessischer Verwaltungsgerichtshof* to decide on the appeal before the legal validity of the contested rule had been clarified, it turned to the Court of Justice. Of the specific questions posed, one is of particular relevance in the present context: whether the procedure by which the Council conferred powers on the Commission to adopt implementing measures was compatible 'with the Community structure and the institutional balance, as regards both the relationship between the institutions and the exercise of their respective powers.' To some extent this question had already been answered in the affirmative by the Court in Case 41/69 *Chemiefarma NV v Commission* (see above 2.4.5.1). But an important difference this time was the 'interposition' between the Council and the Commission of an organ which had not been provided for by the EEC Treaty: the management committee.[253] Setting out to answer the question, the Court focused on two particular claims, which were then dealt with separately. The first was that the EEC Treaty assigned the powers that had been used to adopt the disputed rule with the Council and that they could not, therefore, be conferred on the Commission. In support of this allegation the argument had been advanced that the specific, subject-related provision of the EEC Treaty, Article 43, required the Council to consult the European Parliament, and that this was not taken up in the procedure the Commission had to follow.[254] This, indeed, was an argument which had

---

[252] Note that the Court classified Article 16(1) of Council Regulation 19/62/EEC, explaining that the issue of the licence should be subject to the lodging of a deposit, as 'a special measure of application intended to implement a part of the provisions envisaged in paragraph (1).' Thus, an implementing measure adopted by the Council itself.

[253] Cf. Case 25/70, above Ch 2, n 244, at p. 1171 (paragraph 8).

[254] See Article 43 EEC (1958).

already been raised in the European Parliament and the Court was not unaware of its interest in the matter.[255] Nevertheless, the Court did not invite the European Parliament, as it had on previous occasions, to give its view.[256] This can probably be explained by the fact that the argument had been extensively examined in the Jozeau-Marigné Report and finally discarded (see above 2.4.4).

There can be no doubt that the Court was very familiar with that Report and used the reasoning therein to phrase its findings.[257] Thus, when the Court clarified its position with respect to the first allegation, it emphasized, in words almost identical to those of the Jozeau-Marigné Report, that a distinction had to be made 'between the measures directly based on the Treaty itself and derived law intended to ensure their implementation.' That, the Court said, followed from the legislative scheme of the EEC Treaty, reflected in particular in Article 155 (1958). Probably no less important, it noted also that the distinction had been confirmed in consistent practice.[258] For these reasons, it could not be a requirement that 'all the details' were dealt with in the regulations adopted by the Council on the basis of Article 43 EEC. If only 'the basic elements of the matter' had been established that way, provisions implementing those regulations could be adopted in accordance with a simplified procedure by the Council (thus choosing to reserve the implementing powers for itself) or by the Commission, subject to a delegation of implementing powers under Article 155 EEC (1958).[259] Applying the above reasoning to the case before it, the Court stated that the contested rule did not go 'beyond the limits' of the type of measure that could be permitted for implementing Council

---

[255] See the Opinion of Advocate General Dutheillet de Lamothe in Case 25/70 *Einfuhr- und Vorratsstelle für Getreide und Futtermittel v Köster, Berodt & Co.* [1970] ECR 1140, in particular at pp. 1142–1143.

[256] See e.g. Case 101/63, *Wagner v Fohrmann and Krier* [1964] ECR 195, at p. 198. See further Bradley, above Ch 2, n 216, at p. 244.

[257] This, indeed, was emphasized by Advocate General Dutheillet de Lamothe. As stated in his Opinion, the allegation that the adoption of implementing measures by the Commission in collaboration with management committees should put the institutional balance in question was 'refuted in a masterly fashion by the legal committee of the Parliament in the report of Monsieur Jozeau-Marigné who is, by a happy combination, both a parliamentarian and an excellent lawyer.' See the Opinion of Advocate General Dutheillet de Lamothe in Case 25/70, above Ch 2, n 244, in particular at pp. 1142–1143. Cf. Bradley, above Ch 2, n 216, at p. 244.

[258] See paragraph 6 of the Judgment (above Ch 2, n 244).

[259] See paragraph 6 of the Judgment (above Ch 2, n 244).

Regulation 19/62/EEC.[260] This indeed was one of the crucial points in respect of which the Court may be said to have departed from the reasoning in the Jozeau-Marigné Report. The meaning the Report gave to the notion of implementing measures was so narrow that it is far from certain that it would have included a rule like the present one, constituting an at least quasi-penal sanction.[261] In sharp contrast, the view taken by the Court was one aimed at maximizing the usefulness of implementing measures, at least within the field of the common agricultural policy.[262] This, indeed, was clarified at a later stage of the ruling, when the Court explained that an interpretation which restricted 'the guarantees of effectiveness' provided for by Council Regulation 19/62/ EEC would have the effect of disturbing 'the harmonious functioning' of the system for import and export of cereals.[263]

Having thus given its support, once again, for a wide interpretation of the scope of implementing measures and having clarified the criteria for application of the principle of delegation, the Court went on to discuss the second allegation: that the procedure requiring the Commission to co-operate with a management committee constituted 'an interference in the Commission's right of decision, to such an extent as to put in issue the independence of that institution.'[264] Like the first allegation, this one was also dismissed by the Court. This was not very surprising. As had been emphasized in the Jozeau-Marigné Report, the role of committees was an integral aspect of a general trend, characterized by 'an increase in the tasks facing the Commission.' Therefore, when the Court made up its mind not to oppose or complicate but to promote the transfer of implementing powers to the Commission, it must have been aware of the political reality: that there was little use for a principle of delegation of powers which could not accommodate the demand for a 'close co-operation' between the Commission and the Member States (cf. above 2.2.2.3).

It may be recalled, in this context, that, when the first management committees were introduced in 1962, this was not seen as a definite arrangement and several Governments felt that the last word had not been said (see above 2.2.2.3). But in order to keep up with the tight

---

[260] See paragraph 7 of the Judgment (above Ch 2, n 244).

[261] Cf. the Jozeau-Marigné Report, above Ch 2, n 216, at pp. 13–14 (paragraph 21).

[262] Cf. Türk, above Ch 1, n 11, at p. 170.

[263] See paragraphs 16 and 17 of the Judgment (above Ch 2, n 244).

[264] See paragraph 8 of the Judgment (above Ch 2, n 244).

schedule for establishment of a common market, an agreement was reached to postpone any discussion on matters of principle until the end of the transitional period. This would prove to be a triumph of pragmatism over ideologies. When the time had come to decide whether to retain or amend the arrangement for co-operation between the Commission and the management committees, the Governments no longer found it controversial. The token of that was the adoption on 18 December 1969 of Council Regulation 2602/69/EEC. Here it was stated—briefly but clearly—that the experience had demonstrated that '[t]he provisions governing the procedure to be followed by the Management Committees established in the various sectors of the common organisation of agricultural markets shall be retained beyond expiry of the transitional period.'[265]

Against the background of the fact both that the management committees had proved to be a workable form for co-operation between the Commission and the Member States, and that not only the Council but also the Commission and the European Parliament had come out in favour of them, the Court could hardly have been expected to condemn them.[266] The most interesting aspect of the problem, therefore, was what legal reasoning could be found to arrive at the conclusion everyone was expecting. This time the Court also let itself be guided by the Jozeau-Marigné Report. Enlarging upon the finding in that Report that Article 155 EEC (1958) did not oblige but only permitted the Council to confer implementing powers on the Commission, the Court explained:

Article 155 provides that the Commission shall exercise the powers conferred on it by the Council for the implementation of the rules laid down by the latter. This provision, the use of which is optional, enables the Council to determine any detailed rules to which the Commission is subject in exercising the power conferred on it. The so-called management committee procedure forms part of the detailed rules to which the Council may legitimately subject a delegation of power to the Commission. It follows from an analysis of the machinery set up by Articles 25 and 26 of Regulation No 19 that the task of the management committee is to give its opinions on draft measures proposed by the Commission, which may adopt immediately applicable measures whatever

---

[265] See Council Regulation 2602/69/EEC of 18 December 1969 on retaining the management committee procedure (OJ 1969 L 324/23).

[266] Cf. Türk, above Ch 1, n 11, at p. 172.

the opinion of the management committee. Where the committee issues a contrary opinion, the only obligation on the Commission is to communicate to the Council the measures taken. The function of the management committee is to ensure permanent consultation in order to guide the Commission in the exercise of the powers conferred on it by the Council and to enable the latter to substitute its own action for that of the Commission. The management committee does not, therefore, have the power to take a decision in place of the Commission or the Council. Consequently, without distorting the Community structure and the institutional balance, the management committee machinery enables the Council to delegate to the Commission an implementing power of appreciable scope, subject to its power to take the decision itself if necessary.[267]

Clearly, this argument was not far-fetched but, on the contrary, well in line with the reasoning applied in Case 9/56 *Meroni & Co. S.p.A. v High Authority of the ECSC* (see above 2.2.2.2). It has been noted, previously, that in this case the Court was only prepared to accept a delegation of powers to an organ which was not a Community Institution if strict requirements were satisfied with respect both to the manner in which the delegation was made and the scope of the powers involved. But importantly, the Court indicated very clearly that those requirements would not apply to an arrangement which permitted a Community Institution to 'take over' the deliberations of that organ as its own: this could not qualify as a delegation in the strict sense and a Community Institution would retain full responsibility.[268] It may be noted that the continuous validity of that final consideration was also affirmed in the present case. As emphasized by the Court, the implementing measures resulting from the co-operation between the Commission and management committees were always capable of giving rise 'either to an application for annulment under Article 173 or to a reference for a preliminary ruling under Article 177 of the Treaty.'[269]

---

[267] See paragraph 9 of the Judgment (above Ch 2, n 244).

[268] Cf. the observation of Advocate General Dutheillet de Lamothe (at p. 1143) that 'the Council would transgress the limits laid down for it in the Treaty only if it conferred on the management committee some power of decision.' Cf. also the Council's own observation (at p. 1166) that '[t]he detailed rules of the Management Committee procedure do not have the effect of putting the powers conferred on the Commission in issue: they introduce, it is true, the deliberations of a committee but in the exercise of the powers conferred on it the Commission remains the master of its own decision: it is never obliged to follow the opinion of the Committee...'.

[269] See Case 25/70, above Ch 2, n 244, at p. 1171.

2.5   The end of the transitional period

2.5.1   *Economic and social turbulence*

In spite of the success in a number of areas of co-operation, towards the end of the transitional period there was open talk of 'crisis, paralysis and even disintegration.'[270] A major reason for this was to be found in the economic and social turbulence which had not only hit the Community but much of the Western World. Nowhere in the Community were the problems greater than in France. Following student riots and strikes which involved more than one third of its labour force the country was brought to a standstill.[271] Public order was only restored after General de Gaulle decided to dissolve the *Assemblée Nationale* and—assisted by the armed forces—to call new elections.

Two weeks before the elections the French Government told the Commission and the other Governments that it would have to introduce safeguard measures, including quantitative restrictions on imports and subsidies for exports.[272] Although formally asking for authorization in accordance with the EEC Treaty, the French Government made it clear that it was not going to accept anything but an affirmative answer.[273] Their trump card was the imminent date for completion of customs union. As Prime Minister Georges Pompidou announced to the French press on 19 June 1968, '[t]here is no question of France shirking the commitments accepted for 1 July, provided, of course, that we can have the immediate and temporary safeguard measures which are essential in certain sectors.'[274]

The significance of events in France for the development in the Community is not easily measured. In the elections on 30 June 1968 the orthodox gaullists won a landslide victory and the next day they hosted celebrations for completion of customs union.[275] The General's regime

[270] See Third General Report on the Activities of the European Communities 1969 (Office for Official Publications 1970), at p. 11.

[271] See *Bulletin EC* 2-1969, at p. 16; and *Europe (bulletin quotidien)* 20, 21, 22, and 31 May 1968. See, in general, Chapsal, J., *La vie politique sous la V° Republique* (Paris Presses Universitaires de France 1990).

[272] See *Europe (bulletin quotidien)* 13 June 1968. See also the statement by Commission President Jean Rey to the European Parliament on 3 July 1968, in *Bulletin EC* 8-1968, at p. 9; and Editorial Comments (1968–69) 6 *CMLRev* 355, at pp. 356–358.

[273] Cf. Articles 108 and 206 EEC (1958).   [274] See *Bulletin EC* 8-1969, at p. 24.

[275] See *Bulletin EC* 7-1968; and Editorial Comments (1968–69) 5 *CMLRev*, at pp. 356–358.

had been shaken to its roots but it emerged from the crisis more firmly established than ever before. Within days of the elections the Commission authorized the French Government to proceed with the safeguard measures.[276] The Commission did not try to hide the fact that its decision had been based on political rather than legal considerations.[277] Whether this was an expression of sympathy or the successful result of a threat to block the completion of the customs union will never be known. Nevertheless, the decision was received with gratitude. In his declaration to the *Assemblée Nationale*, the new Prime Minister, Couve de Murville, made it completely clear that it was vital for France to keep up with its commitment to customs union and 'not to do anything which could bring the old demons of malthusianism and of protectionism back to life.'[278]

If there was hope that the French 'storm' was now over, it was shattered a few months later when the French Government announced new protective measures and eventually decided to devalue the Franc.[279] At the same time the German Government decided—unilaterally— to impose a levy on the import of agricultural products and perhaps more importantly to order the *Bundesbank* to revaluate the Mark.[280] The decisions of the French and German Governments unleashed financial speculation which affected the stability of the other currencies as well as the system of common agricultural prices.[281] As one commentator concluded, the point had now been reached at which 'the Member States must be prepared to accept a higher level of integration of their monetary and economic policies than at present exists, if they want to prevent the Community from gradually dissolving into a structure which can be called the "common market" in name only, but which is, in fact, no more than the sum of the six separate economies.'[282]

---

[276] See Commission Decision 68/274/EEC of 5 July 1968 authorising the Republic of France to charge a tax on the import of products relevant for the pork sector (OJ 1968 L 158/16): and Commission Decision 68/301/EEC of 23 July 1968 authorising the Republic of France to take certain safeguard measures in conformity with Article 108(3) of the Treaty (OJ 1968 178/15). See *Europe (bulletin quotidien)* 1 July 1968 and *Bulletin EC* 8-1968, at p. 25.

[277] See *Bulletin EC* 8-1968, at pp. 14–16.   [278] See *Europe (bulletin quotidien)* 17 July 1968.

[279] See *Europe (bulletin quotidien)* 26 November 1968 and *Bulletin EC* 1-1969, at p. 16.

[280] See *Bulletin EC* 8-1968, at pp. 10–25. See also Editorial Comments (1968–69) 6 *CMLRev* 430, at pp. 432–433.   [281] See Editorial Comments, above Ch 2, n 280, at p. 432.

[282] See Editorial Comments, above Ch 2, n 280, at p. 433.

2.5.2 A call for co-ordination of economic and monetary policies

Since 1944, monetary stability in the Western World had been sought to be guaranteed by the system built up around the International Monetary Fund. In essence this was based on the idea that a country suffering from a payments deficit could draw loans from the Fund enabling it to regain equilibrium.[283] The loans were subject to conditions which were supposed to ensure that the deficit country adopted an appropriate economic policy. Like the GATT, this system—based on the supremacy of the Dollar—gave special privileges to the United States, and for that reason, was attacked by the French Commissioner Raymond Barre. In his view, it had not only failed to react to the United States' payments deficit (see above 2.4.1) but actually aggravated the effect this had on the Member States of the Community. The core of the problem, Barre said, was that the economy of Europe had now become too dependent upon that of the United States.[284]

Therefore, even if improvements could be made to the international system, Barre suggested that the time had come to reconsider it and to make an effort instead to set up a 'true financial and monetary market which would be constituted by real European currencies and not by the Eurodollar.'[285] Painfully aware of the situation, the Governments admitted—some with more willingness than others—that Barre was right

---

[283] See From Rome to Maastricht: a brief history of EMU, at internet http://europa.eu.int/scadplus.

[284] See e.g. the address by Commissioner Raymond Barre to the French Chamber of Industry and Commerce on 14 January 1970, in *Bulletin EC* 2-1970, at pp. 13–14. In this it was stated that '[t]oday the currency of Europe is in fact the dollar; the Federal Reserve system is in fact the dollar; the Federal Reserve system is in fact the final lender to the European central banks; there is no European capital market, but there is a Eurodollar market; European industrial structures tend increasingly to be moulded by the investments of American firms; European technology is too fragmented to challenge transatlantic technology. I am not saying all this out of shallow anti-Americanism, for which I personally have no use, but because these are facts.' See also his first speech before the European Parliament on 23 January 1968, in *Bulletin EC* 2-1968, at pp. 20–21.

[285] See in general the so-called Barre Report, Commission Memorandum of 12 February 1969 on the co-ordination of the economic policies and the monetary co-operation within the Community (COM (69) 150). Quotation from Couve de Murville in his speech to the Franco-German Circle in Düsseldorf on 27 January 1970, in *Bulletin EC* 3-1970, at p. 113. Cf. Article 2 EEC (1958) according to which the objectives of the EEC should be achieved 'by establishing a common market and by approximating the national economic policies'. Most efforts having been centred on the first of these, seemingly, the time had now come to proceed to the latter. In respect of the international efforts it may be noted that a conference on reform of the system built

and that now, more than ever, there was a need to join forces.[286] Notwithstanding this, the Council still seemed to suffer from paralysis. As one of the Commission Vice-Presidents, Sicco Mansholt, resentfully pointed out in an interview given to *Der Spiegel*, '[t]he Council of Ministers is no longer a real political organisation but has become more and more of a club where the technical questions are discussed.'[287]

Although the economic depression was set to last for several years, during the last few months of the transitional period the climate improved. One reason for this was General de Gaulle's resignation on 28 April 1969.[288] Another was the initiative taken by his successor, Georges Pompidou, who called for a 'Summit Meeting of Heads of State or Government'.[289] Initially met with suspicion, as time went on the attitude changed and hopes were expressed that this could serve to lift the Community out of its political inertia.[290]

The Summit Meeting was opened on 1 December 1969 in The Hague, in the same *Ridderzaal* where Sir Winston Churchill two decades earlier had convinced the World that 'Europe requires all that Frenchmen, all that Germans, and all that every one of us can give.'[291] Doing his utmost to underline that on this occasion too decisions had to be taken which would change the future, President Pompidou urged his colleagues to 'get down to discussing the real issue and choose between allowing the Community to wither away or giving it a fresh lease of life.'[292]

When the final communiqué was issued the following day, the result was better than expected.[293] The overall positive factor was a declaration in which the Heads of State or Government reaffirmed 'their belief in the political objectives which give the Community its full meaning and scope, their determination to carry their under-takings through to the

up around the IMF was held in Stockholm on 29 March 1968. See *Europe (bulletin quotidien)* 29 March 1968.

[286] See e.g. *Europe (bulletin quotidian)* 13 March and 1 and 2 April 1968.

[287] See *Der Spiegel* 24 November 1969. Reference in *Bulletin EC* 1-1970, at p. 121.

[288] Following his defeat in a national referendum on 27 April 1969. See, in general, Chapsal, above Ch 2, n 271.   [289] See *Bulletin EC* 1-1970, at p. 7.

[290] See Editorial Comments (1970) 7 *CMLRev* 1, at p. 1.

[291] Speech by Winston Churchill at the Congress of Europe on 7 May 1948, in Churchill, W. S., *Europe Unite* (Cassel 1950), at p. 313.

[292] See the statement by Georges Pompidou on the first day of the Summit Meeting, in *Bulletin EC* 2-1970, at p. 34.

[293] See the final communiqué of 2 December 1969, in *Bulletin EC* 1-1970, at pp. 11–16.

end, and their confidence in the final success of their efforts.'[294] In more concrete terms, an agreement had been reached to close the transitional period by the establishment of a definitive arrangement for the financing of the common agricultural policy and a system which would give the Community its own resources, and, then, to proceed towards new challenges: to work out a plan for the creation of economic and monetary union and to re-open the negotiations for enlargement.

During the weeks following the Summit Meeting everyone appeared to be driven by a new spirit and there were 'more meetings by day and night than the Community had ever before known in a comparable stretch of time.'[295] As reported by the Commission, the unanimous feeling when the last meeting of the transitional period broke up was that 'a great step forward had been made and that the Community's latest crisis had been overcome.'[296]

But in spite of the optimism it had to be admitted that the new spirit was the result of an intergovernmental effort rather than the product of the institutional machinery set up by the EEC Treaty. Whatever the differences might have been between them in terms of appearances and manner, this meant that Georges Pompidou had managed to win broad support for the notion of co-operation which had always been the hallmark of Charles de Gaulle. As the French Government's spokesman confidently concluded after the Summit Meeting, '[i]t is not institutions which create a common policy, it is concurrent political wills which make co-operation possible, and the rest is added of itself.'[297]

This, indeed, was as good a premonition as any of the scanty years that lay ahead. Addressing the task which was to become the most important for the Community during the next phase of its existence, the Commission commented cautiously that '[t]he Community institutions, and the Council in particular, will find that they will very soon have to examine the conditions under which they operate and take the necessary steps. They will also have to decide how representatives of the various walks of life can be brought to share in the task of elaborating and implementing the common policies.'[298]

---

[294] See *Bulletin EC* 1-1970, at p. 12.

[295] See General Report 1969, above Ch 2, n 270, at p. 16.

[296] See General Report 1969, above Ch 2, n 270, at p. 17.

[297] Broadcast of 8 December 1969 as referred to in *Bulletin EC* 1-1970, at p. 124.

[298] See General Report 1969, above Ch 2, n 270, at p. 20.

The Dark Ages

'The problem is often not to find good new ideas, but to ensure that good old ones are put into practice.'[1]

3.1 Introduction

3.1.1 The pattern of evolution

The Community embarked upon its next stage of existence with the same enthusiasm with which it had concluded the previous and the agreement which had been reached by the Heads of State or Government in The Hague was soon confirmed by concrete results (see above 2.5.2). In this respect nothing was more important than the adoption by the Council of two inter-linked decisions which established a definitive arrangement for the financing of the common agricultural policy and a system that would give the Community its own budgetary resources (see below 3.2.2.2). The adoption of these Decisions seemed finally to have put to rest a life-long conflict and attention could now be focused on the new challenges: the project for creation of economic and monetary union, and enlargement (see below 3.2.1 and 3.2.2).

But in spite of initial optimism it was not long before the Community was caught up again in the desperation which had haunted it before (see above 2.5.1). This time it was not going to lose its grip lightly. For most

---

[1] The Report of the Three Wise Men presented to the European Council on 8 November 1979 (see below Ch 3, n 145). Quote from *Bulletin EC* 11-1979, at p. 13.

people, therefore, the period under study in this chapter has come to be thought of as the years of political paralysis or even the 'Dark Ages'. Their impression is only confirmed by the fact that, for lawyers, the very same period is the most glorious one; when the Court of Justice stepped forward to 'help' the Community and its Member States to make progress towards an integration based, not on legislation, but on principles of law.[2]

It is sometimes taken for granted that the problem which beset the Community during its Dark Ages had its root in the Luxembourg Compromise and a consequential failure of the Council to effectuate the passage to decision-making by qualified majority voting (see above 2.1.1 and 2.3.4).[3] But to believe that an explanation could be found in such simple terms is mistaken. Even if it had been possible to force action by strict application of the provisions of the EEC Treaty which permitted or even prescribed qualified majority voting, this had been of little use in those few but important fields where unanimity was still a formal requirement. This was the case not only with the common commercial policy and the harmonization of conditions for trade (cf. above 2.4.1 and 2.4.3), but also with the project for creation of economic and monetary union, and, indeed, enlargement.

During the transitional period, the Community suffered because some Governments were unwilling to make the sacrifices needed to make progress in fields of co-operation that were important to other Governments unless those Governments first made the sacrifices needed to make progress in fields that were important to them. Therefore, the

---

[2] See e.g. Case 11/70 *Internationale Handelsgesellschaft mbH v Einfuhr- und Vorratsstelle für Getreide und Futtermittel* [1970] ECR 1125 and Case 106/77 *Amministrazione delle Finanze dello Stato v Simmenthal SpA* [1978] ECR 629: both clarifying the principle of supremacy of Community law; Case 41/74 *Van Duyn v Home Office* [1974] ECR 1337 and Case 148/78 *Pubblico Ministerio v Ratti* [1979] ECR 1629: both clarifying the principle of direct effect of non-implemented Directives; and Case 8/74 *Procureur du Roi v Dassonville et al.* [1974] ECR 837, Case 120/78 *Rewe-Zentral AG v Bundesmonopolverwaltung für Branntwein* [1979] ECR 649, Case 2/74 *Reyners v Belgian State* [1974] ECR 631, Case 33/74 *Van Binsbergen v Bestuur van de Bedrijfsvereniging voor de Metaalnijverheid* [1974] ECR 1299: all ensuring a wide application of the provisions of the EEC Treaty relating to the free movements of goods, persons (establishment), and services. For a discussion on the 'activist' Court, see, in particular, Weiler, J. H. H., The Transformation of Europe (1991) 100 *YaleLJ* 2403.

[3] See e.g. Nicoll, W., The Luxembourg Compromise (1984) 22 *JCMS* 35; Noël, É., The Single European Act (1988) 24 *GO* 3; Vasey, above Ch 2, n 140; and Teasdale, above Ch 2, n 107.

conclusion had been reached that a 'formula of synchronisation' needed to be followed, which would make it possible to approach the differing interests along parallel lines (see above 2.3.1). The significance of that formula was re-affirmed in the negotiations which led to the adoption of the Luxembourg Compromise. Here all Governments found reasons to agree that their co-operation, as a whole, would only function if solutions could be found which were acceptable to everyone. For that reason, the potential for using qualified majority voting to override the interests of a minority was conceived as a *question d'école* rather than an *eventualité concrète* (see above 2.3.4).

Importantly, the continuing validity of this attitude or insight was manifested by the Summit Meeting in The Hague. Here the French President, Georges Pompidou, managed to win a broad support for an inter-governmental model of co-operation which had not been envisaged in the EEC Treaty. In spite of some initial suspicions, once an agreement had been reached from which all of them stood to profit, the Heads of State or Government seemed convinced about the power of concurrent political wills: over the following years they were to meet each other on a regular basis and in 1975 the new habit was institutionalized in the form of a European Council (see below 3.3.1.1). Further evidence of this 'pattern of evolution' could be found in the rather positive reactions to another of the French President's initiatives, that of starting 'with what already exists and create a Confederation of States resolved to harmonise their policy and integrate their economies.'[4]

---

[4] In accordance with this so-called Pompidou Plan, set out by the French President in a press conference on 21 January 1971, '[t]his pattern of evolution poses a number of problems, none of which I am prepared to ignore. Firstly, how can the Council of Ministers take its decisions? Now I would ask everyone, especially our partners in the Six, to consider how coalition governments function. When everyone agrees on an issue, all is well; if not, there is a majority and a minority. In the latter case, either the minority decides that the matter is not vital and concedes defeat, or it takes the opposite view and breaks up the coalition. It is obvious that in the kind of Europe we are envisaging, this must not happen, otherwise the whole thing will collapse. I therefore believe that important decisions can be taken only by unanimous agreement; that the important thing here is political clarity rather than a set of regulations, and that if this is not recognised everything will be destroyed.' For the full text, see *Bulletin EC* 3-1971, at pp. 99–100. Even if the Pompidou Plan was only seen as 'a halfway house' it was generally welcomed and, indeed, felt to be 'worthy of consideration.' See *Bulletin EC* 3-1971, at pp. 100–101; and *Bulletin EC* 4-1971, at p. 154.

3.1.2 A political paralysis?

Even if Pompidou's plan for a Confederation of States was eventually never realized, for many years it was to provide the basis for expectations and a stubborn, even self-destructive, unwillingness to give up the belief in the absolute power of concurrent wills. This chapter will focus on the rather painful path the Community had to travel before all its Govern-ments were ready to reconsider that belief and admit their need for a model of co-operation which enabled them to force action: by use of qualified majority and, indeed, by transfer of far-reaching responsibilities to the Commission. But before that a few more words should be said about the problem that the institutional reform was intended to remedy.

Perhaps most striking is the fact that the supposed paralysis was far from total. On the contrary. Throughout the duration of the period studied in this Chapter the institutional machinery continued to churn out legislation at a steady rate (cf. above 1.2.1).[5] Like today, much of the legislation produced fell within the field of the common agricultural policy and involved matters of little or no political value. But to a sur-prising extent, more controversial matters were also tackled. It may be noted, in that respect, that, during the worst part of the period (1975 to 1985), 154 regulations and 47 directives were adopted by the Council on the basis of its residual competence in Article 235 EEC (1958), formally requiring it to act by unanimity.[6] The content of that legislation ranged from the establishment of new organs with their own legal personality to the introduction of new fields of co-operation, such as protection of environment and consumers.[7]

---

[5] To take just one example, in 1978 the Council adopted 428 regulations and 66 directives: this, in fact, was more than it adopted in 2000 or, indeed, in 1970 (see above 1.2.1). For a detailed study of the Commission's proposals during the period 1974–1980 see Krislow, S., Ehlermann, C.-D., and Weiler, J. H. H., The Political Organs and the Decision Making Process in the United States and the European Community, in Cappelletti, M., Seccombe, M., and Weiler, J. H. H. (Eds.), *Integration Through Law: Methods, Tools and Institutions* (De Gruyter 1986), at pp. 3–110.

[6] Source CELEX. See, for a similar conclusion, Weiler, above Ch 3, n 2; and Usher, The Development of Community Powers after the Single European Act, in White, R. and Smythe, B. (Eds.), *Current Issues in European and International Law: Essays in Memory of Frank Dowick* (Sweet & Maxwell 1990).

[7] See e.g. Council Regulation 337/75/EEC of 10 February 1975 establishing a European Centre for the Development of Vocational Training (OJ 1975 L 39/1); Council Directive 78/659/EEC of 18 July 1978 on the quality of fresh waters needing protection or improvement in order to support fish life (OJ 1978 L 222/1); and Council Directive 79/581/EEC of 19 June 1979

Against this background, the conclusion must be drawn that the problem was not one of a general failure to act. But what then was the problem? This question cannot be answered easily and below only a partial explanation is offered, focusing on the development or, indeed, the lack of development in some specific fields of co-operation. The claim is that the hopes invested in these fields were so great that failure to fulfil them had consequences for the work in general. The specific fields which will be examined are the new challenges established at the Summit Meeting in The Hague (see above 2.5.2): the project for creation of economic and monetary union and the enlargement. The first allowed an extension of the list of objectives to include matters which were so fundamental to the economy of each Member State that any signal of hesitation was reason enough for the Governments to back off. The second introduced a new extreme into the scale of interests which had to be reconciled: the United Kingdom. The combined effect was volatile—especially for a Community which lived by a belief in the absolute power of concurrent wills.

3.2   The failure to deal with new challenges

3.2.1   *A plan for economic and monetary union*

Following the agreement reached at the Summit Meeting in The Hague to work out a plan for the creation of economic and monetary union (see above 2.5.2), on 5 March 1970 a memorandum was presented by the Commission which laid down the principles that were to furnish a basis for further discussion.[8] The Memorandum was almost immediately handed over to a group of experts, headed by the Luxembourg Prime

on consumer protection in the indication of the prices of foodstuffs (OJ 1979 L 158/19). Other examples are co-ordination of monetary policy and equal treatment. See e.g. Council Regulation 3181/78/EEC of 18 December 1978 relating to the European Monetary System (OJ 1978 L 379/2); and Council Directive 76/207/EEC of 9 February 1976 on the implementation of the principle of equal treatment for men and women as regards access to employment, vocational training and promotion, and working conditions (OJ 1976 L 39/40).

[8] See Commission Memorandum of 4 March 1970: a plan for the phased establishment of an economic and monetary union, in *Bulletin EC* Supplement 3-1970. See also the earlier Barre Report, above Ch 2, n 285.

Minister Pierre Werner, which was instructed to evaluate it and to specify the concrete measures required for initiation of the plan. A final version of the subsequent report was presented on 8 October 1970.[9] Overall, this so-called Werner Report supported the idea that the project for creation of economic and monetary union should get started and concluded that it could be completed by the end of 1980. But it was emphasized—in line with the Commission Memorandum—that the project would only be successful if it was embarked upon with a firm intention to carry it through and if the necessary powers were given to 'effective and properly supervised institutions, capable of acting quickly in specific cases.'[10]

When the Werner Report was discussed in the Council, it became clear that several Governments were far from ready to make the type of commitments called for.[11] Not only was there opposition to some of the institutional suggestions but also a fundamental disagreement as to the objective of the whole exercise.[12] In spite of this, it soon became clear that nothing would stop the Governments from going ahead with the project to which they had already subscribed in The Hague. The way forward was pointed out by President Pompidou in a press conference on 21 January 1971:

Progress must be made in deed, not just in word—the project must prove itself as it goes along. From this point of view, as regards economic and monetary union, the spirit of The Hague means embarking resolutely upon the first stage, rather than having theoretical discussions on what may happen, if all goes well, after 1980.[13]

This method of postponing the discussion on matters of principle in order to keep to a tight schedule was nothing new; on the contrary, it was something which the Community had learnt to live with during the transitional period (see e.g. above 2.4.4). Hopeful, therefore, that it would be possible to resolve disagreements on the way, the Governments

---

[9] See Report of the Werner Group to the Council and the Commission of 8 October 1970 concerning the realisation by stages of the economic and monetary union in the Community (OJ 1970 C 136/1). See also *Bulletin EC* Supplement 11-1970.   [10] See *Bulletin EC* 1-1971, at p. 144.

[11] The Werner Report (above Ch 3, n 9) was discussed for the first time on 14 December 1970. See in general Fourth General Report on the Activities of the European Communities 1970 (Office for Official Publications 1971), at pp. 65–88.

[12] See e.g. the criticism by the French Foreign Minister, Maurice Schumann, in *Bulletin EC* 1-1971, at p. 145.   [13] See *Bulletin EC* 3-1971, at pp. 99–100.

decided to launch the project for creation of economic and monetary union.[14] But since they were not sure exactly where this would lead them, their commitment was only manifested in the adoption on 22 March 1971 of a non-binding Resolution. This Resolution set out to seek to ensure a degree of co-ordination of economic and monetary policies and, parallel to that, to intensify the efforts to reach agreement within the Council on legislation aimed at the 'acceleration of effective liberalisation of persons, goods, services and capital and inter-penetration of the economies' by harmonization of taxation.[15] At the same time, an attempt was made to secure a degree of monetary stability through an informal arrangement, based on the idea that the Central Banks should apply more narrow margins for fluctuation of their currencies than required by the system built up around the IMF (see above 2.5.2).

Only a few months after its initiation, the project for creation of economic and monetary union was hit by the first serious setback. Faced with a massive inflow of dollars, the German and Dutch Governments refused to rely on the common fluctuation arrangement but decided, instead, to let their currencies float.[16] This was evidence that the arrangement as such was not capable of dealing with the type of situations it was intended to address and, even more seriously, that there was a fundamental lack of political resolve.

It was noted, in the previous chapter, that this type of problem was far from limited to the Community (see above 2.5.2), and, at the same time as attempts were being made to get the project for creation of economic and monetary union off the ground, the system built up around the IMF was

---

[14] See e.g. General Report 1971, above Ch 3, n 11, at p. IX. See, in general, Man, G. de, The Economic and Monetary Union after Four Years: Results and Prospects (1975) 12 *CMLRev* 193, at p. 198.

[15] See Resolution of the Council and of the Representatives of the Governments of the Member States of 22 March 1971 on the attainment by stages of economic and monetary union in the Community (OJ 1971 C 28/1). On the same day a series of measures was adopted relating to the co-ordination of economic and monetary policies. See Council Decision 71/141/EEC of 22 March 1971 on the strengthening of the co-ordination of short-term economic policies of the Member States of the European Economic Community (OJ 1971 L 73/12); Council Decision 71/142/EEC of 22 March 1971 on the strengthening of co-operation between the central banks of the Member States of the European Economic Community (OJ 1971 L 73/14); and Council Decision 71/143/EEC of 22 March 1971 setting up machinery for medium-term financial assistance (OJ 1971 L 73/15).

[16] See *Bulletin EC* 7-1971, at pp. 126–129. Cf. Resolution of the Council of 9 May 1971 concerning the monetary situation (OJ 1971 C 58/1).

about to crash-land. This, indeed, was one reason why the Member States of the Community had rallied around the idea of economic and monetary union in the first place. One of the events which was felt to be most damaging for the international system was the decision by the United States Government on 15 August 1971 to let the Dollar float and to adopt a series of protective trade measures.[17] The repercussions were world-wide: a few weeks later the decision was taken by the Japanese Government to let the Yen float, followed by the Soviet Government's decision to alter the parity of the Rouble.[18]

The more evident it became that the IMF system was not capable of dealing with the problems at hand, the greater the awareness grew within the Community that a fresh effort had to be made to agree on common action.[19] But in spite of this, there was little sign that good intentions and, indeed, an increasing number of proposals would be transformed into concrete action. A small step forward was taken on 21 March 1972 with the adoption of a new Resolution in which the Governments stated their ambition to place the process towards economic and monetary union back on its feet.[20] This implied a promise to re-examine existing proposals and a new agreement to seek monetary stability, this time through the introduction of the so-called snake arrangement, intended to discourage the inflow of dollars through the introduction of a mechanism for joint floating of currencies.[21] But more important was the successful conclusion of the negotiations for the first enlargement. Apparently unable, themselves, to make progress in the creation of economic and monetary union, the Member States came to invest their hopes, instead, in the newcomers: Denmark, Ireland, and, in particular, the United Kingdom. With their entry, it was felt, the Community would be given 'a genuine strengthening which will not fail to find expression first of all in the reactivation of the economic and monetary union.'[22]

---

[17] See *Bulletin EC* 7-1971, at p. 127 and 11-1971, at pp. 125–129.

[18] See *Bulletin EC* 11-1971, at pp. 125–129.

[19] See *Bulletin EC* 11-1971, at pp. 122–127 and 4-1972, at p. 134.

[20] See Resolution of the Council and of the Representatives of the Governments of the Member States of 21 March 1972 on the application of the Resolution of 22 March 1971 on the attainment by stages of economic and monetary union in the Community (OJ 1972 C 38/3).

[21] See Council Directive 72/156/EEC of 21 March 1972 on regulating international capital flows and neutralising their undesirable effects on domestic liquidity (OJ 1972 L 91/13).

[22] See the Commission Report on Enlarged Community—Outcome of the Negotiations with the Applicant States, in *Bulletin EC* Supplement 1-1972, at pp. 47 and 50.

3.2.2   The first enlargement

3.2.2.1   The cloud of mutual suspicion

As early as 1958, negotiations had been started on the possibility of bringing about an association between the Member States of the Community and some other European States (the other members of the OECD) in the form of a free trade area.[23] The most active stance was taken by the British Government which, unfortunately, had something less extensive in mind than that required by the Community and, in particular, the French Government.[24] The difference of views was well reflected by the British negotiator, Reginald Maudling, reporting home that if the French got what they wanted, 'when the Free Trade Area comes into being there will be no freedom and very little trade.'[25] Not surprisingly, the negotiations came to an abrupt end on 14 November 1958 when the new French President, General de Gaulle, declared that it would not be possible to reach any agreement along the lines envisaged by the British.[26]

Following the break-down of the negotiations for a free trade area, seven of the non-Member States which had been involved decided to go their own way and, as a result of that, the Treaty establishing a European Free Trade Association (EFTA) was signed in Stockholm on 20 November 1959.[27] The intention was that this should provide its signatories with an intermediate framework for economic co-operation and, above all, a joint basis for further negotiations with the Member States of the Community.[28] But whatever their original intention had been, after

[23] See Kapteyn and VerLoren van Themaat, above Ch 1, n 36, at p. 18.

[24] Most importantly, the French Government insisted on an arrangement including a common customs tariff and harmonization in the economic and social spheres. See Malmborg, M. af, *Den ståndaktiga nationalstaten: Sverige och den västeuropeiska integrationen 1945–1959* (Lund University Press 1994), at pp. 297 and 305–307.

[25] See Letter from Maudling to Macmillan 30 September 1958, Prime Minister's Office (PREM) 1958 11/2532. Reference in Malmborg, above Ch 3, n 24, at p. 329.

[26] See Malmborg, above Ch 3, n 24, at pp. 325 and 332; and Kapteyn and VerLoren van Themaat, above Ch 1, n 36, at p. 18. See, in general, Lynch, F., *De Gaulle's First Veto: France, the Rebuff and the Free Trade Area*, EUI Working Paper HEC No 98/8 (European University Institute 1998).

[27] Greece and Turkey associated themselves with the EEC in agreements of 9 July 1961 and 12 September 1963 respectively. See Kapteyn and VerLoren van Themaat, above Ch 1, n 36, at p. 18.

[28] See Resolution adopted in Stockholm 19–20 November 1959, in *Utrikesfrågor: Offentliga dokument m.m. rörande viktigare svenska utrikespolitiska frågor 1959* (Kungliga Utrikesdepartementet 1959), at pp. 103–105. Reference in Malmborg, above Ch 3, n 24, at p. 384.

a few years a radical change took place in the attitude of the British Government. This culminated in the Prime Minister, Harold Macmillan, making an application for full membership on 9 August 1961.[29] Denmark, Ireland, and Norway followed the British example.[30] Once again the hopes were dashed by a sudden move of the French President. To the disappointment of most people on both sides of the table, it had to be stated, therefore, that differences of opinion made any further negotiations impossible (see above 2.3.1).

It is clear that the question of enlargement, in particular by the accession of the United Kingdom, was a pawn in the Member States' game concerning the Community's relationship with the outside world. Thus, for example, those Member States which were strong supporters of a liberalized international market, most notably Germany, had reached the conclusion that it was better to have the United Kingdom within the Community rather than outside, as a competitor (see above 2.1.2). But in France there were strong demands for protectionism and a deep-rooted fear of an international market dominated by the United States. Since Harold Macmillan had made no secret of his country's fundamental loyalty to the United States, the French Government seemed convinced, therefore, that '[w]ith the United Kingdom, the American horse would be dragged into the European Troy.'[31]

More than four years after the first failure, the British Government considered the time ripe to make a fresh attempt and on 10 May 1967 a new application for accession was submitted by the new Prime Minister, Harold Wilson.[32] The United Kingdom was now suffering from serious problems with its balance of payments and 'the enormous economic advantages which enlargement would bring' were seen as a cure.[33] But the application was far from unconditional and there were several problems to which the British Government demanded a satisfactory solution.

[29] See *Bulletin EEC* 9/10-1961, at pp. 5–23.

[30] The other parties to EFTA made a new request for negotiations with a view to the establishment of an association or some other economic arrangement. See Kapteyn and VerLoren van Themaat, above Ch 1, n 36, at p. 18.

[31] See Kapteyn and VerLoren van Themaat, above Ch 1, n 36, at p. 19. Cf. *Europe* (bulletin quotidien) 9 February and 13 March 1968. See, in general, Milward, A. (Ed.), *The Rise and Fall of a National Strategy*, at pp. 145–163 (Frank Cass 2002).

[32] See Fifth General Report on the Activities of the European Communities 1971 (Office for Official Publications 1972), at p. 8.

[33] See Declaration by Deputy Prime Minister George Brown on 4 July 1967, in General Report 1971, above Ch 3, n 32, at p. 8.

None of these was more imperative than that stemming from the fear that the common agricultural policy would place an unfair economic burden on the United Kingdom.[34] The root of this fear was to be found in the fact that a Member State which, like the United Kingdom, was used to import a large quantity of agricultural products from outside the Community had to pay a high price for its imports but, since it itself had a small agricultural sector, would only receive very little in return. Once again the British application was followed by those of Denmark, Ireland, and Norway.[35]

The reactions within the Community to the British application were divided. Although no fundamental objections were raised to the enlargement as such, it soon became clear that it was blocked by the French Government which required that the British economy be restored to health before its application could be considered.[36] This in turn evoked negative reactions in a number of fields of co-operation. According to the Commission, the disagreement over the question of enlargement was even a direct reason for the general deterioration in the atmosphere of the Community.[37]

It has been seen above that the situation changed at the Summit Meeting in The Hague (see above 2.5.2). After having reached agreement to settle the question which had haunted the Community for most of its existence, that of replacing the Member States' financial contributions by a system of own resources, the Heads of State or Government declared that the time had come to prepare for enlargement: '[i]n so far as the applicant States accept the Treaties and their political objective, the decisions taken since the entry into force of the Treaties and the options made in the sphere of development, the Heads of State or Government have indicated their agreement to the opening of negotiations between the Community on the one hand and the applicant States on the other.'[38]

3.2.2.2   A choice between everything or nothing

The Intergovernmental Conference within which the negotiations for accession were to take place was commenced in Luxembourg on

---

[34] See Kapteyn and VerLoren van Themaat, above Ch 1, n 36, at p. 20.

[35] See General Report 1971, above Ch 3, n 32, at p. 8.

[36] See Kapteyn and VerLoren van Themaat, above Ch 1, n 36, at p. 20.

[37] See General Report 1968, above Ch 2, n 173, at pp. 14–15; and General Report 1971, above Ch 3, n 32, at pp. 10–13.

[38] See point 13 of the final communiqué, above Ch 2, n 293, at pp. 11–16. For a general discussion, see Groeben, W. von der, *The European Community: the Formative Years* (European Perspectives 1985).

30 June 1970.[39] The date had been carefully chosen. Only a few weeks earlier the Council had adopted its inter-linked Decisions laying down a definitive arrangement for the financing of the common agricultural policy and introducing a system which would give the Community its 'own' resources (see above 3.1.1).[40] A further circumstance, the significance of which cannot be underestimated, was the change of political leadership in the United Kingdom: from the Labour Government of Harold Wilson to the Conservative Government of Edward Heath.

Quite clearly, Harold Wilson's concern with the common agricultural policy had been sufficient reason for the French Government to resist enlargement until it had been given guarantees that the achievements of the transitional period could not be easily torn up. It may be recalled in this context that the EEC Treaty enabled the Council to adopt, amend, and repeal legislation relating to the common agricultural policy by qualified majority and that this had been the triggering factor for the crisis which led to the Luxembourg Compromise (see above 2.3.2).[41] With the adoption of the Decision on the Community's own resources, basing itself on a steady income from the common agricultural policy, the French Government could now afford to be more generous. Irrespective of the future usefulness of the Luxembourg Compromise, not even the EEC Treaty would permit any changes to be made to the Decision on the Community's own resources unless those were unanimously agreed to.[42]

[39] See General Report 1970, above Ch 3, n 11, at p. 256.

[40] See, respectively, Council Regulation 70/729/EEC of 21 April 1970 on the financing of the common agricultural policy (OJ 1970 L 94/13); and Council Decision 70/243/ECSC/EEC/ EAEC of 21 April 1970 on the replacement of financial contributions from Member States by the Communities' own resources (OJ 1970 L 94/19). According to the new system, the Member States' financial contributions to the Community were to be replaced by its own resources based on the revenue from agricultural levies and, gradually, customs duties (and eventually also from the revenue of a uniform system for value-added tax). It may be noted that the Decision on the Community's own resources was accompanied by an agreement to strengthen the budgetary powers of the European Parliament. See Treaty of 22 April 1970 amending certain budgetary provisions of the Treaties establishing the European Communities (OJ 1971 L 2/1).

[41] See Article 43 EEC (1958). It may be pointed out that the significance of the veto stemming from the Luxembourg Compromise in respect of the question of the financing of the common agricultural policy was reaffirmed and even 'improved' in the agreement which had been reached at the Summit Meeting in The Hague. As explained in the final communiqué, the acceptance of the financial arrangement 'does not exclude its adaptation by unanimous vote, in an enlarged Community, on condition that the principles of this arrangement are not watered down.' See point 7 of the final communiqué, above Ch 2, n 293, at pp. 11–16.

[42] See Article 210 EEC (1958). This required also ratification by the national parliaments.

In addition to that, the Applicant States were required to make a formal acceptance of the common agricultural policy—and all other matters which had now been settled—before the negotiations could get started. This indeed had been an essential part of the agreement reached at the Summit Meeting in The Hague and at the opening of the negotiations it was stated, therefore, that 'the solution of any problems of adjustment which arise must be sought in the establishment of transitional measures and not in changes of existing rules.'[43] Faced with the choice between everything or nothing, the Governments of the Applicant States accepted the terms and confirmed that they would focus their efforts on measures which could make their passage to full membership as painless as possible.[44]

During the months which followed it became clear that all concerned were anxious to keep the negotiations moving at a brisk pace and, most importantly, that the British and the French Governments had made up their minds that the cloud of mutual suspicion which separated them should not be permitted to block a success. It would appear that the most crucial point was passed on 20 and 21 May 1971 when Edward Heath went to Paris for a meeting *en tête à tête* with Georges Pompidou. As reported by the British Prime Minister on his return to London, he had been able to convince the French President that the intentions and expectations of the British Government were not in conflict with those of the French but indeed were very much the same.[45] Of particular importance for the French, no doubt, was the Prime Minister's reassurance that the United Kingdom had 'no intention of trying to destroy the common agricultural policy from within.'[46] Within weeks of the

[43] See General Report 1971, above Ch 3, n 32, at p. 14.

[44] See General Report 1971, above Ch 3, n 32, at p. 15; and General Report 1970, above Ch 3, n 11, at p. 265.

[45] So, for example, Edward Heath explained to the House of Commons on 24 May 1971 that it had been 'heartening to discover how close were the views of the French and the British Governments on the development of Europe and its role in the world' and that an agreement had been reached 'about the sort of Europe we want to see ... It is a Europe which, by its unity, will be of a size and nature and in equal position with the United States, Japan or the Soviet Union, to enter into international trading arrangements and international financial arrangements and to use its influence in the world.' See Debates of the House of Commons on 24 May 1971 (Hansard), Session 1970–71, Volume 818 (HMSO 1971), at columns 32 and 38.

[46] See Parliamentary Debate of 24 May 1971, above Ch 3, n 45, at columns 34 and 37. Quote from *Bulletin EC* 7/8-1973, at p. 116. Cf. also the Commission's report Enlarged Community, above Ch 3, n 22, at pp. 34 and 47–48.

meeting in Paris all matters of any great significance for the negotiations had been settled in agreements on transitional measures.[47]

3.2.2.3   The debates in the House of Commons

In spite of the apparent ease with which the negotiations proceeded, there was a growing preoccupation that their result would not be well received by the British people (of which 59% declared themselves opposed to accession).[48] According to Harold Wilson, now Leader of the Opposition, it was, therefore, 'more important to get the right terms slowly than to get the wrong terms quickly.'[49] As he had been in 1967, he remained very much concerned with 'the price which British housewives will have to pay to subsidise the Community's agricultural policy.'[50] This is not the place for speculation about the likelihood that the British Government might have achieved better terms of accession. But as has been noted above, the scope for the negotiations had been radically delimited by the requirement that the Applicant States must not seek any changes of existing rules. It is not likely, therefore, that an attempt to press for the type of result Harold Wilson wished to see would have been more successful than it had been in 1967. It is even less likely that any terms could have been negotiated which would have satisfied the most fundamental reason for the lack of public support: the common fear that accession to the Community would entail a loss of national sovereignty. As borne out by debates in the House of Commons, this indeed was a fear which was shared by many MPs and the question was raised, therefore, whether it was not 'indefensible to try to force through this drastic constitutional change without a further appeal to the electorate?'[51]

It is submitted that the way in which this question was dealt with is a crucial factor for understanding the problems on which the Community was to focus its attention during many years to follow. The first aspect of the question—requesting an appeal to the electorate—was simply disposed of by classifying the accession as an issue of international relations in respect of which the MPs could not escape their individual

---

[47] See the Commission's report Enlarged Community, above Ch 3, n 22, at pp. 34 and 47–48.

[48] See Parliamentary Debate of 24 May 1971, above Ch 3, n 45, at column 40.

[49] Harold Wilson on 26 April 1971. Quote from *Bulletin EC* 6-1971, at p. 130.

[50] Harold Wilson on 26 April 1971. Quote from *Bulletin EC* 6-1971, at p. 130.

[51] Parliamentary Debate of 24 May 1971, above Ch 3, n 45, at column 42.

responsibility.[52] The second aspect of the question—expressing the concern that accession would lead to a loss of national sovereignty and amount, therefore, to a constitutional change—was dealt with by convincing the MPs that the political understanding which had emerged from the meeting between Edward Heath and Georges Pompidou (see above 3.2.2.2) would guarantee that the Community should never develop beyond their control. As Edward Heath explained to the House of Commons on 24 May 1971:

We discussed the development of the European Community and the working of its institutions. We agreed in particular that the identity of national states should be maintained in the framework of the developing Community. This means, of course, that, though the European Commission has made and will continue to make a valuable contribution, the Council of Ministers should continue to be the forum in which important decisions are taken and the processes of harmonisation should not override essential national interests. We were in agreement that the maintenance and strengthening of the fabric of co-operation in such a Community requires that decisions should in practice be taken by unanimous agreement when vital national interests of any one or more members are at stake. This is indeed entirely in accordance with the views I have long held. It provides a clear assurance, just as the history of the Community provides clear evidence, that joining the Community does not entail a loss of national identity or an erosion of essential national sovereignty.[53]

Seemingly satisfied with the 'right' their Government would have to use the veto in the Council, the MPs soon proved themselves prepared to approve accession on the terms which had been negotiated and, after completion of the ratification procedure, the United Kingdom, and, with it, Ireland and Denmark, became Member States of the Community

[52] Thus, for example, Edward Heath explained to the House of Commons on 24 May 1971 that 'I have always made it plain that it is Parliament's responsibility to decide this issue, as it is to decide every other issue of international relations. If honourable Members do not wish to accept their responsibilities, that is a matter for them. I have always taken the view, as a member of Parliament, that it is my responsibility fully to report on these matters to my constituents and to consult them, but I have always taken the view of Burke, who represented the constituency of the right honourable Member for Bristol, South East (Mr Benn), that one owes them one's judgment as well as one's energy.' See Parliamentary Debate of 24 May 1971, above Ch 3, n 45, at column 41.

[53] See Parliamentary Debate of 24 May 1971, above Ch 3, n 45, at columns 32 and 33. Cf. also columns 39 and 43.

on 1 January 1973 (Norway did not accede, a referendum on 26 September 1972 having gone against membership).[54]

3.2.3 L'Europe, c'est moi: *a return to national policies*

3.2.3.1 *A lack of mutual trust in common action*

The successful conclusion of the negotiations for enlargement meant that one of the greatest causes of disagreement had been overcome and there was much hope that it would now be possible to concentrate on the project for creation of economic and monetary union.[55] But in spite of the initial enthusiasm, the first year of the enlarged Community came to be characterized by 'brutal change and rapid transformation.'[56] Although avoiding here any attempt to explain the exact reasons for this, it shall be pointed out that the international situation—with the monetary instability added to by an oil crisis—was such that it was felt to require more unity than ever but at the same time made it very difficult to give up national control: the stakes were simply too high.[57] There is no better way to describe the state in which the Community found itself than as a rapidly growing lack of mutual trust, close to fear, to join in common action. Clearly, this would have been less hard to cope with if ideas of the right way forward had been more convergent. But over the years it had become

[54] See Act of 22 January 1972 concerning the conditions for accession and the adjustments to the Treaties (OJ 1972 L 73/1). A first vote approving accession was taken in the House of Commons on 28 October 1971. See the Commission's report Enlarged Community, above Ch 3, n 22, at pp. 48 and 63.

[55] See e.g. the Commission's report Enlarged Community, above Ch 3, n 22, at pp. 47 and 50; and the comments made by the President of the European Parliament, Walter Behrendt, after the first Summit Meeting with the Heads of State or Government of the new Member States in Paris on 19 and 20 October 1972, in *Bulletin EC* 10-1972, at p. 24.

[56] See the address by Commission Vice-President Carlo Scarascia Mugnozza to the European Parliament on 12 February 1974, in Seventh General Report on the Activities of the European Communities 1973 (Office for Official Publications 1974), at p. XV. Some examples of the initial dynamism' can be found in the adoption of Council Directive 73/148/EEC of 21 May 1973 on the abolition of restrictions on movement and residence within the Community for nationals of Member States with regard to establishment and the provision of services (OJ 1973 L 172/14); and Council Directive 73/183/EEC of 28 June 1973 on the abolition of restrictions on freedom of establishment and freedom to provide services in respect of self-employed activities of banks and other financial institutions (OJ 1973 L 194/1).

[57] See e.g. the address by Commission Vice-President Carlo Scarascia Mugnozza, above Ch 3, n 56, at p. XVI.

apparent that some of the Governments were not only far from each other but held ideas which were impossible to reconcile. The dilemma this presented was certainly not going to be easier to resolve after enlargement.

Irrespective of the reassurances Edward Heath had given to Georges Pompidou, once inside the Community the British Government soon made it clear that it would seek to 'improve' the common agricultural policy by opening up the possibilities for trade with the rest of the world. According to the British Minister of Agriculture, Joseph Godber, the changes aimed for were supposed to be 'evolutionary and not revolutionary.'[58] This indeed was what many had hoped for but it was also what the French had always feared. For them the common agricultural policy was a guarantee for employment and social welfare, and as such the most fundamental pillar of the Community edifice. It had worked hard to get the common agricultural policy there in the first place and it would not allow it to be weakened at a time when it was needed the most. Whatever measures the French Government was prepared to consider for improving the common agricultural policy, therefore, they were not likely to be of the same kind as those advocated by the British.[59]

One of the first signs of a re-emergence of old conflicts over the common agricultural policy was seen when the Council met on 16 July 1973 for an examination of a Commission proposal for changes in the common organization of the market in sugar.[60] The proposal suggested introducing the power to cut subsidies for surplus production of sugar—most of which were received by French beet growers—through an arrangement for import of sugar under the so-called Commonwealth Sugar Agreement.[61] Although supported by all other representatives in

---

[58] Speech by the British Minister of Agriculture, Joseph Godber, on 27 August 1973, in *Bulletin EC* 7/8-1973, at p. 116.

[59] It may be noted in this context that a series of Directives for reform of agricultural structures had been adopted by the Council on 17 April 1972. These were based on the idea that the area of farmland in use in the Community should be reduced and that incentives should be created for farmers either to leave farming or modernize their methods. See Council Directive 72/159/EEC of 17 April 1972 on the modernisation of farms (OJ 1972 L 96/1); Council Directive 72/160/EEC of 17 April 1972 concerning measures to encourage the cessation of farming and the reallocation of utilised agricultural area for the purposes of structural improvement (OJ 1972 L 96/9); and Council Directive 72/161/EEC of 17 April 1972 concerning the provision of socio-economic guidance for and the acquisition of occupational skills by persons engaged in agriculture (OJ 1972 L 96/15).

[60] At the time based on Council Regulation 1009/67/EEC (see above Ch 2, n 149).

[61] See *Bulletin EC* 7/8-1973, at pp. 49–50.

:he Council, the French Minister of Agriculture, Jacques Chirac, char-
icterized the proposal as a 'scandalous expression of malthusian policy'
ind as such the result of the French Commissioner, Claude Cheysson,
illowing himself to be convinced by the new British Commissioner,
Christopher Soames, 'who defends the interest of his sugar indus-
:rialist.'[62] It would appear that this protest was reason enough for the
Council to back off. As Jacques Chirac commented some weeks later, '[i]f
[had not shown my anger, the Commission's proposals might have had
lisastrous consequences.'[63]

The hostile attitude adopted by the French Government to this, and a
1umber of other proposals designed to liberalize the common agricultural
policy, gave raise to many bitter comments. Thus, for example, the Dutch
Commissioner, Petrus Lardinois, explained to *Le Figaro* that '[t]he French
ind Mr Chirac must realise that they are not alone in Europe' and the
German Minister of Foreign Affairs, Walter Scheel, explained to *Le
Monde* that '[t]he goal cannot be reached if each of those involved says
L'Europe, c'est moi!'[64] Even if the frustration was understandable, it was also
paradoxical and as such symptomatic for the position in which the
Community found itself. According to the text of the EEC Treaty, the
Council was under no obligation to let itself be blocked by the French.
On the contrary, it was permitted and, arguably, even obliged to forge
ahead by a vote which only required the support of a qualified majority.[65]
Since this was not done, it must be concluded that at least some of the
Council's members were more willing to drop their own demands than to
proceed in a direction which was not supported by all.

3.2.3.2 *A consolidation of the right to veto*

As manifested in the discussions which led to the Luxembourg
Compromise, there was a general agreement in the Council that the
Community could only function in the long run if solutions were found
which were acceptable to everyone (see above 2.3.4). But only the French
insisted that this should give each Government a right to veto proposals
which the EEC Treaty said could be adopted by qualified majority.
During the years which followed the Luxembourg Compromise, therefore, the 'streamlined veto' was fragile. If irritated enough by its abuse, the

[62] See *Bulletin EC* 7/8-1973, at pp. 110–113.   [63] See *Bulletin EC* 7/8-1973, at p. 112.
[64] See *Le Figaro* and *Le Monde* on 11 August 1973. References in *Bulletin EC* 7/8-1973, at p. 112.
[65] See Articles 42 and 43 EEC (1958).

other Governments could choose to vote the French down. Importantly, that situation changed after the enlargement. As had been manifested in the debates of the House of Commons (see above 3.2.2.3), the idea that there was a right to veto in the Council had been crucial for the United Kingdom's acceptance of the terms of accession. With its accession, therefore, it had to be concluded that the 'streamlined veto' had become 'a fact of life.'[66]

Only in this light can it be appreciated how important it had been for the British Prime Minister, but also for the French President, to make sure that they both understood each other and that they could agree on the right way to proceed (cf. above 3.2.2.2): if they could only share the same dream, the question of voting would be of little practical significance. But with the block of the proposals for liberalization of the common agricultural policy, the British Government was brutally brought back to the reality. Although representing the Member State which had most to gain from the proposals being adopted, as the British Government had chosen to base its membership on the right to veto it was in principle forced to resist every attempt to use the vote.

According to the firm belief of Georges Pompidou (and Charles de Gaulle before him), it was not the provisions of the EEC Treaty but the concurrent wills of all Governments which would make the Community successful (cf. above 2.5.2 and 3.1.1). This indeed was also the essence of 'the spirit of The Hague'. When asked, therefore, if the attitude adopted by the French Government to the demand for liberalization of the common agricultural policy would not be detrimental for its relationship with the other Governments he refused to admit that the conflict of interest was beginning to reach unmanageable proportions:

Obviously when we get down to practical issues, to 'give and take' as they say and the problem of a price arises for a cereal or butter, or sugar, or carrots, well obviously and inevitably we do not think alike. It is also abundantly clear that our positions are not quite the same and that consequently we need to harmonise them from time to time, if not often. This is why I put great faith in personal contacts which can only proliferate advantageously.[67]

Whatever hopes there may have been that it would be possible to resolve the growing conflict of interest by 'personal contacts', this needed time, and time was something of which the Community was now running short.

---

[66] The Report of the Three Wise Men (see below Ch 3, n 145). Quote from *Bulletin EC* 11-1979, at p. 50.   [67] See Press conference on 27 September 1973, in *Bulletin EC* 7/8-1973, at p. 115.

During the months which followed 'the sugar dispute' (see above 3.2.3.1), the already serious financial situation was exacerbated by an oil crisis. But in spite of the awareness that this required 'common action coupled with a refusal to let ourselves be divided' the Community failed to react.[68] One of the most disappointing expressions of this could be found in the project for creation of economic and monetary union. Although able for some time to keep their exchange rates within the margins of the 'snake arrangement' (see above 3.2.1), most Governments refused to renounce the use of any major national policy instrument. The final blow came on 17 December 1973 when the Governments failed to reach the agreement needed for transition to the second stage.[69] In effect, this meant that the project for creation of an economic and monetary union had now been put on ice.[70]

It has been emphasized above that much of the difficulty encountered by the Community during the year after its first enlargement was due to the fact that solutions had to be found which were acceptable to all Governments—whether formally required or not—and that at least one Government was unwilling to make the type of concessions this required. But contrary to what may have been expected, this did not necessarily have much to do with the enlargement. The changes to the common agricultural policy which the British Government asked for had been on the agenda of other Governments for years and, it should not be forgotten, were also those proposed by the Commission (see above 3.2.3.1). For that reason it is likely that sooner or later the same difficulties would have presented themselves anyway. Nevertheless, with the enlargement the political balance shifted away from the French. While the British Government was praised for its 'clear desire to contribute to the common work', the French Government found itself more isolated than ever.[71] But this was only a passing state of affairs.

[68] See the address by Commission Vice-President Carlo Scarascia Mugnozza, above Ch 3, n 56, at p. XVI. For an example of the agreement that there was a need for common action, see the Declaration of the Heads of State or Government of the enlarged Community at the Summit Meeting in Paris on 19–20 October 1972, in *Bulletin EC* 10-1972, at pp. 15 and 24.

[69] See General Report 1973, above Ch 3, n 56, at p. 192. See also Commission Communication to the Council of 7 November 1973 on the transition to the second stage of economic and monetary union (OJ 1973 C 114/33). See also *Bulletin EC* 8-1972, at pp. 9–13; and Man, above Ch 3, n 14, at p. 194.

[70] See the Commission's Declaration of 31 January 1974 on the State of the Community, in *Bulletin EC* 1-1974, at p. 5.

[71] Speech by Commission President François-Xavier Ortoli on 5 May 1973, in *Bulletin EC* 5-1973, at p. 123.

3.2.3.3   *The demand for re-negotiation: a triggering factor for reform*

Somewhat ironically, it was the British people who would ensure that the French Government's political leadership of the Community was restored. Only one year after the British accession to the Community a general election was held in the United Kingdom, which resulted in the return of a Labour Government under Harold Wilson.[72] No question had been more important for the election than that of the accession to the Community. As forcefully argued by Harold Wilson in his campaign, 'a profound political mistake made by the Heath Government was to accept the terms of entry to the Common Market and to take us in without the consent of the British people.'[73] For that reason the promise was made that a future Labour Government would 'immediately seek a fundamental re-negotiation of the terms of entry.'[74] Obviously determined to stick to that commitment, once installed the new Government let no time pass before it made it clear to the Community that the time had come to put the errors right.

Addressing the Council on 1 April 1974, Foreign Secretary James Callaghan explained that his Government considered that the terms of accession which had been negotiated at the time of entry did not provide for 'a fair balance of advantages' and that it had decided, therefore, to 'stop further processes of integration' until they had been re-negotiated:

We shall negotiate in good faith and if we are successful in achieving the right terms we shall put them to our people for approval. But if we fail, we shall submit to the British people the reason why we find the terms unacceptable and consult them on the advisability of negotiating the withdrawal of the United Kingdom from the Community ... If renegotiations are successful, it is the policy of the Labour Party that, in view of the unique importance of the decision, the people should have the right to decide the issue through a General Election or a Consultative Referendum ... If renegotiations do not succeed, we shall not regard the Treaty obligations as binding upon us.[75]

When setting out the objectives of re-negotiation, Mr Callaghan explained that these were above all related to the common agricultural

---

[72]   The General Elections of 28 February 1974. See, in general, Lasok, D., Some Legal Aspects of Fundamental Renegotiations (1976) 1 *ELRev* 375, at p. 375.

[73]   Let Us Work Together—Labour's Way out of the Crisis, Labour Party Manifesto, February 1974, at pp. 5–7. Reference in Lasok, above Ch 3, n 72, at p. 376.

[74]   The Labour Party Manifesto, above Ch 3, n 72, at pp. 5–7.

[75]   See *Bulletin EC* 3-1974, point 1104. Cf. Lasok, above Ch 3, n 72, at p. 381.

policy and the project for creation of economic and monetary union. First, in respect of the common agricultural policy, the British Government demanded major changes 'so that it ceases to be a threat to world trade in food products, and so that low-cost producers outside Europe can continue to have access to the British food market.'[76] Stressing the fact that the cost of the common agricultural policy was accounting for 80% of the budget, Callaghan also explained that the British Government would refuse to participate in the system for financing of the Community's own resources in accordance with what had been agreed until it had been fundamentally reformed.[77] As clarified '[n]either the taxes that form the so-called own resources of the Community, nor the purpose, mainly agricultural support, on which the funds are mainly to be spent, are acceptable to us.'[78] Secondly, in respect of economic and monetary union, the British Government was concerned with the fact that the project had been initiated without any agreement on its final objective and felt that a great deal of discussion was required before any further decisions could be taken. It was also emphasized that the British Government would 'reject any kind of international agreement which would compel us to accept increased unemployment for the sake of maintaining a fixed parity, as is required by current proposals for an economic and monetary union.'[79]

[76] See *Bulletin EC* 3-1974, point 1104. As clarified by James Callaghan at the Council session of 4 June 1974, the cost of the common agricultural policy should be reduced in real terms, *inter alia* by discouraging costly surplus production and more trade with the rest of the world: 'the CAP must not become an instrument of excessive protectionism or a threat to world trade through the generation and disposal of surpluses.' One of the situations indicated as an illustration was that which had been intended to be dealt with in the Commission's proposal for changes in the organization of the common market for sugar. See *Bulletin EC* 6-1974, point 1102.

[77] See *Bulletin EC* 3-1974, point 1104.

[78] See *Bulletin EC* 3-1974, point 1104. As James Callaghan emphasized at the Council session of 4 June 1974, the British Government felt that the Community could not develop in the right way, unless there was progress in the direction of economic convergence between the Member States: 'we are not helped by the present Community budget arrangements, involving as they do an increasing and serious transfer of resources from the United Kingdom to other members of the Community ... It is wrong in principle and would defeat the objects of the Community if resource transfers under the budget should promote divergence rather than convergence.' According to the British Government's estimations, by 1980 the United Kingdom would provide 24% of the Community's own resources. See *Bulletin EC* 6-1974, point 1102.

[79] See *Bulletin EC* 3-1974, point 1104. According to James Callaghan, the British Government also believed 'that the monetary problems of the European countries can be resolved only in a world-wide framework.' Cf. also *Bulletin EC* 6-1974, point 1102.

It will be seen below that the new British Government's frankness about the fact that it was not going to play by the rules was a triggering factor for reform. But prior to that it should be pointed out that the demand for re-negotiations was accepted and eventually completed at the Summit Meeting of Heads of State or Government in Dublin on 10 to 12 March 1975.[80] The result was presented to the British people as a great success and when it was asked, therefore, to reply yes or no to the question 'Do you think that the United Kingdom should stay in the European Community (the Common Market)?' 67% voted yes.[81] Although it is doubtful if the result achieved really constituted a 're-negotiation' of the terms of accession, clearly the British Government had managed to force through a number of symbolically significant changes to existing rules.[82] One example of this can be found in the adoption of an 'improved' regulation on the common organization of the market in sugar (see above 3.2.3.1).[83] Another is seen in the adoption of a regulation supplementing the system for the Community's own resources with a corrective mechanism for a Member State faced with an unacceptable situation because of its 'unfair financial burden' (cf. above 3.2.2.2).[84]

The new British Government entered the Council with the same attitude as the French had left it in 1965: knowing what it did not want and resolved not to get it.[85] Still suffering from the French Government's refusal to make concessions, this was the last thing the Community needed. Whatever disagreements there had been—and, as has been seen, there had been many—since the Summit Meeting in The Hague the Community had lived with the belief that it should be possible to resolve them by 'personal contacts' between the Heads of State or Government (cf. above 3.2.3.2). In spite of all the disappointments, it would seem that

[80] See Irving, R. E. M., The United Kingdom Referendum, June 1975 (1976) 1 *ELRev* 3, at p. 4.

[81] This, the first referendum in the United Kingdom, took place on 5 June 1975. See Irving, above Ch 3, n 80, at p. 3; and Lasok above Ch 3, n 72, at p. 377. Cf. also Debates of the House of Commons on 23 January 1975 (Hansard), Session 1974–75 Volume 884 (HMSO 1975), at column 1745.

[82] See *Bulletin EC* 3-1975, point 1103; and, for an analysis of the result, Lasok, above Ch 3, n 72.

[83] See Council Regulation 3330/74/EEC of 19 December 1974 on the common organisation of the market in sugar (OJ 1974 L 359/1).

[84] Eventually manifested in the form of Council Regulation 1172/76/EEC of 17 May 1976 setting up a financial mechanism (OJ 1976 L 131/7). Cf. also Council Regulation 2743/80/EEC of 27 October 1980 amending Regulation (EEC) No 1172/76 setting up a financial mechanism (OJ 1980 L 284/1). See further Kapteyn and VerLoren van Themaat, above Ch 1, n 36, at p. 349.

[85] See, in general, on the attitude of the United Kingdom, Allott, P., Britain and Europe: a Political Analysis (1975) 13 *JCMS* 203.

this belief remained intact at the end of the first year after enlargement. But when the new British Government presented itself, even the most optimistic observer had to admit that there was now a fundamental conflict of interest between two members who were not willing to make sacrifices and what little was left of the spirit of The Hague, therefore, was about to turn into a balance of terror.

During the period that followed, an 'atmosphere developed in which, even on minor issues and in quite humble circles, states could obstruct agreement for reasons which they knew full well to be insufficient, but which were never brought into the open let alone seriously challenged by their colleagues.'[86] Contrary to what is sometimes believed, the problem was not so much that the 'streamlined veto' was often invoked in the course of voting but rather that the likeliness that it would gave rise to an assumption that there was no point in pressing a proposal if it was objected to by one of the Governments (cf. above 3.1.1).[87] According to the Commission Secretary-General, Émile Noël, this in turn led the Council to a systematic recourse to the 'formula of synchronisation' and, thus, to attempt to solve several groups of more or less disparate problems at one stroke (cf. above 2.3.1).[88] The risk implicit in this was that global agreement would be achieved only at the lowest possible level and '[t]here was no protection against this risk other than a collective political will which was often lacking.'[89]

3.3 The way towards institutional reform

3.3.1 Initial suggestions for improvements

3.3.1.1 Agreement on an emergency plan

The malaise which gripped the Community forced attention to be paid to the problems of how decisions were taken, or, all too often, not taken.[90]

---

[86] The Report of the Three Wise Men (see below Ch 3, n 145). Quote from *Bulletin EC* 11-1979, at p. 50. Cf. Eighth General Report on the Activities of the European Communities 1974 (Office for Official Publications 1975), at p. 9.

[87] Seemingly, the veto stemming from the Luxembourg Compromise was only invoked explicitly 13 times between 1973 and 1985. See Noël, above Ch 3, n 3, at pp. 4 and 11. Cf. Teasdale, above Ch 2, n 107, at p. 570.   [88] See Noël, above Ch 3, n 3, at p. 5.

[89] See Noël, above Ch 3, n 3, at p. 5.   [90] See Nicoll, Ch 3, n 3, at p. 37.

Significantly, the first important initiative in this direction was launched the very same day James Callaghan presented the Council with the British demand for re-negotiation. In a joint declaration by the Commission and the Luxembourg Presidency of the Council, an emergency plan was presented which would make it possible to 'guarantee the most important common interests' even if the concepts of the future development were not completely uniform.[91]

The central point of the emergency plan was found in a number of proposals relating to procedural aspects, all of which were based on the idea that situations should be avoided in which the veto could be invoked. Some aimed to leave more room for negotiations in the Committee of Permanent Representatives (Coreper). But, most importantly, the Governments were all called upon to 'make it their business' to enable decisions to be reached in the Council without formal voting, in particular when it was already clear that a majority had emerged, and to make extensive use of the possibility to confer powers on the Commission in accordance with Article 155 EEC (1958). In order to make the latter less difficult for the Governments to accept, they were reminded that 'co-operation between the Commission and the competent national authorities would be ensured by procedures which are based on those of the management or other existing committees in the Community.'

The emergency plan was first discussed by the Council on 4 June 1974. This led to an immediate decision to widen the mandate of the Coreper.[92] Then, only a few weeks later, a 'gentleman's agreement' was reached to accept both the proposal to abstain from formal voting and the proposal to make extensive use of the power to confer implementing powers on the Commission.[93] Following some months of reflection, that agreement was officially confirmed by the Heads of State or Government at the Summit Meeting in Paris on 9 and 10 December 1974. In the communiqué issued after the meeting, a statement was made that the time had come to 'renounce the practice which consists of making agreement on all questions conditional on the unanimous consent of the Member States' and that the Heads of State or Government had agreed 'on the advantage of making use of the provisions of the Treaty of Rome whereby the powers

---

[91] See Joint Declaration by the Presidents of the Council and the Commission of 1 April 1974, in *Bulletin EC* 3-1974, at pp. 9–11.   [92] See *Bulletin EC* 6-1974, at p. 122 (point 2504).

[93] See Speech by Willi Wischnewski to the European Parliament on 27 June 1974. Quote from *Bulletin EC* 6-1974, point 2506. See also point 2505.

of implementation and management arising out of Community rules may be conferred on the Commission.'[94]

In addition to the above, the Summit Meeting in Paris confirmed also the continuing significance of 'personal contacts' and emphasized that more should be done to take an overall approach to the internal and external problems facing the Community and its Member States (cf. above 3.2.3.2).[95] A concrete step in this direction was seen in the simultaneous decision to give the Summit Meetings—a practice which had taken place since 1969 (see above 2.5.2)—their own institutional identity as the so-called European Council. The idea was that this would 'enable Europe's leaders to consult as colleagues and friends, to exchange views, and agree on the broad lines of Europe's development, in an atmosphere of confidential and constructive discussion.'[96] Importantly, the Belgium Prime Minster, Leo Tindemans, was also invited to prepare a report on the possibility of converting the various fields of common interest into some form of European Union.[97] However unrealistic that project must have been judged, at the time, it was clear to everyone that most of the problems they were now busy tackling resulted from the fact that the Governments had never really been able to agree what they were trying to achieve. Therefore, whatever procedural tricks they could be hoped to perform, it was not likely that these would be helpful in the long run, if it was not possible to find a political agenda which could be shared by all.

[94] See the communiqué issued after the Summit Meeting in Paris on 9 and 10 December 1974, in *Bulletin EC* 12-1974, point 1104.

[95] See point 2 of the communiqué (above Ch 3, n 94): 'Recognising the need for an overall approach to the internal problems involved in achieving European unity and the external problems facing Europe, the Heads of Government consider it essential to ensure progress and overall consistency in the activities of the Communities and in the work on political co-operation.'

[96] Edward Heath at the inauguration of the Paul-Henri Spaak Foundation in Brussels on 3 December 1973. Quote from *Bulletin EC* 12-1973, at p. 23. See, in general, Lodge, J., The Role of EEC Summit Conferences (1973–74) 12 *JCMS* 337; Bulmer, S. and Wessel, W., *The European Council* (Macmillan 1987); and Werts, J., *The European Council* (North Holland 1992).

[97] See point 13 of the communiqué (above Ch 3, n 94): '[the Heads of Government] note that the time has come for the Nine to agree as soon as possible on an overall concept of European Union...'. Cf. point 16 of the Declaration of the Heads of State or Government at the Summit Meeting in Paris on 19–20 October 1972, according to which the Heads of State or Government 'assigned themselves the key objective of converting before the end of this decade and in absolute conformity with the signed Treaties, all the relationships between Member States into a European Union.' For that reason the Community Institutions were asked to prepare a report to be submitted to a further Summit Meeting before the end of 1975. See *Bulletin EC* 10-1972, at p. 23.

3.3.1.2   The Tindemans Report

In reply to the invitation of the Heads of State or Government, Leo Tindemans presented his report on a European Union to the European Council on 29 December 1975.[98] But contrary to what some may have hoped for, in the introduction to his report, Tindemans explained that he had declined to try to draw up some sort of Constitution or to describe what a European Union was about. This, he stressed, could only be done over time and required well-functioning institutions. Instead, the Report aimed to identify the measures which had to be taken to overcome the present crisis. Perhaps most important, in that respect, the overall conclusion was drawn that in the end progress could only be made as long as it was possible to arrive at a political consensus.[99] Therefore, like the Heads of State or Government before him (see above 3.3.1.1), Tindemans emphasized that an overall approach would have to be agreed which could provide a framework for relevant action and, then, that this should be accompanied by 'a number of practical measures which must be adopted simultaneously in the various directions entailed by the overall approach.'[100]

Once again the two key proposals for practical measures were those which had already won support: that the Council should let decision-making by qualified majority become normal practice and to make extensive use of the power to confer powers on the Commission in accordance with Article 155 EEC (1958). In respect of the latter, Mr Tindemans emphasized that:

The effectiveness of an institutional system does not just depend on the powers which are conferred on the institutions but also on the way in which they are exercised. In this field there is one principle which I feel is essential if we are to have European Union: that of the delegation of executive powers. Delegation must become the general rule if we wish to develop that degree of efficiency which is vital to the institutional system.[101]

In addition to the above, Leo Tindemans suggested that the hitherto unsuccessful efforts to agree an overall approach with respect to

---

[98] See Report by Leo Tindemans to the European Council on 29 December 1975 entitled European Union (*Bulletin EC* Supplement 1-1976).

[99] See the Tindemans Report, above Ch 3, n 98, at pp. 29–30.

[100] See the Tindemans Report, above Ch 3, n 98, at p. 33.

[101] See the Tindemans Report, above Ch 3, n 98, at pp. 31 and 33.

the project for the creation of economic and monetary union should be given a fresh impetus through the introduction of a formula for differentiation or, as it was officially coined some years later, closer co-operation. Essentially, this envisaged that those Member States which were able and, indeed, willing to make progress should be permitted to 'forge ahead' and that those which 'decided to wait' should be allowed to join in at a later date. The idea was as clever as it was simple. By cutting out those Member States which were standing in the way, it would become much less difficult to arrive at the political consensus needed for progress.[102] Over the years to come the formula for differentiation was to become the key to success with respect to the project for the creation of economic and monetary union. A first important sign of that could be seen on 5 December 1978 when an agreement was reached on the introduction of the so-called European Monetary System (EMS), based on fixed but adjustable exchange rates.[103] Apparently, this was possible thanks to the fact that the System only counted eight Member States as full members and that the one Member State which had always been most doubtful—the United Kingdom—decided to wait.[104]

3.3.2 *The responsiveness of the Court of Justice*

3.3.2.1 *A result-oriented approach*

It has been noted above that the two key proposals for procedural improvements that had been advanced by Leo Tindemans—that the Council should let decision-making by qualified majority become normal

---

[102] See the Tindemans Report, above Ch 3, n 98, at pp. 20–21. In principle a result would be achieved which was equal to an extension of qualified majority voting to matters for which the EEC Treaty often required unanimity. According to Tindemans, his formula for closer co-operation did not mean 'a *Europe à la carte*: each country will be bound by the agreement of all as to the final objective to be achieved in common; it is only the time-scales for achievement which vary.'

[103] See European Council Resolution of 5 December 1978 on the establishment of the European Monetary System (EMS) and related matters, in *Bulletin EC* 12-1978, point 1.1.11. See also Council Regulation 3181/78/EEC of 18 December 1978 relating to the European monetary system (OJ 1978 L 379/2); and Council Regulation 3180/78/EEC of 18 December 1978 changing the value of the unit of account used by the European Monetary Co-operation Fund (OJ 1978 L 379/1). See, in general, Jenkins, R., Thatcher: a Satisfactory Alternative to Delors? (1990) 4 *EurAff* 53.

[104] See *Bulletin EC* 12-1978, point 1.1.1 *et seq*.

practice and to make extensive use of the possibility to confer powers on the Commission—were also those which had won support at the Summit Meeting in Paris (see above 3.3.1). That was no coincidence. Clearly, the role of the Governments in resolving the crisis was as central as it was in causing it. Therefore, there was every reason for Tindemans to stick to the proposals to which the Governments had already committed themselves and to underline their importance. Irrespective of that, whatever tactical considerations may have guided Tindemans, during the period that followed his proposals were to be built on by others. Of particular importance in this respect was a series of reports in which the need for procedural and institutional improvements was addressed in the light of a second and third enlargement. But before these are examined, it should be noted that at a crucial point of the development, with the first indication of a willingness to push the Community out of its crisis, the Court of Justice—once again—proved that it was prepared to respond to the efforts which were being made on the political level.

When the proposal was first advanced by the Commission and the Luxembourg Presidency that the Council should make extensive use of the power to confer powers on the Commission (see above 3.3.1.1), the Governments were explicitly reminded of the fact that 'co-operation between the Commission and the competent national authorities would be ensured by procedures which are based on those of the management or other existing committees in the Community.' Even if they did not state the significance of such procedures as clearly, there can be little doubt that Leo Tindemans and, indeed, the Heads of State or Government had anything else in mind.

The usefulness of 'delegation of powers' as a tool for improvement of the decision-making process had already been well-explored during the transitional period. When first put into practice, in 1962, the underlying considerations had not only focused on the need to ensure productivity— to enable the Council to focus its efforts—but also on the need to ensure uniform application and to turn the initial rivalry with the national administration into a fruitful co-operation (see above 2.2.2 and 2.2.3). For that reason, the requirement that the Commission should follow procedures which provided for participation by committees was an inseparable or even genetic feature of the delegation as such: without that requirement the powers entrusted to the Commission had never been the same. This was forcefully confirmed in 1966 when the French Government presented its demand that 'delegation of powers must not imply that the tasks entrusted to the Commission will then be outside the purview of the Council' (see above 2.3.3.2). Apparently, the demand was accepted. During the following period new forms of committees spread themselves to most fields of activity. This, in turn, made it easier for the Council to entrust the Commission with increasing responsibility. At the end of the transitional period, delegation of powers had become a principle of a constitutional nature and all Community Institutions accepted the fact that this would not have been so if it had not been for the committees (see above 2.4.4 and 2.4.5).

The final approval of the new principle was given by the Court of Justice in Case 41/69 *Chemiefarma NV v Commission* and, shortly thereafter, Case 25/70 *Einfuhr- und Vorratsstelle für Getreide und Futtermittel v Köster, Berodt & Co.* (see above 2.4.5). Here the Court manifested a striking responsiveness to the development under way: to the need to provide the Commission with sufficient powers and the fact that there was little use for a principle of delegation of powers which could not accommodate the demand for participation by committees. A similar responsiveness was demonstrated in a number of cases heard during the period which followed the British demand for re-negotiation and the presentation of the 1974 emergency plan (see above 3.3.1.1).

An early example of this can be found in Case 23/75 *Rey Soda v Cassa Conguaglio Zucchero.*[105] Here the Court confirmed its older rulings and explained that '[w]hen Article 155 of the Treaty provides that "the Commission shall exercise the powers conferred on it by the Council for the implementation of the rules laid down by the latter", it follows from the context of the Treaty in which it must be placed and also from practical requirements that the concept of implementation must be given a wide interpretation.'[106] Like the situation dealt with in Case 25/70, in this case the practical requirements were also those of an efficient management of the common agricultural policy.[107] But the added value was that the Court was now ready to acknowledge that its wide interpretation of the concept of implementation, and thus the scope of the powers the Commission could be permitted to exercise, was inter-linked with the

---

[105] Case 23/75 *Rey Soda v Cassa Conguaglio Zucchero* [1975] ECR 1279. For a commentary, see Catalano, N., annotation (1976) 4 *GiustCiv* 6; See Bradley, above Ch 2, n 58, at p. 701; and Türk, above Ch 1, n 11, at p. 176.   [106] See paragraph 10 of the Judgment (above Ch 3, n 105).

[107] The case concerned the validity of Commission Regulation 834/74/EEC of 5 April 1974 establishing the measures necessary to avoid disturbances in the market for sugar caused by the increase in the prices in this sector for the year 1974–1975 (OJ 1974 L 99/15).

requirement that it had to co-operate with a management committee. In the words of the Court, that provided 'a mechanism which allows the Council to give the Commission an appreciably wide power of implementation whilst reserving where necessary its own right to intervene.'[108] The approach was clearly result-oriented.[109]

3.3.2.2   *The role of regulatory committees: a precondition for progress*

Even if the basic function of all committees was the same—to ensure participation of the national administration—the procedures which regulated their relationship with the Commission had several differences. None was more characteristic than that relating to the committees' power to prevent a measure from being adopted by the Commission. For both advisory and management committees this power was non-existent. Even if the Commission would not comply with their opinion, it was expected to take its decision. Only then, after a measure had been adopted, could the control-function of management committees enter into force, providing the Council with an opportunity to react. The legal significance of this construction had been underlined in Case 25/70 (see above 2.4.5.2). Here the Court explained its approval of management committees with reference to the finding that they were only competent 'to ensure permanent consultation in order to guide the Commission in the exercise of the powers conferred on it by the Council and to enable the latter to *substitute* its own action for that of the Commission' (emphasis added).

In accordance with the procedure for co-operation with regulatory committees, by contrast, the control-function entered into force before a measure had been adopted and the Commission could only take its decision if the opinion was positive. The question whether this procedural difference had any significant influence on the co-operation between the Commission and the committees will be returned to at a later stage (see below 4.3.1.1). What shall be emphasized here is that it was reason enough for some Governments to insist that the procedure for co-operation with regulatory committees should always be followed if there was a risk that matters to be dealt with could have political implications. This had been unambiguously demonstrated in the discussions which led to the establishment of the first regulatory committees in 1968 (see above 2.4.2 and 2.4.3) and repeatedly restated on later occasions.

---

[108]   See paragraph 13 of the Judgment (above Ch 3, n 105).
[109]   See, for a similar conclusion, Türk, above Ch 1, n 11, at p. 176.

Following the presentation of the emergency plan and the subsequent agreement on the advantage of making use of the power to confer powers on the Commission (see above 3.3.1.1), regulatory committees rapidly grew in importance. At the start of 1970 the number of regulatory committees was six. Ten years later the number was 41. Of these 26 had been put in place since 1975.[110] The increase was not very surprising. Even if the Governments had understood that it was necessary to make an effort to improve the preconditions for common action, the political basis was all but solid. Therefore, they were more sensitive than ever to the risk that a delegation of powers 'could create political difficulties or alter the impact of the policy itself in unforeseen ways.'[111] In such circumstances the control-function offered by regulatory committees—the power to prevent a measure from being adopted by the Commission—was a precondition without which some Governments would not have been willing to make any delegation at all.

To the same extent that the establishment of regulatory committees helped to satisfy the anxieties of some, it gave raise to new ones for others. This had been manifested by heated debates within the Council and, above all, in protests voiced by the European Parliament (see e.g. above 2.4.3.2 and 2.4.4). But like the Council also the European Parliament seemed to be torn between its concern with the institutional aspects of the development and the awareness that the alternative would be no development at all. Therefore, rather than seeking to block it by arguing that the establishment of regulatory committees was illegal, the European Parliament was asking for political guarantees that it should not be left behind. The reasoning had been outlined in the Jozeau-Marigné Report (see above 2.4.4). Here the Legal Committee of the European Parliament had reached the conclusion that the Council was not obliged to confer powers on the Commission and, therefore, that the imposition of the condition that a procedure should be followed which merely 'reserved' its right to decide 'at last resort' had to be seen as compatible with the EEC Treaty.

---

[110] Cf. the Jozeau-Marigné Report (above Ch 2, n 216) and the List of Committees published by the Commission in *Bulletin EC* Supplement 2-1980. During the same period the number of advisory committees had grown from 6 to 15 and the number of management committees had grown from 14 to 26. It may be noted also that at the start of 1970 there was one committee operating in accordance with an *ad hoc* procedure, the Committee on Protection against Dumping (see above 2.4.2): in 1980 the number had grown to 3.

[111] The Report of the Three Wise Men, below Ch 3, n 145. Quote from *Bulletin EC* 11-1979, at p. 47.

The significance of this conclusion with respect to the question of the legality of management committees was affirmed by the Court in Case 25/70 (see above 2.4.5.2). But unfortunately, that case fed new doubts with respect to regulatory committees, because of the apparent focus by the Court on the finding that the Commission was never obliged to follow the opinion of the committee and the control-function only permitted the Council to react—*a posteriori*—to a measure which had already been adopted. Whatever the Court had intended or, indeed, not intended, to say by that, the answer to the question of the legality of regulatory committees was far from obvious and there was a need for clarification.

The opportunity presented itself on 1 December 1976 when the Italian *Pretura di Lodi* submitted a reference for a preliminary ruling under Article 177 EEC (1958). But before the particularities involved and the subsequent ruling in Case 5/77 *Carlo Tedeschi v Denkavit Commerciale s.r.l* are explained, there are reasons to outline the context in which it had arisen.[112] This is particularly so since it offers an illustrative example of the problems that beset the Community and the important role of regulatory committees in attempts to resolve them.

Following the completion of customs union on 1 July 1968 and the abolition of duties between the Member States, ever increasing attention came to be focused on other forms of obstacles to the establishment and operation of the common market. In particular, efforts were directed towards the harmonization of national rules laying down the conditions which had to be met before products could be sold. An early expression of this could be found in the programme for action in the veterinary sector (see above 2.4.3.1). But the real opening shot came on 28 May 1969 when the Council launched its General Programme for the elimination of technical barriers to trade which result from disparities between the provisions laid down by law, regulation, or administrative action in Member States.[113] This linked a number of old proposals for directives with new ones—in respect of both industrial and agricultural products— and introduced a commitment on behalf of the Member States not to take any action which could put these proposals at risk.[114]

---

[112] See Case 5/77, below Ch 3, n 122.

[113] See General Programme of 28 May 1969 for the elimination of technical barriers to trade which result from disparities between the provisions laid down by law, regulation or administrative action in Member States (OJ 1969 C 76/1).

[114] See, respectively, Council Resolution of 28 May 1969 drawing up a programme for the elimination of technical barriers to trade in industrial products which result from disparities

In order to guarantee that this 'regime of temporary *status quo*' would not cause a situation in which it would not be possible to tackle unforeseen and urgent problems, the General Programme stressed the need for continuous co-operation with the national administrations. The requirements which had to be satisfied were that this should enable the Commission, with respect to directives which had not yet been adopted, to update its proposals and, with respect to directives which had been adopted, to adapt or adjust them. If need be the co-operation should also enable the Member States to take immediate action, unilaterally, against problems of a particularly important nature. All these considerations were joined together in the decision that the General Programme should embrace the 'solution in principle' that all, or at least most, of the directives should contain a specific provision requiring the Commission to follow a procedure for collaboration with regulatory committees similar to that which had already been established in the field of the common commercial policy (see above 2.4.2).[115] Importantly, this combined the committees' power to prevent a measure from being adopted with a *filet* or 'safety net' intended to ensure that some sort of action would always be taken: if, within a certain period, the Council could not reach agreement on an alternative measure, the Commission would be able to proceed as intended.

The General Programme for the elimination of technical barriers to trade enjoyed a strong support among the Governments and it was not long before a considerable number of directives were agreed upon in the Council. As early as 6 February 1970, a first set of directives had been adopted which aimed at the harmonization of technical requirements for motor-vehicles and on 13 July 1970 another set of directives was adopted with respect to additives in foodstuffs.[116] In all of these, co-operation

between the provisions laid down by Law, Regulation or Administrative Action in Member States (OJ 1969 C 76/1–5); and Council Resolution of 28 May 1969 drawing up a programme for the elimination of technical barriers to trade in foodstuffs which result from disparities between the provisions laid down by Law, Regulation or Administrative Action in Member States (OJ 1969 C 76/5–7).

[115] See Council Resolution of 28 May 1969 on the adaptation to technical progress of the Directives for the elimination of technical barriers to trade which result from disparities between the provisions laid down by Law, Regulation or Administrative Action in Member States (OJ 1969 C 76/8). It may be noted that it was explicitly provided that the committee procedure could be modified 18 months after the first of the directives had entered into force.

[116] See Council Directive 70/156/EEC of 6 February 1970 on the approximation of the laws of the Member States relating to the type-approval of motor vehicles and their trailers

between the Commission and the national administrations had been provided for by use of regulatory committees. The new committees introduced by the above directives were the Committee on the Adjustment to Technical Progress of the Directives on the Removal of Technical Barriers to Trade in the Motor Vehicle Sector and the Standing Committee on Foodstuffs.[117] These were soon followed by others. With respect to the ruling in Case 5/77, the Standing Committee on Feedingstuffs, set up on 20 July 1970, is of particular relevance.[118]

Like other committees envisaged in the General Programme for the elimination of technical barriers to trade, the Standing Committee on Feedingstuffs was also intended to provide a mechanism for co-operation with the national administrations which, in turn, would make it possible to entrust the Commission with rather far-reaching powers to adapt or adjust directives to relevant development (with respect to rules intended to ensure that the quality and composition of feedingstuffs was not such that it could endanger animal and human health). In the first of the envisaged directives, Council Directive 70/373/EEC, the usefulness of that construction was exploited to the full.[119] Here a formal obligation was introduced for the Member States to ensure that national controls of feedingstuffs were carried out in accordance with common methods of sampling and analysis. But significantly, nothing was said in Council Directive 70/373/EEC about the actual contents of those methods. Instead, this was left to be established in directives to be

(OJ 1970 L 42/1); Council Directive 70/157/EEC of 6 February 1970 on the approximation of the laws of the Member States relating to the permissible sound level and the exhaust system of motor vehicles (OJ 1970 42/16); Council Directive 70/357/EEC of 13 July 1970 on the approximation of the laws of the Member States concerning the antioxidants authorised for use in foodstuffs intended for human consumption (OJ 1970 L 157/31); Council Directive 70/358/EEC of 13 July 1970 making a fourth amendment to the Council Directive of 23 October 1962 on the approximation of the rules of the Member States concerning the colouring matters authorised for use in foodstuffs intended for human consumption (OJ 1970 L 157/36); and Council Directive 70/359/EEC of 13 July 1970 making a fifth amendment to the Council Directive of 5 November 1963 on the approximation of the laws of the Member States concerning the preservatives authorised for use in foodstuffs intended for human consumption (OJ 1970 L 157/38).

[117] It may be noted that the latter was given an independent legal basis in Council Decision 69/414/EEC of 13 November 1969 setting up a Standing Committee for Foodstuffs (OJ 1969 L 291/9).

[118] This was also given an independent legal basis, in Council Decision 70/372/EEC of 20 July 1970 setting up a Standing Committee for Feedingstuffs (OJ 1970 L 170/1).

[119] See Council Directive 70/373/EEC of 20 July 1970 on the introduction of Community methods of sampling and analysis for the official control of feedingstuffs (OJ 2002 L 170/2).

adopted by the Commission together with the Standing Committee on Feedingstuffs.

Before long it became clear that the solution opted for in Council Directive 70/373/EEC was not so easy for the Governments to agree on when later directives relating to feedingstuffs were discussed. Therefore, a number of more restrictive variants came to be experimented with. An early example was seen a few months later when Council Directive 70/524/EEC concerning additives in feedingstuffs was adopted.[120] In this Directive, the Council reserved all powers to take decisions for itself and requested the Commission to prepare the relevant proposals in 'close co-operation' with the Standing Committee on Feedingstuffs. A later example of solutions which were more restrictive than envisaged in the General Programme for the elimination of technical barriers to trade was found in Council Directive 74/63/EEC on the fixing of maximum per-mitted levels for undesirable substances in feedingstuffs.[121] In this the original idea was taken up again that the Commission should adjust the directive (the list of undesirable substances and their maximum permitted levels) but the procedure for co-operation with the Standing Committee on Feedingstuffs was formulated like that followed in the veterinary field (see above 2.4.3.2): a procedure which combined the general control-function of regulatory committees—the power to prevent a measure from being adopted by the Commission—with an additional one that enabled the Council to block the entry into force of the 'safety net' by a simple majority. This 'double safety net' was spelt out in the last sentence of Article 10(4):

The Commission shall adopt the measures and implement them forthwith where they are in accordance with the Opinion of the Committee. Where they are not in accordance with the Opinion of the Committee, or if no Opinion is delivered, the Commission shall without delay propose to the Council the measures to be adopted. The Council shall adopt the measures by a qualified majority.

If the Council has not adopted any measures within 15 days of the proposal being submitted to it, the Commission shall adopt the proposed measures and implement them forthwith, *except where the Council has voted by a simple majority against such measures* (emphasis added).

[120] See e.g. Council Directive 70/524/EEC of 23 November 1970 concerning additives in feedingstuffs (OJ 1970 L 270/1).
[121] See Council Directive 74/63/EEC of 17 December 1973 on the fixing of maximum permitted levels for undesirable substances and products in feedingstuffs (OJ 1974 L 38/31).

3.3.2.3   *The principle of delegation of powers redefined*

Returning now to the particularities involved in Case 5/77 *Carlo Tedeschi v Denkavit Commerciale s.r.l.* it should be noted, first, that on 27 July 1976, four months before the reference for a preliminary ruling was submitted to the Court of Justice, the Italian Government asked the Standing Committee on Feedingstuffs to place on the agenda for its next meeting the question whether there was not a need to adjust Council Directive 74/63/EEC, by extending the existing list of undesirable substances to include potassium nitrates.[122] Apparently, high levels of such nitrates had been found in feedingstuffs made from powdered milk and it was believed, not that this could endanger animal and human health, but that producers in some Member States, in particular the Netherlands, had fallen for the 'temptation' to add whey—the cost of which was ten times less than that of powdered milk—to their products and still sell them at the full price. Only a few weeks later a decision was taken by the Italian Government to introduce a limitation on the permitted level of potassium nitrates in animal feedingstuffs and to follow that up with border controls. This was reason enough to give the matter prompt attention: when the Standing Committee on Feedingstuffs met on 6 September 1976 the Commission put forward a proposal which should make it possible to include potassium nitrates in the list of undesirable substances, thus fixing the maximum permitted levels.

But for one reason or another, the proposal was not well-received by most members of the Standing Committee on Feedingstuffs. Therefore, rather than risk proceeding towards an unsuccessful vote, the Commission decided to withdraw its proposal from the agenda and to seek alternative solutions. Most notably, it accelerated the setting up of a consultative body composed of 'highly qualified scientists' who would not be instructed by the Governments, the so-called Scientific Committee for Animal Nutrition (cf. above 1.3.3).[123] This body was then assigned the task of examining whether there were objective reasons to include

---

[122] See Case 5/77 *Carlo Tedeschi v Denkavit Commerciale s.r.l.* [1977] ECR 1555 (Judgment of 9 March 1978). For an explanation of the facts, see in particular the Opinion of Advocate General Henri Mayras, at pp. 1582–1588.

[123] See Commission Decision 76/791/EEC of 24 September 1976 establishing a Scientific Committee for Animal Nutrition (OJ 1976 L 279/35). It may be noted, in that context, that only a few days after the first meeting of the Standing Committee on Feedingstuffs (on 16 September 1976), the Commission initiated a legal procedure under Article 169 EEC (1958) which was intended to convince and, if necessary, force the Italian Government to discontinue its

potassium nitrates in the list of undesirable substances. If this proved to be the case, the Commission and, indeed, the Italian Government would have new reasons to re-address the matter within the Standing Committee on Feedingstuffs.

However clever that move may have been, the Italian Government was not prepared to await the scientific solution to a problem which it felt was first and foremost political. Therefore, it chose not to disrupt its ban on potassium nitrates but to maintain it and invoke, formally, the right to apply safeguard measures. This right was an integral aspect of the 'regime of temporary *status quo*' introduced by the General Programme for the elimination of technical barriers to trade (see above 3.3.2.2) and had also been taken up in specific provisions of most directives. Council Directive 74/63/EEC was no exception. Here the possibility was envisaged for a Member State which considered that a substance not listed in the Directive presented a danger to animal or human health to 'provisionally . . . forbid the presence of that substance' subject to the requirement that it should 'advise the other Member States and the Commission without delay of the measures taken and at the same time give its reasons.'[124] The safeguard measures were to apply until a decision had been taken whether or not to adjust the directive.

In practice, having chosen to invoke the right to apply safeguard measures, the Italian Government forced the Commission to re-address the matter within the Standing Committee on Feedingstuffs. But before that had led to any concrete result, a truck-load of feedingstuffs ordered by Denkavit Commerciale s.r.l. from the Netherlands was stopped at the Italian border. The reason for this was that it contained a level of potassium nitrate which, although permitted by Council Directive 74/63/EEC, exceeded the limitation introduced by the Italian Government. As an immediate result, Denkavit was not able to fulfil its obligations to local buyers. It was after one of these buyers, Carlo Tedeschi, had initiated legal proceedings against Denkavit before the *Pretura di Lodi*, that the matter finally came before the Court of Justice. Of a number of questions posed, one is of particular significance for present purposes: the question whether the right to apply safeguard measures was not,

'infringement' of Council Directive 74/63/EEC (above Ch 3, n 121). See the Judgment at p. 1560 (above Ch 3, n 122).

[124] See Article 5 of Council Directive 74/63/EEC, above Ch 3, n 121.

in fact, illegal since those measures were only intended to be applied provisionally and, at the same time, the procedure which should put an end to them—the procedure for co-operation between the Commission and the Standing Committee on Feedingstuffs—could lead to a situation in which no decision was taken at all.[125] That was the situation in which the Council, after the Commission had failed to obtain a positive opinion from the Standing Committee on Feedingstuffs, would block the entry into force of the 'safety net'.[126]

In its relatively brief answer, the Court admitted that the procedure for co-operation between the Commission and the Standing Committee on Feedingstuffs made it possible to prevent the Commission 'from implementing the proposal rejected by the Council' even if the latter did not put forward an alternative solution.[127] But importantly, this was not considered to have 'the effect of paralysing the Commission or of enabling the national measure adopted provisionally to be prolonged indefinitely.'[128] The reason for that, the Court said, was that the Commission was still able to issue 'any other measure which it considers appropriate.'[129] Therefore, in the end the conclusion was reached that no factor had been disclosed which could affect the validity of the right to apply safeguard measures.[130]

Quite understandably, the ruling in Case 5/77 gave rise to much astonishment in the legal literature. What commentators found particularly difficult to understand is how the Court could say that the Commission was able to issue 'any other measure which it considers appropriate' when the contested procedure—like every procedure for co-operation with regulatory committees—was based on the requirement that it could only adopt the measure that a qualified majority of the committee considered appropriate.[131] The ambiguity was not lessened by the fact that the Court had based its previous approval of the procedure for co-operation with management committees on the finding that the

---

[125] See paragraph 51 of the Judgment (above Ch 3, n 122).

[126] Logically, this would have to be a situation in which the proposal presented by the Commission did not manage to win the support of at least a qualified majority of the votes in the Council (and it was not possible to secure the unanimity required to make amendments), and the dissatisfaction was so great that at least a simple majority of the votes could be raised against the proposal.   [127] See paragraph 54 of the Judgment (above Ch 3, n 122).

[128] See paragraph 56 of the Judgment (above Ch 3, n 122).

[129] See paragraph 55 of the Judgment (above Ch 3, n 122).

[130] See paragraph 57 of the Judgment (above Ch 3, n 122).

[131] See Bradley, above Ch 2, n 58, at p. 711.

Commission was never obliged to follow their opinion and that the control-function only enabled the Council to react—*a posteriori*—by replacing a measure which had already been adopted (see above 2.4.5.2 and 3.3.2.2).

However difficult to understand because of its legal reasoning—or, indeed, lack of legal reasoning—the message sent by the Court in Case 5/77 was crystal clear: the Commission was obliged to focus its efforts on bringing about reconciliation between the differing interests of the Member States. If the Commission remained faithful to that objective, it would always consider appropriate the measure a qualified majority of the committee considered appropriate. This shift from a clear-cut principle of delegation of 'powers' towards a 'duty' to seek a swift end to problematic situations was emphasized in the Opinion of Advocate General Henri Mayras. Mr Mayras rebuked the Commission for not having initiated or completed the procedure for co-operation with the Standing Committee on Feedingstuffs as quickly as possible and for having chosen to consult the Scientific Committee for Animal Nutrition (a body which he seemed to find a lot more objectionable than the Standing Committee on Feedingstuffs).[132]

Whatever sacrifices the Court had to make in its legal reasoning in order to arrive at the final conclusion—that the procedure for co-operation between the Commission and regulatory committees was valid—anything else would have been difficult to defend. When the Commission and the Luxembourg Presidency of the Council had first presented their emergency plan, the need was emphasized to 'guarantee the most important common interests' at a time when everyone—the Court included—was painfully aware of the fact that the political basis for action was all but solid (see above 3.3.1.1). One of these common interests was that manifested in the General Programme for the elimination of technical barriers to trade (see above 3.3.2.1). Since 1969 considerable success had been noted with respect to the implementation of the Programme and the Governments had repeatedly confirmed their commitment through the adoption of new directives.

---

[132] See paragraphs 4 and 5 of the Judgment (above Ch 3, n 122). Seemingly it was the choice to institute and consult the Scientific Committee for Animal Nutrition which was hinted at, when Advocate General Mayras explained that '[t]he European Parliament has, on several occasions, vigorously opposed allowing experts to limit the Commission's decision-making power. It has emphasized that the creation of such committees must not bring about any limitation on the latter's responsibilities.'

Importantly, the success had not been halted by the crisis which consumed so much of the Community's energy.[133] The reasons for this were manifold. But there can be little doubt that the 'solution in principle'—the procedure for co-operation between the Commission and regulatory committees—and, linked to that, the possibility for Member States to apply safeguard measures, was of fundamental importance. If there had been any risk that the Court was not aware of this when it set out to give its ruling, this was effectively erased in observations submitted by the British Government. These can only be described as an ultimatum, in which the Court was told, very clearly, that if it issued 'a judicial pronouncement casting doubt on the validity' of the procedure which enabled a Member State to apply safeguard measures, 'harmonisation legislation in future might prove impossible or at least very difficult.'[134]

---

[133] An example of the concrete results this led to could be seen on 27 July 1976 when the Council adopted 14 Directives on harmonization of national legislation on matters ranging from light-signalling devices on motor vehicles to cosmetic products. All but three of these were based explicitly on the idea that 'any amendments necessary' for adaptation to technical progress should be adopted by the Commission subject to a procedure for co-operation with regulatory committees (only the 'safety net'). See e.g. Council Directive 76/756/EEC of 27 July 1976 on the approximation of the laws of the Member States relating to the installation of lighting and light-signalling devices on motor vehicles and their trailers (OJ 1976 L 262/1); Council Directive 76/767/EEC of 27 July 1976 on the approximation of the laws of the Member States relating to common provisions for pressure vessels and methods for inspecting them (OJ 1976 L 262/153); Council Directive 76/768/EEC of 27 July 1976 on the approximation of the laws of the Member States relating to cosmetic products (OJ 1976 L 262/169); and Council Directive 76/769/EEC of 27 July 1976 on the approximation of the laws of the Member States relating to restrictions on the marketing and use of certain dangerous substances and preparations (OJ 1976 262/201). One example of an apparently less successful result could be seen on 15 July 1975 when the Council launched a programme for harmonization of national legislation relating to the environment. See Council Resolution of 15 July 1975 on the adaptation to technical progress of Directives or other Community rules on the protection and improvement of the environment (OJ 1975 C 168/5). This was based on the 'solution in principle' that use should be made of the opportunity to confer powers on the Commission in accordance with the regulatory committee procedure (IIIa). In spite of that most Directives subsequently adopted by the Council did not confer powers on the Commission. This was only remedied after the conclusion of the 1985 Intergovernmental Conference (or rather 1990–91). See e.g. Council Directive 75/442/EEC of 15 July 1975 on waste (OJ 1975 L 194/39) and the later Council Directive 91/156/EEC of 18 March 1991 amending Directive 75/442/EEC on waste (OJ 1991 L 78/32).

[134] See Case 5/77, above Ch 3, n 122, at p. 1565.

3.3.3 *The second and third enlargement*

3.3.3.1 *The Fresco Report*

The enlargement of the Community did not stop with the move from the Six into the Nine. During the remaining part of the period under discussion, first Greece applied to accede in 1975 and became the tenth Member State on 1 January 1981, and then in 1977 Spain and Portugal sought membership and after long and difficult negotiations acceded on 1 January 1986.[135] In preparation for this second and third enlargement, several studies were made of the implications they would have on the functioning of the Community. Against the background of the experiences which had been gained after the first enlargement, these studies all agreed that further enlargement would render existing problems even more serious if they had not been adequately dealt with before. For that reason new proposals for improvements were presented along the lines of those for which some support had already been manifested.

Noteworthy, first, is the Commission's so-called Fresco Report which was submitted on 20 April 1978.[136] In this the suggestion was made that the procedure for adjustment of the EEC Treaty to enlargement should be used 'to adopt the more far-reaching changes required in order to combat the tendency for decision-making procedures to become more cumbersome as a large number of States are involved.'[137] The central proposals were to extend the power to use qualified majority voting in the Council and to provide the Commission with a general competence for exercise of implementing powers.

In respect of the first proposal, the Report took as a starting point the observation that the 'approach' adopted at the Summit Meeting in Paris

---

[135] See Kapteyn and VerLoren van Themaat, above Ch 1, n 36, at p. 21.

[136] See the Commission's Communication to the Council of 20 April 1978 entitled the transitional period and the institutional implications of enlargement (*Bulletin EC* Supplement 2-1978).

[137] See the Fresco Report, above Ch 3, n 136, at pp. 12 and 13. From a legal point of view this meant that the procedure laid down in Article 237 EEC (1958) could be used instead of the procedure laid down in Article 236 EEC (1958). As argued in the Report, there were 'no legal reasons why the concept of adjustment should not be interpreted more broadly than in the past, as long as there is a definite causal link between the adjustments of the Treaties and the enlargement of the Community and as long as it is borne in mind that any change in the fundamental principles of the Treaties can be made only by the special procedure laid down for that purpose.' See the Report at p. 9. Cf. Article 205 EAEC (the position as regards adjustments to the ECSC Treaty was considered to be different and dealt with separately).

(see above 3.3.1.1), i.e. to renounce the practice of making agreement on all questions conditional on unanimous consent, had led to some improvements and that 'a political code of conduct' had emerged which was now accepted by all Governments.[138] But the result of that was not sufficient. Therefore, the suggestion was made that the fields in which this approach could be applied should be extended and that some of the provisions of the EEC Treaty requiring decisions to be taken by unanimity, in particular Article 100 EEC (1958)—the legal basis for harmonization of national legislation affecting the establishment or functioning of the common market—should be amended or, strictly speaking, adjusted so that after enlargement they would only require qualified majority.[139]

Then, in respect of the second proposal, the Report explained that, in spite of all declarations of intent, the Council was still not making adequate use of the opportunity to confer powers on the Commission.[140] In order to come to terms with this, the rather radical idea was presented for a remodelling of Article 155 EEC (1958) so that after enlargement the Commission would be permitted to exercise 'administrative' and 'executive' powers without prior authorization from the Council:

When the Community has a greater number of members it will be even more necessary to relieve the Council and its subsidiary bodies of preparatory work on technical implementation matters and to use decision-making procedures which guarantee flexibility and speed—which have been achieved, as abundant experience shows, whenever a decision has been left to the Commission with the assistance, more and more often, of management and legislative committees. The simplest approach would be to alter the fourth indent of Article 155 of the EEC Treaty (and the fourth indent of Article 124 of the Euratom Treaty) to provide that the Commission shall exercise administrative and executive powers unless the Council decides otherwise. This would introduce into the Community legal order a method of action whose value has been recognised in the many official statements in the past (the

---

[138] See the Fresco Report, above Ch 3, n 136, at p. 12. It may be observed that a certain tendency to make greater use of qualified majority voting had already been noted in 1975. Since then, the Commission has said, '[e]ver greater use is being made of the procedure in all matters which raise no important political questions such as might give a member state a valid reason for demanding a unanimous decision despite the legal possibility of a majority decision.'

[139] See the Fresco Report, above Ch 3, n 136, at pp. 12–15. It was underlined in the Report that it had no intention of reviving the 'old quarrel' about the right to invoke the veto.

[140] See the Fresco Report, above Ch 3, n 136, at p. 16.

most important being the communiqué put out by the Heads of State or Government at the 1974 Summit).[141]

Clearly hoping to make that idea less difficult for the Governments to digest, the Report stressed that it did not mean that they should be left without means to supervise the Commission but that the Council:

... would still have the power to reserve a decision for itself whenever it considered the matter under consideration to be politically sensitive. For implementing measures it could also make provision for committees of Member States' representatives according to the usual procedures, and the possibility of difficult decisions being referred back to the Council itself. The tried and tested arrangements now being used would continue to apply.[142]

3.3.3.2   *The Report of the Three Wise Men*

Only a few months after the Commission had presented the Fresco Report, the European Council instructed the so-called Committee of Three Wise Men to formulate proposals for the 'adjustments to the machinery and procedures of the institutions which are required for the proper operation of the Community' after enlargement.[143] The mandate was understood to mean that the Committee should find solutions which could be implemented swiftly and which did not require any treaty amendments.[144] This may be assumed to denote that at least some Governments were not pleased by the solutions which the Commission had advocated in the Fresco Report. The findings of the Three Wise Men were presented to the European Council on 29 and 30 November 1979 in a 109-page report.[145] As submitted, this provided—and still provides— one of the best analyses which has ever been made of the functioning of the Community, not least because its authors were well familiar with the

---

[141] See the Fresco Report, above Ch 3, n 136, at p. 16. Cf. point 8 of the communiqué issued after the Summit Meeting in Paris on 9 and 10 December 1974, above Ch 3, n 94.

[142] See the Fresco Report, above Ch 3, n 136, at p. 16.

[143] See The European Council meeting in Brussels on 4 and 5 December 1978, in *Bulletin EC* 11-1979, point 1.5.1. Cf. the 'terms of reference' in Annex 1 of the Report of the Three Wise Men, below Ch 3, n 145.

[144] See the foreword of the Report of the Three Wise Men, below Ch 3, n 145, at p. l.

[145] See The Report on European institutions of 8 November 1979 presented by the Committee of Three to the European Council (Office for Official Publications 1979). For a summary, see *Bulletin EC* 11-1979, point 1.5.1.

most important interests involved. They were the former Dutch Prime Minister, Barend Biseheuvel, the former Minister of State in the British (Labour) Government, Edmund Dell, and the former Vice-President of the Commission, Robert Marjolin.

Importantly, in the introduction to their report, the Three Wise Men emphasized that they did not believe a solution to the Community's problems could be found in the simple terms envisaged by their mandate since the deeper causes for previous failures, omissions, and inadequacies in Community performance were not mechanical or procedural:

More important were the political and economic strains that discouraged initiative and limited resources, and the lack of clear guidelines for advance such as existed at an earlier stage. If the general agreements on directions for progress have not been translated into specific action programmes, genuine new 'common policies', it is not because the fora for discussing them were absent. The reasons lie rather in political circumstances and attitudes that sometimes produced conflicting conceptions of the right way forward, and sometimes produced no clear conception at all.[146]

But admitting that the substantive problems could be aggravated by cumbersome machinery—and that this had all too often been the case— they expressed their hope that by correcting what was faulty it should at least be possible to tackle the 'extra handicaps' imposed by inefficiency and dispersion of effort within the machinery itself.[147] The aim which they had set themselves, therefore, was to formulate proposals which could ensure that the Institutions and their procedures, instead of aggravating the existing difficulties, create the best possible administrative conditions for overcoming them. A basic conclusion in this respect was that there was no need to change the balance of institutional powers. In their view, the real task instead was to get existing procedures

---

[146] See the Report of the Three Wise Men, above Ch 3, n 145, at pp. 1–2. As clarified further '[t]he first and foremost important factor is the profound transformation in the economic and political environment of Western Europe in the last ten years ... Even with a more favourable economic background, however, the Community of the 70's could not have escaped two further types of difficulty: those created by the nature of the subject-matter, and those created by membership. The subject-matter of Community activity has multiplied and become more complex since the early days—not least because of the successes of the period of construction ... The three new members of 1973 brought new ideas of their own and new themes they wanted to pursue.' See the Report, at pp. 10–11.

[147] See the Report of the Three Wise Men, above Ch 3, n 145, at pp. 2 and 13.

enforced, and to make the structures operate to the full extent of their capacity.[148] As they explained, therefore:

In choosing criteria of this sort, we have set aside the possibility of constructing an ideal, philosophically consistent 'model' of a Community constitution. Such a model may have been relevant in the past and may be sought again in the future, but it is not a recipe for helping the Community machine to work better here and now. The adjustments which we shall suggest for that purpose are purely practical and on the whole quite limited in scope. The problem is often not to find good new ideas, but to ensure that good old ones are put into practice.[149]

Once again the general idea behind the proposals this led to was that there was a need for clear priorities and that responsibilities and resources should be divided in such a way as to make it possible to carry them out with the maximum economy of effort.[150] In line with developments already under way, the proposals presented by the Three Wise Men were above all intended to increase the frequency of voting by qualified majority in the Council and to reduce the burden on the Council by delegation of responsibilities to the Commission (and also to lower levels in the Council's own organization, most notably the Coreper).[151]

With respect to the procedure for decision-making within the Council, it should be noted, first, that the Three Wise Men suggested that the effects of the commitment entered into at the Summit Meeting in Paris (see above 3.3.1.2) should be improved through the introduction of a working principle in accordance with which, 'in all cases where the Treaty does not impose unanimity, and very important interests are not involved for any State, voting should be the normal practice after an

---

[148] See the Report of the Three Wise Men, above Ch 3, n 145, at p. 34.

[149] See the Report of the Three Wise Men, above Ch 3, n 145, at p. 13.

[150] See the Report of the Three Wise Men, above Ch 3, n 145, at pp. 13 and 91.

[151] Against the background of Mr Tindemans' recommendation that smaller groups of Member States had 'a duty to forge ahead' and the signs which had been seen of such closer co-operation in respect of the project towards economic and monetary union (see above 3.3.1.2), it may be noted that the Three Wise Men found reasons to emphasize that this was a 'model of development' which must not be used more generally. Since that, in their view, would entail a threat to democracy and cohesion, thus creating new problems, they called upon the Commission instead to 'ring a warning bell if what should be a random pattern of differing national commitments ever starts to arrange itself into a two-tier split.' See the Report of the Three Wise Men, above Ch 3, n 145, at pp. 89–91.

appropriate but limited effort for consensus has been made.' This, it was explained, did not mean that an actual vote should always be taken but above all that the mere prospect of resort to vote should encourage the Governments to join in a compromise.[152] Although emphasizing that '[e]ach State must remain the judge of where its very important interests lie' it was suggested also that the manner of appeal to the veto stemming from the Luxembourg Compromise should be better defined.[153] Thus, for example, a Government 'which wants to avert a vote because of very important interests [should] say so clearly and explicitly, and take responsibility for the consequences in the name of its whole Government.'[154] One conclusion which should turn out to be of crucial significance was that the power to judge whether and when a vote should be called should become 'an instrument like any other in the arsenal of an efficient Presidency, to be used flexibly and as necessary in combination with others.'[155]

But whatever improvements it was hoped could be achieved by recourse to qualified majority voting, according to the Three Wise Men the most important step which could be taken to restore the Council's efficiency was to apply a greater selectivity in the choice of cases for action. The argument was that the Council was attempting to do far too much itself and it was necessary, therefore, to seek to distinguish between major and minor issues so as to make it possible to distribute the burden to others.[156] Whereas this indeed was something which had been said before (see above 3.3.1 and 3.3.3.1), it is noteworthy that the Three Wise Men found reasons to deal with the problem caused by disagreements over the conditions for 'delegation' of responsibilities to the Commission:

Delegation may involve the straightforward handing over of a task, or the establishment of a procedure whereby the Commission takes day-to-day decisions in consultation with representatives of Member States (i.e. 'management' and other similar committees). A great many delegations of both kinds have been and continue to be made, but serious difficulties have been encountered recently over the establishment of 'management'-type committees in newer policy fields. It is in the interest of both institutions involved to

---

[152] See the Report of the Three Wise Men, above Ch 3, n 145, at p. 51.

[153] See the Report of the Three Wise Men, above Ch 3, n 145, at p. 51.

[154] See the Report of the Three Wise Men, above Ch 3, n 145, at p. 51.

[155] See the Report of the Three Wise Men, above Ch 3, n 145, at pp. 51–52.

[156] See the Report of the Three Wise Men, above Ch 3, n 145, at pp. 46–47 and 73.

ɔvercome these difficulties if the Council is not to succumb totally to its ɔurdens and if reasonable spare capacity for progress is to be maintained.

However, the anxieties which have caused the problems in specific cases are not hard to understand. When the Community moves into a new area of action States find it difficult to anticipate all of the problems that may arise in execution; apparently small practical implementing decisions could create political difficulties or alter the impact of the policy itself in unforeseen ways. Hence the reluctance of some States to delegate any implementing powers to the Commission unless some kind of emergency procedure for dealing with cases of political difficulty can be agreed. And if anxieties of this kind are not satisfied, no delegation will take place at all.[157]

Significantly, in order to come to terms with the 'serious difficulties' over the establishment of committees and make sure that the possibility to 'delegate' implementing powers to the Commission could be used to enhance efficiency in the Council, the Three Wise Men suggested that a few 'stock formulae' should be worked out to cover each of the separate types of committee, which could then be selected for insertion without dispute in each individual case.[158]

In addition to the above proposals, intended in the first place to improve the work within Council, it should be noted that the Three Wise Men found reasons to focus also on the work within other Institutions. Of particular interest in this respect was the observation that over the years the balance of power between the Commission and the Council had shifted more and more in the latter's favour and that the Commission had now 'lost much of its independent prestige.'[159] Analysing the causes of the Commission's decline, the Three Wise Men concluded first that the same

---

[157] See the Report of the Three Wise Men, above Ch 3, n 145, at p. 47.

[158] See the Report of the Three Wise Men, above Ch 3, n 145, at p. 48.

[159] See the Report of the Three Wise Men, above Ch 3, n 145, at p. 64. It is noteworthy that a short time before the Report of the Three Wise Men was issued, the Report of the Independent Review Body, which concentrated on the Commission's role, was presented. As the terms of reference of the Independent Review Body and the Committee of Wise Men overlap in certain respects, there were several meetings between them. The Report of the Independent Review Body also emphasized that 'over the last ten years the Commission's influence, effectiveness and reputation have declined.' According to the Report, some of the most important reasons for this could be found in the fact that the Commission, after the first enlargement had been 'managed in a manner and with techniques which are inappropriate in present circumstances and can only be more so after further enlargement.' See Commission Communication to the Council on 24 September 1979 entitled Proposals for reform of the Commission of the European Communities and its services, in *Bulletin EC* 9-1979, point 1.3.1. *et seq.*

external factors as had hampered the development of the Community as such had also weakened the Commission. But it was emphasized that these external factors had been accompanied by others, in particular by a lack of coherence and increasing bureaucracy in the Commission's own internal operations.[160]

Against the background of these findings, the Three Wise Men stated very clearly that in their view the role of the Commission was central to the Community as such and that the tendency to reduce its role to that of a secretariat must at all costs be avoided.[161] In order to come to terms with at least some of the problems which beset the Commission, specific proposals were presented for organizational improvements intended to make the Commission more compact and strongly-led (for example to enhance collective deliberations and keep the number of Commissioners to a minimum).[162] Furthermore, it was emphasized that in their view the Commission itself had a responsibility to reassert its political freedom, in particular by framing its initiatives in a more independent manner.[163]

3.3.3.3   *The veto overruled*

When Greece acceded on 1 January 1981 no treaty amendments had been made other than those reflecting directly the increase in the number of Member States (as had also been the case with the first enlargement).[164]

---

[160] See the Report of the Three Wise Men, above Ch 3, n 145, at p. 66.

[161] See the Report of the Three Wise Men, above Ch 3, n 145, at pp. 64 and 71. As similarly noted in the Report of the Independent Review Body (above Ch 3, n 159), 'whatever view is held about the future development of the Community, it is in everyone's interest that the Commission should perform its many tasks efficiently and effectively.'

[162] See the Report of the Three Wise Men, above Ch 3, n 145, at pp. 67–73. Cf. the main recommendations in the Report of the Independent Review Body (above Ch 3, n 159, point 1.3.5): to keep the number of Commissioners to a strict minimum and divide among them portfolios of comparable weight; to reinforce the Presidency so as to allow it to exercise effective co-ordination of the Commission services and ensure a better distribution of staff; to reduce the number of administrative units and strengthen the position of the Directors-General.

[163] See the Report of the Three Wise Men, above Ch 3, n 145, at pp. 71–72. As explained '[i]mproved efficiency demands that each institution should have a clear and coherent policy "line" on the basis of which its dialogue with the other institutions can take place. The Commission's characteristic contribution to this dialogue is to make proposals which convey something more than an approximation of the separate interests of Member States. It should show what kind of actions would best reflect the larger interests of Europe as a whole.'

[164] See Act of 28 May 1979 concerning the conditions of accession of the Hellenic Republic and the adjustments to the Treaties (OJ 1979 L 291/1).

n spite of that a number of improvements were soon observed with respect to the Community's performance and there were new signs that the 'veto culture' had begun to erode.[165] Once again the triggering factor could be found in the uncompromising demands of a British Government. Following general elections on 3 May 1979 the Labour Government had been replaced by a new Conservative Government. Any hopes that this would ease the political situation within the Community were brutally crushed when the new Prime Minister, Margaret Thatcher, made it clear that she was firmly intent on getting her money back.'[166] The situation was brought to a head in 1982 when the British Government threatened to block a decision on increased agricultural spending until an agreement had been reached—once again—to cut its contribution to the system for own resources.[167]

On previous occasions these tactics had always guaranteed success. But this time the Dutch Presidency announced that the matter would have to be put to the vote (thus proving its readiness to comply with the 'working principle' advocated by the Three Wise Men, see above 3.3.3.2).[168] According to the Director-General of the Council's Secretariat General, William Nicoll, the British Government energetically opposed this and claimed that it had a right to invoke the veto since the budgetary consequences of a decision on agricultural spending were a very important national interest.[169] Even though the British Government was immediately supported by its closest allies—the Danish and the Greeks—the others found reasons to stress that it should only be possible to invoke the veto in a matter for which qualified majority voting was provided if the interest at stake was more directly related to the substance of the proposal under consideration.[170] Since in this case it was not, the Council went ahead and adopted the proposal (with the British, Danish, and Greek Governments refusing to take part in the vote).[171]

---

[165] The Thirteenth General Report on the Activities of the European Communities 1979 Office for Official Publications 1980), at p. 26. Cf. Teasdale, above Ch 2, n 107, at p. 571.

[166] See Wallace, H., Distributional Politics: Dividing up the Community Cake, in Wallace, H., Wallace, W., and Webb, C. (Eds.), *Policy Making in the European Community* (Wiley 1983), at pp. 100–105.

[167] See Nicoll, above Ch 3, n 3, at p. 40. See also Vasey, above Ch 2, n 140, at p. 726; Noël, above Ch 3, n 3, at p. 4; and Teasdale, above Ch 2, n 107, at p. 571.

[168] Cf. the Report of the Three Wise Men, above Ch 3, n 145, at pp. 51–52.

[169] See Nicoll, above Ch 3, n 3, at p. 40.   [170] See Vasey, above Ch 2, n 140, at p. 726.

[171] See e.g. Council Regulation 1452/82/EEC of 18 May 1982 fixing cereal prices for the 1982/83 marketing year (OJ 1982 L 164/6).

Following the decision to overrule the British Government, the French Government sought to downplay the general significance of the decision in question, claiming that the decision had no implications for the right to invoke the veto. Their argument was that the right to invoke the veto had never been intended to go so far as to make it possible to create a link with a separate issue—as attempted by the British Government—and that way jeopardize the functioning of a common policy.[172] But irrespective of any explanation, whatever reasoning the French Government gave to explain what they had just done, a precedent had been set the meaning of which was that the vital interest of one Government could now be overruled by the vital interest of other Governments. The significance of this precedent was such that the magic spell had been broken, i.e. for the first time the right to invoke the veto had been questioned and even rejected. Even if it was the French Government which originally insisted on the right to invoke the veto (i.e. the guarantee that nothing should be done against a Government's wish in a question of vital interest), it had now failed to protect that right or principle.[173]

The confusion resulting from the above decision to make use of qualified majority voting was confirmed in a solemn declaration signed at the European Council in Stuttgart on 19 June 1983.[174] In this all Governments made parallel statements on their interpretation of the veto stemming from the Luxembourg Compromise (see above 2.3.4).[175] First, the Governments of Belgium, Germany, Luxembourg, Italy, and the Netherlands explained that they felt that 'the Presidency must have recourse to the vote where the Treaties allow for this.' Then, the French and the Irish Governments declared that in their view 'the President will have recourse to the vote where the Treaties allow for this, while accepting that the vote will be postponed if one or several Member States so request, in the name of defending a vital national interest of direct relevance to the subject under discussion, which they will confirm in

---

[172] See Vasey, above Ch 2, n 140, at p. 726. Apparently, the French negotiators had standing instructions (as had the British) to support any Member State which invoked the veto stemming from the Luxembourg Compromise. But the French Government reversed this overnight, much to the surprise of its negotiators in Brussels.   [173] Cf. Nicoll, above Ch 3, n 3, at pp. 40–41.

[174] Solemn Declaration of the Heads of State or Government of 19 June 1984 on European Union, in *Bulletin EC* 6-1983, at p. 26. Cf. also the German and Italian Governments' so-called Genscher-Colombo Draft European Act, in *Bulletin EC* 11-1983, at p. 9.

[175] It may be noted also that the Governments confirmed their agreement that 'application of the decision-making procedures laid down in the Treaties is of vital importance in order to improve the European Community's capacity to act.'

writing.' The Greek Government stated that 'discussion must continue until a unanimous decision has been reached where vital and essential national interests are at stake and written notification has been given to this effect.' Finally, the British and the Danish Governments came up with a formulation similar to that originally adhered to by the French Government, insisting that 'when a member state considers that its very important interests are at stake, the discussion should continue until unanimous agreement is reached (cf. above 2.3.4).'[176]

3.3.3.4 *The Commission refines its ideas*

During the period which followed the decision to overrule the British Government, there were several events which took the Community closer to an institutional reform. Most important in that respect was the initiative taken by the European Parliament through the adoption of a Draft Treaty on European Union, which in turn helped others—notably the non-gaullist French President François Mitterand and his former Minister of Finance, Commission President Jacques Delors—to initiate an Intergovernmental Conference. But before this is examined, it should be noted briefly that the preparations for the next enlargement—the accession of Spain and Portugal—led the Commission to present two further reports, in which the need for improvements was addressed.[177] The first of these was submitted on 3 December 1982 and the second on 1 March 1983.[178]

The overall conclusion arrived at in both these reports was that the Community was still suffering from a deadlock in the decision-making process and that this would only become more serious after enlargement. In order to come to terms with that, proposals were presented for an adjustment of the EEC Treaty along the lines of the earlier Fresco Report (see above 3.3.3.1). The central proposals were to extend the possibility to use qualified majority voting in the Council into some of the fields currently requiring unanimity and to remodel Article 155 EEC (1958) so

---

[176] See Teasdale, above Ch 2, n 107, at p. 572.

[177] See Act of 12 June 1985 concerning the conditions of accession of the Kingdom of Spain and the Portuguese Republic and the adjustments to the Treaties (OJ 1985 L 302/9).

[178] The so-called Inventory Report and the Fresco II Report. See, respectively, Commission Communication to the European Council on 12 November 1982 entitled Problems of Enlargement—Taking Stock and Proposals (COM (82) 757 final); and Commission Communication to the Council on 1 March 1983 entitled Institutional Implications of Enlargement: More Flexibility in Decision Making (COM (83) 116 final). See also *Bulletin* EC 3-1983, point 2.4.6.

as to provide the Commission with a general competence for exercise of implementing powers. But this time the last of these proposals was refined to clarify that the Council should be permitted to determine what 'procedures' the Commission should follow in each specific case. Importantly, the suggestion had also been picked up from the Report of the Three Wise Men that these procedures should be fixed in an exhaustive list (to be placed in an annex to the EEC Treaty) from which the Council should be able to select without 'the delays necessarily involved in establishing such arrangements' (see above 3.3.3.2).[179]

3.3.4   An inter-institutional campaign for the re-launch of 'Europe'

3.3.4.1   The Draft Treaty on European Union

Parallel to the advance made in the Council with respect to qualified majority voting, increasingly more matters were left to be dealt with by the Commission in close co-operation with committees. A reflection of this could be found in the rapid establishment of new committees: in the period between 1980 and 1984 the number of comitology committees grew from 85 to 154 (cf. above 3.3.2.2).[180] Even if this was a sign of

---

[179] As proposed, the fourth indent of Article 155 EEC (1958) should be replaced by the following text: 'exercise implementing powers in respect of the rules laid down by the Council. Subject to the provisions of Article 205, the Council may provide in such rules that decisions are to be taken in accordance with one of the procedures given in Annex V to this Treaty and may also in specific cases reserve the right to exercise some of the powers directly.' In Annex V, four committee procedures, without variants, are listed (consultative committee, management committee, rules committee, and safeguard committee). See the Fresco II Report, above Ch 3, n 178, at pp. 7 and 11; and Annex II. Cf. *Bulletin EC* Supplement 8-1982, at p. 8. See also Ehlermann, C. D., Compétences d'exécution conférées à la Commission—la nouvelle décision-cadre du Conseil (1988) 316 *RMC* 232, at p. 233; Vos, E., Institutional Frameworks of Community Health and Safety Legislation: Committees, Agencies and Private Bodies (Hart Publishing 1999), at p. 91; and Nicoll, W., Qu'est-ce que la comitologie? (1987) 306 *RMC* 168.

[180] Cf. the List of Committees published by the Commission in *Bulletin EC* Supplement 2-1980 and the Final adoption of the General Budget of the European Communities for the financial year 1984 Annex I, at pp. 351–354 (OJ 1984 L 12/1). The List indicates an increasing reliance on the regulatory committee procedure, in particular with respect to the development of new fields of activity such as the environment (legal basis in Article 100 or 235 EEC (1958)). See e.g. Council Directive 82/501/EEC of 24 June 1982 on the major-accident hazards of certain industrial activities (OJ 1982 L 230/1); Council Directive 82/883/EEC of 3 December 1982 on procedures for the surveillance and monitoring of environments concerned by waste from the titanium dioxide industry (OJ 1982 L 378/1); and Council Directive 82/884/EEC of 3 December

success—that the Council had been willing and able to follow the advice to distinguish better between major and minor issues so as to make it possible to distribute the burden to others'—it was also evidence that the cure was becoming a cause.[181] Already in the Report of the Three Wise Men a warning finger had been pointed at the disputes surrounding the establishment of committees becoming a reason for the *lourdeur* or unwieldiness of the institutional machinery (see above 3.3.2.2). In addition to that, the fear was beginning to find its way back to the agenda of the European Parliament that the establishment of committees and, indeed, their role in the decision-making process was upsetting the balance of powers (cf. above 2.2.3 and 2.4.4).[182]

An early expression of this fear could be found in a resolution adopted on 17 April 1980. Here the European Parliament reiterated its long-held position that the Commission was 'the natural executive organ of the Community' and that the committees must only be given a purely advisory capacity.[183] During subsequent years, the conditions for exercise of implementing powers became a major preoccupation for the European Parliament and various tactics were attempted to eliminate what it saw as unacceptable forms of committees.[184] Perhaps most naturally, the European Parliament used its right to be consulted before new legislation was adopted by the Council to state its view that provisions requiring co-operation with committees should be deleted or at least amended to prescribe procedures which were less restrictive.[185] The result of those

1982 on a limit value for lead in the air (OJ 1982 L 378/15). Cf. also Council Resolution of 7 February 1983 on the continuation and implementation of a policy and action programme on the environment (OJ 1983 C 46/1); Council Resolution of 27 February 1984 on a programme of action on safety and health at work (OJ 1984 C 67/2); and Council Resolution of 7 May 1985 on a new approach to technical harmonisation and standards (OJ 1985 C 136/1).

[181] Cf. the Report of the Three Wise Men, above Ch 3, n 145 (above 3.3.2.2).

[182] It should be noted in this context that in 1979, for the first time, the representatives of the European Parliament were elected by direct universal suffrage. See Act of 20 September 1976 concerning the election of the representatives of the Assembly by direct universal suffrage (OJ 1976 L 278/5).

[183] See European Parliament Resolution of 17 April 1980 on the relations between the European Parliament and the Commission with a view to the forthcoming appointment of a new Commission (OJ 1980 C 117/53). [184] See Bradley, above Ch 2, n 216, at p. 232.

[185] See, for an example of the first, European Parliament Resolution of 10 July 1981 embodying the opinion of the European Parliament on the proposal from the Commission to the Council for a financial regulation on the application of the agreement concerning the implementation of pre-accession aid for Portugal (OJ 1981 C 234/100); and, for an example of the second, European Parliament Resolution of 20 November 1981 embodying the opinion of

efforts will be discussed at great length in the next chapter. Another of the tactics attempted by the European Parliament was to exploit its powers of budgetary control, freezing the funding for committees until specific demands had been satisfied.[186] This helped it to secure information about the work of committees and their organization.[187] Importantly, the use

the European Parliament on the modified proposal from the Commission to the Council for a regulation establishing a Community system for the conservation and management of fishery resources (OJ 1981 C 327/132). It may be noted also that the European Parliament tried to include parliamentary observers in the composition of a committee. See e.g. European Parliament Resolution of 17 May 1983 closing the procedure of consultation of the European Parliament on the proposal from the Commission to the Council for a regulation to implement a Council decision on the tasks of the European Social Fund (OJ 1983 C 161/51). See further Bradley, above Ch 2, n 216, at p. 232.

[186] It may be noted that the European Parliament's powers of budgetary control were increased by the ('Budgetary Powers') Treaty of 22 July 1975 amending certain financial provisions of the Treaty establishing the European Economic Community (OJ 1977 L 359/1) which entered into force on 1 June 1977. Cf. the Report of the Three Wise Men, above Ch 2, n 145, at pp. 74–76, according to which the main change in the relationship between Council and Parliament had come about with the development of the latter's budgetary powers: '. . . since the class of non-obligatory expenditure now constitutes over 20% of the Budget and covers most Community projects and policies apart from the CAP, this puts the Parliament in a strong position to impress its own concept of policy development upon the Council.' It may be noted, furthermore, that it was partly to anticipate and avoid budgetary conflicts that the 'conciliation' procedure was introduced by a joint declaration of the three Institutions in 1975. The conciliation procedure (later referred to as the 'concertation' procedure) provided for joint meetings between the Council and the European Parliament to discuss divergences of view on certain financially significant legislative measures before the latter were adopted. See further Kapteyn and VerLoren van Themaat, above Ch 1, n 36, at pp. 425–427.

[187] This could be seen for the first time on 16 September 1983 when the European Parliament decided to freeze a part of the Commission's funds until the Commission had been able to explain the reasons for a substantial increase in its expenditure for committees. Since the European Parliament was beginning to realize that there was 'no effective centralised system for monitoring the activities of those committees' the Commission was also asked to provide information about the efforts of rationalization it intended to take for the future. See European Parliament Resolution of 16 September 1983 on the cost to the EC budget and effectiveness of committees of a management, advisory and consultative nature (OJ 1983 C 277/195). In reply to this, a few months later a report was presented by the Commission which obviously succeeded in satisfying the European Parliament's most immediate demands and the funds were released. Noteworthy, in particular, was the Commission's explanation that it had decided to limit the reimbursement of travelling expenses for members of the committees to two representatives per Member State and that it would propose dissolving certain committees so as to keep their total number to a minimum. See European Parliament Resolution 10 April 1984 on the rationalisation of the operations of management, advisory and consultative committees, groups of experts and similar bodies financed from the EC budget (OJ 1984 C 127/56).

made by the European Parliament of its powers of budgetary control also became an efficient weapon in the inter-institutional battle which led to the adoption of the second so-called Comitology Decision on 28 June 1999 (see below 4.3.3.4, 4.3.3.5, 4.4.1.3, and 4.4.3.1).

Against the background of the fact that its power to assert a legal right to be involved in the process for adoption of legislation was very limited, the European Parliament came to invest a large part of its energy in the future and the perspective of a fundamental reform. In that respect nothing was to become more important than its adoption on 14 February 1984 of a Draft Treaty on European Union, which—although far too federalist to be realistic—came to give a major impetus to the discussion.[188]

In its Draft Treaty, the European Parliament presented the legal framework it believed was necessary for the common patrimony to be taken over by a European Union. Perhaps most significantly, provisions defining the substantive contents of old and new areas of activity were supplemented by provisions inspired by those found in national constitutions. These concerned 'citizenship' and 'fundamental rights' but also procedural and institutional aspects. A central idea was that new 'laws' should be introduced as the principal form of legislation. The laws, which were to be adopted jointly by the Council and the European Parliament, would 'restrict themselves to determining the fundamental principles governing common action' and explicitly entrust either the Commission (using regulations) or the national administration with the task of their implementation.[189]

It would appear that one of the results the European Parliament hoped to obtain from introducing laws was that it would be possible to get rid of the committees or, at least, ensure that these would only be given a purely advisory capacity. Considering the recent boom in the number of committees and the underlying demands (for co-operation and national control), this was so optimistic that it cannot, seriously, have been meant

[188] See European Parliament Resolution of 14 February 1984 on the Draft Treaty establishing the European Union (OJ 1984 C 77/53). See Noël, above Ch 3, n 3, at p. 4; and Zwaan, J. W. de, The Single European Act: Conclusion of a Unique Document (1986) 23 *CMLRev* 747, at p. 748; and, more generally, Corbett, R., *The European Parliament's Role in Closer EU Integration* (Macmillan Press 1998), at pp. 161–172; Weiler, J. H. H. and Modrall, J., Institutional Reform: Consensus or Majority? (1985) 10 *ELRev* 316; and Demaret, P., Ferri, M., Dewost, J. L., and Ehlermann, C.-D., L'avenir institutionnel des Communautés européennes (1984) 29 *AnnDL* 271.

[189] See Articles 34.1 and 36 of the Draft Treaty on European Union, above Ch 3, n 188.

as anything other than a starting point for further discussion. Some support for that submission can be found in a resolution adopted by the European Parliament on 21 May 1984, only a few months after its Draft Treaty on European Union.[190] In this resolution, the European Parliament attacked the use of regulatory committees when powers were transferred to the Commission to adapt directives to technical and scientific progress on the basis of the argument that this was a violation of 'the general principle common to the laws of the Member States that the delegator should not interfere with the exercise of delegated powers.' But at the same time an awareness shone through that the scope of the powers (which had to be) entrusted to the Commission was so wide that it could not be left without political supervision. Therefore, the insistence on the abolition of regulatory committees was supplemented by the more modest demand for a procedure which would provide the European Parliament with a *droit de regard* similar to that which had been requested already during the transitional period (see above 2.2.3 and 2.4.4).[191]

3.3.4.2   A promise for the future

During the first half of 1984, the Presidency of the Council was held by the French Government and the programme was centred on a claim

---

[190] See European Parliament Resolution of 21 May 1984 on committees for the adaptation of directives to technical and scientific progress (OJ 1984 C 172/6). Based on Report of 5 May 1984 drawn up on behalf of the Legal Affairs Committee on Committees for the Adaptation of Directives to Technical and Scientific Progress (rapporteur: Alan Tyrell) EP Doc 1-205/84. See Bradley, above Ch 2, n 216, at p. 232.

[191] Accordingly, the Commission should be obliged to transmit to the European Parliament every draft measure which it currently sent to regulatory committees, thus giving it the opportunity to express an opinion. The entire project would be subject to deadlines, of two months during which the European Parliament would indicate whether it wished to give an opinion and, if so, of a further three months for formulating the opinion. If and when an opinion was given, the Commission would be required to send it, together with its draft measure, to the Council in cases where it was obliged to refer the matter back to the Council because the committee had given a negative opinion or no opinion. It may be noted that the Commission was also requested to produce a report within a year on the follow-up to the Resolution and that the parliamentary committees were instructed to prepare for 'future action by Parliament to bring the procedure of other regulatory committees into line with that envisaged in the present resolution.' Not surprisingly, the Commission rejected the European Parliament's proposed procedure on the grounds that it would lead to unacceptable delays. See Bradley, above Ch 2, n 216, at p. 232; and Demmke *et al.*, above Ch 2, n 216, at p. 65.

that Europe did not occupy 'the place which could and should belong to it on the international scene.'[192] In contrast to its competitors—most notably the United States and Japan—the Community had not been able to benefit from a change in the financial climate but was still bogged down in internal disputes, the root of which could be found in a common agricultural policy that had become more costly than it could afford. At the one end of the political spectrum there was the British Government, fighting its own war to support the claim for a budget rebate and at the other the French Government itself, whose engagement for the common cause had to be bought on an annual basis at the price of increased spending.[193] In spite of its own heated interest in the matter, the French Government now set out to mediate a solution.

Without going into too much detail, it may be concluded briefly that the French Government managed to conduct the Presidency in such a way as to win broad support for a relatively modest reform of the common agricultural policy (from which it had much to benefit itself).[194] It is submitted that the explanation of the success of the French Government was not so much to be found in the exact terms of that reform as in an ability to focus everyone's attention, and indeed expectation, on a promise for the future: the promise by François Mitterrand to commit his country to the Draft Treaty on European Union (see above 3.3.4.1) and to ensure that 'the main Treaty that binds the European countries together and constitutes their fundamental law' would be consolidated through

---

[192] Statement on the Programme of the French Presidency by Claude Cheysson to the European Parliament on 18 January 1984, in *Bulletin EC* 1-1984, point 3.4.1. Cf. Debates of the European Parliament on 28 March 1984 (OJ 1984 Annex 1-312/157), at p. 124.

[193] See Moravcsik, A., Negotiating the Single European Act: National Interests and Conventional Statecraft in the European Community (1991) 45 *IO* 19, at p. 35.

[194] The reform was aimed at 'modernisation' or 'rationalisation' rather than 'liberalisation'. It may be noted also that the French Presidency managed to make sure that the reform, and the costs it entailed, could be approved by a qualified majority vote. See e.g. *Bulletin EC* 3-1984, points 1.1.1 to 1.1.3 and 1.2.1 to 1.2.7; Debates of the European Parliament on 28 March 1984, above Ch 3, n 192, at pp. 122–158; and Debates of the European Parliament on 24 May 1984 (OJ 1984 Annex 1-314/262) at p. 274. For example, see Council Regulation 1300/84/EEC of 7 May 1984 amending Regulation 1078/77 introducing a system of premiums for the non-marketing of milk and milk products and for the conversion of dairy herds (OJ 1984 L 125/3). It may be noted that the French Government also managed to raise and enforce the qualified majority needed for the adoption of the 'protectionist' Council Regulation 2641/84/EEC of 17 September 1984 on the strengthening of the common commercial policy with regard in particular to protection against illicit commercial practices (OJ 1984 L 252/1).

amendments.[195] In sharp contrast to the British Prime Minister, Margaret Thatcher, who was now only thought of for her obstinacy, the French President succeeded in feeding hope into the Community. Therefore, even if there was reasonable scepticism about his intentions, the promise was nevertheless received with open arms and François Mitterand became the primary spokesman for a re-launch of 'Europe'.[196]

Under the impetus of the French President's new-found enthusiasm, the debate on 'Europe' gathered speed and a first sign of progress came in the meeting of the European Council at Fontainebleau on 18 to 19 June 1984. Here a compromise was finally reached—thanks to an unexpected French willingness to make concessions—on the amount of compensation to be granted to the United Kingdom to reduce its contribution to the budget.[197] That, in turn, opened the way for a decision to stage 'a strong revival' of the Community through a reform intended to give it an economic impulse similar to that given by the programme for establishment of a common market in the 1960s.[198] The preparation of this reform was entrusted to an *ad hoc* committee composed of personal representatives of the Heads of State or Government under the chairmanship of the Irish Senator James Dooge. Even if the decision, in itself, was less ambitious than that envisaged by the European Parliament, it signalled a new kind of momentum: once the British Government had been given what they had always fought for, a sequence of events was

---

[195] See François Mitterand in Debates of the European Parliament on 24 May 1984, above Ch 3, n 194, at p. 262; and Claude Cheysson in Debates of the European Parliament on 28 March 1984, above Ch 3, n 192, at p. 132. An outstanding expression of this *volte face* can be found in the speech in which the French President convinced the European Parliament that 'France, ladies and gentlemen, is available for such an enterprise. I, on its behalf, state its willingness to examine and defend your project, the inspiration behind which it approves. I therefore suggest that preparatory consultations, perhaps leading to a conference of the Member States concerned, be started up.' See François Mitterand in Debates of the European Parliament on 24 May 1984, above Ch 3, n 194, at p. 263 (cf. also p. 258).

[196] See, in general, Moravcsik, above Ch 3, n 193, in particular at p. 31.

[197] See *Bulletin EC* 6-1984, points 1.1.1 to 1.1.7; and Moravcsik, above Ch 3, n 193, at pp. 35–37. According to Moravcsik the British Government was under an implicit threat to agree: Mitterand seemed to choreograph the Fontainbleau summit in a manner designed to remind Thatcher of the possibility of 'differentiation'.

[198] See *Bulletin EC* 6-1984, points 1.1.8 and 1.1.10. See also Gazzo, M. (Ed.), *Towards European Union; from 'Crocodile' to the European Council in Milan* (Agence Europe 1985), at pp. 96–97; Zwaan, above Ch 3, n 188, at p. 748; Noël, above Ch 3, n 3, at p. 4; and Teasdale, above Ch 2, n 107, at p. 573.

triggered which—in due time—would lead to the full transformation of the Community into a European Union (see below 4.3.2).[199]

3.3.4.3   *The programme for completion of an internal market*

The Report of the Dooge Committee was submitted to the European Council meeting in Brussels on 29 and 30 March 1985 (see above 3.3.4.2).[200] In compliance with the directions given one year earlier, the findings had been centred on the prime objective of introducing a programme for completion of 'the internal market'.[201] That would enable an intensification of efforts in the existing fields of activity where progress was still outstanding but also the inclusion—or codification—of new ones, such as monetary policy and protection of environment and consumers (cf. above 3.1.1).[202] Perhaps most importantly, the need was stressed by the Dooge Committee to base the new programme on 'efficient and democratic institutions' and, therefore, to undertake a number of procedural improvements.

The overall submission, in respect of such improvements, was to simplify decision-making in the Council and, at the same time, increase participation by the European Parliament.[203] In line with older suggestions, focus was set on the need to make greater use of qualified majority voting and 'delegation' of implementing powers to the Commission (see above 3.3.1 and 3.3.3). But unfortunately, the members of the Dooge Committee had not been able to agree if this required amendments to the EEC Treaty and, therefore, the calling of an Intergovernmental Conference. The difference of views was particularly evident with regard to the use of qualified majority voting. The proposal supported by most members was the introduction into the EEC Treaty of a 'general principle' that decisions must always be taken by qualified majority voting. In sharp contrast to that, some other members of the Dooge Committee— those representing the British Government and its allies, the Danish and

[199] See Young, H., *This Blessed Plot: Britain and Europe from Churchill to Blair* (Macmillan 1998), at pp. 239–340.
[200] See the Report of the Ad Hoc Committee on Institutional Affairs to the European Council of 19 March 1985, in *Bulletin EC* 3-1985, point 3.5.1 *et seq.*
[201] Parallel to the proposals with respect to the establishment of an internal market, the need was also pointed out for closer ties between the Member States in matters of foreign and security policy.   [202] See the Report of the Dooge Committee, above Ch 3, n 200, point 3.5.1.
[203] Through greater participation in legislation, greater budgetary powers and increased political control over the Commission.

Greek Governments—insisted that it would be sufficient to make better use of existing provisions on qualified majority voting and that a Government must always be permitted to invoke the veto if it considered that very important interests were at stake (cf. above 2.3.4 and 3.3.3.3).[204]

Against the background of this rather profound difference of views, the decision was taken by the European Council to postpone the discussion on what type of procedural improvements should be undertaken, and, instead, to call upon the Commission to present the proposals for legislation that were necessary in order to proceed towards the completion of the internal market.[205] This pragmatic 'method' was nothing new but something which the Community had already learnt to live with during the transitional period (see e.g. above 2.4.4). Importantly, it helped to maintain the momentum and to prevent progress from being blocked by an open clash over matters of principle. But it was also dangerous. This, indeed, had been demonstrated in the context of the premature attempt to create an economic and monetary union, when the inability of the Governments to agree on 'effective and properly supervised institutions' and the decision to let the project 'prove itself as it goes along' had been a major reason for its complete failure (see above 3.2.1).[206]

In spite of all similarities with the earlier decision on economic and monetary union, the present decision to proceed towards the completion of the internal market proved to have a happier ending. An explanation for this can be found in the arrival of a new Commission, which, for the first time in many years, was permitted to play a leading role, both in mediating between the Governments and in formulating and promoting its own political agenda. After the very anonymous Commission of Gaston Thorn, a former Prime Minister of Luxembourg, it was now the turn of a German. But apparently, the German Government felt that they did not have a suitable candidate for the job and, therefore, ceded their choice to France.[207] Following objections by the British Government against the appointment of Claude Cheysson, then Minister of Foreign Affairs (cf. above 3.2.3.1), the choice fell on the Minister of Finance, Jacques Delors, a man the British admired.[208] Jacques Delors had just

---

[204] See Moravcsik, above Ch 3, n 193, at p. 39.

[205] See *Bulletin EC* 3-1985, point 1.2.3. See also Moravcsik, above Ch 3, n 193, at p. 39.

[206] See Man, above Ch 3, n 14, at p. 198.   [207] See Young, above Ch 3, n 199, at pp. 326–327.

[208] See Decision 84/652/EEC/Euratom/ECSC of the representatives of the Governments of the Member States of the European Communities of 4 December 1984 appointing the President of the Commission of the European Communities (OJ 1984 L 341/87). For an examination of the

masterminded a successful reform of the French economy and was thought to be a firm believer in the blessings of a liberalized and de-regulated market: 'though talking left he acted right.'[209]

The significance, for subsequent events, of the political expectations placed on Jacques Delors cannot be underestimated. Of outstanding importance is the fact that this gave Margaret Thatcher reasons to believe that the new Commission would share her ideas of the right way forward and to permit herself—for a crucial moment—to be caught by the wind.[210] As a final token of a budding affinity, the British Prime Minister saw the appointment, by the other Governments, of her own Secretary of State for Trade, Lord Cockfield, to the Commission.[211] Only a few months later, Commissioner Cockfield presented his celebrated White Paper on completion of the internal market before the end of 1992, including 297 time-tabled proposals for the removal of so-called non-tariff barriers to trade: national rules setting differing standards on matters relating to the movement of goods, persons, services, and capital.[212] This was exactly what the British had always wanted.

political game, see Moravcsik, above Ch 3, n 193; Endo, K., *Presidency of the European Commission under Jacques Delors: the Politics of Shared Leadership* (Saint Martin's Press 2000); and Drake, H., Political Leadership and European Integration: The Case of Jacques Delors (1995) 18 *WEP* 140.

[209] See Young, above Ch 3, n 199, at p. 327.

[210] For a discussion of this complex matter, see Young, above Ch 3, n 199, at pp. 320–329.

[211] Apparently, Cockfield had been Thatcher's nominee for Commission President. Moravcsik above Ch 3, n 193, at p. 40. See, in general, Bruce, L., The EC's Lord Cockfield: Bullying Europe Towards Unity (1987) 42 *IntMan* 20. Cf. the maiden speech of the new Commission President, Jacques Delors, before the European Parliament on 14 January 1985 (in which he proclaimed his commitment to the goal of completing the programme for establishment of an internal market by the end of 1992). See *Bulletin EC* 1-1985, points 1.1.1 to 1.1.4.

[212] See the Commission's White Paper of 14 June 1985: Completing the Internal Market (COM (85) 310 final). See also *Bulletin EC* 1-1985, points 1.3.3 and 1.3.4; and *Bulletin EC* 6-1985, points 1.3.1 to 1.3.9. It should be stressed that the ambition to seek the removal of non-tariff barriers to trade was far from new but a core aspect of the Community's inherent obligations, laid down in the original EEC Treaty from 1958 and still valid. But during most of the time which had passed since the end of the transitional period the Governments had been more successful in introducing new barriers than getting rid of old ones. From a practical point of view, this meant that Lord Cockfield had to do little more than to re-compile existing proposals, left to languish in the drawers (cf. above 2.4.3.1, 3.2.1, and 3.3.2.2). But importantly, when the proposals came before Lord Cockfield, the underlying ambition was re-phrased so as to require, not the absolute harmonization of national laws, but only the reduction of existing differences to an acceptable level. Essentially, the White Paper on completion of the internal market envisaged that the harmonization of national laws should be restricted to the adoption of the 'essential requirements' with respect to safety and other public interests; and that the Commission, in co-operation with

3.3.4.4   *A controversial decision*

The White Paper on completion of the internal market was at the centre of the agenda of the European Council meeting in Milan on 28 and 29 June 1985. To the delight of Margaret Thatcher and, indeed, Jacques Delors, it was immediately given a strong support by her fellow Heads of State or Government.[213] For that reason focus came to be set on the question of what type of procedural improvements were needed for the project to be successful.[214] Only three months earlier, when the Dooge Report was first laid before it, the European Council had been forced to admit that there was a profound difference of views on the right answer and the decision had been taken, therefore, to postpone any further discussion (see above 3.3.4.3). Apparently the rather sudden return to the question at a moment when Margaret Thatcher—the person who was most hostile to the institutional reform others felt was indispensable—had *almost* got what she wanted was not a coincidence but a carefully planned tactic to create a 'synergy' and oblige her to commit herself to more than she had intended.[215]

At the beginning of the discussion it looked as if the solution favoured by Margaret Thatcher, to settle for some sort of 'gentlemen's agreement' on extended use of existing provisions (cf. the Dooge Report above

comitology committees, should be responsible for examination of the differing national standards. If a standard was approved, all Member States would have to accept goods conforming to it. Parallel to this, a long term harmonization of national standards should be sought to achieve on a voluntary basis, through the work of industrial standardization bodies. For a comment, see e.g. Weiler, J. H. H., The White Paper and the Application of Community Law; and Schmitt von Sydow, H., The Basic Strategies of the Commission's White Paper, both in Bieber, R., Dehousse, R., Pinder, J., and Weiler, J. H. H. (Eds.), *1992: One European Market—a Critical Analysis of the Commission's Internal Market Strategy* (Nomos 1988).

[213]   See *Bulletin EC* 6-1985, points 1.2.1 to 1.2.10 and point 1.3.9. See also Noël, above Ch 3, n 3, at p. 5; and Zwaan, above Ch 3, n 188, at p. 749. Cf. also Council Resolution of 7 May 1985, above Ch 3, n 180.

[214]   See *Bulletin EC* 6-1985, points 1.2.1 *et seq.* See also Noël, above Ch 3, n 3, at p. 5; and Zwaan, above Ch 3, n 188, at p. 749. Cf. also Council Resolution of 7 May 1985, above Ch 3, n 180.

[215]   See Noël, above Ch 3, n 3, at pp. 4–5. The British Prime Minister had never made any secret of her hostility to any type of procedural improvements which required amendments to the EEC Treaty and, therefore, the calling of an intergovernmental conference. Apparently, her fear was that the calling of an intergovernmental conference could 'open the way for uncontrollable constitutional ventures, themselves likely to be federalistic, certain to be legalistic and, in all, guaranteed to operate against the British interest.' See Young, above Ch 3, n 199, at pp. 330–331. See also Moravcsik, above Ch 3, n 193, at p. 41; Zwaan, above Ch 3, n 188, at p. 749; and Teasdale, above Ch 2, n 107, at p. 573.

3.3.4.2), was to be accepted by the others and she had even begun to think 'how easy it had been' to get her points across.[216] But for her adversaries this was only a prelude to the real game.[217] Under the hand of the Italian Presidency, held by the Prime Minister, Bettino Craxi, the discussion was increasingly focused on the need for a more far-reaching reform and, therefore, an Intergovernmental Conference. Then, without warning, Craxi sprang his little surprise: stressing that the decision to call for an Intergovernmental Conference only required the support of a simple majority, he pressed for a formal vote—which was carried.[218] Following that rather embarrassing defeat, Margaret Thatcher returned to London in a fury. But this did not lead her to make anything so unwise as a pledge to refuse to approve the result of the Intergovernmental Conference. On the contrary, she sent her officials off to negotiate a result that would expedite completion of the internal market. By this means Margaret Thatcher, instead of being the chief obstacle to the reform, became one of its chief architects.

3.4 The fortification of the committee system

3.4.1   The 1985 Intergovernmental Conference

3.4.1.1   An imaginative tactical approach

The Intergovernmental Conference which was to bring about the first important change to the EEC Treaty was opened in Luxembourg on 9 September 1985.[219] Like that which had paved the way for the first enlargement, this Conference was also preceded by the adoption of a new decision on the Community's own resources (cf. above 3.2.2.2).[220] But in

---

[216] See Thatcher, M., *The Downing Street Years* (HarperCollins 1993), at p. 549.

[217] See Noël, above Ch 3, n 3, at p. 6; Young, above Ch 3, n 199, at pp. 331–332; Moravcsik, above Ch 3, n 193, at p. 41; Zwaan, above Ch 3, n 188, at pp. 749–750; and Teasdale, above Ch 2, n 107, at p. 574.

[218] The procedure (this time) was that of Article 236 EEC (1958). But as emphasized when the vote was taken, it would only be possible to adopt the actual result of an intergovernmental conference if unanimously approved and then ratified by all national parliaments. See Noël, above Ch 3, n 3, at p. 6.   [219] See *Bulletin EC* 9-1985, points 1.1.1 *et seq.*

[220] See Council Decision 85/257/EEC of 7 May 1985 on the Communities' system of own resources (OJ 1985 L 128/15). According to the new Decision any Member State bearing an

sharp contrast to the earlier Conference, the Commission, this time, was not only permitted but expected to play an active role. The tone was set in an introductory speech where Jacques Delors told the representatives of the Governments that the time had now come 'to do some straight talking' and outlined the ideas which were to provide a basis for the negotiations.[221] No one present could be mistaken about his intention to place the question of institutional reform at the centre of the agenda:

In actual fact any searching appraisal of the decision-making process or, more accurately, the all-too-frequent non-decision-making process shows the cause of our predicament to be 'unanimity', the dead weight which is crushing the whole Community system. Its menacing presence, even when decisions may be taken by qualified-majority, is producing paralysis. We must cut the Gordian knot, break with the present practice of systematically seeking unanimity and shift to qualified-majority voting in clearly defined cases; this is what the Commission will be proposing in its draft amendments to the Treaty relating to the large single market, technology, economic and social cohesion, and currency.

Finally, we must dig ourselves out of the present impasse constituted by the huge 'grey area' between the Council and the Commission, which is blocking not only the Commission's proposals to the Council but also the measures required to implement Council decisions. There is a grey-area sociology, which must be analysed and modified, not by eliminating the Luxembourg pseudo compromise—and I bow to the views expressed by the Member States—but simply by deciding to switch to qualified-majority voting when the aim is to attain objectives agreed to in principle by all.

The extension of majority voting must be sustained, as you stipulated in Milan, by improving the decision-making machinery within the Council and also by extending the Commission's management powers so as to restore its capacity to act. Here again we should let simplicity be our guide in overcoming the problems of taking and implementing decisions.[222]

However clear Delors was about his intention to place the question of institutional reform at the centre of the agenda, he was also aware of the risk that the Conference would become bogged down if it was introduced

excessive budgetary burden in relation to its relative prosperity would be able to benefit at the appropriate time from a correction. See Kapteyn and VerLoren van Themaat, above Ch 1, n 36, at p. 349.

[221] See Commission Proposal to the IGC 1985, in *Bulletin EC* 9-1985, points 1.1.1 *et seq.*
[222] See Commission Proposal to the IGC 1985, above Ch 3, n 221, point 1.1.1.

as the first item.[223] Therefore, in full agreement with the organizers, the Luxembourg Presidency, the decision was taken to adopt an imaginative tactical approach similar to that which had proven so successful during the run-up (see above 3.3.4.3): to address the question of institutional reform, not as a matter of general relevance, but as an integrated aspect of concrete proposals designed to bring about progress in some of the fields of co-operation where the Governments had shown themselves most willing to agree.[224] The plan was that this would open up a 'dialogue' which would enable the Commission to explain its thinking and take any observations or objections into account before the real negotiations began.[225]

The proposals around which the negotiations came to concentrate could be split between a first set intended to facilitate the transformation of the Community into 'a pertinent and efficient economic entity' and a second aimed at establishing a general agreement on a single framework for economic and political co-operation (a move hoped, by some, to facilitate future progress towards a European Union).[226] Only the first set is of relevance for present purposes. Essentially, this contained the proposals for amendments to the EEC Treaty which would specify the objectives of the relevant fields of co-operation and, then, support their achievement by procedural improvements.[227]

It has been emphasized, above, that the 'minimising' of the institutional reform to a limited number of fields was intended to make it less difficult to agree on than a more revolutionary reform, such as that envisaged in the Draft Treaty on European Union (see above 3.3.4.1). But this did not affect the nature of the procedural improvements aimed for. From the introductory speech by Jacques Delors it could be seen that, in line with all previous suggestions—formalized for the first time in the 1974 emergency plan and most recently restated in the Dooge Report—the focus would be set on the need to extend the possibility to use qualified majority voting in the Council and to improve the preconditions for an efficient exercise of implementing or 'management' powers (see above 3.3.1.1 and 3.3.4.3).[228] In addition to

---

[223] See Zwaan, above Ch 3, n 188, at p. 752.

[224] See Commission Proposal to the IGC 1985, above Ch 3, n 221, point 1.1.2.

[225] See Noël, above Ch 3, n 3, at pp. 6–8.

[226] See Commission Proposal to the IGC 1985, above Ch 3, n 221, point 1.1.1.

[227] See Commission Proposal to the IGC 1985, above Ch 3, n 221, points 1.1.3 to 1.1.7.

[228] See Commission Proposal to the IGC 1985, above Ch 3, n 221, points 1.1.2 to 1.1.16 (see also points 1.1.8 and 1.1.9; and *Bulletin EC* 10-1985, point 1.1.5). For the proposals made by the Member States, see *Bulletin EC* 10-1985, point 1.1.2. See also Noël, above Ch 3, n 3, at pp. 7–8.

that a rather half-hearted attempt was made to enhance the powers of the European Parliament.[229]

3.4.1.2   *The Single European Act*

The Intergovernmental Conference was to be extremely intensive and relatively short. No more than three months after it had started, on 17 December 1985, the result was finalized in the form of the Single European Act.[230] From this document it was clear that the negotiations had remained close to the initial proposals. Structurally, the Single European Act was divided into two separate parts: one containing amendments to the EEC Treaty and another setting out the agreement on a single framework for economic and political co-operation which, five years later, would provide the basis for the negotiations that were to lead to the establishment of a European Union (see below 4.3.2.1). In what follows, the discussion will be restricted to the first part.

It has been seen above that in order to secure the necessary— unanimous—support for an institutional reform, the decision had been taken not to approach it as a matter of general relevance but as an integral aspect of proposals designed to bring about progress in some specific and, indeed, specified fields of co-operation. The fields finally agreed on were the internal market, providing for the establishment and functioning of an area in which the free movement of goods, persons, services, and capital was ensured, and, linked to this, environment, economic, and social

---

[229] According to Noël, the effective participation of the European Parliament in the amended legislative process was seen by a number of delegations and by the Commission as the indispensable complement to the move from unanimity to qualified majority voting in the Council. See Noël, above Ch 3, n 3, at p. 12. But in spite of that, the matter was only dealt with by Jacques Delors in the form of a final reminder. Accordingly: 'I should like to close with a reminder that we need to enhance the prerogatives of the European Parliament . . . if we make a gesture towards Parliament, we shall be justifying its existence and helping to give it greater clout . . . We can do so by giving it more responsibility and involving it in the Community decision-making process.' See Commission Proposal to the IGC 1985, above Ch 3, n 221, point 1.1.1. The proposals concerning the role of the European Parliament were intended not only to give it a stronger right to participation in the process for adoption of legislation in those areas where qualified majority voting would apply but also equal standing to the Council and the Commission in the procedure for judicial review (see above Ch 3, n 221, points 1.1.10 to 1.1.13).

[230] See Single European Act of 28 February 1986 (OJ 1987 L 169/1). The Single European Act was signed, first, at Luxembourg on 17 February 1986 and, then, at The Hague on 28 February 1986. See *Bulletin EC* 11-1985, point 1.1.1 and *Bulletin EC* 12-1985, points 1.1.3 and 1.1.4. See, in general, Ehlermann, C.-D., The Internal Market Following the Single European Act (1987) 24 *CMLRev* 361.

cohesion, and research and technological development. Importantly, these were all fields in which the Governments had already manifested their ability to make progress on the basis of existing provisions of the EEC Treaty.[231] Therefore, the fact that they had been included in the Single European Act was not so much evidence that the Community had been given formal clearance to get involved in previously forbidden matters as a sign that in these fields—and in these fields only—could sufficient support be found for an institutional reform.

Leaving, for the moment, those aspects of the institutional reform which related to the arrangement for exercise of implementing powers, it should be noted that all 'new' fields had been based on a decision-making procedure which provided the Council with an at least partial possibility to use qualified majority voting. This was a remarkable step forward which was to have far-reaching consequences. In that respect no amendment was more important than that inserted into the EEC Treaty as Article 100a. During subsequent years this was to become the principal legal basis for the adoption of harmonizing legislation aimed at 'the establishment and functioning of the internal market.'[232] Since the objectives of the internal market—centred on the free movement of goods, persons, services, and capital—overlapped those of the 'old' common market, this meant that several existing provisions requiring unanimity were to become more or less obsolete.[233]

---

[231] Likewise a formal reference was inserted to the European Monetary System, in operation since 1979 (see above 3.3.1.2).

[232] See Article 18 SEA, inserting a new Article 100a EEC (1987). See also Article 13 SEA, inserting a new Article 8a EEC (1987).

[233] See Moravcsik, above Ch 3, n 193, at p. 43; and Barents, R., The Internal Market Unlimited: Some Observations on the Legal Basis of Community Legislation (1993) 30 *CMLRev* 85. It may be noted that in addition to the above amendments, an explicit right was introduced for Governments outvoted in the Council or wishing to invoke a safeguard clause to retain national legislation for reasons of *exigences importantes* (cf. above 3.3.2.2). The best example could be found in the fourth paragraph of the new Article 100a EEC (1987). There can be no doubt that this was one part of the 'political price' which had to be paid (to Margaret Thatcher) to secure final approval of the institutional reform. Furthermore, it was evidence that the idea of closer co-operation or differentiation—used for the first time in 1979 to make an advance towards economic and monetary union—had now been accepted as a condition for progress in general (see above 3.3.1.2). The formula for closer co-operation, first presented by Leo Tindemans (see above 3.2.4), had since been taken up, developed and promoted first by François Mitterand as 'a Europe of different speeds or variable geometry' and then by Jacques Delors. As explained by Delors in his introductory speech to the Intergovernmental Conference: 'it would be negligent

Parallel to the extension of the power to use qualified majority voting, a limited effort was made to strengthen the role of the European Parliament in some of the 'new' fields through the introduction of the co-operation procedure.[234] This was a refined version of a procedure already applied, in practice, for the adoption of legislation with appreciable financial implications.[235] The important difference with the original consultation procedure was that it provided the European Parliament with an opportunity to have 'a second bite a the cherry' in a situation where the Council was unwilling to comply with its opinion (cf. above 2.1.1).[236] Essentially, the Council had to explain its objections to the opinion in a 'common position' which was then re-communicated to the European Parliament for a second reading. The basic idea was that this would open up for a dialogue. But if, in the end, no agreement was reached with the European Parliament, the Council still had the right to decide (by unanimous vote). Even if the introduction or, rather, codification of the co-operation procedure was a step forward, it was clearly a lot less than the MEPs believed they had reasons to hope for when François Mitterand swore allegiance to their cause (see above 3.3.4.2). But as will be seen in the next chapter, this was not the end of the story but only a beginning (see below 4.3).

3.4.2   A new arrangement for exercise of implementing powers

3.4.2.1   The proposal for amendment of Article 155 EEC

Before the amendments resulting from the Single European Act were introduced into the EEC Treaty, the legal basis for the exercise by the Commission of implementing powers was found in Article 155 EEC.

---

of us to overlook something of vital importance to certain States: differentiation . . . By this I mean that if, within the framework of a policy defined by the Twelve, four, five or six countries all wish to go further or faster than the others to attain a Community objective, the Treaty should not stop them from doing so.' See, in respect of Jacques Delors, *Bulletin EC* 9-1985, at p. 9 (point 1.1.1); and, in respect of François Mitterand, Debates of the European Parliament on 24 May 1984, above Ch 3, n 194. See also Ehlermann, C.-D., Differentiation, Flexibility, Closer Co-operation: The New Provisions of the Amsterdam Treaty (1998) 4 *ELJ* 246.

[234] See, in particular, Article 7 SEA, inserting a new Article 149 EEC (1987).

[235] See the so-called conciliation procedure, above Ch 3, n 186.

[236] See Kapteyn and VerLoren van Themaat, above Ch 1, n 36, at pp. 427–430.

Here an oblique reference was made to the Commission's *duty* to 'exercise the powers conferred on it by the Council for the implementation of the rules laid down by the latter.'[237] In accordance with the established interpretation, this did not entail any corresponding *right* for the Commission to exercise implementing powers (see above 2.4.5 and 3.3.2). The logical consequence of this arrangement was that the Council was not only free to keep the exercise of implementing powers to itself but also, if these powers were conferred on the Commission, to determine 'detailed rules' or conditions, such as those requiring it to collaborate with advisory, management, or regulatory committees (in accordance with the formula *qui peut le plus, peut le moins*).[238]

However reasonable this arrangement may have seemed, in principle, the Commission was far from content. The immediate reasons for its dissatisfaction had been set out in the reports relating to the second and third enlargement (see above 3.3.3.1 and 3.3.3.4) and, then, refined in the proposals to the Intergovernmental Conference. First, it was claimed, the Council had 'become increasingly reluctant to give the Commission the powers it needs' and was all too often trying to deal with matters of an implementing nature itself. Because of this, the proper functioning of the Council was rendered unnecessarily difficult.[239] Then, with respect to the 'conditions' placed upon it, the Commission said that a 'grey area' of committees had emerged which was impairing both efficiency and clear determination of responsibilities.[240] This concern with a 'grey area' had been stressed by its President, Jacques Delors, in his introductory speech to the Intergovernmental Conference (see above 3.4.1.1) and was

---

[237] See Bradley, above Ch 2, n 58, at p. 699.

[238] See Case 25/70, above Ch 2, n 244, at paragraph 9; and Bradley, Ch 2, n 58, at p. 713.

[239] See Commission Proposal to the IGC 1985, above Ch 3, n 221, point 1.1.16; and oral evidence given by Claus-Dieter Ehlermann to the House of Lords, in House of Lords Select Committee on the European Communities, Delegation of Powers to the Commission (final report), Session 1986–87, 3rd Report (16 December 1986), at pp. 18–19 (paragraph 81). Cf. *Bulletin EC* 6-1987, point 2.4.12 (the Commission's implementing powers).

[240] See Commission Proposal to the IGC 1985, above Ch 3, n 221, point 1.1.16. According to the Commission, '[a] whole grey area of committees has emerged within which endless procedural wrangles have counted for more than the solution of basic problems. This has led to considerable loss of time and energy and has seriously undermined effective management and the clear demarcation of the responsibilities of each institution.' See *Bulletin EC* 6-1987, point 2.4.12 (the Commission's implementing powers).

later explained in great detail by the Director-General of the Commission Legal Service, Claus-Dieter Ehlermann:

... over the years we have seen that relatively well-established procedures have been amended more or less slightly, and if you asked me how many different procedures there are I would not be able to give you a clear answer. There are perhaps 10, 20 or 30. It is incredible to see the number of different types of techniques which have evolved over the years. What is so objectionable from the point of view of efficient decision-making is that people systematically re-open the question of what procedure to use and fiddle around with existing techniques in order to limit a little bit more here or there the powers of the Commission, or exercise the right of appeal to the Council. These constant attempts to re-discuss committee procedures are a waste of energy and a waste of resources.[241]

Against the background of the dissatisfaction with the operation of the arrangement for exercise of implementing powers, in its proposals to the Intergovernmental Conference the Commission presented a project based on the suggestion that it should be 'unfettered' from existing constraints.[242] The project, which was directly inspired by ideas elaborated in its previous reports on enlargement, envisaged that an amendment should be made to Article 155 EEC, clarifying that the Commission would be permitted to exercise implementing or 'management' powers without prior authorization from the Council (and that the Council should only be permitted to reserve the right to exercise such powers for itself in 'specific cases'). Parallel to this, the power to determine 'conditions' should be rationalized through the introduction of a limited number of fixed committee procedures (to be placed, not in an annex to the EEC Treaty, as previously suggested, but in normal legislation[243]).

In addition to the above project, the effects of which would not be limited to any specific field of co-operation, a proposal was advanced for the inclusion into the EEC Treaty of a provision which would give the Commission 'special' powers to adopt implementing measures relating

[241] See oral evidence given by Claus-Dieter Ehlermann, above Ch 3, n 239, at p. 18 (paragraph 75).

[242] See Commission Proposal to the IGC 1985, above Ch 3, n 221, point 1.1.16. See also *Bulletin EC* 10-1985, point 1.1.5; and the Nineteenth General Report on the Activities of the European Communities 1985 (Office for Official Publications 1986), at p. 32.

[243] See oral evidence given by Claus-Dieter Ehlermann, above Ch 3, n 239, at p. 27 (paragraph 135); and Ehlermann above Ch 3, n 179, at p. 233.

to the establishment and functioning of the internal market.[244] This would also stipulate that the Commission was to be permitted to exercise implementing powers without prior authorization from the Council (and that the Council should only be permitted to reserve the right to exercise such powers for itself in 'specific cases'). But, importantly, it would restrict the opportunity for the Council to determine 'conditions' to the most liberal type of committee procedure: that of the advisory committee (see below 4.2.2.2).

3.4.2.2 *Article 145 EEC: a more cautious construction*

In the years which had passed since the agreement on an emergency plan in 1974 (see above 3.3.1.1), it had become increasingly clear that there was a general awareness of the advantage of making better use of the opportunity to confer implementing powers on the Commission (see e.g. above 3.3.4.3). But this did not mean that much support could be found for the suggestion that it should be freed from existing constraints. During the transitional period, the Governments had manifested their conviction that the 'delegation of powers must not imply that the tasks entrusted to the Commission will then be outside the purview of the Council' (see e.g. above 2.3.3.2 and 2.3.5.4).[245] Since then, that conviction had grown stronger rather than weaker. This, indeed, was the most obvious conclusion which could be drawn from the fact that so much time was spent on disputes over the right 'conditions' (see above 3.3.3.2) and the rather drastic increase in the number of regulatory committees (see above 3.3.2.2).

Unsurprisingly, therefore, when the arrangement for exercise of implementing powers was discussed by the Intergovernmental Conference, the conclusion was soon reached that in order for it to be possible to agree on any improvements, a more 'cautious' construction had to be opted for than that envisaged in the proposals.[246] This meant, first of all,

---

[244] Accordingly, '[t]he Commission, after receiving the opinions of a consultative committee composed of representatives of the Member States, shall lay down provisions for the implementation of the measures adopted by the Council pursuant to [the co-operation procedure]. The Council, acting unanimously, may however reserve the right in specific cases to lay down certain of those implementing provisions.' See Commission working papers of 16 September and 5 October 1985, in Ehlermann, above Ch 3, n 230, at p. 403 and annex. Cf. oral evidence given by Claus-Dieter Ehlermann, above Ch 3, n 239, at p. 19 (paragraph 83).

[245] See the French Government's Memorandum, above Ch 2, n 122, at pp. 6–7.

[246] See Ehlermann, above Ch 3, n 179, at pp. 233–234. Cf. Noël, above Ch 3, n 3, at p. 8.

that the Commission's apparently rather stubborn insistence on the inclusion of a provision which would give it 'special' powers to adopt implementing measures in the field of the internal market was dropped.[247] Instead a non-binding declaration was adopted in which the Council was requested 'to give the advisory committee procedure in particular a predominant place in the interests of speed and efficiency in the decision-making process, for the exercise of the powers of implementation conferred on the Commission within the field of Article 100a of the EEC Treaty.'[248] Then, with regard to the project intended to grant the Commission a general competence for exercise of implementing powers, this was only accepted in a modified version, manifested in an amendment, not to Article 155 EEC, but to Article 145 EEC. Accordingly:

To ensure that the objectives set out in this Treaty are attained the Council shall,...confer on the Commission, in the acts which the Council adopts, powers for the implementation of the rules which the Council lays down. The Council may impose certain requirements in respect of the exercise of these powers. The Council may also reserve the right, in specific cases, to exercise directly implementing powers itself. The procedures referred to above must be consonant with principles and rules to be laid down in advance by the Council, acting unanimously on a proposal from the Commission and after obtaining the opinion of the European Parliament.[249]

For anyone familiar with the structure of the EEC Treaty, the move from Article 155 EEC (situated in the 'Commission' section) to Article 145 EEC (situated in the 'Council' section) suggests that there was a wish to clarify that, as a matter of principle, the powers enshrined in that provision should be seen as falling within the Council's sphere of

[247] See Ehlermann, above Ch 3, n 230, at p. 403.

[248] Declaration No 1 attached to the Single European Act of 28 February 1986 on the powers of implementation of the Commission (OJ 1987 L 169/24). The full text of the Declaration read as follows: 'The Conference asks the Community authorities to adopt, before the act enters into force, the principles and rules on the basis of which the Commission's powers of implementation will be defined in each case. In this connection the Conference requests the Council to give the advisory committee procedure in particular a predominant place in the interests of speed and efficiency in the decision-making process, for the exercise of the powers of implementation conferred on the Commission within the field of Article 100a of the EEC Treaty.'

[249] See Article 10 SEA, inserting a third indent into Article 145 EEC (1987).

competence and not within the Commission's sphere of competence.[250] Notwithstanding this, the amendment was an important step forward. An often overlooked feature in that respect was that it brought about a codification of existing practices, in particular that of requiring the Commission to comply with 'conditions' (cf. 'certain requirements') and that this, in turn, efficiently erased some reasons for doubts and disputes. But most importantly, two new rules were introduced which, although inserted at a different place in the EEC Treaty, came close to those proposed by the Commission.[251]

According to the first of these rules, the Council was not only enabled but *obliged* to confer 'powers for the implementation' of the legislation it adopted on the Commission (and only the Commission).[252] No reservation had been made in respect of any field of co-operation and, importantly, the meaning of the notion of implementation had been left undefined. The only restriction to the rule was found in an explanation that the Council was permitted to 'reserve the right, in specific cases, to exercise directly implementing powers itself.' Then, according to the second rule, the Council was only permitted to require the Commission to comply with conditions or 'requirements' that were 'consonant with principles and rules' which had been laid down beforehand. The objective this sought to achieve was the rationalization of the use made of advisory,

---

[250] See Ehlermann, above Ch 3, n 179, at p. 233. Cf. also the discussions leading to the Luxembourg Compromise, above 2.3.4.

[251] See *Bulletin EC* 6-1987, point 2.4.13 (the Commission's implementing powers); and Ehlermann, above Ch 3, n 179, at p. 233.

[252] Although a few commentators have gone against mainstream opinion, the above interpretation of the amendment to Article 145 EEC, as placing an obligation on the Council to confer implementing powers on the Commission has been given solid support in the legal literature. See e.g. Ehlermann, above Ch 3, n 179, at p. 233; Jacqué, above Ch 1, n 5, at p. 61; Jacqué, J. P., L'Acte unique européen (1986) 22 *RTDE* 595; Blumann, above Ch 1, n 5; Glaesner, H. J., Die Einheitliche Europäische Akte (1986) 21 *EuR* 2; Bradley, above Ch 2, n 58, at p. 703; Ruyt, J. de, L'Acte Unique Européen: commentaire (Editions de l'Université de Bruxelles 1989), at p. 139; and Schwarze, above Ch 2, n 58, at p. 1205. According to Jacqué, the interpretation is confirmed *a contrario* by the third sentence of the paragraph, which provides that the Council in specific cases 'may' reserve the right to exercise implementing powers to itself. The implication is that in all other cases, power to take implementing measures is conferred on the Commission. According to Bradley, had the authors of the SEA wished to maintain the *status quo*, whereby the Council was able to choose freely whether or not to delegate implementing powers to the Commission and to withdraw them by means of supervisory procedures, there was little need to amend Article 145 EEC, the fourth indent of Article 155 EEC being already sufficient for this purpose. For a contesting interpretation, see Dehousse, above Ch 1, n 11, at p. 322.

management, and regulatory committees—the 'grey area' with which the Commission had been so concerned—through the introduction of a limited number of fixed procedures (cf. above 3.4.2.1).

It is important to note that the relevant 'principles and rules' should be placed in normal legislation, to be adopted 'by the Council, acting unanimously on a proposal from the Commission and after obtaining the opinion of the European Parliament.' This guaranteed a certain flexibility but introduced also a risk, in theory, that a situation could arise in which the Council, if the necessary legislation had not been adopted, would be obliged to confer implementing powers on the Commission without being permitted to require it to collaborate with committees (cf. below 4.2.1.1). But more likely, in practice, several Governments would prefer to defer ratification of the Single European Act until that legislation had been adopted. Therefore, in order to avoid a delay, in the Declaration referred to above all Institutions involved were requested to make sure that the legislation was adopted before the Single European Act entered into force. The way in which this was done and the result will be examined, in great detail, in the following chapter.

4

The Years of Entrenchment

'This innocent looking document, with a rather boring title, does in fact belie its appearance.'[1]

4.1 Introduction

4.1.1 The death of the Luxembourg Compromise?

Even if the Luxembourg Compromise had not been raised, explicitly, during the negotiations which led to the adoption of the Single European Act, the move to qualified majority voting—agreed by all Governments and later ratified by all national parliaments—was a clear indication that systematic recourse to unanimity voting was to be abandoned.[2] In support of this, the practice which had emerged within the Council over the previous few years was codified by an amendment to its rules of procedure (cf. above 3.3.3.3).[3] Here it was clarified that the Council 'shall vote on the initiative of its President' and also that the President 'shall be required to open voting proceedings on the invitation of a member of the Council or of the Commission, provided that a majority of the Council's members so decides.'[4]

[1] Lady Elles, MEP, in the debates on the Commission Proposal of 3 March 1986 for a Council Regulation laying down the procedures for the exercise of implementing powers conferred on the Commission. See Debates of the European Parliament of 9 July 1986 (OJ 1986 Annex No 2-341), at p. 130.　　　　　　　　　　　　[2] See Noël, above Ch 3, n 3, at p. 10.
[3] According to Emile Noël, around 100 decisions had been taken by qualified majority voting in 1986. See Noël, É., *Working Together* (Office for Official Publications 1987), at p. 27.
[4] See Article 5(1) of the Council's Rules of Procedure as resulting from amendment of 20 July 1987 (OJ 1987 L 291/27).

Apparently the move to qualified majority voting was respected. As reported by the Commission on 10 January 1991, '[t]he decision-making process in the Council has improved considerably thanks, firstly, to regular recourse to voting since the end of the Single Act negotiations, and, secondly, to the effect of provisions of the Single Act which extend majority voting.'[5] It has been argued, therefore, that the Luxembourg Compromise effectively died with the Single European Act.[6] However true that may be in theory, in practice more than one Government has continued to insist that it is still alive. Most noteworthy, the British Government has stated its 'support, in principle, for retaining the principle of protecting national interests deriving from the Luxembourg Compromise' whilst the French Government has expressed its view 'that any Member State should still be able to invoke, where necessary, the existence of a significant national interest, thus justifying postponement of the vote and the continuation of negotiations along the lines of the Luxembourg compromise.'[7]

Notwithstanding the success with respect to the use of qualified majority voting, 'the outcome of the Conference fell short of the Commission's hopes.'[8] One of the greatest reasons for its disappointment was the failure to secure 'special' powers to adopt implementing legislation for the achievement of the internal market (cf. above 3.4.2).[9] A similar

[5] See Commission Communication of 10 January 1991, below Ch 4, n 85, at p. 1. See also Twenty-fourth General Report on the Activities of the European Communities 1990 (Office for Official Publications 1991), at p. 359. Here it was said that '[t]he improvement in the Council's decision-making procedure which began with the signing of the Single European Act continued in 1990. Wherever necessary, decisions have been taken by a qualified majority, either by means of a formal vote or by establishing that a majority exists without resorting to a formal vote. The possibility of majority voting has introduced an element of flexibility in the position of the member States, which are forced to reach a consensus.'

[6] See Teasdale, above Ch 2, n 107, at p. 575.

[7] See, for the view of the British Government, its White Paper of 12 March 1996 on the IGC: an Association of Nations; and, for the view of the French Government, the Memorandum on France's guidelines for the 1996 IGC, both in the European Parliament White Paper of 29 March on the 1996 Intergovernmental Conference: Summary of the positions of the Member States of the European Union with a view to the 1996 Intergovernmental Conference (http://www.europa. eu.int/en/agenda/igc-home). See also Miller, V., *Qualified Majority Voting and the Blocking Minority*, House of Commons Research Paper 94/47, at pp. 11–12.

[8] Statement by Commission President Jacques Delors after the meeting on 16 and 17 December 1985, in *Bulletin EC* 12-1985, point 1.1.4.

[9] See Ehlermann, above Ch 3, n 230, at p. 403. Note that Ehlermann observes that the Commission set out its reservation against the SEA in another Declaration attached to the Final Act.

disappointment was voiced by the European Parliament which concluded that the result was 'very far from constituting the genuine reform'
it had been waiting for (cf. above 3.3.4).[10] Therefore, the European
Parliament announced that it had instructed its Political Affairs Committee to make sure that the provisions introduced by the Single
European Act were 'exploited to the very limit' and that all available
means were used to obtain the necessary improvements. This, indeed,
was the battle-cry which would set the tone of inter-institutional relations
for many years to come.

4.1.2   A continuity of institutional reform

Some contemporary commentators have concluded, for example Professor David Edward, that the Single European Act had the positive merit
of setting clear limits to the institutional debate. In his view, '[w]e must
now get used to the idea that the Treaty as amended by the Single Act is
the version of the Treaty which most of us will be teaching and applying
for the rest of our working lives.'[11] Nothing could have been more
mistaken. Not only did Professor Edward himself give up teaching to
become a judge in the Court of Justice, but the EEC Treaty was soon to be
amended again and again and again. During the following 15 years, three
Intergovernmental Conferences were convened and the last of them was
not over before the next one had already been scheduled. Therefore,
rather than setting clear limits to the institutional debate, the Single
European Act marked only the first stage of an ongoing process of reform,
the end of which is still not in sight.

Like the first stage of that process, subsequent stages were also
connected to negotiations for further enlargement (see above 3.3.3). After
the accession of Greece, Spain, and Portugal, many expected a pause of
a decade or more in the enlargement of the Community while the
Governments took stock of their plan for new initiatives. But '[t]he pace
of development in what was formerly known as Eastern Europe soon
forced a revision of that cautious prediction.'[12] In 1990 the former

[10] See Resolution of 16 January 1986 on the position of the European Parliament on the
Single Act approved by the Intergovernmental Conference on 16 and 17 December 1985 (OJ 1986
C 36/144).
[11] See Edward, D., The Impact of the Single Act on the Institutions (1987) 24 *CMLRev* 19,
at pp. 21–22.   [12] See Weatherill and Beaumont, above Ch 1, n 36, at p. 7.

German Democratic Republic became part of the Community, albeit as an extension of the German Federal Republic rather than as a thirteenth Member State. Five years later, after the entry into force of the Treaty on European Union (see below 4.3.2.3), the accession was completed of Austria, Finland, and Sweden.[13] Even before that, an agreement had been reached that any of the associated Central and Eastern European countries which so desired should be granted full membership as soon as they were able to satisfy certain economic and political conditions.[14] Meanwhile, the European Union would make the necessary improvements to its institutional system. This task was addressed by the Intergovernmental Conference which led to the adoption of the Treaty of Amsterdam but, unfortunately, the effort was not sufficient (see below 4.3.6.2). Therefore, a new Conference was convened 'to carry out a comprehensive review' of the institutional system.[15] The result was set out in the Treaty of Nice (see below 5.4.1). Here the conclusion was reached that the way was now open for enlargement but, at the same time, the call was made for 'a deeper and wider debate about the future of the European Union.'[16] For that reason, it was explained, an intergovernmental conference should be convened again in 2004.

The continuity of institutional reform was to provide new opportunities to re-open the discussion on the arrangement for exercise of implementing powers. Therefore, shortly after the first Comitology Decision had been adopted in 1987 (see below 4.2), proposals were presented for revision by the Commission as well as the European Parliament. The proposals were all based on ideas which had previously

---

[13] See the Treaty of 24 June 1994 concerning the accession of the Kingdom of Norway, the Republic of Austria, the Republic of Finland and the Kingdom of Sweden to the European Union (OJ 1994 C 241/9). In the end, for a second time, a referendum in Norway decided against accession. For a general comment, see Jorna, M., The Accession Negotiations with Austria, Sweden, Finland and Norway: A Guided Tour (1995) 20 *ELRev* 131.

[14] See *Bulletin EC* 6-1993, point I.13; and *Bulletin EU* 12-1993, points I.13 and I.39. Hungary and Poland submitted formal requests to accede to the European Union in April 1994; as did Romania and Slovakia in June 1995; Latvia in October 1995; Estonia, Lithuania, and Bulgaria in December 1995; the Czech Republic in January 1996; and Slovenia in June 1996. Beside these countries, Switzerland, Malta, Cyprus, and Turkey had already applied to accede. See, in general, Kapteyn and VerLoren van Themaat, above Ch 1, n 36, at pp. 25–26.

[15] See Protocol No 11 annexed to the Treaty of Amsterdam of 2 October 1997 on the institutions with prospect of enlargement of the European Union (OJ 1997 C 340/111) (Article 2).

[16] See Declaration No 23 annexed to the Treaty of Nice of 26 February 2001 on the future of the Union (OJ 2001 C 80/85).

)een mooted, so it was no surprise that they were rejected for similar
·easons to those raised before. For several years the Community Insti-
:utions dug themselves deeper into their positions on the arrangement for
:xercise of implementing powers: these were the years of entrenchment.
[t was only after a long and devastating battle that a second Comitology
Decision was adopted in 1999 (see below 4.4).

4.2   The first Comitology Decision

4.2.1   The background

4.2.1.1   The Commission presents its proposal

[n 1986 the problem of delays involved in the choice of committee
procedures had become more pressing than ever: there were now more
:han 30 different variants of the basic procedures in operation and
:he Commission complained that it had to 'wage a constant defensive
>attle against the Council's obsession with committees.'[17] The solution
promoted by the Commission, taken up from the Report of the Three
Wise Men (see above 3.3.3.2), was to cut down the range of procedures to
:hose set out in an exhaustive list (from which the Council should be
permitted to choose). As originally envisaged, this list would be set out in
an annex to the EEC Treaty (see above 3.3.3.4).[18] The idea was that this
would make it extremely difficult to change. But in the course of the
[ntergovernmental Conference, the Commission decided to modify its
original proposal and to promote, instead, an arrangement where the list
of procedures would only be fixed in ordinary legislation, thus permitting
greater flexibility (see above 3.4.2.1).[19]

It has been seen in the preceding chapter that this later arrangement
was also that which was finally embraced by the Intergovernmental
Conference (see above 3.4.2.2). Therefore, in the amendment made by the
Single European Act to Article 145 EEC, an explanation was included
:hat the relevant procedures 'must be consonant with principles and rules

---

[17] See Debates of the European Parliament on 9 July 1986 (OJ 1986 Annex 2-341/130).
[18] See the so-called Fresco II Report, above Ch 3, n 178, point 2.4.6.
[19] See oral evidence given by Claus-Dieter Ehlermann, above Ch 3, n 239, at p. 27
paragraph 135).

to be laid down in advance by the Council, acting unanimously on a proposal from the Commission and after obtaining the opinion of the European Parliament.' In practice, this meant that the institutional reform could not be considered complete until the relevant legislation had been put in place.[20] Underlining this, in a declaration attached to the Single European Act, the Intergovernmental Conference asked 'the Community authorities to adopt, before the act enters into force, the principles and rules on the basis of which the Commission's powers of implementation will be defined in each case'.[21]

Acting in response to that request, only a few days after the Single European Act had been signed by the Governments (and parallel to the process for ratification), the Commission presented a proposal for a Council Regulation 'laying down the procedures for the exercise of implementing powers conferred on the Commission.'[22] This, in fact, was the first proposal made under the Single European Act. But since the Single European Act had not yet entered into force, the proposal was not based on the amended Article 145 EEC (1987) but on the existing Article 235 EEC (1987).[23] According to Claus-Dieter Ehlermann, Director-General of the Commission Legal Service and the person responsible for drafting the proposal, this was only 'a technical trick' to allow it to be put forward as quickly as possible.[24] The plan was that the legal basis would then be changed to Article 145 EEC (1987) before the proposal was finally adopted.

As explained in a memorandum placed at the start of the proposal, it had been intended to establish the 'rules' which should govern the requirements imposed in respect of the exercise by the Commission of implementing powers.[25] In compliance with the fundamental concern

---

[20] See oral evidence given by Claus-Dieter Ehlermann, above Ch 3, n 239, at p. 17 (paragraph 74).

[21] See the Declaration on the powers of implementation, above Ch 3, n 248.

[22] See Commission Proposal of 3 March 1986, below Ch 4, n 24. See *Bulletin EC* 1-1986, point 2.4.6, where it is explained *inter alia* that the proposal had already been put to the Council on 29 January 1986. See also Ehlermann, above Ch 3, n 179, at p. 233; and Bradley, above Ch 2, n 58, at p. 695.

[23] Oral evidence given by Claus-Dieter Ehlermann, above Ch 3, n 239, at p. 17 (paragraph 74).

[24] Oral evidence given by Claus-Dieter Ehlermann, above Ch 3, n 239, at p. 17 (paragraph 74). See also the explanatory memorandum to the Commission Proposal of 3 March 1986 for a Council Regulation laying down the procedures for the exercise of implementing powers conferred on the Commission (COM (86) 35 final).

[25] See the explanatory memorandum to the Commission Proposal of 3 March 1986, above Ch 4, n 24.

hat the Council should only be able to choose between a limited number
of fixed procedures, the content of these rules was such as to bring about,
on the one hand, a codification of the three basic types of advisory,
management, and regulatory committee procedures and to prescribe, on
the other, that no other form of procedure would be allowed. Since this
was thought to be difficult enough to achieve no attempt had been made
to formulate any additional 'principles'. The main priority when drafting
the proposal had been to find a solution which could be expected to get
through 'without any watering down or major amendments.'[26] According
to the President of the Commission, Jacques Delors:

The Commission's thinking was that we should try to show the Council of
Ministers that we are reasonable people, that we are not, repeat not, asking a
hundred in the hope of getting fifty, and that when we propose three committees, including the regulatory committee, we are trying to allow for and
show understanding of the misgivings of some countries.[27]

It is clear that Delors' attempt to show that the Commission was not asking
for much was part of a carefully planned tactic. By making the proposal as
simple as possible, excluding 'principles', and including the basic type of the
controversial regulatory committee procedure (see above 2.4.4), the Commission hoped, not only that it should be possible for the Council to accept
it without major amendment, but also that the Council would find it less
difficult in the future to make use of the advisory committee procedure.[28]

Apparently the Commission had been considering seriously the possibility of including 'principles' or criteria in the proposal which would
regulate the choice between the fixed procedures, but it finally decided
not to do so. The background to that decision can be found in the
negotiations of the Intergovernmental Conference. Here the Commission
had been pressing very hard for an express provision that, within the field
of the internal market, use should only be made of the advisory committee procedure (see above 3.4.2.1). But it soon turned out that this
was something which the Governments were not willing to accept. In the
end, therefore, a non-binding declaration was made instead in which the

---

[26] See oral evidence given by Claus-Dieter Ehlermann, above Ch 3, n 239, at p. 25 (paragraph
127); and Debates of the European Parliament of 9 July 1986, above Ch 4, n 1, at p. 118.

[27] See *Bulletin EC* 10-1986, point 2.4.22.

[28] See oral evidence given by Claus-Dieter Ehlermann, above Ch 3, n 239, at pp. 21–23
paragraphs 102 and 111–113).

Intergovernmental Conference requested the Council to 'give the advisory committee procedure in particular a predominant place in the
interests of speed and efficiency' within the ambit of the new Article 100a
EEC (see above 3.4.1.2).[29] Having thus already been given a clear indication of the Governments' position, in its proposal the Commission did
not re-address the question of principles or criteria relating to the choice
of committee procedure.[30] As reported by Claus-Dieter Ehlermann, the
Commission felt that there was a near-certitude that, if a new attempt was
made, 'the Council will not adopt the proposed criteria but will retain
criteria which, from the point of view of the Commission, direct proceedings, almost systematically, to the most unfavourable committees in
order that administrations can retain greater power.'[31]

4.2.1.2   *The debates in the European Parliament*

The 'realistic thinking' which had guided the Commission when drafting
the proposal meant that it had refrained, not only from including principles
relating to the choice of committee procedure, but also from including
principles relating to the European Parliament's demand for a *droit de regard*
(see above 3.3.3). No matter how wise this may have been from a tactical
point of view, it was something which the European Parliament was not
able to digest. An unambiguous sign of the misgivings this gave rise to
could be seen on 9 July 1986 in the session where the European Parliament
was expected to give its formal opinion on the proposal.[32]

In preparation for that debate and then the vote, the MEPs had been
presented with a report from the same Political Affairs Committee that
they had recently instructed to ensure that the Single European Act
would be 'exploited to the very limit' (see above 4.1.2).[33] Essentially, the

---

[29] See the Declaration on the powers of implementation, above Ch 3, n 248. According to
Ehlermann, the Commission had also adopted an internal rule to the end that it would only
accept advisory committees in the area of Article 205 EEC (1987): implementation of the budget.
See oral evidence given by Claus-Dieter Ehlermann, above Ch 3, n 239, at p. 19 (paragraph 83).

[30] See Ehlermann, above Ch 3, n 179, at p. 235; and oral evidence given by Claus-Dieter
Ehlermann, above Ch 3, n 239, at p. 19 (paragraph 83).

[31] See oral evidence given by Claus-Dieter Ehlermann, above Ch 3, n 239, at p. 19 (paragraph 83).

[32] See Debates of the European Parliament of 9 July 1986, above Ch 4, n 1, at pp. 118–135.

[33] See the Report of 2 July 1986 drawn up on behalf of the Political Affairs Committee on the
proposal from the Commission of the European Communities to the Council for a regulation
laying down the procedures for the exercise of implementing powers conferred on the Commission (rapporteur: Klaus Hänsch) EP Doc A2-78/86.

so-called Hänsch Report was based on a reasoning which had now become classic. As the rapporteur, Klaus Hänsch, explained, the Political Affairs Committee had reached the conclusion that the management and the regulatory committee procedures were both an interference with the institutional balance since they enabled the Council to 'take back the power' and thus deprived the European Parliament of its rights to supervisory control—rights which it could only exercise in relation to the Commission.[34]

But aware that the use of such procedures was a precondition without which certain Governments would refuse to leave to the Commission implementing powers, the Political Affairs Committee had not been able to agree to recommend that they should be abandoned. Instead it was argued that the European Parliament should seek to ensure that the use of the management and the regulatory committee procedures would not lead to an erosion of its supervisory powers, or indeed to a circumvention of its right to participation in the legislative process, and amendments to the proposal were tabled accordingly. The first of these provided that the Commission should be required to forward all draft measures it sent to committees to the European Parliament, and the second that if the Council was going to retain the opportunity to take back the power, then the European Parliament must also be involved through consultation.[35]

The debates which ensued revealed that strong feelings were involved and that many MEPs feared that the 'innocent looking document' produced by the Commission, if adopted, would be detrimental.[36] The reaction had not been difficult to predict and in order to avoid any misunderstandings, the Commission, represented by its President,

---

[34] See Debates of the European Parliament of 9 July 1986, above Ch 4, n 1, at pp. 118–119. The European Parliament's rights to supervisory control were set out, in particular, in Articles 137, 142, and 144 EEC (1987).

[35] See Debates of the European Parliament of 9 July 1986, above Ch 4, n 1, at pp. 118–119. In addition to this, the idea was presented that the European Parliament should have a right to ask for the initiation of the so-called conciliation procedure, instead of the normal consultation procedure, when legal acts were about to be adopted which would require the use of committee procedures. The conciliation procedure, which had been introduced on an informal basis at the time of the completion of the system for the Community's own resources, was intended to enable an agreement to be reached between the European Parliament and the Council within a limited period of time. See Joint Declaration of the European Parliament, the Council and the Commission of 4 March 1975 concerning the institution of a conciliation procedure between the European Parliament and the Council (OJ 1975 C 89/1).

[36] See the statement by Lady Elles, MEP, in Debates of the European Parliament of 9 July 1986, above Ch 4, n 1.

Jacques Delors, had been asked to be present and to explain its 'realistic thinking'. But rather than reassuring the MEPs, Jacques Delors only managed to confirm their worst suspicions.[37]

Therefore, when voting on the proposal, the MEPs did not only approve the amendments suggested in the Hänsch Report but also added new ones.[38] Noteworthy, in particular, were amendments aimed at the complete elimination of the regulatory committee procedure, and the introduction of 'criteria' requiring that precedence should be given to the advisory committee procedure within the field of the internal market (cf. above 3.4.2.2), and that the procedures of committees already in operation should be converted so as to conform with the new ones. The European Parliament and the Commission were now worlds apart and Jacques Delors could not withhold his contempt for the MEPs' inability to comprehend the 'realistic thinking' which the proposal had been premised on:

You demand consultation with the Commission but you have ignored what I said this morning. Well, that's your business. As for me, I am sticking to my point of view. That's all. None of my arguments have succeeded in convincing you, on a single point. You always want the maximum.[39]

In spite of the fact that the amendments had been voted through (some of them with a narrow majority), or perhaps because of that, the European Parliament decided not to deliver a formal opinion but to refer the matter back to its Political Affairs Committee.[40] According to Claus-Dieter Ehlermann, this was an attempt to avoid a major conflict with the Commission.[41] Conveniently, the resulting delay could also be used to put pressure on the Commission to adjust its proposal. Even if the opinion

---

[37] See the statement by Commission President Jacques Delors in Debates of the European Parliament of 9 July 1986 above Ch 4, n 1, at pp. 121–123. Generally, Jacques Delors insisted on the need to keep the proposal as simple as possible and refused, categorically, to consider the idea of making any amendments. He said, however, that he was willing to give the commitment 'in the name of the Commission' that proposals tabled in committees should be forwarded to the European Parliament, and that the Commission was prepared to give the European Parliament an annual report of the work in general of committees. See oral evidence given by Claus-Dieter Ehlermann, above Ch 3, n 239, at p. 25 (paragraph 127).   [38] See OJ 1986 C 227/54.

[39] See Debates of the European Parliament of 9 July 1986, above Ch 4, n 1, at p. 155.

[40] See the Report of 20 October 1986 drawn up on behalf of the Political Affairs Committee on the proposal from the Commission for a Council regulation laying down the procedures for the exercise of implementing powers conferred on the Commission (rapporteur: Klaus Hänsch) EP Doc A2-138/86.   [41] See Ehlermann, above Ch 3, n 179, at p. 235.

of the European Parliament was merely consultative, in principle the proposal could not be adopted before it had been delivered (see below 4.4.1). Therefore, anxious as the Commission seemed to be to get the new arrangement off the ground as quickly as possible, the European Parliament was now in possession of a precious pawn.

Whether a proof of loyalty or the redemption of a pawn, after some months the Commission's attitude softened and it was noted that it had reconsidered its position on the amendments adopted on 9 July 1986 and stated its willingness to bring it more into line with the position of Parliament.'[42] The most concrete result of this was a new proposal, in which provisions were included requiring that the advisory committee procedure should be given a predominant place in the field of the internal market and that the procedures of existing committees should be adapted to the new arrangement within a reasonable time.[43] The Commission also stated its willingness to enter into a unilateral commitment 'to ensure comprehensive information for and consultation of Parliament about draft implementing measures which it plans to present to committees' (cf. below 4.2.3.1).[44] Obviously pleased with the development, on 23 October 1986 the European Parliament finally declared itself ready to 'resume its interrupted consideration' of the proposal and delivered its opinion.[45]

4.2.2   The result

4.2.2.1   The new Council Decision 87/373/EEC

The proposal eventually placed before the Council gave rise to lengthy and difficult discussions and it was not until 22 June 1987 that an

---

[42] See European Parliament Resolution of 23 October 1986 closing the procedure for consultation of the European Parliament on the proposal from the Commission to the Council for a regulation laying down the procedures for the exercise of implementing powers conferred on the Commission (OJ 1986 C 297/94).

[43] See Articles 2 and 3 of the amended Commission Proposal of 3 December 1986 for a Council Regulation laying down the procedures for the exercise of implementing powers conferred on the Commission (COM (86) 702 final).

[44] See European Parliament Resolution of 23 October 1986, above Ch 4, n 42. Cf. the statement by Jacques Delors, above Ch 4, n 1. See also Ehlermann, above Ch 3, n 179, at p. 235.

[45] See European Parliament Resolution of 23 October 1986, above Ch 4, n 42. The only point on which the amendments voted on 23 October 1986 distinguished themselves from those voted on 9 July 1986 was that the requirement that procedures of existing committees should be brought into line with the new rules within 'one year' was relaxed to 'an appropriate period'.

agreement could be reached.[46] A few weeks later, after the amendments introduced by the Single European Act had entered into force,[47] the agreement was given legal form through the adoption of Council Decision 87/373/EEC.[48] From the contents of this Decision, it appeared that the efforts of the Commission and the European Parliament had been wasted. Not only had the Council made many changes but close to nothing had remained of the proposal the Decision was supposed to have been based on.[49] None of the changes was more evident than the Council's choice of the form of a decision and not, as proposed by the Commission, the form of a regulation. This was an indication that at least some Governments wished the legal consequences of the new arrangement to be limited to its immediate addressees: the Commission and the Council.[50] Arguably, this way it was hoped to avoid the risk that it could be considered to entail obligations for the national administrations and to confer rights on individuals.

Another change related to the application of the new arrangement to already existing committees. The 'realistic thinking' of the Commission had been based on an awareness that each aspect dealt with in the proposal would open up a discussion in the Council and that the rules which

[46] See *Bulletin EC* 6-1987, points 2.4.14 and 2.4.15 (the Commission's implementing powers); Twentieth General Report on the Activities of the European Communities 1986 (Office for Official Publications 1987), at pp. 35–36; and Ehlermann, above Ch 3, n 179, at p. 235. Only a few days before the agreement was reached, the European Parliament 'urgently' requested the Council to accept the proposal so as to meet the objective of the Intergovernmental Conference to strengthen the executive powers of the Commission. See European Parliament Resolution of 17 June 1987 on the Single European Act (OJ 1987 C 190/75).

[47] In spite of the fact that the Single European Act had already been finalized on 17 December 1985 (cf. above 3.4.1.2), because of a legal action alleging that the ratification procedure followed by the Irish Government was unconstitutional, it did not enter into force until 1 July 1987. See General Report 1986, above Ch 4, n 46, at p. 34.

[48] See Council Decision 87/373/EEC of 13 July 1987 laying down the procedures for the exercise of implementing powers conferred on the Commission (OJ 1987 L 197/33). Significantly, Council Decision 87/373/EEC was the first legal act adopted after the coming into force of the SEA. As had been envisaged from the start, its legal basis was that of the amended Article 145 EEC (1987). See *Bulletin EC* 6-1987, point 2.4.11 (the Commission's implementing powers); and Ehlermann, above Ch 3, n 179, at p. 232.

[49] Undoubtedly, this was a manifest breach of the procedural requirement for re-consultation of the European Parliament. Cf. below 4.4.1.

[50] Cf. Article 249 EC (1987) in which the legal characteristics and effects of the various instruments are explained (see above 1.2.1). Accordingly, the Decision is only binding 'upon those to whom it is addressed.'

would eventually be agreed could very well be such that the Commission would be better off without them (see below 4.2.1.1). Proving the Commission right, in that respect, the Council had not only ignored the provision insisted upon by the European Parliament, that the procedures of existing committees should be adjusted within a reasonable time, but inserted an explanation that the Decision should 'not affect the procedures for the exercise of the powers conferred on the Commission in acts which predate its entry into force' and that it would be possible to retain the procedures when these acts were amended in the future.[51] This meant that the practical significance of the new arrangement was going to be 'much more apparent than real.'[52]

4.2.2.2 *The fixed committee procedures*

With respect to the rules regulating the relationship between the Commission and the Council, a number of new elements were introduced. Noteworthy, first, is an introductory provision in which it was clarified that the Council should specify the 'essential elements' of the implementing powers conferred on the Commission (and *a contrario* that the Commission could not exercise such powers unless this had been done).[53] According to Claus-Dieter Ehlermann, this had little legal significance since an identical, or at least similar, requirement had already been established by the Court of Justice in Case 25/70 *Einfuhr- und Vorratsstelle für Getreide und Futtermittel v Köster, Berodt & Co* (see above 2.4.5.2).[54]

---

[51] According to Article 4 of the Decision, '[t]his Decision shall not affect the procedures for the exercise of the powers conferred on the Commission in acts which predate its entry into force. Where such acts are amended or extended the Council may adapt the procedures laid down by these acts to conform with those set out in Articles 2 and 3 or retain the existing procedures.'

[52] See Commission Communication of 10 January 1991, below Ch 4, n 85, at p. 12.

[53] See Article 1(1) of Council Decision 87/373/EEC, above Ch 4, n 48.

[54] See Ehlermann, above Ch 3, n 179, at p. 236. In Article 1(1) of Council Decision 87/373/EEC (see above Ch 4, n 48) it was laid down that, '[o]ther than in specific cases where it reserves the right to exercise directly implementing powers itself, the Council shall, in the acts which it adopts, confer on the Commission powers for the implementation of the rules which it lays down. The Council shall specify *the essential elements of these powers*.' (emphasis added). The wording should be compared with the Court's ruling in Case 25/70 (see above Ch 2, n 244), in which it was (only) explained that a distinction had to be made 'between rules which, since they are essential to the subject matter envisaged, must be reserved to the Council's power, and those which being merely of an implementing nature may be delegated to the Commission.' Arguably, Article 1(1) of Council Decision 87/373/EEC (see above Ch 4, n 48) was an attempt to go even further. Support for that submission is found in the Court's ruling in Case C-240/90

But politically the new provision could be read as a statement that a unanimous Council was keen to preserve the flexible nature of implementing powers, to establish any boundaries only on a case-by-case basis, and to avoid, therefore, any type of general definitions or 'principles' similar to those found in most national constitutions (restricting the scope of implementing powers a national parliament may delegate to a Government).[55]

Then, secondly, the basic committee procedures proposed by the Commission had been enriched by the inclusion of additional and more restrictive variants to the management and regulatory committee procedures.[56] In addition, a special procedure—not explicitly involving the use of committees—had been introduced for the exercise of implementing powers when so-called safeguard measures were involved.[57] Since the procedures laid down in the Decision were to be the only ones which the Council could choose between when implementing powers were conferred on the Commission, their main features should be set out in some detail.

The fixed advisory committee procedure The advisory committee procedure was characterized by the fact that the committee's opinion was not formally binding on the Commission. But it should take 'the utmost account' of the opinion and inform the committee of the manner in which this had been done. Although expected to deliver the opinion by unanimity, 'if necessary' the committee could proceed to a vote by simple

Germany v Commission. Here the argument (of the German Government) that Article 1 of Council Decision 87/373/EEC required the Council to specify the essential elements of the powers conferred on the Commission was rejected. According to the Court: '[t]hat argument does not carry conviction either. It is clear from the aforementioned Köster judgment that since the Council has laid down in its basic regulation the essential rules governing the matter in question, it may delegate to the Commission general implementing power without having to specify the essential components of the delegated power; for that purpose, provision drafted in general terms provides a sufficient basis for the authorising act ... That principle is not affected by the aforementioned decision. As a means of secondary law it cannot add to the rules of the Treaty, which do not require the Council to specify the essential components of the implementing powers delegated to the Commission.' See Case C-240/90 *Germany v Commission* [1992] ECR I-5383 (Judgment of 27 October 1992), paragraphs 41 to 42. It may be noted that Article 1(1) of Council Decision 99/468/EC (see below 4.4.2) explains that '[t]hese provisions shall stipulate *the essential elements of the powers thus conferred.*' (emphasis added). This does not seem to say anything different than before.

[55] See Ehlermann, above Ch 3, n 179, at p. 236.

[56] See Article 2 of Council Decision 87/373/EEC, above Ch 4, n 48.

[57] See Article 3 of Council Decision 87/373/EEC, above Ch 4, n 48.

majority. This had not been proposed by the Commission, and has been seen by some as an attempt to put more pressure on it to accept the committee's views.[58] Essentially, this was the procedure which was applied in fields where the Governments could agree that the Commission should be left with most discretion and that had been used for the first time in 1962 in the field of competition (see above 2.2.2: the Advisory Committee on Restrictive Practices and Dominant Positions). Obviously unwilling to make it a binding commitment—as the European Parliament had insisted—in a declaration attached to the Decision, the Council promised that this procedure should be given 'a predominant place' within the field of the internal market (see above 4.2.1.2).[59]

The fixed management committee procedure The management committee procedure was characterized by the power it gave the committee to 'appeal' an implementing measure to the Council. According to the procedure, the Commission would adopt an implementing measure which would apply immediately. Only then would the committee give its opinion. If this was negative, the Commission would communicate the measure to the Council which could modify or annul it. The basic variant of the procedure (IIa) was that which had been used in the field of the common agricultural policy since 1962 (see above 2.2.2: the Management Committees for Cereals *etc.*). Here, the Commission was given the right to choose whether or not to suspend the application of a measure on appeal to the Council. The significance of that was practical rather than formal. If the Commission should choose not to suspend the application of a measure on appeal, it would be difficult, politically, for the Council to modify or annul it. The more restrictive variant of the procedure (IIb) was that which had been used for the first time in 1975 in the field of regional development (the Regional Development Fund Committee).[60] Here the Commission was obliged to suspend the application of a measure on appeal.

[58] See Blumann, above Ch 1, n 5, at pp. 53–54. See also Bradley, above Ch 2, n 58, at p. 704. As argued by Bradley, an indicative vote could equally well be seen as adding value to the consultation procedure, by forcing the administrations of the Member States, which will ultimately be responsible for the concrete application of the measure, to take a position prior to its adoption. Note also that each delegation had a right to ask to have its position recorded in the minutes.

[59] See Ehlermann, above Ch 3, n 179, at p. 237. Cf. the Declaration on the powers of implementation, above Ch 3, n 248.

[60] See Council Regulation 724/75/EEC of the Council of 18 March 1975 establishing a European Regional Development Fund (OJ 1975 L 73/1).

The fixed regulatory committee procedure The regulatory committee procedure was characterized by the power it gave the committee to prevent an implementing measure from being adopted. According to the procedure, the Commission could only adopt an implementing measure, in the first instance, if the committee had given a positive opinion. If no opinion was given or the opinion was negative, however, the Commission had to submit a 'proposal' on the measure to be taken to the Council. The only real difference between this proposal and a proposal submitted within the normal legislative process was that the Council was under no obligation to take the view of the European Parliament into account. So, for example, the Council could adopt the proposal by qualified majority and amend it by unanimity.[61] The basic variant of the procedure (IIIa) was that of the so-called *filet* or 'safety net' which had been used for the first time in 1968 in the field of customs legislation (see above 2.4.2: the Committee on Origin of Goods). This provided that if the Council had not adopted the proposal within a limited period, then the power returned to the Commission which should adopt the proposed measure itself. The more restrictive variant of the procedure (IIIb) was that of the so-called *contre-filet* or 'double safety net' which had also been used for the first time in 1968, in the field of veterinary legislation (see above 2.4.3: the Standing Veterinary Committee). This added an opportunity for the Council (by simple majority) to 'decide against' the proposed measure, thus preventing the power from returning to the Commission. Although repeatedly argued against by both the Commission and the European Parliament, all Governments agreed that this variant would be indispensable in future conferrals of implementing powers on the Commission in politically sensitive fields.[62]

The fixed safeguard procedure The safeguard procedure that had been fixed was intended to be applied when the Council gave the Commission powers to introduce safeguard measures. According to the procedure, the Commission would notify both the Council and the Member States of its decision whether or not to introduce such measures. It could also be stipulated by the Council that the Commission, before adopting its decision, must consult the Member States in accordance with

[61] See e.g. Commission Communication of 10 January 1991, below Ch 4, n 85, at p. 4. Cf. Bradley, above Ch 1, n 76, at pp. 76–77. But, as pointed out by Bradley, the Council could only amend the Commission proposal by unanimity (subject to the general rule in Article 250(1) EC (2003)).

[62] See Ehlermann, above Ch 3, n 179, at p. 237.

procedures to be determined in each case. Any Member State could refer the Commission's decision to the Council within a time limit to be determined in the act in question. There were two variants of what could happen next. The basic variant of the procedure (IVa) provided that the decision adopted by the Commission should continue to apply if the Council (by qualified majority) had not taken a different decision within a limited period. The alternative variant of the procedure (IVb) provided that the Council (by qualified majority) could confirm, amend, or revoke the decision adopted by the Commission and that it was deemed to be revoked if the Council had not acted within a limited period. In contrast to the other procedures, the safeguard procedure did not explicitly require the use of any committee. Nevertheless, it is clear that when the procedure had been used in the past, for example in 1968 in the field of anti-dumping, an *ad hoc* type of committee had been used to ensure continuous consultations between the Commission and the Member States (see above 2.4.2: the Committee on Protection against Dumping).[63] It would appear that this was also the way in which the procedure was intended to be used in the future.[64]

4.2.3 *The reactions*

4.2.3.1 *An alarm bell for resistance*

As has been seen above, the Commission, when preparing the proposal, had concentrated its efforts on an attempt to come up with a solution which would reduce the number of different committee procedures the Council could choose between to the three basic types of advisory, management, and regulatory committee procedures. The hope was that this was a solution the Council would be willing to accept 'without any

[63] It may be noted that this practice, in turn, had its root in the solution chosen in Council Decision of 9 October 1961 concerning a consultation procedure in respect of the negotiation of agreements concerning commercial relations between Member States and third countries (OJ 1961 71/1273).

[64] See, for an example of variant IVa, Council Regulation 12/98/EC of 11 December 1997 laying down the conditions under which non-resident carriers may operate national road passenger transport services within a member state (OJ 1998 L 4/10); and, for an example of variant IVb, Council Regulation 519/94/EC of 7 March 1994 on common rules for imports from certain third countries (OJ 1994 L 67/89). See also Commission Communication of 10 January 1991, below Ch 4, n 85, at p. 12; and Ehlermann, above Ch 3, n 179, at p. 237.

watering down or major amendments' (see above 4.2.1.1). Judged in the light of that ambition the final result was a failure: not only had a provision been inserted explicitly authorizing the continuous operation of old committee procedures (see above 4.2.2.1) but the list from which procedures were to be chosen in the future had been extended so as to include the restrictive variant of the regulatory committee procedure and the safeguard procedure (see above 4.2.2.2). Therefore, for the Commission it was not possible to accept Council Decision 87/373/EEC without reservations. Its reasons for dissatisfaction were specified in a statement recorded in the Council's protocol:

1. As far as the regulatory committee is concerned, the Commission deplores the fact that the Council has adopted the *contre-filet* procedure which may result in the Commission's being prevented from adopting its proposed implementing measures where the Council fails to reach a decision. The Commission would have preferred the Council to confine itself to the *filet* procedure which allows the Council to adopt or amend the implementing measures proposed by the Commission within a certain time limit, leaving the Commission free to adopt the measures itself in the absence of a Council decision.
2. The Commission would reaffirm its reservations concerning variant (b) of the safeguard procedure, which provides no guarantee that a decision will be taken. It fears that continued recourse to this formula will do nothing to ease the Commission's task in relation to day-to-day management of the common commercial policy.
3. The Commission deplores the Council's failure to fix a deadline, however remote, for bringing the numerous existing committees into line with the principles of the framework decisions. It is essential that they be adapted over a realistic time span, to clarify and simplify current procedures.[65]

Apparently, this statement was later followed up by the Commission when proposals for new legislation were submitted to the Council. By refusing to include the contested procedures (IIIb and IVb) in its proposals, the Commission forced the Council, if it wished to use them, to make formal amendments (something which required unanimity).[66] But forceful as the

---

[65] See *Bulletin EC* 6-1987, point 2.4.14 (the Commission's implementing powers); and Twenty-first General Report on the Activities of the European Communities 1987 (Office for Official Publications 1988), at p. 31.

[66] See Corbett above Ch 3, n 188, at p. 258. The procedure which the Council had to comply with if it wished to amend a proposal is laid down in Article 250(1) EC (2003).

Commission's reaction may have seemed, it should not be overestimated. If sufficiently unhappy with the way things were going, it could have prevented the Decision from being adopted by withdrawing its proposal. This, indeed, was a weapon which the Commission had found reasons to use in the past and also one which its President had not hesitated to brandish before the European Parliament.[67] But this did not happen. It would seem, therefore, that the Commission was more eager to proceed 'to the order of the day' than to provoke an open conflict (cf. above 2.4.4).

Not very surprisingly, the European Parliament immediately took a more active stance against Council Decision 87/373/EEC. Only a minimum account had been taken of its demands when the proposal was drafted and, in the end, they were completely ignored. For the European Parliament, therefore, the Decision became 'an alarm bell' for resistance.[68] During the initial stage of what was to develop into a long-lasting and destructive battle, different tactics were attempted. Perhaps most naturally, the European Parliament took the opportunity, when consulted on (amended) proposals for legislation, to state its opinion that provisions requiring use of committee procedures should be deleted or at least replaced by provisions requiring less restrictive ones.[69] This, in fact, was one of the tactics the European Parliament had often attempted in the past (see above 3.3.4.1). But from now onwards it was to be applied systematically and specific guidelines were adopted which the plenary (i.e. that part or function of the European Parliament where all MEPs meet to discuss and ultimately vote) was told to follow:

1. In first reading, Parliament should systematically delete any provisions for procedure III(a) or (b) and replace it by procedure II(a) or (b), or, for proposals concerning the internal market put forward under Article 100a

---

[67] Proclaiming that the Commission would 'fight to the bitter end' for its proposal, in the session where the European Parliament delivered its opinion on the proposal, Delors explained that he 'may well withdraw the proposal if confidence is not reposed in the realism, pragmatism and professionalism of the Commission. If we are pressed too far, there will be no proposal on the table any more. And then it will be seen that if Europe is making no headway it is the fault of the Council, and indeed Coreper.' See *Bulletin EC* 10-1986, point 2.4.22.

[68] See European Parliament Resolution of 8 July 1987 on the Council Decision of 22 June 1987 on the implementing powers of the Commission (OJ 1987 C 246/42). Here the Decision was described as 'an alarm bell demonstrating the manifest lack of political will on the part of the Member States to give practical effect to the objectives of the SEA on the eve of its coming into force.'

[69] See Corbett above Ch 3, n 188, at p. 258; and Bradley above Ch 2, n 216, at p. 232.

of the EEC Treaty, procedure I. Alternatively, when the subject matter is particularly important or sensitive, Parliament could provide for decisions to be made by the legislative procedure instead.

2. In second reading, Parliament should continue to oppose any provisions in a common position for procedure III(b), but III(a) could be accepted exceptionally, as a compromise, except for proposals concerning the internal market put forward under Article 100a of the EEC Treaty, where II(b) should be maximum acceptable compromise.[70]

Unfortunately, for the European Parliament, its right to participate in the adoption of legislation—whether stemming from the original consultation procedure or the co-operation procedure—did not entail any obligation for the Council to comply with its opinion (see above 3.4.1.2). Therefore, parallel with the above, other tactics were explored. Perhaps most drastic, in that respect, was an action brought before the Court of Justice on 2 October 1987 in which it was claimed that Council Decision 87/373/EEC was unlawful since the Council, when adopting it, had infringed the amended Article 145 EEC (1987): Case 302/87 *European Parliament v Council*.[71] The reasoning deserves some further explanation.

Prior to the Single European Act, the lawfulness of committee procedures had been based on Article 155 EEC and the idea that the Council was free to confer or not to confer implementing powers on the Commission (see above 2.4.5.2). A logical consequence of this was that the Council was also free to set conditions: *qui peut le plus, peut le moins*. But in accordance with the amended Article 145 EEC, an obligation had been introduced for the Council to confer implementing powers on the Commission, with the exemption only for 'specific cases' (see above 3.4.2.2). According to the European Parliament, this meant that the Commission now disposed of 'originating and autonomous powers in regard to the implementation . . . which must be clearly distinguished from the powers granted to it under the system of delegation' provided for in Article 155

---

[70] The guidelines were adopted by 'the meeting of chairmen of parliamentary committees' and subsequently approved by the so-called Enlarged Bureau. See Corbett above Ch 3, n 188, at p. 258. Cf. Bradley above Ch 2, n 216, at pp. 232 and 236.

[71] See Case 302/87 *European Parliament v Council* [1988] ECR 5615 (Judgment of 27 September 1988). For a commentary see Jacqué, J.-P., annotation (1989) 25 *RTDE* 225, at p. 225; Weiler, J. H. H., Pride and Prejudice: Parliament v. Council (1989) 14 *ELRev* 334, at p. 334; and Hilf, M., annotation (1990) 25 *EuR* 273, at p. 273. This was the first application ever made by the European Parliament under Article 173 EEC (1987). Cf. above Ch 3, n 229.

EEC (1987).[72] Under such circumstances, for the Council to adopt a decision based on the use of committee procedures which reserved to itself 'the last word' in more than specific cases was an illegal attempt to impose conditions and, therefore, an interference with the institutional balance.[73] Whether a good argument or not, it was clearly too hot for the Court to handle: one year after the application had been submitted it was dismissed on procedural grounds without anything being said about the substance.[74]

One of the few successful tactics employed by the European Parliament was to direct its claims, not against the Council, but against its presumed ally: the Commission. During the debates which preceded the adoption of Council Decision 87/373/EEC the Commission had explained its willingness to ensure for the European Parliament information and consultation on matters placed before committees (see above 4.2.1.2). This, indeed, was a promise which the European Parliament had

---

[72] See Case 302/87, above Ch 4, n 71, at p. 5620. For a similar argument, see Schwarze, above Ch 2, n 58, at pp. 1205–1206. Cf. Bradley, above Ch 2, n 58, at p. 714. The interpretation put forward by Bradley is that if the EEC Treaty accords the Council the right to exercise implementing powers only in exceptional cases, it guarantees that in all other cases these powers are exercised by the Commission, under the supervision of the European Parliament, rather than the Council and committees.

[73] Most significant, in this respect, was the 'classic' argument that the management and regulatory committee procedures made it possible for the Council to exercise implementing powers which belonged to the Commission and that the European Parliament was deprived, therefore, of its rights to exercise supervisory powers. Other arguments supporting the claim that Council Decision 87/373/EEC (see above Ch 4, n 48) should be annulled were that the provision requiring the Council to specify 'the essential elements' gave the Council 'a discretion to lay down the criteria enabling it to challenge the general implementing powers conferred on the Commission' and that the provision reserving the right to maintain existing procedures was a violation of the new principle that 'rules and principles' had to be laid 'in advance.' In addition to the above, the claim was made by the European Parliament that the Decision was substantially different from the proposal and that so many amendments had been made by the Council that the European Parliament should have been provided with an opportunity for re-consultation (cf. below 4.3.4).

[74] According to the Court, 'the applicable provisions [of the EEC Treaty], as they stand at present, do not enable the Court to recognise the capacity of the European Parliament to bring an action for annulment.' See Case 302/87, above Ch 4, n 71, at p. 5644 (paragraph 28). It may be noted that the Commission, through its President, indicated that it considered that the European Parliament did have a right to standing. See Commission Report of 28 September 1989, below Ch 4, n 85, at p. 5. Furthermore, several commentators saw the ruling as distinctly at odds with previous case law relating to the institutional balance of powers. See, in particular, Weiler, above Ch 4, n 71; and Bradley, K., The Variable Evolution of the Standing of the European Parliament in Proceedings before the Court of Justice (1988) 8 *YBEL* 27.

every intention of making sure the Commission would keep. Following the adoption of Council Decision 87/373/EEC, its President, Lord Plumb, sent a letter to Jacques Delors, in which the exact terms were set out of an agreement that, as a general rule, all 'draft decisions relating to legislative documents' should be forwarded by the Commission to the European Parliament at the same time as they were forwarded to the committees.[75] These terms were accepted by Delors in a letter sent back to Lord Plumb on 14 March 1988.[76] Even if this so-called Plumb-Delors Agreement was not sufficient to appease the European Parliament, it was an important step forward: for the first time a formal concession had been made to its life-long demand for a *droit de regard* (see above 2.2.3, 2.4.4, and 3.3.4.1).

4.2.3.2 *A general principle of division of powers*

More or less parallel with the European Parliament's unsuccessful challenge of Council Decision 87/373/EEC before the Court of Justice, another case was initiated in which it was called upon to adjudicate in a long-standing dispute between the Commission and the Council over the use of the management committee procedure when implementing decisions were adopted involving budgetary spending. Even if the precise matter involved was rather particular, the subsequent ruling had general significance: not only did it erase every doubt as to the legality of the Decision, but it made it clear that the arrangement for exercise of implementing powers had become a central element of the institutional and, indeed, constitutional legal order.[77]

---

[75] According to the Plumb-Delors Agreement: '[w]ith the exception of routine management documents with a limited period of validity and documents whose adoption is complicated by considerations of secrecy or urgency, draft decisions relating to legislative documents will be forwarded to Parliament, for information, at the same time that they are forwarded to the committees in question, and in the same working languages.' See Bradley, above Ch 2, n 216, at p. 236. Parallel to the agreement a new provision was inserted into the European Parliament's Rules of Procedure, effective from the entry into force of the SEA, charging its President to refer any implementing measures or proposals tabled by the Commission to the relevant parliamentary committee.   [76] See Bradley, above Ch 2, n 216, at p. 236.

[77] See Case 16/88 *Commission v Council* [1989] ECR 3457 (Judgment of 24 October 1989). For a commentary, see Blumann, C., annotation (1990) 26 *RTDE* 173; and Forman, J., annotation (1990) 27 *CMLRev* 872. For an overview of the underlying conflict, see Ehlermann, C.-D. and Minch, M., Conflicts between the Community Institutions within the Budgetary Procedure: Article 205 of the EEC Treaty (1981) 16 *EuR* 23. Cf. also the Opinion of Advocate General Darmon in Case 16/88, paragraphs 20 to 24 and 42.

The background to the ruling in Case 16/88 *Commission v Council* is found in Council Regulation 3252/87/EEC on the co-ordination and promotion of research in the fisheries sector, adopted a few months after the entry into force of the Single European Act and Council Decision 87/373/EEC.[78] In this regulation, provision had been made for the Council to establish certain research programmes (and research co-ordination programmes) and, then, for the Commission to ensure that the programmes were 'carried out' by concluding contracts with research centres and organizing seminars, conferences, and study trips. For those purposes, the Commission was required to co-operate with the 'Standing Committee for the Fishing Industry' in accordance with a management committee procedure (IIa).

But as argued by the Commission, the powers needed for it to comply with the tasks set out in the Regulation had already been granted in Article 205 EEC (1987). This required it 'to implement the budget... on *its own responsibility* and within the limits of the appropriations, having regard to the principles of sound financial management' (emphasis added).[79] As a consequence, there was no need for such powers to be conferred specifically upon it by the Council. In doing so, and imposing an additional obligation to comply with a management committee procedure, the Council had not only applied Article 145 EEC (1987) wrongly but had violated Article 205 EEC (1987), thus interfering with the institutional balance.[80] The Council, for its part, contended that a clear distinction had to be drawn between the arrangement for exercise of implementing powers as now provided for in Article 145 EEC (1987) and the budgetary powers governed by Article 205 EEC (1987). In its view, these were not on the same level: a decision implementing the budget was not possible until a substantive decision, whether general in nature or individual, had been taken giving the expenditure a legal basis.[81]

In its ruling, the Court stressed that the provisions of the EEC Treaty which specify the powers of the institutions to act in the various fields of

[78] See Council Regulation 3252/87/EEC of 19 October 1987 on the co-ordination and promotion of research in the fisheries sector (OJ 1987 L 314/17).

[79] See Case 16/88, above Ch 4, n 77, at p. 3461. Article 205 EEC (1987) should be read in conjunction with Article 155 EEC (1987), according to which the Commission 'shall... have its own power of decision and participate in the shaping of measures taken by the Council and by the European Parliament in the manner provided for in this Treaty.'

[80] See paragraph 5 of the Judgment (above Ch 4, n 77).

[81] See paragraph 6 of the Judgment (above Ch 4, n 77).

co-operation may confer directly on the Commission its own powers of decision.[82] But it explained that the Commission was wrong to maintain that this had anything to do with Article 205 EEC (1987) or the question whether Article 145 EEC (1987) could be relied upon by the Council to confer implementing powers on the Commission to adopt decisions involving budgetary spending. As the Council contended, these articles did not operate on the same level: the responsibility of the Commission for implementing the budget was not such 'as to modify the division of powers resulting from the various provisions of the Treaty which authorise the Council and the Commission to adopt generally applicable or individual measures within special areas... and from the institutional provisions' of Article 145 EEC (1987).[83] For this reason the Court dismissed the application. The Court clarified the meaning of Article 145 EEC (1987) and the new arrangement for exercise of implementing powers:

The concept of implementation for the purposes of that article comprises both the drawing up of implementing rules and the application of rules to specific cases by means of acts of individual application. Since the Treaty uses the word 'implementation' without restricting it by the addition of any further qualification, that term cannot be interpreted so as to exclude acts of individual application.

Under the system established by the Treaty as it stood before the Single European Act, the Court ruled, in its judgment of 17 December 1970 in Case 25/70 *Einfuhr- und Vorratsstelle v Köster*... that if the Council could confer implementing powers on the Commission under Article 155 of the Treaty it could also make the exercise of those powers subject to a management committee procedure which enabled the Council to take the decision itself if it saw fit and that the legality of the management committee procedure could not be disputed in relation to the institutional structure of the Community.

The Council's right to make the exercise of the powers which it confers on the Commission subject to certain procedures was expressly preserved in the amendments made to Article 145 of the Treaty by the Single European Act. Those procedures must be consonant with the rules laid down in advance and after obtaining the opinion of the European Parliament. They were laid down by Council Decision 87/373 of 13 July 1987.[84]

---

[82] See paragraph 9 of the Judgment (above Ch 4, n 77). Examples listed by the Court were Articles 90(3), 91, 93(2), and 115 EEC (1987).

[83] See paragraph 16 of the Judgment (above Ch 4, n 77).

[84] See paragraphs 11 to 13 of the Judgment (above Ch 4, n 77).

4.3 The inter-institutional battle

4.3.1 The operation of the new arrangement for exercise of implementing powers

4.3.1.1 The Commission provides an analysis

During the following years, the Commission often took the opportunity to express its discontent with the new arrangement for exercise of implementing powers. Noteworthy, in particular, are two special reports in which it stated itself to be 'still deeply concerned by developments in this area' which, it said, ran counter to the spirit of the Single European Act and were likely to compromise the efficiency of the internal market programme (see above 3.3.4.3).[85] According to these reports the Council had not kept its previous promise to give the advisory committee procedure a predominant place within the field of the internal market (see above 4.2.2.2) but, instead, the Council had 'almost systematically' amended proposals for legislation so as to replace that procedure by the regulatory committee procedure.[86] Furthermore, the Council had extended the use of the most restrictive variant of the regulatory committee procedure—that based on the *contre-filet* mechanism—into fields of co-operation where this was not customary (see above 4.2.2.2).[87]

[85] See Commission Report to the European Parliament of 28 September 1989: delegation of executive powers to the Commission (SEC (89) 1591 final); and Commission Communication to the Council of 10 January 1991: conferment of implementing powers on the Commission (SEC (90) 2589 final). Quote from the Commission Communication of 10 January 1991, at p. 1. It may be noted that through this second report the Commission fulfilled its part of a review provided for in Article 5 of Council Decision 87/373/EEC, above Ch 4, n 48. Here it was stated that '[t]he Council shall review the procedures provided for in this Decision on the basis of a report submitted by the Commission before 31 December 1990.' Cf. also Commission Communication to the Council of 10 July 1989: the Council's delegation of executive powers to the Commission (SEC (89) 1143 final).

[86] According to the Commission, the Council only opted for the advisory committee procedure for 12 of the 37 proposals adopted in the field of the internal market. See Commission Report of 28 September 1989, above Ch 4, n 85, at p. 8, and Commission Communication of 10 January 1991, above Ch 4, n 85, at p. 7. It may be noted, in this context, that many of the central documents adopted by the Council with regard to the internal market programme, for example Council Resolution of 7 May 1985, above Ch 3, n 180, were based on the idea that significant powers should be conferred on the Commission subject to the requirement that it must co-operate with committees following a regulatory committee procedure. Cf. also General Programme of 28 May 1969, above Ch 3, n 113.

[87] In spite of the fact that the Commission had never proposed that variant (IIIb), the Council had decided to introduce it 37 times (examples of areas it was introduced were research, banking,

This led the Commission to the conclusion that 'the Council's tendency, when delegating powers, to attach a blocking mechanism whereby it can prevent a decision being taken has, far from waning, actually grown since the Single Act entered into force.'[88] For the Commission, this was difficult to understand since, in its view, there were no objective reasons for the insistence on a blocking mechanism designed to prevent it from abusing implementing powers:

An analysis of the many cases in which the Commission has exercised executive powers for many years now reveals no abuse whatsoever on the Commission's part. On the contrary, it demonstrates that the Commission has always been able to secure the backing of experts representing the Member States on the various committees... Consequently, instances of the Commission having to refer proposed measures to the Council in the absence of support from national experts are virtually non-existent and the Council has never had to use the blocking mechanism designed to prevent the Commission intervening in the event of the Council failing to take a decision.[89]

It should be noted that this analysis was based on the finding that the Commission had managed to secure a favourable opinion from the committee in 98% of the cases in which the regulatory committee procedure had been involved since the coming into force of the new arrangement. In the remaining 2% of the cases, where the matter had been referred to the Council, a decision had 'virtually always' been taken by the Council and recourse to the disputed *contre-filet* mechanism had not proved necessary.[90] The finding with respect to the management committee procedure was similar. Only in eight out of 16,248 cases dealt with during the period 1962 to 1978 had the opinion been negative (and of these only two had led the Council to introduce modifications).[91] According to the Commission,

and environment). See Commission Communication of 10 January 1991, above Ch 4, n 85, at p. 7. It may be noted in this context that on 8 July 1987 the Commission had adopted a decision in which it stated that it would never recommend a IIIb procedure in a proposal for a legal act. See COM (87) Min 881 item XI A.

[88] See Commission Communication of 10 January 1991, above Ch 4, n 85, at p. 11.

[89] See Commission Report of 28 September 1989, above Ch 4, n 85, at pp. 10–11.

[90] See Commission Report of 28 September 1989, above Ch 4, n 85, at pp. 8–9.

[91] In 15,094 cases the opinion had been favourable and in 1,156 cases there had been a failure to give an opinion. Seemingly, the statistics relating to the management committee procedure only relate to the field of common agricultural policy. See Commission Report of 28 September 1989, above Ch 4, n 85, at p. 9.

this pattern was confirmed by recent statistics, showing that no negative opinions had been delivered for years.[92]

4.3.1.2   A call for further reform

At the same time as the Commission refined its criticism of the new arrangement for exercise of implementing powers and the way it was applied—or not applied—by the Council, there was a growing concern in the European Parliament as to whether the Commission was 'keeping its side of the bargain.'[93] The focus was on the operation of the Plumb-Delors Agreement and the Commission's promise to forward to it the more important matters dealt with by the committees (see above 4.2.3). Since this type of inter-institutional commitment was unknown to the EEC Treaty it was far from clear whether it had any legal effects and if so what those were.[94] In practice, therefore, the 'right' granted to the European Parliament rested only on the Commission's will and ability.

This soon proved to be problematic. Firstly, the number of matters actually transmitted by the Commission was relatively small. According to figures compiled by the European Parliament Secretariat, only 171 out of 400 relevant draft measures were transmitted during the first three years and these were concentrated in the fields of the common agricultural policy and customs union and were highly technical in nature—in spite of the fact that this period included the run-up to the internal market.[95] Secondly, the European Parliament was given little or no indication of the time constraints involved in each case.[96] This made it

---

[92] According to the Commission, of 1,792 cases dealt with in 1988, there had been 1,665 favourable opinions and 127 failures to give an opinion. See Commission Report of 28 September 1989, above Ch 4, n 85, at p. 9.   [93] See Bradley, above Ch 2, n 216, at p. 237.

[94] See Bradley, above Ch 2, n 216, at p. 237. As Bradley pointed out, inter-institutional agreements are not mentioned in the EEC/EC Treaty as a source of law. According to him, in the light of the case law, it could be argued that inter-institutional agreements are legally binding only where parties actually had the intention to be legally bound. See Case C-58/94 *Netherlands v Council* [1996] ECR I-2169 (Judgment of 30 April 1996), at paragraph 27 and Case C-25/94 *Commission v Council* [1996] ECR I-1469 (Judgment of 19 March 1996), at paragraphs 48–50.

[95] See Report of 19 November 1990 drawn up on behalf of the Committee on Institutional Affairs on the executive powers of the Commission (comitology) and the role of the Commission in the Community's external relations (rapporteur: Panayolis Roumeliotis) EP Doc A3-310/90, at p. 5. Cf. Bradley, above Ch 2, n 216, at p. 237.

[96] See the Roumeliotis Report, above Ch 4, n 95, at p. 5. Cf. Bradley, above Ch 2, n 216, at p. 237.

difficult to react: during the first three years it had taken a position in plenary on just one matter.[97]

The concern of the European Parliament with the operation of the Plumb-Delors Agreement was set out in a resolution adopted on 13 December 1990.[98] Here the Commission was requested to improve its performance 'in the interests of providing effective information to and the effective consultation of the European Parliament.'[99] Importantly, it was also admitted that the European Parliament itself had not managed to secure an adequate follow-up. Nevertheless, whatever the improvements that had to be made in the relationship between the European Parliament and the Commission, these would never be enough to come to terms with the most fundamental problems. In this respect, the findings presented by the Commission in its special reports were taken up in the Resolution to deplore (once again) the use of regulatory committee procedures and to reassert that the Commission was an executive body 'not by delegation but by right' (see above 4.3.1.1). As the European Parliament emphasized, it would take a further reform of the EEC Treaty to 'guarantee the effectiveness of the decision-making process and compliance with the democratic principle of the separation of powers and control of executive power.'

4.3.2   The 1991 Intergovernmental Conference

4.3.2.1   A limited ambition

The opportunity for further institutional reform came with the Intergovernmental Conference that opened in Rome on 15 December 1990. Only five years had passed since the agreement had been reached on the Single European Act and the experience which had been gained since then had barely been evaluated. Therefore, the aim was to complete or

---

[97] See European Parliament Resolution of 19 April 1991 on infant formulae and follow-up milks (OJ 1991 C 129/226). This was adopted after the European Parliament's Environment and Consumer Protection Committee had explained its view in a plenary hearing that the draft measure was not sufficiently strict. In response, the Commission modified its proposal significantly. The final result could be seen in Commission Directive 91/321/EEC of 14 May 1991 on infant formulae and follow-on formulae (OJ 1991 L 175/35). See further Corbett, R., Jacobs, F., and Shackleton, M., *The European Parliament* (Harlow 1992), at p. 234.

[98] See European Parliament Resolution of 13 December 1990, below Ch 4, n 102; and the Roumeliotis Report, above Ch 4, n 95.

[99] See the Roumeliotis Report above Ch 4, n 95, at p. 5.

complement the previous reform rather than to initiate a new one. In other words, the time had come to proceed to the second and final step of the process for establishment of a European Union. Overall, the tasks which the Governments had set themselves were to clarify their agreement on a single framework for economic and political co-operation (see above 3.4.1.2) and to improve the institutional system, in the light of experience, so as to make it more efficient and democratic.[100] Once again the focus was to be on the need to extend the opportunity to use qualified majority voting in the Council, to improve the preconditions for an efficient exercise of implementing powers, and, finally, to enhance the powers of the European Parliament (cf. above 3.3.4.3 and 3.4.1.1).

In respect of the issue which is most relevant for present purposes, the exercise of implementing powers, it has already been noted that the Commission and the European Parliament were far from content with the arrangement that had been adopted by the previous Conference (see above 4.2.3). The developments which had taken place since then had only strengthened their convictions (see above 4.3.1). Therefore, even if important differences of opinion persisted, the Commission and the European Parliament were brought together by a strong feeling that something still had to be changed. A fundamental point of departure for both of them was the insistence on an arrangement which gave the Commission a greater responsibility of its own: for the Commission, this was a precondition for speed and efficiency and for the European Parliament it was the natural reaction against a development which it felt would lead to the erosion of its supervisory powers and right to participation in the process for adoption of legislation.

Encouraged by the support of the European Parliament and, perhaps more importantly, by some initial signs of governmental approval, the Commission presented, in its contribution to the Intergovernmental Conference, a proposal aimed at a fundamental overhaul of the existing arrangement for exercise of implementing powers. This was the proposal to introduce a hierarchy of legal acts similar to that existing in the national systems.[101] Based on ideas which had been set out by the

---

[100] The agenda was laid down by the European Council in Dublin on 25 and 26 June 1990 and in Rome on 14 and 15 December 1990. See General Report 1990, above Ch 4, n 5.

[101] See Commission Contributions to the IGC 1991, in *Bulletin EC* Supplement 2-1991. It may be noted that both the European Council in Dublin on 25 and 26 June 1990 and the European Council in Rome on 14 and 15 December 1990 had come out in favour of giving the Commission a greater executive part to play in the implementation of Community policies.

European Parliament as early as in 1984 in its Draft Treaty on European Union (see above 3.3.4.1), the proposal was so ambitious that it must have been intended to initiate a debate rather than to present a solution which the Governments could realistically be expected to accept.[102] Nevertheless, since it sought to deal with several of those aspects which are central to the present discussion and, it is submitted, is likely to reappear in the future, it is worth closer examination.

4.3.2.2   *The proposal for a hierarchy of legal acts*

In general terms the proposal presented by the Commission meant that a number of amendments should be made to the EEC Treaty which would enable a clear distinction to be made between different types of legal acts in accordance with their substance or quality and to link that to the procedure for their adoption. As an integral aspect of this, it was argued that the opportunity should be taken to do away with the Directive (which the Commission felt had developed into 'a hybrid instrument of ambiguous status') and to introduce instead a new category of legal act: the Law.[103] Clearly, the proposal had been designed to ensure the Commission a greater responsibility for the adoption of implementing measures of general and permanent effect. But when trying to 'sell' the idea, the Commission preferred to emphasize that it would place institutional relations on 'a balanced footing' and strengthen the role of the European Parliament by removing 'matters of detail' from its agenda.[104]

The most central element of the proposal was to be found in the notion of 'implementation' which was negatively, and indeed vaguely, defined. As set out in a proposed amendment to Article 189 EEC, the new Laws would be

[102] See European Parliament Resolution of 14 February 1984 on the Draft Treaty establishing the European Union (OJ 1984 C 77/53). See also, more directly linked to the up-coming Intergovernmental Conference, European Parliament Resolution of 11 July 1990 on the Intergovernmental Conference in the context of the Parliament's strategy for European Union (OJ 1990 C 231/97); European Parliament Resolution of 12 December 1990 on the constitutional basis of European Union (OJ 1991 C 19/65), in particular paragraphs 45–49; and European Parliament Resolution of 13 December 1990 on the executive powers of the Commission (commitology) and the role of the Commission in the Community's external relations (OJ 1991 C 19/273).

[103] See Commission Contributions to the IGC 1991, in *Bulletin EC* Supplement 2-1991, point 3.2.2.

[104] Another 'selling' argument was that the proposal, if adopted, should 'make it possible to clarify the system of legal acts, thereby making it easier for national parliaments and authorities to take them into consideration, and to ensure that the principle of subsidiarity was adhered to.' See Commission Contributions to the IGC 1991, above Ch 4, n 103.

used in all fields of co-operation to determine 'the fundamental principles, general guidelines and basic elements of the measures to be taken for their implementation.'[105] All other matters should be considered as 'implementation' and would be covered by regulations or decisions.[106] The practical significance of this was above all a procedural one: whereas the adoption of Laws should be reserved for the Council and the European Parliament, acting together in accordance with a new co-decision procedure, the adoption of regulations and decisions would be left to the Commission.[107]

In order to provide an unambiguous basis for its greater responsibility, in the proposal the Commission had taken up the idea again that an amendment should be made to Article 155 EEC (see above 3.4.2).[108] Since this required that the amendment which had been made to Article 145 EEC by the Single European Act be deleted—and with it the legal basis for the Council to require 'some kind of emergency procedure for dealing with cases of political difficulty'—a new Article 189b EEC would need to be introduced instead according to which:

A law may provide that, in the exercise of the powers referred to in the fourth indent of Article 155, the Commission shall be assisted by an advisory

[105] According to a proposed amendment to Article 189 EEC (1987): '[a] law shall have general application. It shall be binding in its entirety; any provisions which do not call for implementing measures shall be directly applicable in all Member States. Action to be taken to apply the provisions of this Treaty shall be defined by laws. Laws shall determine the fundamental principles, general guidelines and basic elements of the measures to be taken for their implementation. Laws shall determine *inter alia* the rights and obligations of individuals and firms and the nature of the guarantees they should enjoy in every Member State.' See Commission Contributions to the IGC 1991, above Ch 4, n 103. It is noteworthy that an explicit reference was made to the words used by the Court of Justice in Case 25/70, above Ch 2, n 244. Cf. also the ruling in the pending Case C-240/90 above Ch 4, n 54.

[106] See Commission Contributions to the IGC 1991, above Ch 4, n 103.

[107] See the proposed Article 189a EEC. In comparison with the co-operation procedure introduced by the SEA the new co-decision procedure would put the Council and the European Parliament on an equal basis by granting them both express power of rejection at the final stage of the procedure, which would prevent an act being adopted. See Commission Contributions to the IGC 1991, above Ch 4, n 103, points 3.2.2 and 3.3.2.

[108] See Commission Contributions to the IGC 1991, above Ch 4, n 103, at p. 117 (and point 3.2.4). According to the proposal, Article 155 EEC (1987) would be amended so as to provide that: 'In order to ensure the proper functioning of the Union, the Commission shall ... adopt, in the manner provided for in Article 189b, the regulations and take the decisions necessary to implement laws, without prejudice to the provisions of Article 189b(1) conferring a power of substitution on the European Parliament and the Council. It shall also adopt the administrative provisions necessary to implement the regulations.'

committee composed of representatives of the Member States, whose role shall be to deliver an opinion on the draft of the measures to be taken; where the measure to be taken is a regulation, a law may provide that the Commissions shall be assisted by a management committee and that in the event of the Committee delivering a negative opinion by the majority provided for in the first indent of the second subparagraph of Article 148(2), the Council acting by a qualified majority, may take a different decision within a given period.[109]

One of the implications of this was that the regulatory committee procedure would be abolished. This 'loss' the proposal sought to compensate through the establishment of a new 'substitution mechanism' of which the Council and the European Parliament could avail themselves at the stage preceding entry into force of a regulation.[110] In principle this meant that the Council and the European Parliament would be permitted to act in place of the Commission if they considered that the Commission was exceeding its powers or straying from the guidelines. According to the envisaged procedure, which would apply as an alternative to the use of advisory or regulatory committee procedures, the Commission would forward the text of the Regulation to the Council and the European Parliament.[111] Within a limited period, the Council and the European Parliament would then be able to block its entry into force. If either institution exercised this option the Commission could adopt a new regulation itself or present a proposal for a regulation which would be adopted in the same way as a law.[112]

---

[109] The second paragraph of the proposed Article 189b EEC. See Commission Contributions to the IGC 1991, above Ch 4, n 103, point 3.2.4. Quote from the Report of the Three Wise Men, above Ch 3, n 145, at p. 47.

[110] See Commission Contributions to the IGC 1991, above Ch 4, n 103, point 3.2.5.1.

[111] See the first paragraph of the proposed Article 189b(1) EEC according to which: '1. Where a regulation implements a law, a power of substitution shall be reserved to the European Parliament and the Council in all cases where no provision is made for recourse to one of the procedures referred to in paragraph 2. The following procedure shall apply: (i) the Commission shall adopt the regulation in question and forward it to the European Parliament and the Council; (ii) the Commission regulations shall enter into force on expiry of a period of two months reckoned from the date of transmission unless the European Parliament, by a majority of its members, or the Council, acting by a qualified majority, rejects the measure within that period; (iii) in that event the Commission may either adopt a new regulation, which shall be subject to the substitution procedure, or submit a proposal for a regulation; in the latter case the procedure laid down in Article 189a shall apply.'

[112] See Commission Contributions to the IGC 1991, above Ch 4, n 103, point 3.2.5.1. As reasoned by the Commission, this solution would come into play above all in cases of a

For the sake of clarity, it should be noted that the proposal envisaged that the implementation of a law, even if it was presumed to be a matter for the Commission, should also be able to be entrusted 'in whole or in part to the Member States, acting in accordance with their own constitutional requirements.'[113] As the President of the Commission, Jacques Delors, emphasized, 'here the task would be to adopt the essential function of the directive, to give it its original meaning, leaving the choice of ways to attain the objective open; in this case, national parliaments are necessarily involved in the Community process, instead of being, as all too often at present, mere recording chambers.'[114] In such cases each law would specify the division of tasks between the Member States, on the one hand, and the Commission, on the other.[115]

4.3.2.3 The Treaty on European Union

When the result of the Intergovernmental Conference—the new Treaty on European Union (EU)—was signed in Maastricht on 7 February 1992, it became clear that the Governments had been far from willing to accept the logic underlying the proposal for a hierarchy of legal acts.[116] Not only had the amendments suggested by the Commission been completely ignored but a declaration had been made in which the Governments manifested their unanimous support for the existing order of legal acts.[117] In this Declaration it was emphasized 'that it must be for each Member State to determine how the provisions of Community law can best be

wide divergence of opinion between the European Parliament and the Council or between one of these institutions and the Commission.

[113] The last sentence of the proposed amendment to Article 189 EEC. See Commission Contributions to the IGC 1991, above Ch 4, n 103, point 3.2.3.

[114] See Contribution to the debate on the Principle of Subsidiarity, held at the European Institute for Public Administration (EIPA); Maastricht on 21 March 1991. Reference in Jacqué, above Ch 1, n 5, at p. 59. Cf. Commission Contributions to the IGC 1991, above Ch 4, n 103, point 3.2.3.

[115] See Commission Contributions to the IGC 1991, above Ch 4, n 103, point 3.2.3. As explained by the Commission, the main criteria applicable to this division of tasks will be the extent of the need for uniformity given the objective to be achieved to comply with a law—that is to say the requirements of non-discrimination and legal certainty—and the relative complexity of the matter being dealt with.

[116] See Treaty of 7 February 1992 on European Union (OJ 1992 C 191/1). Cf. Jacqué, above Ch 1, n 5, at p. 67.

[117] See Declaration No 19 attached to the Treaty of 7 February 1992 on European Union on the implementation of Community law (OJ 1992 C 191/102).

enforced in the light of its own particular institutions, legal system and other circumstances.'

But clear as this may seem, the Governments were obviously aware of the likelihood that a number of problems would persist and that it would be necessary, therefore, to consider a further reform. For that reason, a provision had been included in the Treaty on European Union in which it was explained that a new intergovernmental conference would be convened in 1996.[118] This would permit the Governments to make a new examination of the question 'to what extent it might be possible to review the classification of Community acts with a view to establishing an appropriate hierarchy between the different categories of act.'[119]

Even if it had left the existing arrangement for exercise of implementing powers untouched, the Treaty on European Union was to have far-reaching implications for the future development. The reason for this was to be found in the establishment of the so-called co-decision procedure.[120] Under the original consultation procedure and the later co-operation procedure, the Council was given sole responsibility to decide the content of legislation (see above 3.4.1.2). It was quite natural, therefore, that the Council should also be permitted to decide the conditions for the exercise of implementing powers. These were but one part of the contents of, for example, a regulation. Through the introduction of the new co-decision procedure, however, the European Parliament was granted an opportunity to participate in the negotiations and, if necessary, block legislation from being adopted. For the first time, therefore, the European Parliament was in a position to assert its demands.

Before the implications of the new co-decision procedure for the exercise of implementing powers are examined, it should be noted, briefly, that prior to the entry into force of the Treaty on European Union, another attempt was made to ease the tension, along similar lines to the Plumb-Delors Agreement (see above 4.2.3). In an agreement concluded between the new President of the European Parliament, Egon Klepsch, and the Commissioner responsible for regional policy, Bruce Millan, the Commission promised that it would forward to the

---

[118] See Article N(2) EU (1993), in which it was explained that '[a] conference of representatives of the governments of the Member States shall be convened in 1996.'

[119] See Declaration No 16 attached to the Treaty of 7 February 1992 on European Union on the hierarchy of Community Acts (OJ 1992 C 191/101).   [120] See Article 189b EC (1993).

European Parliament all draft measures relating to the implementation of structural funds.[121] According to the terms of the Klepsch-Millan Agreement, the Commission would also 'take the European Parliament's requests into consideration whenever possible in order to take them into account when deciding on each initiative.'

4.3.3 The implications of the new co-decision procedure

4.3.3.1 An intensification of resistance

The Treaty on European Union entered into force on 1 November 1993. Only a few weeks later a resolution was adopted in which the European Parliament set out its views on the implications of the co-decision procedure for the future exercise of implementing powers.[122] As explained therein, the new procedure was fundamentally different from the existing consultation and co-operation procedure since it implied the 'full equality' of the European Parliament.[123] Therefore, it was no longer acceptable for the Council—one of the two branches of the legislative authority—to reserve an exclusive competence over the exercise powers of political supervision. Within those fields where the co-decision procedure was to apply, the Council was now obliged to secure the support of the European Parliament, both when laying down conditions (type of

---

[121] See Code of Conduct of 12 July 1993 on the implementation of structural policies by the Commission (OJ 1993 C 255/19).

[122] See European Parliament Resolution of 16 December 1993 on questions of commitology relating to the entry into force of the Maastricht Treaty (OJ 1994 C 20/176). Based on Report of 6 December 1993 drawn up on behalf of the Committee on Institutional Affairs on questions of committology relating to the entry into force of the Maastricht Treaty (rapporteur: Biagio de Giovanni) EP Doc A3-417/93 (see also Report of 15 July 1994 drawn up on behalf of the delegation to the Conciliation Committee on the text confirmed by the Council following the conciliation procedure on the proposal for a European Parliament and Council Directive on the application of Open Network Provision (ONP) to voice telephony (rapporteur: Imelda Read) EP Doc A4-1/94, p. 11). See Bradley, above Ch 2, n 216, at pp. 237–238; and Blumann, C., *Le Parlement européen et la comitologie: une complication pour la Conférence inter-gouvernementale de 1996* (1996) 32 *RTDE* 1, at pp. 8–11.

[123] Cf. the Read Report, above Ch 4, n 122, at pp. 9 and 10: '[t]hus the co-decision procedure is fundamentally different in nature from the co-operation procedure; it is a joint act of the Council and Parliament following a shuttle procedure in which the two institutions are on an equal footing. Parliament no longer delivers an opinion which the Council may or may not accept, as it alone sees fit; Parliament participates as of right in the preparation of legislation.'

committee procedure to be followed) and when deciding on matters transferred to it if the Commission had not been given the necessary support of a committee operating under the management or regulatory committee procedure (see above 4.2.2.2).

Obviously eager to escape the narrow framework introduced by the Single European Act, the European Parliament argued further that the exercise of implementing powers with respect to acts adopted under the co-decision procedure could not be considered to fall within the scope of Article 145 EC (1993), since this Article referred only to 'acts which the Council adopts' alone (see above 3.4.2.2). According to the European Parliament, this meant that there was now a lacunae in the EC Treaty: if everything had been done correctly, '[w]hen the draftsmen . . . decided to introduce co-decision into the Maastricht Treaty, Articles 145 and 155 should have immediately been amended, technically speaking, but this did not occur.'[124] This, indeed, was an omission which would have to be dealt with as soon as a new opportunity arose for revision of the EC Treaty (cf. above 4.3.2.3). But pending this, a 'general decision' needed to be agreed which could provide a temporary basis for the exercise of implementing powers with respect to acts adopted under the co-decision procedure.

Not surprisingly, the European Parliament had a rather clear idea of what the contents of that general decision ought to be. First, it should permit only the establishment of 'consultative committees' consisting of national experts 'with responsibility for advising the Commission specifically on the impact of the decisions in the various national or local systems.' Then, irrespective of the establishment of such committees, the European Parliament needed to be granted a legal right to be informed about matters expected to lead to the adoption of implementing 'legislation' and to state its opinion (cf. above 4.2.3.1). Parallel to this *droit de regard*, a mechanism would be introduced—similar to that foreseen by the Commission in its proposal for a hierarchy of legal acts—which would enable the Council and the European Parliament to cancel implementing legislation and, then, require the Commission 'to formulate a new decision, taking account of any guidelines approved by the two arms of the legislative authority' (see above 4.3.2.2).[125]

---

[124]   See Debates of the European Parliament on 15 September 1998 (OJ 1998 C 313/17).

[125]   One important difference from the solution envisaged by the Commission was that the European Parliament wanted the substitution mechanism to be 'general' (while the Commission only wanted it to be an alternative to the committee procedures). Another important difference was that it should only enable the Council or the European Parliament to request the other

4.3.3.2   A breakdown in institutional co-operation

The ideas expressed by the European Parliament were well-received by the Commission, which promised to look into the possibility of revising the existing rules.[126] But, apparently, this was not sufficient. The Council had always been frosty with regard to the suggestion that the European Parliament should be permitted to share its powers of political supervision and there were no signs of any willingness to accept the argument that the exercise of implementing powers with respect to acts adopted under the co-decision procedure could not be considered to fall within the scope of Article 145 EC (1993).[127] Therefore, weary of waiting for whatever miracle the Commission might be hoped to perform, the European Parliament decided to launch an offensive which would force the Council to take its demands seriously.[128]

Since the entry into force of Council Decision 87/7373/EEC, the European Parliament had systematically sought to use its right of participation in the adoption of legislation to delete any provision for a regulatory committee procedure and to replace it by a less restrictive one (see above 4.2.3.1). But as long as it lacked the formal power to assert its view this would rarely lead to any visible result (see above 3.4.1.2). Importantly, through the introduction of the new co-decision procedure, the European Parliament was enabled to take an active part in the negotiations on legislation and, if it was not satisfied, block the adoption. This was the opportunity it had always been waiting for: during the first year of operation of the co-decision procedure 'the issue was fought out on each individual item of legislation' and disputes over 'comitology' became a central feature of most negotiations.[129]

nstitution to 'agree to repeal' the implementing legislation. As envisaged by the European Parliament, 'the Council, by a qualified majority, or Parliament, by a majority of the votes of its component members, may ask the other institution to cancel an implementing legislative decision of the Commission; if the other institution, by the above mentioned majority, agrees to the proposal, the implementing legislative decision should be cancelled and the Commission should be required to formulate a new decision, taking account of any guidelines approved by the two arms of the legislative authority; the cancelling proposal should not have a suspensive effect on the Commission's decision.'

[126] See the explanatory memorandum of the Draft Inter-Institutional Agreement of 19 April 1994, below Ch 4, n 139.

[127] See Jacqué, above Ch 1, n 5, at pp. 67–68. See also Corbett, above Ch 3, n 188, at p. 348.

[128] See e.g. Corbett, above Ch 3, n 188, at pp. 258 and 347; and Bradley, above Ch 2, n 216, at p. 238.   [129] See Corbett, above Ch 3, n 188, at pp. 258 and 347–348.

The precedent was set in the very first case dealt with under the co-decision procedure: the proposal for a Council Directive on the application of open network provision (ONP) to voice telephony.[130] In conformity with most existing legislation on harmonization of conditions for trade, the proposal envisaged a continuous co-operation with the national administration (cf. above 3.3.2.2). This was manifested, most notably, in a provision where powers were conferred on the Commission to determine 'the modifications necessary to adapt... the Directive to new technological developments or to changes in market demand' in accordance with an advisory committee procedure. This was in line with the intention to give that procedure 'a predominant place' within the field of the internal market (see above 4.2.2.2) and fully backed by the European Parliament. But nevertheless the Council took the position that the proposal should be amended so as to replace the advisory committee procedure by a regulatory committee procedure (IIIa).[131] The position taken by the Council in this case reflected what had often happened in previous cases, i.e. the solution embraced by the legislation in its final form or version.[132] But this time, before the

---

[130] See Corbett, R., Jacobs, F., and Shackleton, M., *The European Parliament* (John Harper Publishing 2000), at p. 258; Jacqué, above Ch 1, n 5, at p. 64; and Falke and Winter, above Ch 1, n 11, at pp. 564–565. See Commission Proposal of 28 August 1992 for a Council Directive on the application of open network provision (ONP) to voice telephony (OJ 1992 C 263/20) and amended Commission Proposal of 7 May 1993 for a Council Directive on the application of open network provision (ONP) to voice telephony (OJ 1993 C 147/12). It may be noted that the proposed Directive was part of a wider policy aimed at the harmonization of conditions for access by all users to public telephone networks. Prior steps had been taken through the adoption, first, of the 'framework' Council Directive 90/387/EEC of 28 June 1990 on the establishment of the internal market for telecommunications services through the implementation of open network provision (OJ 1990 L 192/1) and, then, of Council Directive 92/44/EEC of 5 June 1992 on the application of open network provision (ONP) to leased lines (OJ 1992 L 165/27). See *Bulletin EC* 7/8-1992, paragraph 1.3.86; *Bulletin EC* 11-1992, paragraph 1.3.92; and *Bulletin EC* 3-1993, paragraph 1.2.75. Cf. also Council Resolution of 17 December 1992 on the assessment of the situation in the Community telecommunications sector (OJ 1993 C 2/5); and Council Resolution of 22 July 1993 on the review of the situation in the telecommunications sector and the need for further development in that market (OJ 1993 C 213/1).

[131] In respect of the relevant cases of exercise of implementing powers (adaptation to technological development or changes in market demand). In some other cases the advisory committee procedure would continue to apply. See *Bulletin EC* 5-1993, paragraph 1.2.77; and *Bulletin EC* 6-1993, paragraph 1.2.124.

[132] See, for example, the solution that had been adopted in respect of the previous Council Directive 90/387/EEC, above Ch 4, n 130; and Council Directive 92/44/EEC, above Ch 4,

Council could adopt an amended proposal the co-decision procedure entered into force.[133]

In a second opinion on 19 January 1994 the European Parliament asked for a number of amendments to be made which would give force to its demands as stated recently in the Resolution on the implications of the co-decision procedure for the future exercise of implementing powers (see above 4.3.3.1): a shift back to the original advisory committee procedure, the inclusion of provisions which would secure its *droit de regard*, and a substitution mechanism.[134] None of these amendments were accepted by the Council (or indeed the Commission).[135] Therefore, as required by the co-decision procedure, a 'conciliation committee' was convened to negotiate a solution. The importance of the matter was underlined by the fact that the delegation of the European Parliament was headed by its President, Egon Klepsch.[136]

130, against which the EP had unsuccessfully protested (subject to the co-operation procedure). See European Parliament Resolution of 26 May 1989 embodying the opinion of the European Parliament on the proposal from the Commission to the Council for a directive on the establishment of the internal market for telecommunications services through the implementation of Open Network Provision (OJ 1989 C 158/300); and European Parliament Resolution of 13 October 1991 embodying the opinion of the European Parliament on the Commission proposal for a Council Directive on the application of open network provision to leased lines (OJ 1991 C 305/61).

[133] The entry into force of the new Treaty entailed a change of legal basis and/or legislative procedure for certain Commission proposals pending before Parliament and the Council. See the List of proposals pending before the Council on 31 October 1993 for which entry into force of the Treaty on European Union will require a change in the legal base and/or a change in procedure (COM (93) 570 final). See also *Bulletin EU* 1/2-1994, point 1.7.5.

[134] See European Parliament Resolution of 19 January 1994 embodying the opinion of the European Parliament on the common position established by the Council with a view to the adoption of a European Parliament and Council directive on the application of open network provision (ONP) to voice telephony (OJ 1994 C 44/93).

[135] Apparently the Commission also rejected the amendments which were aimed at giving the European Parliament a supervisory role with respect to the exercise of implementing powers (a *droit de regard* and a substitution mechanism). The reasons were, first, that it felt that 'any changes to comitology procedures require an inter-institutional agreement which would cover in a horizontal way issues of comitology in the context of co-decision' and, second, that it considered it 'inappropriate to consult the European Parliament on detailed technical changes' (and that 'any significant major changes' would be dealt with in the normal legislative process). See the explanatory memorandum in the Opinion of the Commission of 1 March 1994 on the European Parliament's amendments to the Council's common position (COM (94) 48 final), at p. 2.

[136] See the Read Report, above Ch 4, n 122, at pp. 6–7.

But it soon became clear that the Council was not willing or, indeed, able to make any concessions and that the European Parliament was firmly intent to stick to its demands. Therefore, the final meeting of the conciliation committee ended in a deadlock. As a result, the Council formally reaffirmed its initial position which, in turn, was rejected by the European Parliament in a third and final reading on 19 July 1994.[137] Even if the European Parliament—for the first time in history—had managed to exercise a decisive influence over the legislative process, it was no triumph: much time and energy had been spent on an important proposal which, in the end, was not adopted.

4.3.3.3   *The proposal for a settlement*

It has been noted above that the Commission had promised the European Parliament to look into the possibility of revising the existing rules for exercise of implementing powers. Quite understandably, the ruthlessness with which the ONP-proposal was sacrificed helped the Commission to honour its commitment. In the debates preceding the vote on a second opinion (see above 4.3.3.2), an awareness had been demonstrated that this might only be the first in a series of events. Here the Commissioner responsible for telecommunications, Martin Bangemann, had tried to save his proposal by urging the MEPs not to fight their battle against 'comitology' on an individual item and to concentrate on the need for an appropriate horizontal solution.[138]

The first concrete step towards such a solution was taken a few months later when the Commission—in the midst of the unsuccessful negotiations on the ONP-proposal—presented a draft inter-institutional agreement 'on the rules for exercising the powers to implement acts adopted jointly by the European Parliament and the Council.'[139] This

---

[137] See European Parliament Decision of 19 July 1994 on the text confirmed by the Council following the conciliation procedure on the proposal for a European Parliament and Council Directive on the application of open network provision (ONP) to voice telephony (OJ 1994 C 261/13). Based on the Read Report, above Ch 4, n 122. See *Bulletin EU* 1/2-1994, paragraph 1.2.102; *Bulletin EU* 3-1994, paragraph 1.2.102; and *Bulletin EU* 7/8-1994, paragraph 1.2.101.

[138] See *Europe* (bulletin quotidien) 19 January 1994, at p. 9.

[139] See Draft Inter-Institutional Agreement between the European Parliament, the Council and the Commission of 19 April 1994 on the rules for exercising the powers to implement acts adopted jointly by the European Parliament and the Council in accordance with the procedure laid down in Article 189b of the EC Treaty (SEC(94) 645 final). See Jacqué, above Ch 1, n 5, at p. 68; Monar, J., Inter-institutional Agreements: the Phenomenon and its New Dynamics

supported the argument that there was a lacuna in the EC Treaty which would have to be dealt with by the next Intergovernmental Conference and suggested a temporary solution (cf. above 4.3.3.1). Accordingly a rule would be established, by means of inter-institutional agreement, which provided, by analogy with Article 145 EC (1993), that implementing powers with respect to acts adopted under the co-decision procedure would be conferred on the Commission and that special 'principles and rules' would be established for the use of committee procedures.

The key element of the envisaged principles and rules was found in a qualitative distinction between implementing acts as containing either legislative' or 'non-legislative' measures. Over the years, the European Parliament had made it clear that it had no wish 'to interfere in the details of the Commission's executive operations' and that it was only interested in matters which were politically significant.[140] As suggested by the Commission, therefore, the existing types of advisory and management committee procedure could be used for the adoption of implementing acts containing non-legislative measures and there was no need for modification (but, importantly, the restrictive variant of the management procedure (IIb) and the regulatory committee procedure should be excluded). For the adoption of implementing acts containing legislative measures a new type of procedure would be introduced in accordance with which draft measures were to be submitted to both an advisory committee and the European Parliament. Then, taking 'full account' of their opinions, the Commission would adopt the measure which was to apply immediately. In addition, a substitution mechanism would be introduced which would make it possible for the Council and the European Parliament to agree to repeal an implementing act. In this formulation, the substitution mechanism combined some of the Commission's older ideas with those of the European Parliament (see above 4.3.2.2 and 4.3.3.2).[141]

after Maastricht (1994) 31 *CMLRev* 693 and Snyder, F., Inter-institutional Agreements: Forms and Constitutional Limitations, in Winter, G., *Sources and Categories of European Union Law: a comparative and reform perspective* (Nomos 1996), at p. 453.

[140] Debates of the European Parliament of 9 July 1986 above Ch 4, n 1, at pp. 118–119. Cf. also the Plumb-Delors Agreement of 14 March 1988, above Ch 4, n 75; and European Parliament Resolution of 16 December 1993, above Ch 4, n 122.

[141] In that case the Commission could adopt a new implementing act or present a proposal for an act to be adopted by the Council and the European Parliament in accordance with the co-decision procedure. Note the main differences: i. shorter period (one month instead of two in

Although presented as a pragmatic attempt to resolve the 'differences of opinion' that were presently impeding the operation of the co-decision procedure, the agreement, if accepted, would have left the mediator, the Commission itself, in a stronger position than it had been in before. Clearly, this was a development which the Governments were not very enthusiastic about (cf. above 4.3.2.3), and not surprisingly, therefore, the draft agreement was rejected.[142] The suspicions regarding the Commission's own interest in the matter were spelt out some years later by the Director of the Council Legal Service, Jean-Paul Jacqué. In his view, 'under the cover of contributing to resolving a dispute, the Commission was first and foremost seeking to free itself of the constraints of Council Decision 87/373/EEC and secure largely uncontrolled implementing powers to itself.'[143] It should be noted also that the Council was far from willing to accept the basic argument that there was a lacuna in the EC Treaty but insisted that Article 145 EC (1993) applied 'to all Council acts, including those adopted in accordance with the [co-decision] procedure.'[144]

its proposal to the IGC), thus intended to keep up the speed; ii. the Council and the European Parliament would have to agree (not in its proposal to the IGC but taken up from the European Parliament); iii. the Commission could adopt a new implementing act, which would be subject to the same procedure, or present a proposal for an act to be adopted by the Council and the European Parliament in accordance with the co-decision procedure (basically the same as the Commission proposal to the IGC but different from the proposal of the European Parliament, according to which the Commission would be required to formulate a new decision, taking account of any guidelines approved by the Council and the European Parliament).

[142] Apparently, the Council was particularly concerned with the fact that the solution envisaged in the draft agreement would have made it very difficult to reject an implementing measure adopted by the Commission, since it required agreement from the European Parliament and the Council, something likely to happen very rarely. See Jacqué, above Ch 1, n 5, at p. 68.

[143] Jacqué, above Ch 1, n 5, at p. 68.

[144] See Jacqué, above Ch 1, n 5, at pp. 67–68. According to Jean-Paul Jacqué: 'in formal terms, acts adopted according to the [co-decision] procedure are indeed acts adopted by the Council, as shown by the wording used in all the legal bases that refer to the [co-decision] procedure: "the Council, deciding in accordance with the Article [co-decision] procedure." There is, therefore, no question of a Treaty lacunae, and Article [202] EC does apply to all Council acts, including those adopted in accordance with the [co-decision] procedure.' For a comment see Bradley, above Ch 1, n 76, at p. 72; and Corbett, above Ch 3, n 188, at p. 348. It should be noted that this argument has recently been rejected by the Court of Justice. According to the Court: 'Article 202 EC must be held to refer both to measures adopted by the Council alone and to measures adopted by the Council together with the European Parliament under the co-decision procedure.' See Case C-378/00 *Commission v European Parliament and Council* [2003] ECR I-937 (Judgment of 21 January 2003), paragraph 40; and Case C-259/95 *European Parliament v Council* [1997] ECR I-5303 (Judgment of 2 October 1997), paragraphs 24 and 26.

4.3.3.4 A Modus Vivendi: *the terms of a temporary cease-fire*

However right the Council may have been in its suspicions about the Commission trying to use the battle over 'comitology' to move its own position forward, there was a growing 'risk of permanent conflict' which needed to be avoided.[145] Therefore, following a period of intense discussions under the German Presidency, the Council finally managed to come up with a proposal for a cease-fire which was acceptable to everyone.[146] First of all, the Governments committed themselves to examine the question of the exercise of implementing powers in respect of acts adopted under the co-decision procedure in the Intergovernmental Conference scheduled for 1996 (see above 4.3.2.3). Then, for the intermediate period, a *Modus Vivendi* would be established, the terms of which would meet the demand of the European Parliament for a *droit de regard* but preserve the existing arrangement for exercise of implementing powers.

The *Modus Vivendi* was signed on 20 December 1994 by the President of the Council, Klaus Kinkel, the President of the European Parliament, Nicole Fontaine, and the President to the Commission, Jacques Delors.[147] Only a few days before, a budgetary decision had been taken by the European Parliament to place a substantial share of the proposed funding for committees in the reserve (see below 4.3.3.5). This, indeed, provided a strong incentive for the speedy handling of the matter. Essentially, the provisions of the *Modus Vivendi* were focused on a set of 'guidelines' for the adoption of draft implementing acts of a general nature.[148] Accordingly:

4. The appropriate committee of the European Parliament shall be sent, at the same time and under the same conditions as the committee referred to in the basic act, any draft general implementing act submitted by the Commission and the timetable for it. The Commission shall notify the

[145] See General Report on the Activities of the European Union 1994 (Office for Official Publications 1995), at p. 411 (point 1175).

[146] See General Report 1994, above Ch 4, n 145, p. 411 (point 1175); and Bradley above Ch 2, n 216, at p. 239.

[147] See *Modus Vivendi* of 20 December 1994 between the European Parliament, the Council and the Commission concerning the implementing measures for acts adopted in accordance with the procedure laid down in Article 189b of the EC Treaty (OJ 1996 C 102/1). See *Bulletin EU* 12-1994; and General Report 1994, above Ch 4, n 145, p. 411 (point 1175).

[148] It may be noted that, according to the *Modus Vivendi* (above Ch 4, n 147), the 'guidelines' should 'in no way prejudice the positions of principle expressed by the three institutions.' Cf. the view of Kieran Bradley at the European Parliament Legal Service, according to which the preference for a *Modus Vivendi*, as opposed to inter-institutional agreement, could be read as indicating

appropriate European Parliament committee if a specific measure needs to be adopted urgently and shall also notify it of any other possible difficulty. The appropriate European Parliament committee shall undertake to use urgent procedure where necessary. The Commission shall inform the appropriate European Parliament committee when measures adopted or envisaged by the Commission are not in accordance with the opinion delivered by the committee referred to in the basic act or when, in the absence of an opinion, the Commission must submit a proposal to the Council regarding a measure to be taken.

5. The Council shall adopt a draft general implementing act which has been referred to it in accordance with an implementing procedure only after:

—informing the European Parliament, setting a reasonable time limit for obtaining its opinion, and

—in the event of an unfavourable opinion, taking due account of the European Parliament's point of view without delay, in order to seek a solution in the appropriate framework.

The act shall in any case be adopted by the deadlines laid down in the specific provisions of the basic act.

6. In the context of this *modus vivendi*, the Commission shall take account as far as possible of any comments by the European Parliament and shall keep it informed at every stage of the procedure of the action which it intends to take on them, so as to enable the Parliament to assume its own responsibilities in full knowledge of the facts.

It is clear that these guidelines included elements which had never been formalized in the two older agreements (cf. above 4.2.3.1 and 4.3.2.3). Noteworthy, in that respect, was the undertaking by the Council not to 'adopt a draft general implementing act which has been referred to it in accordance with an implementing procedure' without first informing the European Parliament and providing it with an opportunity to state its opinion. Even if the situations to which this was to apply were extremely rare (see above 4.3.1.1), the symbolic significance was considerable: for the first time the Council had agreed to place itself under a direct obligation to the European Parliament.[149]

'a failure to agree on the parameters of the dispute, with an acceptance of the fact that political life and legislative activity must nonetheless go on.' Bradley, above Ch 1, n 76, at p. 72. Bradley argues, however, that the *Modus Vivendi* was capable of having binding legal effects (at pp. 73–74).

[149] For a concrete example of a parliamentary consultation under the *Modus Vivendi* (above Ch 4, n 147), see European Parliament Resolution of 14 May 1998 embodying Parliament's opinion on the proposal for a Council Regulation concerning the compulsory indication on the labelling of certain foodstuffs produced from genetically modified organisms (OJ 1998 C 167/187).

As a solution to the most immediate problems, the *Modus Vivendi* was successful and achieved the aim of bringing about a temporary cease-fire. This was soon confirmed in the discussions on a Directive on the application of open network provision to voice telephony (cf. above 4.3.3.2). Following a declaration by the European Parliament that it was willing to consider 'an *ad hoc* solution' to the problem of comitology, on 1 February 1995 a new proposal was submitted by the Commission.[150] Like the original one, this proposal also envisaged that the Commission should be empowered to determine 'the modifications necessary to adapt [the Directive] to technological developments or to changes in market demand' in accordance with the advisory committee procedure. Once again the Council took the position that the proposal should be amended so as to provide instead for a regulatory committee procedure (IIIa). This was something which the European Parliament now found less difficult to digest and its only demand was that a *note explicative* should be included in the Preamble of the Directive in which a reference was made to the fact that an agreement had been reached on a *Modus Vivendi* concerning the exercise of implementing powers with respect to acts adopted in accordance with the co-decision procedure.[151] This was accepted by the Council and the Directive was finally adopted.[152]

4.3.4   The Court of Justice strikes a balance

4.3.4.1   A continuous threat to efficiency

Even if the *Modus Vivendi* was a step forward for the European Parliament, the fact remained that it had got very little of what it had

---

[150] See, respectively, European Parliament Resolution of 30 September 1994 on the need for further action by the Community in the field of ONP-voice telephony (OJ 1994 C 305/147); and Commission Proposal of 1 February 1995 for a European Parliament and Council Directive on the application of open network provision (ONP) to voice telephony (OJ 1995 C 122/4). See *Bulletin EU* 1/2-1995, paragraph 1.3.10.

[151] See European Parliament Decision 95/231/EC of 26 October 1995 on the common position established by the Council with a view to the adoption of a European Parliament and Council Directive on the application of open network provision (ONP) to voice telephony (OJ 1995 C 308/112).

[152] See European Parliament and Council Directive 95/62/EC of 13 December 1995 on the application of open network provision (ONP) to voice telephony (OJ 1995 L 321/6). It may be noted also that the Directive included a so-called review clause according to which: '[t]he European Parliament and the Council shall decide by 1 January 1998, on the basis of a proposal

requested.[153] Therefore, when approving the *Modus Vivendi*, the European Parliament adopted a restrained tone, describing it as 'a pragmatic and provisional means of dealing with the problems raised by the application of the [co-decision procedure] on the understanding that a definitive and fully democratic solution to these problems must be found at the 1996 Intergovernmental Conference.'[154] The full implications of this were to be seen a few years later when the European Parliament, unsatisfied with the way the matter had been dealt with in the Intergovernmental Conference (see below 4.3.6.3), found reasons to manifest the need for a more permanent solution and to sacrifice new proposals for legislation in order to sustain its demands.[155] One of the more significant examples of this can be found in the unsuccessful negotiations on a proposal of 17 July 1995 intended to improve the regulatory framework within the field of financial services (cf. below 5.4.1).[156] Almost three years after it had been presented, the proposal was finally rejected by the European Parliament: once again the stumbling block was comitology and the Council's insistence that the Commission should only be empowered to exercise

which the Commission will submit to them in good time, on the revision of this Directive to adapt it to the requirements of market liberalization.' See later European Parliament and Council Directive 98/10/EC of 26 February 1998 on the application of open network provision (ONP) to voice telephony and on universal service for telecommunications in a competitive environment (OJ 1998 L 101/24).

[153] See Jacqué, above Ch 1, n 5, at p. 69; and Bradley, above Ch 1, n 76, at p. 73.

[154] See European Parliament Resolution of 18 January 1995 on a decision of the European Parliament, the Council and the Commission on the detailed provisions governing the exercise of the European Parliament's right of inquiry and a *modus vivendi* between the European Parliament, the Council and the Commission concerning the implementing measures for acts adopted in accordance with the procedure laid down in Article 189b of the EC Treaty (OJ 1995 C 43/37).

[155] See e.g. Corbett, Jacobs, and Shackleton, above Ch 4, n 130, at p. 259; and the General Report on the Activities of the European Union 1998 (Office for Official Publications 1999), point 1027. Accordingly, 'a closer examination of the [co-decision] procedures shows that Parliament and the Council are divided above all on institutional matters, particularly the executive powers conferred on the Commission (committee procedure) and declarations entered in the minutes, on budget questions and on a number of political problems connected for example with ethics, the environment, consumer protection, health and social policy.'

[156] See Commission Proposal of 17 July 1995 for a European Parliament and Council Directive amending Council Directive 93/6/EEC of 15 March 1993 on the capital adequacy of investment firms and credit institutions and Council Directive 93/22/EEC of 10 May 1993 on investment services in the securities field (OJ 1995 C 253/19).

implementing powers subject to a regulatory committee procedure (cf. above 4.3.3.2).[157]

Importantly, the dissatisfaction of the European Parliament was far from limited to the situation now covered by the *Modus Vivendi*—the exercise of implementing powers within the field of application of the co-decision procedure—but it extended also to the situation in those 'old' fields where the consultation and co-operation procedures continued to apply.[158] Here, the *Modus Vivendi* had provided no reason for the European Parliament to give up its resistance, not even temporarily. Therefore, in order to put some weight behind its otherwise ineffectual demands with respect to comitology, the European Parliament began to make extensive use of its 'power to delay' (see above 4.4.1.3), in particular by postponing votes and insisting on re-consultation whenever amendments were introduced by the Council. An illustration of this can be found in the history of Council Directive 96/62/EC on ambient air quality assessment and management. The original proposal had been submitted by the Commission on 4 July 1994, but it was not until 22 May 1996 that the European Parliament delivered its final opinion.[159] Another illustration can be taken from the saga of Council Regulation 2053/93/EC/Euratom on the provision of technical assistance to economic reform and recovery in the independent States of the former Soviet Union and Mongolia. This will be returned to below (see below 4.3.4.2).

However justified the European Parliament's concern with comitology may have been, the harder it fought the more was done by the Council and, indeed, the Commission to circumvent it and to have matters of potential controversy dealt with in the form of implementing legislation. Somewhat paradoxically, therefore, the European Parliament became

---

[157] For an overview of the history of the proposal see the Legislative Observatory of the European Parliament (OEIL), at internet http://www.europarl.eu.int. See also *Bulletin EU* 4-1997, points 1.2.34 and 1.3.46.   [158] See Bradley, above Ch 2, n 216, at p. 232.

[159] See, for example, the history of Commission Proposal of 4 July 1994 for a Council Directive on ambient air quality assessment and management (OJ 1994 C 216/4). The proposal was approved by the European Parliament subject to amendments aimed *inter alia* at the replacement of a regulatory committee procedure responsible for updating the directive in line with scientific and technical progress by an advisory committee procedure. See European Parliament Decision 96/155/EC of 22 May 1996 on the common position established by the Council with a view to the adoption of a Council Directive on ambient air quality assessment and management (OJ 1996 C 166/63). Unsurprisingly, when the proposal was finally adopted by the Council, the amendments were ignored. See Council Directive 96/62/EC of 27 September 1996 on ambient air quality assessment and management (OJ 1996 L 296/55).

a driving force behind the very development it most wanted to resist. The usefulness of the simplified procedures for adoption of implementing legislation as a means to circumvent the European Parliament was acknowledged by Advocate General Philippe Léger on 14 February 1995. He stated that, '[t]he possibility of delegating is thus one element in the balance of powers between the Parliament and the other institutions which may find it a way of excluding the Parliament from the legislative process.'[160]

Even if everyone was aware of the practical considerations underlying the wish to circumvent the European Parliament, from a legal point of view this was only tolerated if the matters dealt with did not go beyond the limits of what could reasonably be characterized as 'implementation' and if the requirement was respected that 'the basic elements of the matter' were established in accordance with the normal procedures for adoption of legislation (see above 2.4.5.2). This was also emphasized by Philippe Léger. In his view, it was the 'ancillary or subordinate' character of implementing legislation which justified 'less formality in deciding on it.'[161] This meant that the opportunity to use the procedures for adoption of implementing legislation as a means of circumventing the European Parliament and, indeed, the opportunity for the European Parliament to resist this depended on a delicate balance, and the only one competent to strike that balance was the Court of Justice.

In its ruling on 29 October 1980 in Case 138/79 *Roquette Frères v Council*, the Court had explained that participation of the European Parliament in the process for adoption of legislation was an 'essential factor in the institutional balance' and an 'essential formality', disregard of which meant that the legislation in question was void.[162] For a long time, however, the legal significance of this was rather limited, since the European Parliament, if its right to participation was violated, had no standing to defend it before the Court. This, indeed, was manifested by the ruling in Case 302/87 *European Parliament v Council* in which the Court explained that the EEC Treaty did not enable it 'to recognise the capacity

---

[160] See the Opinion of Advocate General Léger in Case C-417/93, below Ch 4, n 180, at p. 1208 (paragraph 107).

[161] See the Opinion of Advocate General Léger in Case C-417/93, below, Ch 4, n 180, at p. 1208 (paragraph 107).

[162] See Case 138/79 *Roquette Frères v Council* [1980] ECR 3333 (Judgment of 29 October 1980), at p. 3360 (paragraph 33). See also Case 139/79 *Maizena v Council* [1980] ECR 3393 (Judgment of 29 October 1980), paragraph 34.

of the European Parliament to bring an action for annulment' (see above 4.2.3.1). If it wanted to defend its right by legal action, it had to rely on others and, then, take the opportunity to make an intervention.[163]

But, less than two years after its ruling in Case 302/87, the Court changed its mind and declared that an annulment action at the suit of the European Parliament was, indeed, admissible 'provided that the action seeks only to safeguard its prerogatives and that it is founded only on submissions alleging their infringement.'[164] The European Parliament did not delay in responding: in the next few years the Court of Justice was virtually flooded by applications from the European Parliament. Many of these related to matters of substance and the choice of legal basis for legislation, with the European Parliament attempting to push as much as possible towards fields of co-operation where its own position was more generously defined (from fields where the consultation procedure applied to fields where the co-operation procedure applied and, then, to fields where the co-decision procedure applied).[165] But more importantly, for present purposes, the applications were also concerned with procedural matters, with the European Parliament seeking to secure interpretations which would make it difficult for the Council and the Commission to circumvent it by means of the simplified procedures for adoption of implementing legislation.

4.3.4.2   A wide notion of implementation

In several rulings during the 1990s, the Court reconfirmed that the participation of the European Parliament in the adoption of legislation

---

[163] See e.g. Case 138/79, above Ch 4, n 162; Case 16/88, above Ch 4, n 77 (above 4.2.3.2); and Case C-155/91 *Commission v Council* [1993] ECR I-939 (Judgment of 17 March 1993), at p. 969. In the latter case the European Parliament intervened to seek the annulment of Council Directive 91/156/EEC (see above Ch 3, n 133) on the ground that the regulatory committee procedure provided for therein did not comply with the EEC Treaty. The Court found that the plea was based on grounds which were 'entirely unconnected' with those relied upon by the Commission and concluded that the intervention was inadmissible. See also Case 41/69, above Ch 2, n 237; Case 25/70, above Ch 2, n 244; and Case 5/77, above Ch 3, n 122. Cf. Bradley, above Ch 2, n 237, at p. 54.

[164] See Case C-70/88, above Ch 1, n 81, at p. 2073. For a discussion, see Bradley, K., Sense and Sensibility: Parliament v. Council Continued (1991) 16 *ELRev* 245. Importantly, this was also codified by the Treaty on European Union, in an amendment to Article 173 EC. Cf. above Ch 3, n 229.

[165] See e.g. Case C-187/93 *European Parliament v Council* [1994] ECR I-2857 (Judgment of 28 June 1994) and Case C-42/97 *European Parliament v Council* [1999] I-869 (Judgment of 23 February 1999).

was an essential factor in the institutional balance and specified that 'the duty to consult the Parliament in the cases provided for by the Treaty includes a requirement that the Parliament be re-consulted on each occasion on which the text finally adopted, viewed as a whole, departs substantially from the text on which the Parliament has already been consulted.'[166] But however comforting this may have sounded to the European Parliament, the Court also made it clear that it was not prepared to support the fight against the Council and the Commission. Instead, the result of many rulings were often such as to make it more difficult for the European Parliament to defend its position.

Thus, for example, the Court took the sting out of the notorious 'power to delay' by stating that the European Parliament was not entitled to complain when legislation was adopted before it had stated an opinion if it had 'failed to discharge its obligation to co-operate sincerely with the Council.'[167] The Court also reduced the usefulness to the European Parliament of its right to re-consultation when amendments were made to a proposal for legislation, by excluding from it the most controversial form of amendments: those relating to the type of committee procedure (see above 4.2.3.1 and 4.3.4.1). Although admitting that the choice of one type of committee or another may have 'a decisive influence' on the actual operation of an arrangement for exercise of implementing powers, the Court did not consider it so substantial as to justify re-consultation if 'the overall balance' of the powers allocated to the Commission and the Council was not 'decisively affected' by that choice.[168]

But most importantly, in a number of rulings the Court struck the balance between the notion of 'implementation'—the scope for legislation adopted in accordance with simplified procedures—and 'the basic elements'—requiring the use of normal procedures—in such a way as to encourage rather than prevent the Council and the Commission from outflanking the European Parliament. Of particular significance, in that

---

[166] Case C-417/93, below Ch 4, n 180. See also Case C-65/90 *European Parliament v Council* [1992] ECR I-4593, paragraph 16; Case C-388/92 *European Parliament v Council* [1994] ECR I-2067, paragraph 19; and Case C-65/93 *European Parliament v Council* [1995] ECR I-643, paragraph 21 (Judgment of 30 March 1995). Cf. also Case 41/69, above Ch 2, n 237, paragraph 178.

[167] See Case C-65/93, above Ch 4, n 166, paragraph 28. It may be noted that according to the Court (paragraph 23): 'inter-institutional dialogue, on which the consultation procedure in particular is based, is subject to the same mutual duties of sincere co-operation as those which govern relations between Member States and the Community institutions.' See also Case 204/86 *Greece v Council* [1988] ECR 5323 (Judgment of 27 September 1988), paragraph 16.

[168] See e.g. Case C-417/93, below Ch 4, n 180, at paragraphs 25 and 26.

respect, were the rulings in Case C-156/93 *European Parliament v Commission* and Case C-417/93 *European Parliament v Council.*

The background to Case C-156/93 *European Parliament v Commission*[169] is found in Council Regulation 2092/91/EEC on organic production of agricultural products.[170] In this Regulation, the conditions were set out under which the labelling and advertising of agricultural products may refer to organic production methods. These included the requirement that the product must not contain or must not have been treated with substances other than those set out in a so-called 'limitative list' (a list that appears in legislation of a technical nature. It contains the substances or items that are permitted or legal and all substances or items which do not appear in the list are thus illegal) placed in an Annex to the Regulation. The list would be established and updated in implementing legislation adopted by the Commission in co-operation with the 'Standing Committee on Organic Farming', following a regulatory committee procedure (IIIa).[171]

Importantly, when the European Parliament voted its opinion on the proposal which led to the adoption of Council Regulation 2092/91/EEC,[172] concerns were expressed that the use of genetically-modified micro-organisms (GMMOs) should be excluded from organic farming (and, as usual, that the regulatory committee procedure should be replaced by a management committee procedure).[173] In response to that, the Commission explained that it shared the concerns and assured the European Parliament that 'the technical work will be started so that an

---

[169] See Case C-156/93 *European Parliament v Commission* [1995] ECR I-2019 (Judgment of 13 July 1995). For a commentary see Nuffel, P. van, annotation (1995) 1 *ColJEL* 530; Constantinesco, V., annotation (1996) 123 *JDrInt* 459; and Schlacke, S., annotation (1995) 110 *DVer* 1288.

[170] See Council Regulation 2092/91/EEC of 24 June 1991 on organic production of agricultural products and indications referring thereto on agricultural products and foodstuffs (OJ 1991 L 198/1).

[171] See Article 5 of Council Regulation 2092/91/EEC, above Ch 4, n 170.

[172] See Commission Proposal of 4 December 1989 for a Council Regulation on organic production of agricultural products and indications referring thereto on agricultural products and foodstuffs (OJ 1990 C 4/4).

[173] See European Parliament Resolution of 12 March 1991 embodying the opinion of the European Parliament on the Commission proposal for a Council regulation on organic production of agricultural products and indications referring thereto on agricultural products and foodstuffs (OJ 1991 C 106/27). Based on the Report of 19 November 1990 drawn up on behalf of the Committee on Agriculture and Fisheries and Rural Development on the proposal from the Commission to the Council for a regulation on organic production of agricultural products and indications referring thereto on agricultural products and foodstuffs (rapporteur: Solange Fernex) EP Doc A3-311/90.

appropriate ruling can be examined.'[174] Apparently, this led the European Parliament to expect that the Commission, once the Regulation had been adopted, would submit a proposal for revision, which would provide them with a new opportunity to state their opinion on the use of GMMOs in organic farming.[175] But when the envisaged implementing legislation was adopted by the Commission, GMMOs were included.[176]

Quite understandably the European Parliament felt betrayed and lodged an application with the Court in which it argued that the Commission had exceeded its powers, effectively amending Council Regulation 2092/91/EEC in a manner which aimed to avoid the normal procedure for settling the matter.[177] But the Court found no reason to discontinue its result-oriented approach and dismissed the application (cf. above 3.3.2.1). As stated in its ruling of 13 July 1995, the inclusion of GMMOs in the limitative list did not go beyond 'the framework for implementation of the principles laid down by the basic regulation adopted following consultation of the Parliament' and was therefore possible to decide upon under a 'different' procedure.[178] The finding was supported by the conclusion that the Council's passivity with regard to the concerns expressed by the European Parliament, i.e. the non-inclusion in its Regulation of an explicit prohibition against GMMOs, was an expression of intention and, indeed, political will.[179]

In the parallel ruling in Case C-417/93 *European Parliament v Council*, the notion of implementation was interpreted so widely as to permit provisions not in an Annex but in the main text of a regulation adopted under a normal procedure to be amended under a simplified procedure.[180]

---

[174] See paragraph 28 of Case 156/93, above Ch 4, n 169.

[175] See paragraph 28 of Case 156/93, above Ch 4, n 169.

[176] See Commission Regulation 207/93/EEC of 29 January 1993 defining the content of Annex VI to Regulation 2092/91/EEC on organic production of agricultural products and indications referring thereto on agricultural products and foodstuffs and laying down detailed rules for implementing the provisions of Article 5(4) thereto (OJ 1993 L 25/5). The Regulation inserted a special clause into the limitative list which explained that the Commission and the Standing Committee on Organic Farming could include various forms of GMMOs by means of individual decisions.

[177] The procedure provided for in Article 43 EEC (1993) was the consultation procedure. See paragraphs 12 and 16 of Case 156/93, above Ch 4, n 169.

[178] See paragraphs 18 and 22 of Case 156/93, above Ch 4, n 169.

[179] See paragraph 24 of Case 156/93, above Ch 4, n 169.

[180] See Case C-417/93, *European Parliament v Council* [1995] ECR I-1185 (Judgment of 10 May 1995). For a commentary, see Búrca, G. de, annotation (1996) 33 *CMLRev* 1051; and

This case related to the Commission Proposal of 25 November 1992 for a Council Regulation concerning the provision of technical assistance to economic reform and recovery in the independent States of the former Union of Soviet Socialist Republics and Mongolia.[181] The proposal, which was a follow-up measure to the previous TACIS-Programme (the Programme for Technical Assistance for the Commonwealth of Independent States), was sent to the European Parliament for consultation on 5 March 1993.[182] In line with most other proposals for legislation, this proposal envisaged that the Commission should be entrusted with the responsibility for exercise of implementing powers in co-operation with a comitology committee, the TACIS-Committee, following a management committee procedure. But the European Parliament was aware that the Council had the intention, once again, to include an amendment which would replace the management committee procedure by a regulatory committee procedure (cf. above 4.3.1.1 and 4.3.3.2).[183] Therefore, after a period of repeated examination, lengthy discussions in plenary sitting and repeated postponement of the vote, the European Parliament decided to reject the proposal *in toto*.[184]

Five days after the European Parliament had rejected it, the proposal was adopted by the Council. In comparison with the original proposal,

Smijter, F. de, annotation (1995) 1 *RMUE* 203; Nuffel, above Ch 4, n 169; and Constantinesco, above Ch 4, n 169.

[181] See Commission Proposal of 25 November 1992 for a Council Regulation concerning the provision of technical assistance to economic reform and recovery in the independent States of the former Union of Soviet Socialist Republics and Mongolia (OJ 1993 C 48/13).

[182] Subject to Article 235 EEC (1993) and, thus, the consultation procedure. For the 1991–92 TACIS-Programme, see Council Regulation 2157/91/EEC/Euratom of 15 July 1991 concerning the provision of technical assistance to economic reform and recovery in the Union of Soviet Socialist Republics (OJ 1991 L 201/2).

[183] As explained by Advocate General Philippe Léger: '[i]t is essential to note at this point that the Council's proposal to introduce a type III committee was known to the Parliament and that the question of comitology was absolutely *central* to the debates before the Parliament, since several members of the Parliament attributed delays in making finance available and in taking decisions to the existence of a management committee in the 1991–1992 TACIS programme. It was the point of contention between the Council and the Parliament which was ultimately to lead the latter to reject the proposal.' See the Opinion of Advocate-General Léger in Case C-417/93, above Ch 4, n 180, at pp. 1205–1206 (paragraphs 95 and 97).

[184] See European Parliament Resolution of 14 July 1993 embodying the opinion of the European Parliament on the proposal for a Council regulation concerning the provision of technical assistance to economic reform and recovery in the independent States of the former Union of Soviet Socialist Republics and Mongolia (OJ 1993 C 255/81).

the final result, Council Regulation 2053/93/EEC/Euratom concerning the provision of technical assistance to economic reform and recovery in the independent States of the former Soviet Union and Mongolia, contained several amendments.[185] With respect to the exercise of implementing powers, the Council had not only replaced the management committee procedure by a regulatory committee procedure but had also introduced a supplementary procedure which said that the maximum amount for certain public contracts, set at 300,000 ECU, 'may be revised by the Council on the basis of a Commission proposal' without any involvement of the European Parliament.[186]

Less than three months after Council Regulation 2053/93/EEC/ Euratom was adopted, on 12 October 1993, the European Parliament brought an action for its annulment in the Court of Justice. Of particular relevance for present purposes was the claim that the supplementary procedure was unlawful since '[s]uch a procedure for amendment, differing from that required for the adoption of the original legislation, leads to an erosion of the Parliament's prerogatives.'[187] The claim was certainly not unreasonable. But the Court nevertheless preferred to stretch the meaning of its previous rulings rather than to interfere with the solution agreed in the Council.

As the Court explained in its ruling of 10 May 1995, from a legal point of view the situation at hand was not so different from that dealt with in Case 25/70 *Einfuhr- und Vorratsstelle für Getreide und Futtermittel v Köster, Berodt & Co.* (see above 2.4.5.2).[188] Here the Court had confirmed the legality of a regulation adopted by the Commission with reference to the fact that it could not be a requirement that 'all the details' be dealt with in a regulation adopted by the Council under the normal procedure (consultation procedure). If only 'the basic elements of the matter' had been established that way, the provisions implementing a regulation could be

---

[185] Council Regulation 2053/93/EC/Euratom of 19 July 1993 concerning the provision of technical assistance to economic reform and recovery in the independent States of the former Soviet Union and Mongolia (OJ 1993 L 187/1).

[186] See Article 7(2) of Council Regulation 2053/93/EEC/Euratom, above Ch 4, n 185.

[187] See paragraph 29 of the Judgment (above Ch 4, n 180).

[188] See the reference in paragraph 30 of the Judgment (above Ch 4, n 180) to Case 25/70, above Ch 2, n 244, paragraph 6; and Case 46/86 *Romkes v Officer van Justitie* [1987] ECR 2671 (Judgment of 16 June 1987), paragraph 16. In the latter case the Court emphasized that implementing legislation adopted by the Commission or, indeed, the Council itself, may not jeopardize the essential elements of the basic legislation, without violating the prerogatives of the European Parliament.

adopted under a simplified procedure, by the Council, reserving the exercise of implementing powers for itself, or by the Commission, subject to a delegation of implementing powers.[189]

Applying that ruling to the case before it, the Court focused its assessment of the procedure for revision of the maximum amount for public contracts on the question of whether it could be regarded as 'essential' for the principles or the scheme of the Regulation as a whole (cf. 'the basic elements of the matter') and concluded that it was merely part of the arrangements for its implementation.[190] Consequently, the Council had also been 'entitled to consider that the revision of the threshold in question fell within its implementing powers, which are not subject to the procedure laid down by articles in the EEC and Euratom Treaties on the basis of which the contested regulation was adopted.'[191]

The implications of the rulings in Case C-156/93 *European Parliament v Commission* and Case C-417/93 *European Parliament v Council* were far-reaching: even if a provision was placed in legislation adopted under a normal procedure, it could be considered to be implementing in nature and, therefore, possible for the Council or, indeed, Commission to modify under a simplified procedure which excluded participation of the European Parliament.[192] The principal significance of this was not limited to those fields of activity where the consultation procedure applied but was general, thus extending also to those fields where the co-operation and co-decision procedure applied.[193] Therefore, whatever

[189] See paragraph 30 of the Judgment (above Ch 4, n 180). As now restated by the Court, this should be read so that 'the procedure by which the Council adopts regulations relating to a Community policy, on a proposal from the Commission and after consulting the Parliament, applies solely to the basic regulations containing the essential elements of the matter to be dealt with and the provisions implementing those regulations may be adopted by the Council according to a different procedure.'

[190] See paragraph 32 of the Judgment (above Ch 4, n 180). Cf. Advocate General Léger who considered that the contested procedure 'calls in question neither the principles nor the scheme of the regulation and does not go beyond "implementing powers" which alone may be delegated.' See the Opinion of Advocate General Léger in Case 417/93, at p. 1209 (paragraph 115).

[191] See paragraph 33 of the Judgment (above Ch 4, n 180).

[192] See Jacqué, above Ch 1, n 5, at p. 62; Türk, above Ch 1, n 11, at p. 175; and Türk, written evidence, in the 1998–99 House of Lords Paper on Comitology, below Ch 4, n 297, at p. 65.

[193] Additional support for that submission was provided by the Court of Justice in its ruling in Case C-259/95 above Ch 4, n 144, 4.3.3.3. Here the Court reached the conclusion that the fact that an initial decision had been jointly adopted by the European Parliament and the Council did not preclude the Council from adopting a decision amending the initial decision alone. The decisions involved were, respectively, European Parliament and Council Decision 94/3092/EC

the Court's intentions had been, it had not only confirmed the legality of a few concrete measures clearly designed to circumvent the European Parliament but had also provided the Council and the Commission with a weapon for the future.

4.3.5   The power of budgetary control

To the surprise only of a few over-enthusiastic commentators,[194] the 'rights' granted to the European Parliament under the *Modus Vivendi* soon proved to be suffering from the same practical problems as those granted to it under the Plumb-Delors and Klepsch-Millan Agreements (which continued to apply).[195] During the period leading up to the 1996 Intergovernmental Conference, no more than 166 out of 491 relevant measures were transmitted to the European Parliament.[196] This led to the conclusion that the Commission—in spite of its officially supportive attitude—had not made much of an effort to establish the routines required.[197] For the European Parliament, which had now picked up steam, this was unacceptable and it decided, therefore, to tighten the Commission's belt.

In 1983 the European Parliament had discovered that it could use its budgetary powers to press the Commission 'to keep the matter of committees under review, and to keep proper minutes of all meetings, showing

of 7 December 1994 introducing a Community system of information on home and leisure accidents (OJ 1994 L 331/1); and Council Decision 95/184/EC of 22 May 1995 amending Decision 3092/94/EC introducing a Community system of information on home and leisure accidents (OJ 1995 L 120/36).

[194] See Demmke *et al.*, above Ch 2, n 216, at p. 75. In their view the *Modus Vivendi* represented clear progress in comparison with the Plumb-Delors Agreement 'in particular as to how all measures of a general nature had to be transmitted to the European Parliament by the Commission.' See also Ciavarini-Azzi, above Ch 1, n 26, at p. 55. According to him the *Modus Vivendi* had 'without doubt enabled the Parliament to enjoy greater access to information on the subject.'

[195] See paragraph 6 of the Code of Conduct annexed to the Resolution of 15 March 1995 on the Commission's annual programme of work (OJ 1995 C 89/69).

[196] See Working Document of the European Parliament Committee on Budgets of 30 April 1996 on developments on the Comitology dossier (PE 216.965). See Bradley, above Ch 2, n 216, at pp. 237 and 240.

[197] See Bradley, above Ch 2, n 216, at p. 240. As asserted by Bradley, the Commission did not only fail to supply the European Parliament with sufficient information but also with sufficient time for it to adopt a position. Cf. Working Document of the European Parliament Institutional Committee of 12 September 1996 on the *Modus Vivendi* concerning the implementing measures for acts (PE 218.255).

attendance, duration and opinions delivered' (see above 3.3.4.1).[198] This, indeed, was a tactic which it would revert to again on several occasions.[199] Of particular significance for present purposes was the decision taken by the European Parliament on 15 December 1994 to place 90% of the proposed funding for committees in the reserve while demanding from the Commission a list of the matters these committees had been involved in during the previous year (cf. above 4.3.3.4).[200]

The Commission responded swiftly, with a 1,918 page report listing 355 committees involved in the exercise of implementing powers.[201] As a result, the European Parliament released half of the funds.[202] The other half was only released after a study had been made of the information supplied. In this study it was noted that the information had not been sufficient to enable an evaluation of whether the committees had acted within their mandate and that it had not even been possible to determine how often certain committees had met, or what had been their opinion on the draft measures they examined.[203]

Following up on that study, on 26 October 1995 a resolution was adopted by the European Parliament in which the Commission was requested to improve its internal procedures and 'to set out guidelines for all executive committees ... so that not only are the dates of the meetings and terms of the advice tendered clear, including the legislative and decisional references, but also the voting breakdown is provided in the event of a vote, and the decision taken by the Commission is transmitted, where it differs from the advice tendered.'[204] The demand was also made that, as a rule,

---

[198] Bradley, above Ch 2, n 216, at p. 242.

[199] See, in general, on the use made by the European Parliament of its budgetary powers, Corbett, above Ch 3, n 188, at pp. 93–113.

[200] See European Parliament Resolution of 15 December 1994 on the draft general budget of the European Communities for the 1995 financial year (OJ 1995 C 18/145).

[201] See Budget 1995: Comitology—Decisions taken in 1994 by committees listed in Annex I to Part A of section III of the General Budget for the European Union for 1994, Commission Documents XIX/A7/67/95 (volumes I and II) and XIX/A7/117/95 (addendum).

[202] See OJ 1995 C 89/1 and OJ 1995 C 249/26.

[203] See the Report of 25 July 1995 drawn up on behalf of the Committee on Budgets on the Commission's response to Parliament's request for information on the 1994 activities of executive committees (rapporteur: Terence Wynn) EP Doc A4-189/95. See Demmke *et al.*, above Ch 2, n 216, at p. 78.

[204] See European Parliament Resolution of 26 October 1995 on the Commission's response to Parliament's request for information on the 1994 activities of executive committees (OJ 1995 C 308/133).

committees should meet in public, and that their agendas and minutes, as well as a declaration of the financial interests of their members, should be published.

Once again the Commission failed to assuage the dissatisfaction, and as a result the European Parliament decided to continue to place the expenditure for committees in the budgetary reserve. The controversy was only brought to an end on 27 September 1996 when an agreement was concluded between the Chairman of the European Parliament Budget Committee, Detlev Samland, and the Commission Secretary General, David Williamson.[205] On the basis of that agreement the European Parliament decided to shelve the matter until it had 'taken cognisance' of the outcome of the Intergovernmental Conference.[206] According to the terms of the Samland-Williamson Agreement:

(a) in order to keep the European Parliament informed of the work of the executive committees, the Commission shall make available to Parliament, in good time in advance of committee discussions, the annotated agendas for each meeting of management and regulatory committees;

(b) the Commission shall make available to Parliament the results of votes in management and regulatory committees (votes for and against and abstentions);

(c) the Commission will require all members of management and regulatory committees, other than public service officials, to sign, on appointment, a declaration that there is no conflict between their membership of the committee concerned and their personal interests; in the event of such conflict arising during the work of the committee, they will inform the chairman of the committee and will not participate in the discussion on the issue; the chairman of the committee will point out that this obligation applies to all members;

(d) if Parliament or a parliamentary committee wishes to attend the discussion on certain items on the agenda of a committee, the chairman will put the request to the committee, which may take a decision; if the committee

---

[205] The so-called Samland-Williamson Agreement concluded between the Chairman of the European Parliament's budget committee and the Secretary General of the Commission. Set out in paragraph 72 of the European Parliament's Resolution of 24 October 1996 on the Draft General budget of the European Communities for the Financial Year 1997 (OJ 1996 C 347/125). See further the 1998–99 House of Lords Paper on Comitology, below Ch 4, n 297, at pp. 12–14; and Bradley, above Ch 2, n 216, at p. 243.

[206] See paragraph 74 of the European Parliament Resolution of 24 October 1996, above Ch 4, n 205.

does not accept the request, the chairman must give reasons for the decision; Parliament may wish to publicise such reasons.

4.3.6 The 1996 Intergovernmental Conference

4.3.6.1 The Westendorp Report

Through the adoption of the Single European Act in 1986 the first stage was initiated of an institutional reform intended to be completed a few years later. The second stage was embarked upon through the adoption of the Treaty on European Union in 1992. But contrary to what had originally been intended, this left a number of matters in a provisional state of resolution and provided for a revision in 1996 (see above 4.3.2.3).[207] The preparations for the new Intergovernmental Conference were begun more or less immediately. Less than a year after the entry into force of the Treaty on European Union a decision was taken by the European Council to set up a 'Reflection Group' to examine the functioning of the institutional system and the potential for improvement.[208] The Chairman was to be the Spanish State Secretary for European Affairs, Carlos Westendorp.

The Reflection Group started its work on 2 June 1995 with a meeting in Messina, where 40 years before the historic Conference had been held that led to the adoption of the EEC Treaty.[209] According to the instructions, the Reflection Group was to focus its deliberations on questions for which revision had been stipulated at the time of adoption of the Treaty on European Union, such as an extension of the scope of the co-decision procedure (i.e. the 'classic' items of qualified majority voting in the Council and increased involvement of the European Parliament),[210] or the establishment of 'an appropriate' hierarchy of legal

[207] See Article N(2) EU (1993). Cf. also Article M EU (1993), according to which the planned revision should not entail any questioning of the existing *acquis communautaire.*

[208] See Presidency Conclusions of the European Council meeting on 24 and 25 June 1994 (Corfu), at internet http://www.europa.eu.int; and General Report 1994, above Ch 4, n 145, at p. 412 (point 1176). The Reflection Group consisted of representatives of the Governments' Foreign Ministries and of the Commission President. In addition, two representatives of the European Parliament were to 'take part'.

[209] See *Historique de la Conference Intergouvernementale 1996* (http://www.europa.eu.int).

[210] See Article 189b(8) EC (1993), according to which '[t]he scope of the procedure under this Article may be widened, in accordance with the procedure provided for in Article N(2) of the Treaty on European Union, on the basis of a report to be submitted to the Council by the Commission by 1996 at the latest.'

acts, and also questions which had been earmarked for assessment at a later point, such as a revision of the rules for exercise of implementing powers (see above 4.3.2.3).[211]

Most of the questions the Reflection Group was expected to deal with had already been discussed on a number of occasions and it was clear to everyone that several Governments held strong views which they were not going to reconsider lightly. For some, this was reason enough to insist that a debate on fundamental or constitutional issues should be avoided and that only such amendments should be considered which were absolutely necessary in order to tidy-up and clear the way for further enlargements.[212] Although objected to in some quarters, in particular by the European Parliament,[213] this minimalist approach was to prevail. An early indication to that end could be found on 27 June 1995 when the European Council told the Reflection Group to 'bear in mind' the advantages of seeking improvements that would not require any treaty amendment.[214]

The final result of the discussions in the Reflection Group were presented in a report submitted to the European Council on 15 December 1995.[215] In principle, this so-called Westendorp Report fixed the major themes on which the negotiations in the Intergovernmental Conference were to centre: bringing the European Union closer to the citizens, a strong external identity, and efficient Institutions with regard to enlargement. Avoiding here the risks incumbent in any attempt to pass an overall judgment on the work of the Reflection Group, the focus will be on the findings in respect of the questions that are most relevant for our present purposes: the establishment of a hierarchy of legal acts and a revision of the rules for exercise of implementing powers.

---

[211] See General Report 1994, above Ch 4, n 145, at p. 412 (point 1176). For an outline of the preparations see the White Paper of the European Parliament's Task Force on the 1996 Intergovernmental Conference, volume II (http://europa.eu.int/en/agenda/igc-home).

[212] For a summary of the different positions, see the Task Force White Paper, above Ch 4, n 211. Cf. the Presidency Conclusions of the European Council meeting on 9 and 10 December 1994 (Essen), at internet http://www.europa.eu.int.

[213] See, in particular, the European Parliament Resolution of 17 May 1995 on the functioning of the Treaty on European Union with a view to the 1996 Intergovernmental Conference (OJ 1995 C 151/56). Cf. also the Commission Report of 10 May 1995 on the Operation of the Treaty on European Union (SEC (95) 731).

[214] See the Presidency Conclusions of the European Council meeting on 26 and 27 June 1995 (Cannes), at internet http://www.europa.eu.int.

[215] See the Presidency Conclusions of the European Council meeting on 15 and 16 December 1995 (Madrid), at internet http://www.europa.eu.int and *Historique de la Conférence Intergouvernementale 1996*, above Ch 4, n 209.

It has been seen above that the Commission and the European Parliament were far from satisfied with the arrangement for exercise of implementing powers that had been agreed by the Inter-governmental Conference which led to the adoption of the Single European Act (see above 4.2.3.1 and 4.3.1). Therefore, in spite of their differences of opinion, the Commission and the European Parliament were united in stating that something had to be changed. The result could be seen in the proposal for establishment of a hierarchy of legal acts, based on a clear distinction between the responsibility of the Council and the European Parliament, on the one hand, and that of the Commission, on the other (see above 4.3.2.2). This placed the demand for a revision of the rules for exercise of implementing powers within a project so ambitious that it must have been aimed, first and foremost, to open up a debate. In that respect, the proposal was also successful. Even if it was rejected in 1991, it had made its way to the agenda for 1996.

As explained in the Westendorp Report, two conflicting positions had emerged with respect to the inter-linked questions of the establishment of a hierarchy of legal acts and a revision of the rules for exercise of implementing powers.[216] The first position was that embraced by a number of representatives who favoured the introduction of a hierarchy of legal acts similar to that which had been proposed and were willing, therefore, to replace the existing rules for exercise of implementing powers with rules that would give the Commission full implementing powers (subject to control by both the Council and the European Parliament). In their view, this would above all serve to clarify the functions of the Community Institutions.

The second position was that taken by those who were opposed to the introduction of this type of hierarchy of legal acts. These seem to have constituted a large majority.[217] Although not denying that this could bring clarity, they refuted the logic, which they felt was based on the idea of separation of powers within a state.[218] Those who took this position

---

[216] See the Report from the Chairman of the Reflection Group on the 1996 Intergovernmental Conference of 5 December 1995: A Strategy for Europe (Office for Official Publications 1995), at pp. 30, 35–36 (paragraphs 111 and 126 to 128). See also Bradley, above Ch 1, n 76, at p. 76.

[217] The Westendorp Report did not specify what position had been taken by which representatives. But clearly, the most energetic representative of this position was the British Government. See, for example, *Positions des Etats membres sur les thèmes à l'ordre du jour de la Conférence intergouvernementale 1996* (http://europa.eu.int/en/agenda/igc-home).

[218] See the Westendorp Report, above Ch 4, n 216, at p. 35 (paragraph 126). As stated: 'Those who are opposed to this system do not deny its clarity, but refute its logic, which is based on the

were also refusing to grant the Commission what they referred to as executive powers since they believed that it would disturb the institutional balance. But admitting that existing committee procedures were 'complicated and confused' they declared themselves prepared to consider 'simplified committee procedures which would not undermine the Council's executive functions.'[219] In their view this would not require a reform of the EC Treaty, but only a revision of Council Decision 87/373/EEC. Therefore, it should not be discussed within the Intergovernmental Conference.

The European Council warmly welcomed the Westendorp Report and judged it to be a good basis for the work of the Intergovernmental Conference.[220] But before that could be started, the European Parliament had to be consulted (this was now laid down as a requirement in the EU Treaty).[221] Obviously determined not to lose any time, the European Council demanded that this should be done as rapidly as possible.[222] The European Parliament lived up to these expectations and the Resolution embodying its opinion was adopted on 13 March 1996.[223] This expressed support for the convening of the Intergovernmental Conference as such

idea of separation of powers within a State, since this approach would transform the Council into a second legislative chamber and Commission into the European executive. Their view is that the Union has its own particular nature which is suited to a characteristic classification of acts: Regulations, Directives, Decisions and Recommendations. They feel, however, that within this characteristic system it is possible to clarify the functions of each of the institutions while maintaining the balance between them. In this context, they recommend a return to the original spirit of the Treaty through greater attention to the quality of each act and a use of the Directive which is more in line with its genuine purpose.' Interestingly, it was also argued that the introduction of the co-decision procedure meant that the debate on the hierarchy of acts had lost its previous importance.

[219] See the Westendorp Report, above Ch 4, n 216, at pp. 35–36 (paragraphs 127 and 128).

[220] The Presidency Conclusions of 15 and 16 December 1995, above Ch 4, n 215. See General Report on the Activities of the European Union 1995 (Office for Official Publications 1996), at p. 423 (point 1027).   [221] See Article N(1) EU (1993).

[222] See General Report 1995, above Ch 4, n 220, at p. 423 (point 1027).

[223] See European Parliament Resolution of 13 March 1996 embodying (i) Parliament's opinion on the convening of the Intergovernmental Conference, and (ii) an evaluation of the work of the Reflection Group and a definition of the political priorities of the European Parliament with a view to the Intergovernmental Conference (OJ 1996 C 96/77). This was based on the Report of 5 March 1996 drawn up on behalf of the Committee on Institutional Affairs on (i) Parliament's Opinion on the convening of the IGC and (ii) evaluation of the work of the Reflection Group and definition of the political priorities of the European Parliament with a view to the Intergovernmental Conference (rapporteurs: Raymonde Dury and Hanja Maij-Weggen) EP Doc A4-68/96.

but emphasized that the Westendorp Report could not be considered to constitute a sufficient basis since it contained 'some shortcomings and negative options and no unanimous agreement on the major issues.'[224] Of particular concern in this respect was the lack of suggestions for reform of the legislative procedure. According to the long-held view of the European Parliament, there was not only a need to extend the scope of the co-decision procedure but also to simplify 'the existing maze of commitology procedures' and to introduce a hierarchy of legal acts.[225]

4.3.6.2 *The Treaty of Amsterdam*

The Intergovernmental Conference commenced in Turin on 29 March 1996 and finalized in Amsterdam little more than a year later.[226] Even if the result, manifested in the Treaty of Amsterdam, was more humble than that of the previous two Conferences, it was certainly not insignificant.[227] For the first time a general opportunity had been provided for groups of Member States to engage in closer co-operation (cf. above 3.3.1.2)[228] and, in an attempt to improve the public image of the European Union, a right had been established for its citizens to have access to documents.[229] Perhaps most remarkably, a number of changes were also

---

[224] See, in general, Blumann, above Ch 4, n 122.

[225] See paragraph 21.6 of the European Parliament Resolution of 13 March 1996, above Ch 4, n 223; and paragraph 32 of the European Parliament Resolution of 17 May 1995, above Ch 4, n 213. In essence, the proposal presented by the European Parliament meant that the overall responsibility for implementing measures would be transferred to the Commission and that both management and regulatory committee procedures would be abolished. The Council and the European Parliament would be notified of the measures proposed. In addition, a substitution mechanism would be introduced which would enable the Council and the European Parliament to reject the measure proposed, irrespective of each other, and to call for new implementing measures or the initiation of a full legislative procedure. It may be noted that the proposal presented by the European Parliament was largely supported by the Commission. But the Commission was willing to keep the three basic forms of committee procedures if only the variants of the procedures were dropped. See Commission Opinion of 29 February 1996: Reinforcing Political Union and Preparing for Enlargement (COM (96) 90 final), at pp. 13–14 (paragraphs 21–22).

[226] See the retrospective site at internet http://europa.eu.int/en/agenda/igc-home.

[227] See Treaty of Amsterdam of 2 October 1997 amending the Treaty on European Union, the Treaties establishing the European Communities and certain related acts (OJ 1997 C 340/1).

[228] See the new Articles 40 and 43 to 45 EU (1999) and the new Article 11 EC (1999).

[229] See the new Article 255 EC (1999). As explained therein, the general principles and conditions governing this right of access to documents would be determined within two years of the entry into force of the Treaty of Amsterdam. See European Parliament and Council

agreed which would strengthen the role of the European Parliament, including a new right to approve the appointment of the President of the Commission and an extension of the application of the co-decision procedure (which was also simplified).[230]

But somewhat paradoxically, nothing had been done to meet the demands of the European Parliament with respect to the arrangement for exercise of implementing powers. Still unwilling to consider any amendment to Article 145 EC, now renumbered Article 202 EC, the Governments restricted themselves to the solution which had already won broad support within the Reflection Group: a revision of Council Decision 87/373/EEC. Therefore, in a declaration attached to the Treaty of Amsterdam, the Commission was requested to submit a proposal for amendments by the end of 1998.[231] Quite clearly, this was not going to be an easy task. In spite of the fact that the basic arrangement had been left unchanged, the Commission had to come up with 'a text bringing the Community implementation system more closely into line with the new institutional balance.'[232] This had not only to be acceptable to all Governments but to a European Parliament which was now beginning to get impatient (cf. above 4.3.4.1); if not, the inter-institutional battle would soon flare up again.[233]

Regulation 1049/01/EC of 30 May 2001 regarding public access to European Parliament, Council and Commission documents (OJ 2001 L 145/43).

[230] See, respectively, Articles 214 and 251 EC (1999). For an explanation of the simplified co-decision procedure, see Craig and Búrca, above Ch 1, n 9, at pp. 144–147. It should be noted that the European Parliament, although pleased with the changes relating to the co-decision procedure, expressed its disappointment that the institutional reform was not sufficient to proceed with enlargement. It requested, therefore, that a further revision of the treaties should be undertaken. See the European Parliament Resolution of 19 November 1997 on the Amsterdam Treaty (OJ 1997 C 371/99); and the European Parliament Resolution of 26 June 1997 on the meeting of the European Council on 16 and 17 June in Amsterdam (OJ 1997 C 222/17). Importantly, the view that the institutional reform was not sufficient was also stated in a Protocol attached to the Treaty of Amsterdam. In this the Governments explained that before enlargement a new Intergovernmental Conference should be convened 'in order to carry out a comprehensive review of the provisions of the Treaties on the composition and functioning of the institutions.' See Article 2 of Protocol No 11, above Ch 4, n 15.

[231] See Declaration No 31 annexed to the Amsterdam Treaty of 2 October 1997 on the Council Decision of 13 July 1987 (OJ 1997 C 340/137). Cf. Jacqué above Ch 1, n 5, at p. 69.

[232] Ciavarini-Azzi, above Ch 1, n 26, at p. 55.

[233] It should be pointed out that the European Parliament only accepted the Treaty of Amsterdam, and recommended that Member States ratify it, subject to a number of conditions. One of these was that the European Parliament should be involved in drafting and finalizing the

4.4 The second Comitology Decision

4.4.1 *The background*

4.4.1.1 *The Commission presents its proposal*

The proposal the Commission had been asked to prepare was finalized on 24 June 1998.[234] Apparently, it had not felt obliged to stick to the terms of the Declaration attached to the Treaty of Amsterdam (see above 4.3.5.3); instead of making mere amendments to Council Decision 87/373/EEC the proposal was aimed at the adoption of an entirely new decision. But the significance of this was more apparent than real. Since the Intergovernmental Conference had left Article 202 (ex 145) EC unchanged, the room for manoeuvre was very limited.[235] Therefore, the aim had only been to reconstruct the existing system of committees in a way which would make it 'less complex, less opaque and more open to parliamentary control.'[236] In accordance with that, the content of the proposal could be divided into three different categories.

The first of these consisted of some provisions aimed at making the system 'less complex'. The aim was to reform or modify the rules regulating the work of already existing committees so that these committees and new or future committees would be subject to the same rules.[237] In fact this was what the Commission had sought to achieve in 1986: the only

new Comitology Decision and that it should receive its agreement. See the European Parliament Resolution of 19 November 1997, above Ch 4, n 230. Cf. the European Parliament Resolution of 16 January 1997 on the general outline for a draft revision of the Treaties (OJ 1997 C 33/66) in which the European Parliament expressed its strong regret that the Dutch Presidency had failed to prepare 'most of the key institutional issues' facing the Conference, in particular the reform of the committee system; and the European Parliament Resolution of 11 June 1997 on the draft treaty drawn up by the Dutch Presidency (OJ 1997 C 200/70), in which the European Parliament expressed its discontent with the planned Declaration that the committee system should only be dealt with by means of revision of Council Decision 87/373/EEC, above Ch 4, n 48.

[234] See Commission Proposal of 24 June 1998 for a Council Decision laying down the procedures for the exercise of implementing powers conferred on the Commission (OJ 1998 C 279/5). For an analysis, see Kortenberg, H., Comitologie: le retour (1998) 34 *RTDE* 317.

[235] See Ciavarini-Azzi, above Ch 1, n 26, at p. 55.

[236] See the statement by the Commission Vice-President Neil Kinnock in the Debates of the European Parliament on 5 May 1999 (OJ 1999 C 279/160). See also *Bulletin EU* 6-1998, point 1.9.6.

[237] See Articles 3 to 5 and 8 of the Commission Proposal of 24 June 1998, above Ch 4, n 234.

difference this time was that no attempt had been made to get rid of the safeguard procedure (cf. above 4.2.2.2). Furthermore, the proposal envisaged that certain procedural modifications should be made. Overall these were rather modest. An important exception to that, however, were the modifications to the regulatory committee procedure. These constituted the second category.

In accordance with the regulatory committee procedure, as had been fixed by Council Decision 87/373/EEC, if a draft implementing measure was not explicitly approved by the committee, the Commission had to place the matter before the Council in the form of a 'proposal' (see above 4.2.2.2). The only difference between such a proposal and an ordinary proposal for legislation was that the Council was under no obligation to provide the European Parliament with an opportunity to state its opinion (or, indeed, to take its opinion into account). But as now envisaged by the Commission, its duty to place the matter before the Council (cf. 'shall') would be replaced by a right to present a proposal within the normal legislative process (cf. 'may').[238] The solution was as elegant as it was simple. In one stroke the Commission would get rid of the controversial *contre-filet* mechanism, strengthen its own right of initiative, and make the system 'more open to parliamentary control.'

The third category consisted of a number of provisions aimed at making the committee system 'less opaque' or, in other words, more transparent. Essentially, two different aspects were dealt with. The first was that manifested in the introduction of principles or 'criteria' on the basis of which a choice should be made between the different procedures. This had been considered by the Commission in 1986. But, anxious to come up with a proposal which could be expected to get through 'without any watering down or major amendments', the Commission had found it wiser to abstain. Apparently, it had felt that the risk was too great that the Council would only satisfy itself with criteria which would 'direct proceedings, almost systematically, to the most unfavourable committees' (see above 4.2.1.1). In the end, a non-binding promise had been obtained, instead, that the Council should give the advisory committee procedure 'a predominant place' within the high priority field of the internal market

---

[238] According to Article 5 of the Commission Proposal of 24 June 1998 (above Ch 4, n 234): '[i]f the measures envisaged are not in accordance with the opinion of the committee, or if no opinion is delivered, the Commission shall not adopt the measures envisaged. In that event, it may present a proposal relating to the measures to be taken, in accordance with the Treaty.'

(see above 4.2.2.2). This soon proved to be of little practical importance: only a few years after the entry into force of Council Decision 87/373/ EEC the conclusion was drawn that the Council was 'almost systematically' replacing the advisory committee procedures proposed by the Commission with regulatory committee procedures (see above 4.3.1.1).

Against this background, there cannot be much doubt that the criteria envisaged in the proposal for a new decision were not only intended to make the system more transparent but also to reinforce the Commission's autonomy. Importantly, the idea this time was not to link the choice of committee procedure to a certain field of co-operation—as the advisory committee procedure was supposed to be given a predominant place within the field of the internal market—but to link it to the substantive scope or quality of the measures to be taken.[239]

Even if it was not stated clearly by the Commission, the underlying logic was similar to that of its proposal for a hierarchy of legal acts: the substantive scope of the measures to be taken would also determine how the balance between 'the legislative authority' and 'the executive authority' should be struck (see above 4.3.2.2).[240] Also, this time the notion of implementation and, therefore, the substantive scope of the measures to be

---

[239] See Article 2 of the Commission Proposal of 24 June 1998, above Ch 4, n 234. Accordingly, '[i]mplementation and management measures, and in particular those relating to common policies such as the common agricultural policy, to the implementation of programmes with significant budgetary implications, or to the grant of substantial financial support, shall be adopted by use of the management procedure. Measures of general scope designed to apply, update or adapt essential provisions of basic instruments shall be adopted by the use of regulatory procedure. The advisory procedure shall be applied where the management or regulatory procedure is not or is no longer considered appropriate. The safeguard procedure may be applied where the power to decide on such measures is conferred on the Commission.' It may be noted that the proposal for introduction of a hierarchy of legal acts presented by the Commission in 1991 envisaged the abolition of the regulatory committee procedure (see above 4.3.2.2).

[240] See e.g. the explanation by Marcelino Oreja that 'for the first time, it is proposed to relate the choice of procedure to the nature of the decisions to be adopted. Procedures in the management committee will guarantee a speedy decision on matters of financial and agricultural management, whilst granting the committee a significant right of investigation. It is anticipated that the regulatory committee will deal with general issues relating to key aspects of legislation, and it will be much stricter with the Commission. The issue of adapting to technical progress is a good example. The procedure should, obviously, be much stricter for the Commission, and should allow the legislative authority plenty of scope to intervene. Lastly, the advisory committee will deal with all other issues which the legislative authority considers straightforward.' See the statement by Commissioner Marcelino Oreja in the Debates of the European Parliament on 15 September 1998, above Ch 4, n 124.

taken by the executive authority was very wide. This, indeed, was manifested in the criterion which required that '[m]easures of general scope designed to apply, update or adapt essential provisions of basic instruments' should be adopted by use of the regulatory committee procedure. Since those measures were most likely to interest the legislative authority, '[t]he procedure should, obviously, be much stricter for the Commission, and should allow the legislative authority plenty of scope to intervene.'[241]

The second aspect addressed was that of the European Parliament's right to be kept informed on a regular basis. Here, the objective the Commission had set itself was to bring about a simplification of the existing situation through the introduction of rules which provided for the 'central elements' of the *Modus Vivendi* and the inter-institutional agreements.[242] Accordingly, the European Parliament would be entitled to receive agendas for committee meetings, draft implementing measures submitted to committees within the fields of application of the co-decision procedure, and the results of voting. It would also be kept informed about matters transferred to the Council. Clearly, this was less than the European Parliament had already been promised. Most notably, the requirement in the *Modus Vivendi* that account should be taken of the European Parliament's position was missing (see above 4.3.3.4).[243] But as argued by the Commission, it would still be a step forward: in contrast to those political understandings, the new rules would be law and thus legally-binding.[244] It was not clear from the proposal how the rules were to be put into practice. Apparently it was felt that it would be possible to sort this out in a separate agreement between the European Parliament, the Commission, and the Council or, alternatively, between the European Parliament and the Commission.[245]

---

[241] See the statement by Commissioner Marcelino Oreja in the Debates of the European Parliament on 15 September 1998, above Ch 4, n 124.

[242] See Article 7 of the Commission Proposal of 24 June 1998 above Ch 4, n 234.

[243] For an analysis of the differences between the proposed rules and the *Modus Vivendi* and the inter-institutional agreements, see Türk, written evidence, in the 1998–99 House of Lords Paper on Comitology, below Ch 4, n 297, at pp. 66–67. Cf. also the oral evidence given by Richard Corbett, at p. 27 (paragraph 120).

[244] See the statement by Commissioner Marcelino Oreja in the Debates of the European Parliament on 15 September 1998, above Ch 4, n 124. See also the oral evidence given by Hervé Dupuy to the House of Lords, in the 1998–99 House of Lords Paper on Comitology, below Ch 4, n 297, at p. 8 (paragraph 49); and the oral evidence given by Claire-Françoise Durand, at p. 9 (paragraph 53). See also Ciavarini-Azzi, above Ch 1, n 26, at p. 56.

[245] According to Marcelino Oreja, '[t]he Commission awaits Parliament's proposals, in the hope that an agreement can be reached which would be part of the decision itself.

4.4.1.2 *The Aglietta Report*

The proposal for a new comitology decision was formally submitted to the Council on 17 July 1998 and a few weeks later the process was initiated for consultation of the European Parliament (cf. above 3.4.2.2).[246] The European Parliament was well prepared. On 3 August 1998, a report on the proposal was finalized by its Committee on Institutional Affairs.[247] This swiftness was not surprising: the Committee on Institutional Affairs was the successor of the Political Affairs Committee that had been responsible for the examination of the proposal which led to the adoption of the old Decision in 1987 (see above 4.2.1.2) and the problem of comitology was a permanent item on its agenda. As explained in the so-called Aglietta Report, there were a number of reasons for the European Parliament to object to the existing arrangements. Some of these were related to the fact that there were 'so many committees, and agendas and procedures that are difficult to get hold of, that it is opaque and not transparent for the wider public.'[248] But even more alarming was the risk that it would undermine the co-decision procedure.

As early as 1962 the European Parliament had expressed its concern at the potential scope of matters dealt with by the Commission in co-operation with committees (see above 2.2.3). According to its reasoning, if matters of legislative bearing could be adopted in the form of an implementing measure, this would upset the institutional balance. Only a few years later such suspicions were confirmed by the Jozeau-Marigné

Alternatively, it would form part of the agreement between Parliament, the Commission and the Council or, if appropriate, of an agreement between the European Parliament and the Commission. In an attempt to launch negotiations towards such an agreement, the Commission has circulated the draft declaration, which recognises that the European Parliament has an important part to play.' See the statement by Commissioner Marcelino Oreja in the Debates of the European Parliament on 15 September 1998, above Ch 4, n 124. According to Neil Kinnock, it had been envisaged that 'an inter-institutional agreement could subsequently be concluded to clarify how this provision would actually operate in practice.' See the statement by Commission Vice-President Neil Kinnock in the Debates of the European Parliament on 5 May 1999, above Ch 4, n 236.

[246] See *Bulletin EU* 6-1998, point 1.9.6.

[247] Report of 3 August 1998 drawn up on behalf of the Committee on Institutional Affairs on the modification of the procedures for the exercise of implementing powers conferred on the Commission—comitology (rapporteur: Maria Adelaide Aglietta) EP Doc A4-292/98.

[248] See e.g. the oral evidence given by Richard Corbett to the House of Lords, in the 1998–99 House of Lords Paper on Comitology, below Ch 4, n 297, at p. 24; and the statement by Richard Corbett in the Debates of the European Parliament on 15 September 1998, above Ch 4, n 124.

Report (see above 2.4.4). Here evidence was presented that implementing measures were far from limited to day-to-day management but could very well involve matters of fundamental political significance. Quite naturally, this 'sliding in powers' was less difficult for the European Parliament to live with as long as its right to participation in the adoption of legislation was limited to that provided for under the consultation procedure (see above 2.1.1). But with the introduction of the co-operation procedure and, then, the co-decision procedure the situation became intolerable (see above 3.4.1.2 and 4.3.2.3), reaching a peak in 1993. On the basis of a strategy drawn up by the Committee on Institutional Affairs, the European Parliament launched an offensive which it had no intention of abandoning until agreement had been reached on an adequate solution (see above 4.3.3).

In spite of the fact that it had brought about a further strengthening of the co-decision procedure (through the simplification and the extension of its field of application), the Treaty of Amsterdam had done nothing to accommodate the European Parliament's worries about the arrangement for exercise of implementing powers. According to the Aglietta Report, this was paradoxical: many matters which the European Parliament felt it should have a say on were dealt with in the form of implementing measures and, therefore, the scope for action under the co-decision procedure was increasingly restricted to the adoption of measures with a very general content. The changes made to the co-decision procedure by the Treaty of Amsterdam unambiguously expressed the equality between the Council and the European Parliament. Therefore—as had been emphasized in 1993 (see above 4.3.3)—the Council and the European Parliament had also to exercise political supervision over the exercise of implementing powers together. According to the rapporteur, Maria Adelaide Aglietta:

The European Parliament's initiative on comitology stems from problems of transparency and respect for legislative procedures raised by the current system, all the more unacceptable today with a Treaty of Amsterdam which has redefined the role of the European Parliament in the co-decision procedure, bringing it up to parity with the Council. It is therefore evident, not least in the absence of a modification to Article 202, formerly Article 145—which refers to the acts adopted by the Council and not the acts adopted jointly by the European Parliament and the Council—that comitology is a grey area, with virtually no rules. In the framing of new rules, it is necessary to bear in

nind the increased responsibility of the European Parliament,... In
)articular, I believe that responsibility for the delegation of executive power
:o the Commission and the controls on executive activity should be
;hared equally by the legislative authority, in other words by the European
?arliament and the Council in the area of co-decision.[249]

\against the background of the demands of the European Parliament, it
was not possible for the Committee on Institutional Affairs to reach any
)ther conclusion than that the proposal presented by the Commission
was far from sufficient: 'even if a few steps forward have been taken with
:his proposal, the main concerns and requests from the European Par-
iament have been somewhat sidestepped.'[250] The greatest source of
liscontent was to be found in the rather half-hearted attempt made by the
Commission to deal with the sliding in powers, meaning that an increasing
1umber of matters of political significance would be dealt with outside the
1ormal legislative process in accordance with procedures from which the
European Parliament itself was excluded. According to the Report, there
were two fundamental principles lacking from the proposal:

The first principle is to guarantee full respect for the legislative procedure, in
)rder to avoid a legislative act being adopted outside the regular co-decision
)rocedure. This is something which all those who want the process to be
:ransparent and democratic have at heart. From this point of view, the def-
nition of an executive act which is given in the Commission proposal is
worrying, because it goes in the opposite direction to respect for the need for a
nore precise determination of the respective roles: the executive role of the
:he Commission, on the one hand, and the legislative role of the Council and
:he European Parliament on the other. In contrast to the Commission, we
)elieve that an implementing rule cannot be amended, adapted or updated, these
)eing the key elements of the basic legislative acts, including the annexes, and
when we talk about 'technical adaptations', we know perfectly well that, very
)ften, key elements of the legislation are dealt with in the annexes. I think that if
:onfusion remains in the executive sphere which is codified in the new decision,
t will be inevitable that the basic acts become increasingly general rules—and
:his is a risk for everyone, not just the European Parliament—and that the
:ommittees see their role in the defining of key elements of legislation
ncreasingly strengthened, which is what we are seeking to overcome.

[249] See the statement by Maria Adelaide Aglietta in the Debates of the European Parliament
)n 15 September 1998, above Ch 4, n 124.

[250] See the statement by Maria Adelaide Aglietta in the Debates of the European Parliament
)n 15 September 1998, above Ch 4, n 124.

The other essential principle for a correct and democratic balance between the different institutions is that the European Parliament should have the possibility of exercising real control over the implementing rules, in other words of intervening within a limited period to possibly contest the legitimacy or the procedural substance of the rule. This would obviously mean that the Commission may have to revoke or change that rule, but it will be able to discuss the most appropriate way of achieving control by the European Parliament without this involving any interference in the executive role of the Commission or a slowing-down of the executive process in such a way as to prejudice citizens' rights.[251]

The fundamental principles requested in the Aglietta Report had certainly not been unknown to the Commission when it drafted the proposal. They corresponded to the position taken by the European Parliament in the discussions which led to the adoption of the first Comitology Decision in 1987 (see above 4.2.1.2) and had been voiced on a regular basis since the introduction of the co-decision procedure (see above 4.3.3 and 4.3.5).[252] But the most difficult task for the Commission had not been to understand the demands of the European Parliament but to accommodate them within a solution which could be accepted by the other parties involved. First, there was the Council. Several Governments had already manifested their lack of support for anything but a modest revision of the existing arrangement and the procedure prescribed by the EC Treaty required unanimity (see above 4.3.4.3). Then of course, there was the Commission itself. Even if it had not been stated very openly, the Commission was concerned that the parliamentary demands would conflict with its own vested interests. This was above all reflected in the attitude adopted by the Commission towards the demand that the European Parliament should be provided with an opportunity to contest the legitimacy or the procedural substance of an implementing measure.

As early as 1962 the claim had been made by the European Parliament that it was entitled 'to discuss its position publicly and promote it' (see above 2.2.3). Parallel with the strengthening of its legislative powers, the

---

[251] See the statement by Maria Adelaide Aglietta in the Debates of the European Parliament on 15 September 1998, above Ch 4, n 124.

[252] The demand for a more precise determination of the responsibilities of 'the legislative authority' and 'the executive authority' was also a key aspect of the European Parliament's insistence on a hierarchy of legal acts. See for example the European Parliament Resolution of 14 February 1984, above Ch 4, n 102; and the European Parliament Resolution of 17 May 1995, above Ch 4, n 213.

:laim was refined and in 1993 it was finally absorbed by the proposal for ι substitution mechanism which would enable the Council and the European Parliament to repeal an implementing measure on equal :erms (see above 4.3.3.1). In spite of the fact that the Commission had previously shown some sign of support for that suggestion (see above 4.3.2.2 and 4.3.3.3), in its proposal an entirely different solution had been ɔpted for. This was the solution embraced by the 'radical' reform of the :egulatory committee procedure.[253]

It has been noted above that the reform of the regulatory committee procedure did not foresee any power to contest an implementing measure ɔther than that left to the committee (see above 4.4.1.1). Only in situations where the committee made use of that power could the European Parliament hope to be able to exercise some influence. The practical significance was minimal. Not only were these situations 'virtually ιon-existent' (see above 4.3.1.1), but if, exceptionally, they did occur, the natter would still not come before the European Parliament by default ɔut only as the result of a decision by the Commission to present a normal proposal for legislation.[254]

4.4.1.3 A demand for further negotiations

Unsurprisingly, when the Aglietta Report was first debated in the European Parliament on 15 September 1998, it immediately won strong

---

[253] As emphasized by Marcelino Oreja: 'I should like to stress the radical nature of the reform which the regulatory procedure is undergoing. If the committee and the Commission cannot reach agreement, the measure at issue may only be approved by the legislative authority, that is o say, under the co-decision procedure of the European Parliament and the Council.' See the statement by Commissioner Marcelino Oreja in the Debates of the European Parliament on 15 September 1998, above Ch 4, n 124.

[254] According to Marcelino Oreja, the existing system had worked well from a strictly echnical point of view: '[o]nly in a small number of cases have difficulties arisen over the idoption of a decision, thus requiring it to be referred back to the Council—for regulatory procedures, only in 32 of the 3,000 legal acts over the last five years. The number of decisions finally approved by the Council and not by the Commission is well below 5%.' An at least partial explanation of the reasoning behind the solution was given by Marcelino Oreja: 'It is clear to me :hat the Parliament must not assume an executive role. I am sure it has no intention of becoming some kind of alternative power, or of taking part in an activity which must remain entirely within :he Commission's competence if it is to be useful and efficient. It is for the Commission to use its nitiative and fulfil its responsibilities, studying each individual case and ruling on the legitimacy and appropriateness of adopting an executive decision. It follows from these principles that it is 'or the Commission to rule whether, on the contrary, a new legislative procedure should be

support and MEPs from all camps took the opportunity to urge their colleagues 'to be very careful with regard to any olive branches held out by the Commission.'[255] The demand for a reform of the committee system was a legacy which had been passed on from one generation of MEPs to another for as long as any of them could remember. Now faced with an opportunity to sort the system out once and for all, it was not difficult for them to wait a little longer. Therefore, instead of an Opinion which would have closed the procedure for consultation of the European Parliament, a resolution was adopted in which the 'guidelines' were laid down for further negotiations with the Commission and the Council.[256] The strategy had once again been drawn up by the Committee on Institutional Affairs. As explained by Ms Aglietta:

The European Parliament has decided to act at two points: to begin negoti-ations with the Council and the Commission as soon as possible on the basis of

initiated.' See the statement by Commissioner Marcelino Oreja in the Debates of the European Parliament on 15 September 1998, above Ch 4, n 124. Cf. the Swedish Government's Position PM of 20 November 1998, above Ch 1, n 25.

[255] See the statement by Brian Crowley in the Debates of the European Parliament of 15 September 1998, above Ch 4, n 124.

[256] See European Parliament Resolution of 16 September 1998 on the modification of the procedures for the exercise of implementing powers conferred on the Commission— comitology (OJ 1998 C 313/101). See *Bulletin EU* 9-1998, point 1.8.2. The 'guidelines' for the negotiations were set out in point 1 of the Resolution. Accordingly a result should be sought which would be:

> guaranteeing full respect for the legislative procedure in order to prevent a legislative act (including the revision and updating of acts adopted under the co-decision procedure and the amending of annexes, insofar as these are general in scope) from being adopted as an implementing measure outside the regular co-decision procedure. Total compliance with the legislative procedure becomes increasingly important as the field of application of the co-decision procedure is extended;

> ensuring a balance between the institutions following the modification of the co-decision procedure, so as to guarantee real equality between the Council and the Parliament, both in establishing the delegation of implementing powers to the Commission and in the exercise of the power of control of the legislative authority (the Council and the Parliament) over an implementing measure;

> defining the Commission's degree of autonomy in implementing the provisions by assigning more specific powers, by specifying implementing provisions in the relevant legislation, whilst simultaneously ensuring that the legislative authority (the Parliament and the Council) do not intervene in implementing measures.

he resolution we are discussing today and—with the negotiations started or ndeed swiftly completed—to express its final opinion on the Commission's proposal. A satisfactory conclusion of the negotiations also depends on the willingness of the Commission and, above all, the Council to discuss Parliament's requests openly and without hindrance, as well as the willingness of Parliament to understand the reasoning of the Commission and the Council.[257]

n accordance with the consultation procedure, the European Parliament wanted to state its opinion on a proposal presented by the Commission before the Council could adopt it. Moreover, if substantial modifications were made to the proposal—by the Commission or the Council—the European Parliament ought to be re-consulted (save where the modifications corresponded to those suggested by the European Parliament).[258] Even if this procedure did not oblige the Commission or the Council to comply with the opinion of the European Parliament, it was an 'essential formality' which they should not be permitted to disregard.[259] In the past, the European Parliament had learnt to use its limited rights under the consultation procedure as a 'power to delay' (cf. above 4.2.1.2).[260] Quite naturally, the strength of this power was premised on the other parties' wish to reach a rapid settlement of the matter at hand. This, indeed, had been seen in the discussions which led to the adoption of the first Comitology Decision in 1987: both the Commission and the Governments had felt that the institution of 'principles and rules' for the exercise of implementing powers was a precondition for initiation

---

[257] See the statement by Maria Adelaide Aglietta in the Debates of the European Parliament of 15 September 1998, above Ch 4, n 124.

[258] See e.g. Case C-65/90, above Ch 4, n 166, at p. 4621. For an explanation of the legal situation, see Kapteyn and VerLoren van Themaat, above Ch 1, n 36, at pp. 419–424.

[259] See Case 138/79, above Ch 4, n 162. Here it was stated by the Court of Justice that the requirement for consultation of the European Parliament reflected 'the fundamental democratic principle that the peoples should take part in the exercise of power through the intermediary of a representative assembly. Due consultation of the Parliament in the case provided for by the Treaty therefore constitutes an essential formality disregard of which means that the measure concerned is void.'

[260] Naturally, the right of the European Parliament to state its Opinion is not intended to be abused. But in practice, the distinguishing line between a slow but serious consultation and a deliberate delay is a fine one. The legal formula intended to strike the balance was laid down by the Court of Justice in Case C-65/93 (above Ch 4, n 166), at pp. 668–669. Accordingly, 'the institutional dialogue, on which the consultation procedure in particular is based, is subject to the same mutual duties of sincere co-operation as those which govern relations between Member States and the Community institutions.'

of the programme for establishment of an internal market (see above 3.4.2.2 and 4.2.1.1).

Clearly, the strength of the 'power to delay' was not as great in the present situation. Not only had the Court of Justice decided that the requirement for consultation of the European Parliament did not apply if it 'failed to discharge its obligation to co-operate sincerely with the Council' (see above 4.3.4.2) but it was the European Parliament itself which insisted on reform and the other parties could be expected to be less sensitive to the pressure. Therefore, in order to put some additional weight behind its words, the European Parliament decided to make use of other available means. Of particular importance, in that respect, was its power of budgetary control (cf. above 4.3.5). Following the debates on 15 September 1998, the statement was made by the European Parliament that it would 'consider the appropriateness of placing commitology funding in reserve in the 1999 budget if the modification of the Council Decision fails to take due account of Parliament's positions.'[261] Two months later, in the midst of the negotiations, the decision was taken to go from words to deeds and to put just over half of the appropriations for committees in the reserve, 'in order to maintain pressure on all sides to come to an equitable and effective solution on the new commitology structure.'[262]

The first sign of progress could be seen on 24 March 1999 when the Committee on Institutional Affairs presented an up-dated version of its Aglietta Report.[263] The timing was crucial. Less than two weeks before,

---

[261] This was in particular stated by Jens-Peter Bonde in the Debates of the European Parliament on 15 September 1998, above Ch 4, n 124. The broad support for this suggestion was reflected in point 3 of the European Parliament Resolution of 16 September 1998 (see above Ch 4, n 256), in which it was stated that the European Parliament should 'consider the appropriateness of placing commitology funding in reserve in the 1999 budget if the modification of the Council decision fails to take due account of Parliament's positions.' See also *Bulletin EU* 10-1998, point 1.5.4.

[262] See European Parliament Resolution of 17 December 1998 on the Draft General Budget of the European Union for the Financial Year 1999 as modified by the Council (OJ 1999 C 98/212), point 30. Based on the Report of 10 December 1998 drawn up on behalf of the Committee on Budgets on the Draft General Budget of the European Union for the Financial Year 1999 (rapporteur: Barbara Dührkop Dührkop) EP Doc A4-500/98. See also *Bulletin EU* 11-1998, point 1.5.2; and *Bulletin EU* 12-1998, point 1.5.2.

[263] See the Report of 24 March 1999 drawn up on behalf of the Committee on Institutional Affairs on the proposal for a Council Decision laying down the procedures for the exercise of implementing powers conferred on the Commission (rapporteur: Maria Adelaide Aglietta) EP Doc A4-169/99.

the Commission responsible for the much criticized proposal for reform of the committee system had resigned.[264] With respect to its contents, the second Aglietta Report was more or less identical to the first one: this time the need was stressed for a solution which would give the European Parliament an equal share of the powers of political supervision over implementing acts adopted within the field of the application of the co-decision procedure. But, importantly, the conclusion was reached that the inter-institutional negotiations, insisted upon by the European Parliament, had now reached a point where it was possible to state an opinion.

For this reason, the Committee on Institutional Affairs had prepared a draft resolution in which the original proposal was approved subject to a number of amendments. The amendments were well in line with previous statements and envisaged, above all, the complete abolition of the regulatory committee procedure, a delimitation of the substantive scope of implementing measures (the insertion of an explanation that implementing measures should not be used to 'update or adapt essential provisions' of basic instruments[265]), the introduction of a mechanism for 'protection of the legislative sphere' (consisting of a right to revoke a decision, within the fields of application of the co-decision procedure and, within other fields, a more limited right to 'blow the whistle'[266]), a wider right to information, and, finally, the adoption of a uniform set of rules for the internal workings of all committees.

---

[264] See *Bulletin EU* 3-1999, point 1.10.12.

[265] Cf. the European Parliament Resolution of 16 September 1998 (see above Ch 4, n 256) in which it was stated that: 'acts which modify, update or supplement the essential aspects of a legislative provision cannot be considered implementing measures.' See the oral evidence given by Richard Corbett to the House of Lords, in the 1998–99 House of Lords Paper on Comitology, below Ch 4, n 297, at p. 28 (paragraphs 128–129); and the written evidence submitted by Alexander Türk, at p. 65.

[266] The amendments that aimed to bring about a 'protection of the legislative sphere' corresponded to older demands for establishment of a substitution mechanism. Essentially, the 'right to revoke' within fields of application of the co-decision procedure envisaged that it should be possible for the Council and the European Parliament, independently of each other, to revoke an implementing measure within a limited period of time. If so the Commission would amend the implementing measure or present a normal legislative proposal. The 'right to blow the whistle' within all other fields meant that the European Parliament would be entitled to ask the Commission to substitute a (draft) implementing measure with a normal legislative proposal and that the Commission would be obliged to take account of the position of the European Parliament 'as far as possible'.

4.4.1.4   The European Parliament delivers its opinion

The second Aglietta Report and the draft Resolution were debated in the European Parliament on 5 May 1999, the same day it approved the nomination of Romano Prodi for President of a new Commission.[267] It is unlikely that the coincidence was unintentional. Romano Prodi was a man with both political and academic credentials: he was a Professor of Economics and had recently resigned as Italian Prime Minister. Clearly, the expectations were high among many MEPs that this was the man who would bring about many of the improvements they had been waiting for. The promises made when he presented them with his 'vision of the European venture' matched their expectations: if appointed and approved, his Commission would make transparency and the opening-up of the Institutions its 'top priorities.'[268] Even before his Commission had yet been instituted, Professor Prodi managed to fuel the MEPs with hope, not only for matters to be dealt with in the future, but also for current ones. Of those, none was more important than the reform of the committee system.

The last time the reform of the committee system had been debated by the MEPs, quite naturally, the Commission had been represented by Marcelino Oreja, the Commissioner responsible for relations with the European Parliament. Now, on 5 May 1999, it was represented by the Commissioner responsible for transport, Neil Kinnock. The shift was not as strange as it may have seemed. Mr Kinnock was one of the few members of the old Commission who remained in the new Commission, in which he would be responsible for administrative reform.

As Neil Kinnock explained, the demands made by the European Parliament with regard to the reform of the committee system were strongly supported by the Commission, which was confident that several of them would be agreed in Council. The only important aspect left to be dealt with was the protection of 'the legislative prerogatives' and, linked to that, the future of the regulatory committee procedure

---

[267] See European Parliament Resolution of 5 May 1999 on the nomination of the Commission President (OJ 1999 C 279/171). See *Bulletin EU* 5-1999, point 1.9.15. It may be noted also that less than a week before, on 1 May 1999, the Treaty of Amsterdam had finally entered into force (see above Ch 4, n 227).

[268] See the address by Romano Prodi to the European Parliament on 4 May, in *Bulletin EU* 5-1999, point 2.3.1. Cf. also the address by Romano Prodi to the European Parliament on 13 April 1999, in *Bulletin EU* 5-1999, point 2.2.1.

(cf. above 4.4.1.3).[269] Apparently, the Council still refused to make any concessions and the Commission offered the European Parliament a right to 'blow the whistle' based on a unilateral commitment.[270] But this was not sufficient. A similar solution had already been provided in the *Modus Vivendi* and experience had proved that it was 'little short of a disaster.'[271] Therefore, the European Parliament would not settle for anything less than a legally-binding mechanism for protection of the legislative sphere. If this were not obtained, the inter-institutional conflict would continue. This, indeed, was underlined by Richard Corbett, one of the MEPs who had been most actively involved in the negotiations:

I warn the Council that although it has made progress on transparency, if the working group continues to be so restrictive on Parliament's rights to intervene, then there will be no agreement and we will continue in legislative procedure after legislative procedure to block the comitology measures and resist the adoption of such restrictive measures and we will be very restrictive on voting the budgets and the credits to allow comitology-type committees to continue to meet. We are not seeking to take powers to ourselves to intervene in the detail but we are seeking to have the safeguard. That safeguard is very important. It is the principle on which we will insist and unless agreement is reached in this matter I can tell Council that co-decision procedure after co-decision procedure will have to go all the way to conciliation and time after time there will be difficulty on this problem.[272]

---

[269] See the statement by Commissioner Neil Kinnock in the Debates of the European Parliament on 5 May 1999 above Ch 4, n 236. Cf. also the statement by the representative of the Committee on Institutional Affairs, Biagio De Giovanni, in the Debates of the European Parliament on 5 May 1999, above Ch 4, n 236.

[270] See Ciavarini-Azzi, above Ch 1, n 26, at p. 56.

[271] See the *Modus Vivendi*, above Ch 4, n 147 (and also the Klepsch-Millan Agreement, above Ch 4, n 121). In respect of the practical experience, see e.g. the Opinion of the Committee on the Environment, Public Health and Consumer Protection, in Report of 30 March 1999 drawn up on the behalf of the Committee on Institutional Affairs on the proposal for a Council Decision laying down the procedures for the exercise of implementing powers conferred on the Commission (rapporteur: Maria Adelaide Aglietta) EP Doc A4-169/99. Cf. however, the statement by Richard Corbett in the Debates of the European Parliament of 5 May 1999, above Ch 4, n 236: '[i]f you look at the way we have used this power in the informal procedures that already exist, it is actually very unusual for parliaments to intervene and to blow the whistle. We have done it occasionally—infant formulae milk is a notable example. We blew the whistle, the Commission entered into a dialogue with us, changed its proposal and that was ultimately what was adopted. It worked.'

[272] See the statement by Richard Corbett in the Debates of the European Parliament on 5 May 1999, above Ch 4, n 236.

Unsatisfying as it may have been that this problem had not yet been resolved, it was not likely that it could be hoped to achieve anything more through further negotiations. Whether they liked it or not, therefore, the MEPs felt that they had to leave the next move to the Council. But before delivering their opinion, the MEPs were given some advice from Neil Kinnock which would turn out to be of crucial significance. They were advised to make sure that they got their priorities right. The logic underlying this advice was that the Council would be more likely to accept the demand for a mechanism for protection of the legislative sphere if the MEPs were willing to reconsider their categorical rejection of the regulatory committee procedure. According to Mr Kinnock, new formulae had been suggested which he thought would be acceptable, not only to the Commission but also to the European Parliament,'provided that there is no double safety net or *contre-filet* which would give the Council the means of rejecting a proposed executive measure.'

At the end of the session, a resolution was adopted in which the European Parliament approved the proposal for a new comitology decision subject to a number of amendments.[273] These were more or less the same as those which had been proposed in the second report of the Committee on Institutional Affairs (see above 4.4.1.3). But an important difference could be found with respect to the regulatory committee procedure. Accordingly, 'maintaining regulatory committees would be unacceptable *unless* the double safety-net procedure were abandoned, while guaranteeing effective decision-making procedures and avoiding a system which might result in no decisions being taken.' (emphasis added). This, indeed, was evidence that the MEPs were not only competent to make demands but also to bargain and the link to Mr Kinnock's advice was obvious. At the same time, it was a statement of both historical and constitutional significance: for the first time ever, the European Parliament had admitted a readiness to accept the regulatory committee procedure.

4.4.2   The result

4.4.2.1   The new Council Decision 99/468/EC

After the European Parliament had adopted its opinion, the discussions within the Council were intensified and, finally, on 21 June 1999 an

---

[273] See European Parliament Resolution of 6 May 1999 embodying Parliament's opinion on the proposal for a Council Decision laying down the procedures for the exercise of

agreement was reached.[274] One week later the new Comitology Decision was adopted: Council Decision 99/468/EC laying down the procedures for the exercise of implementing powers conferred on the Commission.[275] Even if a number of amendments had been made, the contents of the Decision could be split into the same three categories as the proposal on which it was based (see above 4.4.1.1). The first contained provisions which were intended to make the committee system less complex (see below 4.4.2.2). In line with the proposal, these focused on the simplification of the fixed committee procedures and an adjustment or 'streamlining' of the variety of procedures in operation.

The second category included provisions which were expected to make the system more open to parliamentary control (see below 4.4.2.3). It has already been noted that the solution envisaged by the Commission, integrated into a reform of the regulatory committee procedure, had been unacceptable to both the European Parliament and the Council (see above 4.4.1.5). In the end, therefore, a different solution was opted for. Supplementary to a more modest and, indeed, less elegant reform of the regulatory committee procedure, a power was introduced for the European Parliament to intervene in defence of its legislative prerogative.

The third category, finally, contained provisions which were aimed to make the committee system less opaque or, in other words, more transparent (see below 4.4.2.4). These were based on the ideas manifested in the proposal that criteria should be established for the choice of committee procedure and that the European Parliament should be granted a legal right to information. Although not foreseen in the proposal, some rules were also introduced relating to more general aspects of transparency.

4.4.2.2 A system less complex

In its proposal the Commission had sought to bring about simplification of the fixed committee procedures through the abolition of the restrictive

---

implementing powers conferred on the Commission (OJ 1999 C 279/404). See also *Bulletin EU* 5-1999, point 1.8.9.

[274] Council meeting (General Affairs) of 21–22 June 1999 (Presse 198 No 9008/99).

[275] Council Decision 99/468/EC of 28 June 1999 laying down the procedures for the exercise of implementing powers conferred on the Commission (OJ 1999 L 184/23). For a commentary, see Lenaerts K. and Verhoeven, A., Towards a Legal Framework for Executive Rule-Making in the EU? The Contribution of the New Comitology Decision (2000) 37 *CMLRev* 645.

variants and, parallel to that, certain procedural modifications.[276] These were clearly aimed at bringing about a strengthening of its own position.[277] Unsurprisingly, therefore, the Council's reaction was not very enthusiastic and the modifications were rejected. Instead, a more limited simplification was agreed on in respect of the two most important types of procedure: the management and regulatory committee procedure.[278]

The simplified management committee procedure The management committee procedure had been designed to be used in situations where there was a need for rapid action. In contrast to the other procedures, therefore, the Commission would adopt an implementing measure—which would apply immediately—before the committee had given its formal opinion. If, later, the opinion should turn out to be negative, the Commission would have to communicate the measure to the Council which was entitled to modify or annul it. The practical significance of that power, however, was restricted by the fact that the measures had already begun to apply: for each passing day it would become more difficult for the Council to modify or annul it. Under the old Comitology Decision this had been dealt with so that the Commission could be either permitted (cf. 'may') or obliged (cf. 'shall') to suspend the application of a measure on 'appeal' (see above 4.2.2.2).

In the new Decision, the Council had approached the management committee procedure a little more courageously than the safeguard procedure: the restrictive variant had been deleted.[279] But the practical significance of this manoeuvre was more apparent than real. Parallel to the abolition of the restrictive variant, one element from that variant was transferred to the new simplified procedure. This was the rule that the period during which the Council would be permitted to modify or annul an implementing measure (i.e. the period during which the Commission could suspend its application) could be as long as three months. Under the

---

[276] See above 4.4.1.1.

[277] Cf. the advisory committee procedure: that paragraph 3 should be deleted ('[t]he opinion shall be recorded in the minutes; in addition, each Member State shall have the right to ask to have its position recorded in the minutes'); and the management committee procedure: that paragraph 3 should state that 'the Commission *may* adopt measures which shall apply immediately...' (emphasis added).

[278] For the advisory committee procedure and the safeguard procedure, see, respectively, Articles 3 and 6 of Council Decision 99/468/EC above Ch 4, n 275.

[279] See Article 4 of Council Decision 99/468/EC, above Ch 4, n 275.

basic form of the old management committee procedure, this period had been limited to one month. Another, essential, element from the abolished variant was found in the Preamble of the new Decision. This explained that in situations 'where non-urgent measures are referred to the Council, the Commission should exercise its discretion to defer application of the measures.' The combined effect of this was that the power to make use of the more restrictive variant had certainly not ceased to exist but merely lost its official recognition.

A cause for even deeper concern with regard to the 'transparency' of the management committee procedure could be found in a declaration attached to the new Decision, in which the Commission promised not to abandon its 'constant practice... to try to secure a satisfactory decision which will also muster the widest possible support within the Committee.'[280] This was a clear indication that the power of the committee to influence the final product stretched far beyond its formal opinion. If this was complied with—which it apparently had been in the past—the opinion of the committee would be positive and the question whether the Commission was obliged or only permitted to defer application of an implementing measure on appeal would be of no practical relevance.

The simplified regulatory committee procedure The most substantial changes were those relating to the regulatory committee procedure.[281] It has been seen above that this, indeed, had been one of the most problematic matters dealt with not only in the negotiations with the European Parliament but also in the discussions within the Council itself. Contrary to what may have been expected, the greatest problem had not been the European Parliament's persistent insistence that the procedure should be abolished altogether but that one of the Governments—the Danish— was not willing to give up 'the possibility for the Council to veto

---

[280] See the statement by the Commission on Article 4 in Declarations on Council Decision 99/468/EC of 28 June 1999 laying down the procedures for the exercise of implementing powers conferred on the Commission (OJ 1999 C 203/1). According to the relevant statement, '[u]nder the management procedure, the Commission would recall that its constant practice is to try to secure a satisfactory decision which will also muster the widest possible support within the Committee. The Commission will take account of the position of the members of the Committee and act in such a way as to avoid going against any predominant position which might emerge against the appropriateness of an implementing measure.' Cf. the statement by the Commission on Article 5, below Ch 4, n 288.

[281] See Article 5 of Council Decision 99/468/EC, above Ch 4, n 275.

a Commission proposal by simple majority in sensitive fields' (i.e. the *contre-filet* mechanism).[282] After the European Parliament had adopted its opinion, the discussions within the Council were intensified.[283] The efforts of the German Presidency were, first, focused on finding a solution which would secure a regulatory committee procedure that could be 'effectively used' and at the same time avoid any further inter-institutional conflict, and, then, on convincing the 'stubborn' Government that this solution was the best available. These efforts were not wasted. Only a week before the end of the German Presidency agreement was finally reached.[284]

Like the old regulatory committee procedure (see above 4.2.2.2) the new simplified one was also based on the idea that the committee should actively approve a draft implementing measure before the Commission could adopt it. If not, the Commission had to submit a proposal which the Council could adopt (and presumably also amend[285]) or 'oppose' by qualified majority.[286] The latter was a novelty which had been introduced in place of the *contre-filet* mechanism, thus satisfying the demands of the Commission and the European Parliament.[287] Accordingly, if the Council should 'oppose' the proposal, the Commission would have to re-examine it and either re-submit its proposal—in original or amended version—or present a new proposal within the normal legislative process. The objective would be to find a 'balanced' solution and the Commission, therefore, had promised to 'act in such a way as to avoid going against any predominant position which might emerge within the Council against the appropriateness of an implementing measure.'[288] In addition to the

---

[282] Council meeting (General Affairs) of 31 May 1999 on Comitology (Presse 171-G No 8657/99).   [283] See Council meeting of 21–22 June 1999, above Ch 4, n 274.

[284] See Council meeting of 21–22 June 1999, above Ch 4, n 274.

[285] The Council could, however, only amend the Commission proposal by unanimity (subject to the rule of amendments in Article 250(1) EC (1999).

[286] If the Council could remain passive, the *filet*-mechanism would continue to apply, requiring the Commission itself to adopt the proposal at the end of a given period.

[287] Cf. the explanation in the Preamble that the simplified regulatory committee procedure would comply 'in full with the Commission's right of initiative in legislative matters.'

[288] See the statement by the Commission on Article 5 in Declarations on Council Decision 99/468/EC, above Ch 4, n 280. According to the statement: '[i]n the review of proposals for implementing measures concerning particularly sensitive sectors, the Commission, in order to find a balanced solution, will act in such a way as to avoid going against any predominant position which might emerge within the Council against the appropriateness of an implementing measure.'

above, a more limited power was inserted for the European Parliament to manifest its discontent with a draft implementing measure or a proposal. But that will be examined in the part concerning parliamentary control (see below 4.4.2.3).

The adjustment of the procedures of existing committees In 1986 the possibility had been foreseen by the Commission and the European Parliament of aligning the procedures of existing committees with those that were about to be fixed. But to their disappointment, the Council decided not only to ignore that possibility but to insert a provision authorizing the continuous operation of old procedures (see above 4.2.2.1). In order to rectify this, and ensure that the procedures to be laid down in the new Decision would be the only ones in operation, the Commission had included, in its proposal, a provision requiring the Council and the European Parliament to adjust 'without delay ... provisions relating to committees assisting the Commission in the exercise of implementing powers provided for by instruments predating this Decision in order to align them on it.'[289] The reaction this time was a little more enthusiastic. Although refusing to make it a binding commitment, in a declaration the Council agreed that the adoption of the new Decision should be followed by an adjustment of old procedures 'on a case by case basis, in the course of normal revision of legislation.'[290] Seemingly concerned that the European Parliament would take the opportunity to reopen debates on matters of substance, the Council (and the Commission) emphasized that the forth-coming manoeuvre must not have 'the effect of jeopardising attainment of the objectives of the basic instrument or the effectiveness of Community

---

[289] See Article 8 of the Commission Proposal of 24 June 1998, above Ch 4, n 234.

[290] See statement by the Council and Commission in Declarations on Council Decision 99/468/EC, above Ch 4, n 280. Cf. European Parliament and Council Regulation 1882/03/EC of 29 September 2003 adapting to Council Decision 99/468/EC the provisions relating to committees which assist the Commission in the exercise of its implementing powers laid down in instruments subject to the procedure referred to in Article 251 of the EC Treaty (OJ 2003 L 284/1); Council Regulation 806/03/EC of 14 April 2003 adapting to Decision 99/468/EC the provisions relating to committees which assist the Commission in the exercise of its implementing powers laid down in Council instruments adopted in accordance with the consultation procedure—qualified majority (OJ 2003 L 122/1); and Council Regulation 807/03/EC of 14 April 2003 adapting to Decision 99/468/EC the provisions relating to committees which assist the Commission in the exercise of its implementing powers laid down in Council instruments adopted in accordance with the consultation procedure—unanimity (OJ 2003 L 122/36).

action.' The message was crystal clear: if the MEPs did not behave themselves, the adjustment would immediately be discontinued.[291]

4.4.2.3   A system more open to parliamentary control

The European Parliament's concern about the committee system was based on the fear of a sliding in powers: matters of fundamental political significance were increasingly dealt with outside the normal legislative process in accordance with procedures where the European Parliament itself had no influence (see above 4.4.1.2 and 4.4.1.3). The only real power to prevent this was entrusted with the Council. For the European Parliament that was unacceptable, especially within the field of the application of the co-decision procedure. Since this procedure had given the European Parliament equality in the normal legislative process, it was entitled also to equality in the exercise of powers of political supervision over implementing measures. The concerns and demands of the European Parliament were certainly not unknown to the Commission. But nevertheless, when the Commission drafted the proposal for a new decision the effort to make the committee system 'more open to parliamentary control' had been limited to a simplification of the regulatory committee procedure, the practical significance of which would be near to nothing for the European Parliament (see above 4.4.1.1 and 4.4.1.2).

It has been seen above that the demand of the European Parliament for equality in the exercise of powers of political supervision was the most difficult matter dealt with in the negotiations (see above 4.4.1.3 and 4.4.1.5). After stubborn resistance, the Council finally surrendered and the European Parliament won its most important victory.[292] There can be little doubt that the decisive factor had been the threat of a prolonged and intensified inter-institutional conflict (see above 4.4.1.4). According to the solution finally adopted, the European Parliament would be permitted to 'blow the whistle' if it felt that a draft implementing measure[293] or a

---

[291] Cf. Ciavarini-Azzi above Ch 1, n 26, at p. 56. For a discussion on some of the (practical) problems with adjustment, see the written evidence submitted by Statewatch to the House of Lords, in the 1998–99 House of Lords Paper on Comitology, below Ch 4, n 297, at p. 56.

[292] See Ciavarini-Azzi, above Ch 1, n 26, at p. 56.

[293] The general right to intervention must be presumed to apply to all types of committee procedures. In the case of the management committee procedure, the application of the right to intervention is explicitly provided for in Article 4(3) of Council Decision 99/468/EC. But it is not clear from the text of the Decision if the European Parliament shall indicate its objection

proposal submitted to the Council under the regulatory committee procedure was exceeding the powers conferred on the Commission in a basic instrument adopted under the co-decision procedure. The meaning of this was explained, most clearly, with respect to the first case. Here the Commission would have to re-examine the measure in the light of the parliamentary position (taking it 'into account') and either submit a new draft measure, continue with the procedure, or present a proposal for normal legislation (cf. below 4.4.3.2).[294] It would also keep the European Parliament informed of the choice of action and its reasons. With respect to the second case, concerning proposals submitted under the regulatory committee procedure, it was stated that the Council should only act on the proposal (i.e. adopt it or object to it) if this was appropriate 'in view of' the parliamentary position. The exact meaning of this was far from clear.[295]

4.4.2.4 A system more transparent

The third category of content consisted of provisions aimed at making the committee system more transparent. Overall, these were based on the ideas embraced by the Commission in the proposal: that criteria should be established for the choice between the fixed committee procedures and that existing 'political understandings' should be replaced by a legal right for the European Parliament to be kept informed about committee procedures. In addition to that some provisions were introduced which would respond to the criticism that the committee system had made the fog around decision-making even thicker in the eyes of the public. The move was not as surprising as it may have seemed. During the last few years, a group of Governments had been pressing hard for the introduction of rules that would make the workings of the European Union

before or after the measure has been submitted to the committee. In Article 8 of the Decision reference is only made to 'draft implementing measures, the adoption of which is contemplated and which have been submitted' to a committee. According to the management committee procedure, however, the implementing measure is only formally 'submitted' to the committee after it has been adopted.

[294] See Article 8 of Council Decision 99/468/EC, above Ch 4, n 275. It was also explained that the parliamentary position would be stated in a resolution, setting out the grounds on which it was based.

[295] See Article 5(5) to (6) of Council Decision 99/468/EC, above Ch 4, n 275. Cf. the *Modus Vivendi* (above Ch 4, n 147) according to which the Council should take 'due account' of the position of the European Parliament 'in order to seek a solution in the appropriate framework.'

more transparent. In that wider context, the ambition to open the committee system up in the eyes of the public was but one small step.

The criteria relating to the choice of committee procedure The proposal to establish criteria relating to the choice of committee procedure presented the Council with a rather delicate problem. Undoubtedly, such criteria would help to achieve consistency and predictability and their establishment, therefore, would be an important measure of reform.[296] But at the same time there were several conflicting ideas about what the actual content of the criteria should be. One extreme, in that respect, was the position taken by the European Parliament, which insisted on criteria which would enable a clear-cut distinction between 'legislative' and 'implementing' measures (see above 4.3.4.2 and 4.4.1.3). Another extreme was the position taken by those who rejected the logic of the European Parliament and insisted on criteria that were open-ended (see above 4.3.4.2). No better representative of this position can be found than the House of Lords Select Committee on the European Communities. In its opinion on the proposal for a new comitology decision, the Select Committee emphasized that the EC Treaty did 'not follow or impose any rigid doctrine of the formal separation of powers' and recommended that the substantive scope of implementing measures had to remain flexible:

Any criteria must be generally acceptable, readily understandable and workable. There must not be a risk that their practical application would give rise to the sort of time-consuming debate between the institutions which they are intended to remove. Nor must they create unnecessary opportunities for challenge on legal grounds. They must be capable of being applied to the wide variety of subject matter dealt with by Comitology committees (from intervention prices under the CAP to, in the future, rules affecting civil liberties under the new Title IV of the EC Treaty establishing an 'area of freedom, security and justice'). They must not be too prescriptive, and they should permit differences of policy (for example, as currently exists in the relation to the supervision of substantial spending decisions). Allowance has also to be made for the nature and extent as well as the development of the Commission's experience and capabilities. Under the current regime, for example, the regulatory procedure may be used on the grounds of the novelty of the

---

[296] See the Preamble of Council Decision 99/468/EC, above Ch 4, n 275. Cf. the Opinion of the House of Lords, in the 1998–99 House of Lords Paper on Comitology, below Ch 4, n 297, at p. 33 (paragraph 165).

subject-matter. As mentioned, one of the key interests to be protected is that of the Member States. There will remain matters on which there are sensitivities, at least until the Commission has shown itself capable of exercising the powers in question completely.[297]

According to the House of Lords Select Committee, it was not likely that the criteria required could be accurately and concisely translated into legal text. Therefore, some sort of 'guidelines' should be agreed instead in a political rather than a legal text.[298] A major advantage of this was that it should be possible to provide, at least some, consistency and predictability and, at the same time, avoid the risk of 'unnecessary opportunities for challenge on legal grounds.'[299] Essentially this was also the solution opted for by the Council. The only difference was that, in the end, the guidelines were still called criteria and that they were left in the text of the new Decision. The trick which made this possible was to insert an explanation that the criteria should only be of 'a non-binding nature' (not in the text of the new Decision but in its Preamble).[300]

In respect of their substance, the criteria adopted did not depart greatly from those which had been proposed by the Commission. Noteworthy, first, were the criteria relating to the management committee and safeguard procedures. These provided that the former should be used for the adoption of 'management measures' and the latter for (all) situations 'where the basic instrument confers on the Commission the power to decide on safeguard measures.'[301] A certain clarification of the meaning of management measures was given through the examples of measures 'such as those relating to the application of the common agricultural and

---

[297] It may be noted that support for this standpoint was found in Case 16/88 *Commission v Council* (see above Ch 4, n 77). See the Opinion of the House of Lords, in House of Lords Select Committee on the European Communities, Delegation of Powers to the Commission: Reforming Comitology, Session 1998–99, 3rd Report (2 February 1999), at pp. 32–33 (paragraphs 163–164). It may be noted that a very similar view has been stated by the Swedish Government. See Position PM of 20 November 1998, above Ch 1, n 25.

[298] See the Opinion of the House of Lords, in the 1998–99 House of Lords Paper on Comitology, above Ch 4, n 297, at p. 33 (paragraph 165).

[299] Quote from the 1998–99 House of Lords Paper on Comitology, above Ch 4, n 297.

[300] See point 5 of the Preamble to Council Decision 99/468/EC, above Ch 4, n 275.

[301] See Articles 2(a) and 6 of Council Decision 99/468/EC, above Ch 4, n 275. In the proposal it was envisaged that the criteria relating to all procedures should be placed in Article 2. But for unknown reasons the Council decided to place the criteria relating to the safeguard procedure in Article 6.

common fisheries policies, or to the implementation of programmes with substantial budgetary implications.'

Perhaps most importantly, the criteria relating to the regulatory committee procedure provided that this should be used for the adoption of 'measures of general scope designed to apply essential provisions of basic instruments' or to 'adapt or update' certain non-essential provisions of basic instruments. This was narrower than that proposed by the Commission and a concession to the demands of the European Parliament (see above 4.4.1.3). But at the same time it was clear that the criteria would be wide enough to ensure that the regulatory committee procedure could be used for the adoption measures of legislative bearing.[302]

The final criteria were those relating to the advisory committee procedure. Here the triumph of flexibility over predictability was total. In the text adopted by the Council, the criteria envisaged in the proposal, that the advisory committee procedure should be applied in all situations where the management and regulatory committee procedures were not considered appropriate (cf. 'without prejudice to'), had been supplemented by the requirement that the procedure should also be 'considered to be the most appropriate.'[303] A logical consequence of this is that if the advisory committee procedure was not considered to be the most appropriate, then the management or regulatory committee procedure could be used.

The European Parliament's right to information   In its proposal, the Commission had indicated a willingness to 'tidy up' the *Modus Vivendi* and the inter-institutional agreements through the introduction of a right for the European Parliament to be informed about committee procedures on a regular basis (see above 4.4.1.1). The basic idea was that the previous

---

[302] See Article 2(b) of Council Decision 99/468/EC, above Ch 4, n 275. The most important difference with the proposal was that 'essential provisions of basic instruments' should only be possible to 'apply' and not to 'update or adapt'. The practical significance of this is far from clear. For an explanation of the European Parliament's view on the difference between 'apply' and 'adapt' see the oral evidence given by Richard Corbett to the House of Lords, in the 1998–99 House of Lords Paper on Comitology, above Ch 4, n 297, at p. 28 (paragraph 129). Cf. the European Parliament Resolution of 16 September 1998: 'acts which modify, update or supplement the essential aspects of a legislative provision cannot be considered implementing measures.' (above Ch 4, n 256).

[303] See Article 2(c) of Council Decision 99/468/EC, above Ch 4, n 275, according to which the advisory committee procedure, 'without prejudice to points (a) and (b), . . . shall be used in any case in which it is considered to be the most appropriate.'

promises would be replaced by a legally-binding commitment. Accordingly, the European Parliament would be entitled to receive agendas for committee meetings, draft implementing measures submitted to committees within fields of application of the co-decision procedure, and the results of voting. It would also be kept informed about matters transferred from the Commission to the Council. This was exactly the type of improvement upon which the Council and the Governments had been hoping to focus. In the negotiations, therefore, there was little or no objection. Instead the European Parliament was encouraged to ask for more. When the new Decision was finally adopted the list of items which it would now be entitled to receive had been extended to include, in addition to the above, 'summary records of committee meetings, and lists of the authorities and organisations to which the persons designated by the Member States to represent them belong.'[304] Significantly, it was made clear in the text that the responsibility for providing the information should rest with the Commission.

The new rules on informing the public Supplementary to the European Parliament's right to information, rules were also inserted on informing the public. These had not been envisaged in the proposal but were the result of amendments insisted upon by a group of Governments who had set themselves the objective of making the workings of the European Union more transparent.[305] First of all, a requirement was laid down that all committees should adopt or adapt their rules of procedure on the basis of a standard set of rules.[306] Then it was explained that the Commission should draw up a list of all committees and present an annual report on their working.[307] The standard rules of procedure, the list of committees, and the annual report were all to be published in the Official Journal. In addition, the Commission was also given the responsibility for the setting-up of a public register containing the

---

[304] See Article 7(3) of Council Decision 99/468/EC, above Ch 4, n 275. Cf. also Article 5(4) in which it was specified that the Commission shall inform the European Parliament of proposals submitted to the Council under the regulatory committee procedure. It may be noted that the new items were taken up essentially from the Samland-Williamson Agreement (see above 4.3.3).

[305] See e.g. the Swedish Government's Position PM of 20 November 1998, above Ch 1, n 25. Cf. also the European Parliament Resolution of 16 September 1998 (above Ch 4, n 256), in which the European Parliament emphasized that the need to simplify the committee system (also) corresponded to the principle of transparency as that had been incorporated in Article 255 EC (1999). [306] See Article 7(1) of Council Decision 99/468/EC, above Ch 4, n 275.

[307] See Article 7(4) of Council Decision 99/468/EC, above Ch 4, n 275.

references for all documents sent to the European Parliament.[308] Finally, the rule was established that '[t]he principles and conditions on public access to documents applicable to the Commission shall apply to the committees.'[309] This meant that a matter which had been disputed for some years had now been settled.

On 24 June 1997, a Dutch company, Rothmans International BV, brought an application to the Court of First Instance that a decision by the Commission to refuse it access to the minutes of the 'Customs Code Committee' should be annulled.[310] The application was soon supported in an intervention by one of the most energetic crusaders for transparency, the Swedish Government, which insisted that the Customs Code Committee and all other committees operating within the committee system must be regarded as 'an integral part of the Commission.'[311] If not, the work of these committees would fall outside the scope of the new rules on public access and an individual wishing to obtain access to documents would be dependent on the committees' exercise of their own discretion, without any possibility of judicial review.[312] The Commission contended that the minutes of the Customs Code Committee were not covered by the rules on public access to its documents and that the application should be dismissed.[313] In its view, the argument that the committees must be regarded as an integral part of the Commission was a 'misconstruction' of their role, functions, and place within the institutional framework.[314] Even if the Commission provided

---

[308] See Article 7(5) of Council Decision 99/468/EC, above Ch 4, n 275. Cf. European Ombudsman Decision of 29 January 1999 (paragraph 2.4), in which the Commission was requested to keep a public register of documents in its holding (see below Ch 4, n 318). In the complaint, it had been alleged that the Commission's failure to establish a register for Commission documents amounted to maladministration because it severely restricted citizens' ability to make use of the rules on access to documents (laid down in Commission Decision 94/90, below Ch 4, n 313, and according to which the public shall have the widest possible access to Commission documents).

[309] See Article 7(2) of Council Decision 99/468/EC, above Ch 4, n 275.

[310] See Case T-188/97 *Rothmans International BV v Commission* [1999] ECR II-2463 (Judgment of 19 July 1999). [311] See paragraph 49 of the Judgment (above Ch 4, n 310).

[312] See paragraph 50 of the Judgment (above Ch 4, n 310).

[313] See Commission Decision 94/90/EC of 8 February 1994 on public access to Commission documents (OJ 1994 L 46/58). This was based on the Code of Conduct of 6 December 1993 concerning public access to Council and Commission documents (OJ 1993 L 340/41).

[314] See paragraph 45 of the Judgment (above Ch 4, n 310).

'the secretarial services', the committees were solely responsible for their deliberations.[315]

Less than two weeks after the initiation of Case T-188/97 *Rothmans International BV v Commission*, a similar complaint was made to the European Ombudsman.[316] The ensuing inquiry led the Ombudsman, after careful consideration, to request an opinion from the Council. Like the Commission before it, the Council replied that it could not be considered to be responsible and that documents relating to the committees were not covered by the rules on public access to its documents.[317] It added that normally it would not be physically in possession of the documents in question. Apparently, the otherwise valiant Ombudsman had now run up against a problem he preferred not to interfere with. In the end, therefore, it was explained that it was 'not justified to continue the inquiry into this grievance' since the Court of First Instance would give an authoritative answer in due time.[318]

The European Ombudsman was not the only one who preferred not to interfere with the problem of responsibility over the comitology committees. The Court of First Instance also made an effort to avoid it, at least until a solution had been agreed within the Council. At an early stage of the negotiations for a new comitology decision, the Swedish Government gave voice to its intention not to fix its position on public access to committee documents before the Court of First Instance had given its ruling in Case T-188/97.[319] Eventually, that intention had to be abandoned. When the new Decision was adopted, more than two years

[315] See paragraph 44 of the Judgment (above Ch 4, n 310).

[316] See European Ombudsman Decision of 29 January 1999, below Ch 4, n 318. Here it was claimed that the Commission was acting unlawfully by imposing automatic confidentiality on documents relating to committees operating within the committee system (the complainant claimed that the documents were in fact covered by the Commission's rules on public access to documents).

[317] See Council Decision 93/731/EC of 20 December 1993 on public access to Council documents (OJ 1993 L 340/43). This was also based on the Code of Conduct of 6 December 1993, above Ch 4, n 313.

[318] See European Ombudsman Decision of 29 January 1999 on complaint 633/97/PD against the Commission (http://www.euro-ombudsman.eu.int), paragraph 1.3.

[319] See the Swedish Government's Position PM of 20 November 1998, above Ch 1, n 25. Accordingly, '[o]f great significance for our position [on public access to committee documents] is the result of the so-called Rothmans case, in which the EC Court has to examine the Commission's interpretation that comitology committees are autonomous and, as a consequence, not liable under the Commission's rules for access to documents.'

had passed since Rothmans International BV brought its application to the Court of First Instance. But a few weeks later, the day after the new Decision entered into force, the Court of First Instance finally gave its ruling.[320] This emphasized—in line with the new Decision—that the committees operating within the committee system had no own administration, budget, archives, or premises, still less an address of their own, and that the formal responsibility, therefore, must lie with the Commission.[321]

4.4.3   *The reactions*

4.4.3.1   *Agreement on rules of good conduct*

At the initial stage of the negotiations with the Commission and the Council, the European Parliament had decided to enter a significant part of the appropriations for committees in the budgetary reserves (see above 4.4.1). This was a tactical move, intended 'to maintain pressure on all sides to come to an equitable and effective solution on the new commitology structure.' The European Parliament was obviously not too displeased with the result: following the adoption of Council Decision 99/468/EC the appropriations were released.[322] Two things were emphasized.[323] The first, that the endorsement by the European Parliament of the new Decision did not prejudge its positions on matters of principle, and the second, that there were still some 'rules of good conduct' for implementation of the Decision to be drawn up in an inter-institutional agreement. Leaving the first statement to be discussed, briefly, at the end of this chapter, in the following paragraphs the focus will be on the significance of the second.

At the time when the Commission presented its proposal, it had been foreseen that clarifications of how the rules on information would operate in practice could be made in a separate agreement (see above 4.4.1). During the negotiations, it became increasingly clear that this power would be used and that the agreement would only be concluded between the European Parliament and the Commission. The major advantage of

---

[320] See Case T-188/97, above Ch 4, n 310.

[321] See paragraphs 58 to 62 of the Judgment (above Ch 4, n 316).

[322] See General Report on the Activities of the European Union 1999 (Office for Official Publications 2000), point 982.   [323] See General Report 1999, above Ch 4, n 322, point 982.

this approach was that it would become easier to focus the negotiations, between the Institutions and also within the Council, on more fundamental matters, such as the reform of the regulatory committee procedure.[324] The first concrete signs that the envisaged agreement was on its way could be seen at a 'trilogue' on 6 October 1999. Here it was decided that the negotiations should be started as soon as possible and that the agreement should be finalized in the form of an exchange of letters between the European Parliament President, Nicole Fontaine and the new Commission President, Romano Prodi.[325] Once started, the negotiations were to be relatively short: the result was presented to the MEPs on 16 February 2000,[326] and the next day the agreement was approved.[327]

Essentially two types of issues had been dealt with in the Fontaine-Prodi Agreement. The first of these was the completion of the simplification operation (cf. above 4.4.1). It has already been noted that not all elements of the *Modus Vivendi* and the inter-institutional agreements had

[324] According to Monica Frassoni (rapporteur): '[d]uring the protracted inter-institutional negotiations it was understood that the European Parliament and Commission would conclude an inter-institutional agreement on the procedures for implementing certain aspects of the new decision. On the one hand, certain points which the Council did not intend to incorporate into the decision were to be made explicit and, on the other, the system for providing information about implementing measures and monitoring them was to be organised more precisely.' See the statement by Monica Frassoni in the Debates of the European Parliament on 16 February 2000 (OJ 2000 C 339/57).

[325] See the statement by Monica Frassoni in the Debates of the European Parliament on 16 February 2000, above Ch 4, n 324. Seemingly, it was also agreed that a reference to this exchange of letters should subsequently be made in the 'framework agreement' between the European Parliament and the Commission on which negotiations have not yet begun. See later the Framework Agreement of 5 July 2000 on relations between the European Parliament and the Commission, published in *Bulletin EU* 7/8-2000, point 2.2.1. See also point 1.9.1.

[326] See Agreement between the European Parliament and the Commission on procedures for implementing Council Decision 99/468/EC of 28 June 1999 laying down the procedures for the exercise of implementing powers conferred on the Commission (OJ 2000 L 256/19). See also the General Report on the Activities of the European Union 2000 (Office for Official Publications 2001), point 1100; and *Bulletin EU* 1/2-2000, point 1.9.3.

[327] See European Parliament Resolution of 17 February 2000 on the agreement between the European Parliament and the Commission on procedures for implementing Council Decision 1999/468/EC of 28 June 1999 laying down the procedures for the exercise of implementing powers conferred on the Commission (OJ 2000 C 339/269). Based on the Report of 31 January 2000 drawn up on behalf of the Committee on Constitutional Affairs on the agreement between the European Parliament and the Commission on procedures for implementing the new Council Decision of 28 June 1999—commitology (rapporteur: Monica Frassoni) EP Doc A5-21/00.

been taken up in the Decision. The majority of these were of marginal significance and the European Parliament had been prepared to renounce them voluntarily.[328] But a few elements were re-routed to the Fontaine-Prodi Agreement. Noteworthy in that respect was the requirement that the Commission should forward 'specific draft measures for implementing basic instruments which, although not adopted under the co-decision procedure, are of particular importance to the European Parliament.'[329] With the adoption of the Fontaine-Prodi Agreement all elements of the old instruments had been dealt with; those which had not been taken up by the Comitology Decision had either been renounced or re-routed.[330] The benefits of that could be found in the declaration that the European Parliament and the Commission now considered the *Modus Vivendi*, the Plumb-Delors Agreement, and the Samland-Williamson Agreement 'superseded and thus of no effect in so far as they themselves are concerned.'[331]

[328] Cf. the statement by Richard Corbett (Committee on Rules of Procedure): '[o]verall we have a system which has made some progress. The supplementary aspects that arise from the inter-institutional agreement with the Commission are welcome, but that could not change the basic decision of the Council. Even here, we have renounced voluntarily—because this did not happen automatically—the Plumb-Delors agreement as part of the overall compromise. We have been willing to relinquish the provisions in that. We shall have to be very vigilant on what used to be covered by that agreement and is not fully covered by the new decision. We must be very vigilant.' See the statement by Richard Corbett in the Debates of the European Parliament on 16 February 2000, above Ch 4, n 324.

[329] See paragraph 2 of the Fontaine-Prodi Agreement (above Ch 4, n 326). Essentially, this requirement had been taken up from the Plumb-Delors Agreement (see above 4.2.3). Another example can be found in the explanation that the European Parliament would receive the relevant information 'at the same time as the members of the committees and on the same terms.' See paragraph 1 of the Agreement. This had previously been stated, most clearly, in the *Modus Vivendi* (see above 4.3.3). It should be noted also that a reference was made to the recent ruling of the Court of First Instance in Case T-188/97 (above Ch 4, n 310), in which the general right was recognized to request access to the minutes of committee meetings from the Commission.

[330] It would seem that the only element which had been renounced was the promise made in the Samland-Williamson Agreement that the European Parliament should be able to request that it send an observer to attend the discussion of certain items on the agenda of a committee (see above 4.3.3). Cf. however, the statement that '[w]e should not draw the conclusion that because all these provisions of previous agreements are not in the current text they will be overruled for good.' Presumably, this was an implicit reference to the standard rules of procedure which were to be proposed by the Commission. See the oral evidence given by Claire-Françoise Durand to the House of Lords, in the 1998–99 House of Lords Paper on Comitology, above Ch 4, n 297, at p. 9 (paragraph 50).

[331] See paragraph 3 of the Fontaine-Prodi Agreement (above Ch 4, n 326). Presumably, this meant that the Klepsch-Millan Agreement (see above 4.3.2) should not be considered to have been superseded.

The second type of issue which had been dealt with in the Fontaine-Prodi Agreement was the clarification of how 'the system for providing information about implementing measures and monitoring them was to be organised more precisely.'[332] The right to information which had been laid down in the Comitology Decision required the Commission to inform the European Parliament of committee proceedings on a regular basis.[333] For the European Parliament, this meant a considerable step forward. In contrast to the previous right, based on political understanding, the new one was law and legally binding. But this did not mean that everything had changed. Past experience had shown that both the Commission and the European Parliament had serious difficulties dealing with the flow of information: documents had been supplied and received unsystematically, and the procedures were generally thought of as a 'huge paper chase'.[334] Therefore, in an attempt to come to terms with the problem, the Fontaine-Prodi Agreement provided that in the future all relevant information should be forwarded electronically.[335] In practice, this meant that use should be

---

[332] See Monica Frassoni in the Debates of the European Parliament on 16 February 2000, above Ch 4, n 324.

[333] See Article 7(3) of Council Decision 99/468/EC, above Ch 4, n 275.

[334] See the oral evidence given by Bryan Cassidy to the House of Lords, in the 1998–99 House of Lords Paper on Comitology, above Ch 4, n 297, at p. 26 (paragraph 113). According to Monica Frassoni, '[h]itherto, such information had been supplied on paper and unsystematically, and was of no use to our services; and indeed this was often the fault of Parliament itself.' See the statement by Monica Frassoni in the Debates of the European Parliament on 16 February 2000, above Ch 4, n 324. Cf. above 4.3.1 and 4.3.3. Cf. also that according to the European Parliament Committee on the Environment, Public Health and Consumer Protection 'the problems with the *Modus Vivendi* lie less in the text than in the practice. The central theme running through the [criticism] concerns information flow: too little relevant information, too late. Large numbers of documents are sent to the Environment Committee secretariat, which has to register, distribute and archive them. But key information is often missing. Moreover, documents are forwarded by a central Commission unit rather than by the responsible service, often without the latter service being identified. This arrangement seems unnecessarily cumbersome, untransparent and time-consuming given the exceedingly short time-limits for Parliament's response.' See the Opinion of the Committee on the Environment, Public Health and Consumer Protection, in the (Third) Aglietta Report of 30 March 1999, above Ch 4, n 271.

[335] See paragraph 4 of the Fontaine-Prodi Agreement (above Ch 4, n 326). Accordingly, '[o]nce the appropriate technical arrangements have been made, the documents referred to in Article 7(3) of Decision 1999/468/EC will be forwarded electronically. Confidential documents will be processed in accordance with internal administrative procedures drawn up by each institution with a view to providing all the requisite guarantees.'

made of the Internet and that the European Parliament would be given (limited) access to the CIRCA-base managed by the Commission Data Centre in Luxembourg.[336]

In the Fontaine-Prodi Agreement, certain clarifications were also made in respect of the power given to the European Parliament to 'blow the whistle' if it felt that an implementing measure was exceeding the powers conferred on the Commission in a basic instrument adopted under the co-decision procedure (see above 4.4.2.3). This had also been embraced by the previous political understanding and the experience had been far from satisfactory (see above 4.4.2.3). The most apparent problem was that the European Parliament needed much more time to prepare its position than the Commission thought it could afford to give. In order to clarify the conditions for exercise of the right of intervention, in the Fontaine-Prodi Agreement the general rule was laid down that the European Parliament would have to state its protest, in plenary, within one month after the date of receipt of the final draft of an implementing measure.[337]

4.4.3.2   The European Parliament less united

The MEPs' determination to fight an inter-institutional battle had been a strong 'incentive' for the other parties to consider their demands and negotiate a new comitology decision. This had been seen, first, in the agreement on a temporary cease-fire (see above 4.3.3), and, then, in the final discussion in the Council, where the prospect of avoiding 'any further inter-institutional conflict' was so tempting that even the most resistant Government could be convinced to give up the *contre-filet* mechanism (see

---

[336] See the statement by Monica Frassoni in the Debates of the European Parliament on 16 February 2000, above Ch 4, n 324. The facilities of CIRCA (Communication and Information Resource Centre for Administrations) are not publicly accessible. But some basic information can be found at the homepage of IDA (Interchange of Data between Administrations), at internet http://europa.eu.int/ISPO/ida.

[337] See paragraph 6 of the Fontaine-Prodi Agreement (above Ch 4, n 326). See also paragraph 7, according to which '[i]n urgent cases, and in the case of measures relating to day-to-day administrative matters and/or having a limited period of validity, the time limit will be shorter. That time limit may be very short in extremely urgent cases, and in particular on public health grounds.' In these special cases, a simplified procedure would be applied. In addition to this clarification in respect of the time-limits, it was also pointed out that the formal responsibility for informing the European Parliament of the action the Commission intends to take on a resolution should lie with the Commissioner in charge. See paragraph 8 of the Agreement.

above 4.4.2).[338] Even if there had been some give-and-take, the MEPs were fairly pleased with the result. The new Comitology Decision constituted 'a real step forward in comparison with the previous situation' and, with the approval of the Fontaine-Prodi Agreement, they were finally entitled to take a breather.[339] As one of the members of the Committee on Institutional Affairs, Monica Frassoni, stated, this had marked 'the end of a saga which has kept Parliament busy for two years, along with a few enthusiasts scattered among the various institutions of the Union, whom many people do not hesitate to call masochists.'[340]

Against the background of the inter-institutional battle, the question which now remained to be answered was whether the result which had been achieved was sufficient to bring the battle to an end. Even if the European Parliament had received the new Comitology Decision as a great step forward, it had certainly not managed to satisfy all its demands. For this reason, when the budgetary reserves were released, it had been emphasized that the endorsement by the European Parliament of the new Decision did not prejudge its positions on matters of principle. Exactly what these positions were, however, was no longer clear: this, indeed, was the object with which the European Parliament had been trading in the negotiations. No better example can be found than its sudden willingness to reconsider the life-long demand for abolition of the regulatory committee procedure (see above 4.4.1). In contrast to the initial situation, where the MEPs had been standing united, there were now signs of a split between those, like Monica Frassoni, who felt that the fight was over, and the old school of hard-liners, represented by one of the members of the Committee on Rules of Procedure, Richard Corbett. According to him:

Overall we have a system which has made some progress. The supplementary aspects that arise from the inter-institutional agreement with the Commission

---

[338] Cf. the statement by the Commission that the 'various innovations' of the new Comitology Decision (see above Ch 4, n 275) were 'intended to end the recurrent conflicts between Parliament and the Council in this area and should facilitate the adoption of legislation under the co-decision procedure.' See *Bulletin EU* 6-1999, point 1.8.3.

[339] See point C of the European Parliament Resolution of 17 February 2000 (see above Ch 4, n 327), according to which 'the new decision on the committee procedure only partly meets the expectations of the European Parliament, but nonetheless constitutes a real step forward in comparison with the previous situation.'

[340] See the statement by Monica Frassoni in the Debates of the European Parliament on 16 February 2000, above Ch 4, n 324.

are welcome, but that could not change the basic decision of the Council ... So it is a step forward. My group reluctantly accepts it as a step forward. We are not as enthusiastic about compromising as Mrs Frassoni. We recognise that there are limitations and the issue will no doubt come back in a few years' time. If we want a Union that is democratic and transparent to the fullest degree we will have to revisit this subject.[341]

---

[341] See the statement by Richard Corbett in the Debates of the European Parliament on 16 February 2000, above Ch 4, n 324.

The Time for Change?

5.1 Introduction

In this final chapter, the answer to the question what comitology really is will be sought (cf. above 1.4.1 and 1.4.2). For that reason an extensive summary will be made of the findings in Chapters 2 to 4. This, it is submitted, makes it possible to discern a pattern: a rather surprising consistency with which the actors involved have taken their positions in the development of the committee system. It also makes it possible to discern which actors and positions have dominated the development and, indeed, the crucial moments of change, when prior positions have been reconsidered or even abandoned. Even if some findings are presented which concern more general aspects of the development of the committee system, the focus will be on the actors and their positions. The reason for this is that the assessment has shown that the answer to the question what comitology really is depends on one's perspective. Finally, the overall conclusions will be discussed in the context of some recent events which are likely to have implications for the future of the committee system and, indeed, the legal and political order which it is a part of.

5.2 Summary

5.2.1 The general development

During the period which followed upon the entry into force of the EEC Treaty in 1958, the so-called Transitional Period, most efforts were directed towards the establishment of a common market based on a common agricultural policy, a common commercial policy, and a common transport policy. The negotiations which would lead to the adoption of the legislation this required were at the top of the agenda from the very start. Before long it was realized that the common agricultural policy had to be given highest priority and that any hesitation in this field would risk compromising achievements elsewhere.

Following three years of intense negotiations within the Council, agreement was finally reached on a set of regulations laying down a common organization of agricultural markets. One of the questions which had provoked most difficulty concerned the exercise of implementing powers. The way towards resolution was only opened up after a compromise had been reached that the responsibility for adoption of measures of a 'practical nature' would be shared between the Commission and a new type of organ—management committees—which would bring together representatives of the national administrations. The solution opted for stressed the sole right of the Commission to take formal decisions but permitted the new committees to be actively involved in the deliberations and to supervise the result: if a decision was objected to, it would be placed before the Council which would then be enabled to replace it with another.

Even if this solution meant that the immediate problem with respect to the exercise of implementing powers had been overcome, several Governments felt that the last word had not been said. Therefore, it was agreed that the Council would return to the matter in a few years' time and decide 'in the light of experience' whether the procedure for co-operation between the Commission and management committees should be retained or amended. This would prove to be a triumph for pragmatism over ideologies: when the time did come to decide the Governments no longer found the procedure controversial and the decision was taken that it should 'be retained beyond expiry of the transitional period.'

The next, important stage of the development was initiated during the spring of 1965 when the Presidency of the Council was held by France. One matter which had to be dealt with concerned the financing of the common agricultural policy. For some, in particular the French Government, this was a very pedestrian question. But for others, in particular the Commission, it was an opportunity to provoke a debate on matters of principal and, indeed, constitutional significance. Following heated debates the last session of the Presidency ended in deadlock. Only a few days later, the French Government announced that it would withdraw its representation from the Council. Although initially unclear exactly what the French Government was hoping to obtain as a result of its *politique de la chaise vide*, it soon became evident that its grievances did not in the first place relate to the financing of the common agricultural policy but to the role played by the Commission. During the following months the French Government explained that some sort of agreement had to be reached within the Council on its relationship with the Commission.

The most well-known part of the agreement asked for concerned an envisaged shift from unanimous to qualified majority voting in the Council. But of greater significance for present purposes was the French Government's discontent with the Commission's 'habit' of making proposals for legislation which, instead of dealing with the substance of the problems posed, merely gave itself implementing powers without specifying what measures it would take. Even if the French Government accepted the need for some sort of delegation of powers, it demanded that the executive powers thus vested in the Commission should be precisely circumscribed and leave no room for discretion or autonomous responsibility, failing which the balance of powers, which is a feature of the institutional structure of the Community and a basic guarantee provided by the Treaty, would not be respected.'

It was not until early 1966 that a compromise was finally reached within the Council. According to the public statement in which it was set out, all Governments except the French were willing to accept that, whenever very important interests of one or more Governments were at stake, the Council would endeavour, within a reasonable time, to reach solutions which could be adopted by all of them. The French Government went further, requiring that in the same situation 'the discussion must be continued until unanimous agreement is reached.' The fact that the exact meaning of this 'agreement to disagree' was not clear had little practical significance: at an early stage of the negotiations the conclusion had been reached by the Governments that the Community would only function if solutions could be found which were acceptable to all of them. More important, therefore, was a series of 'methods of co-operation' to be adopted by the Council after a future exchange of views with the Commission. These were well in line with those demanded by the French and stated, for example, that the Commission would consult all Governments before presenting new proposals. One of the few points which were not retained was that relating to the French demand that implementing powers vested in the Commission should leave no room for autonomous responsibility. This did not mean that the matter had not been considered but that the conclusion had been reached that the necessary improvements did not require any 'exchange of views' with the Commission.

The crisis of the empty chair was to cast its shadow over the Community for many years to come. This was the result of a development over time for which additional factors, such as the accession of the United Kingdom, were decisive. But in a more limited perspective, a number of immediate reactions can be identified. Of particular significance in that respect was the subsequent development with respect to the responsibility for exercise of implementing powers. Within a few years the use of management committees became normal practice in most fields of activity and a new stricter procedure was introduced which only permitted the Commission to adopt implementing measures which had been approved by a committee in a positive opinion. Initially, the committees operating under the new procedure were only conceived of as another form of the older management committees. But it was soon observed that they were often used in situations where the Commission was empowered to adopt measures of a permanent and, indeed, general nature. For this reason their label soon became that of regulatory committees.

1970 marked the conclusion of the transitional period and the beginning of the next stage of the Community's existence. But in spite of some initial optimism, it was not long before the Community was caught up again in the desperation which had haunted it before. This time it was not going to lose its grip lightly. For most people, therefore, the period that lay ahead has come to be thought of as the years of political paralysis or even the Dark Ages. It has been emphasized that it is not easy to conclude exactly what the problem was and, therefore, an attempt has only been made to offer a partial explanation, focusing on the development with respect to the two major challenges that lay ahead: the creation of economic and monetary union and enlargement. The claim is that the hopes invested were so great that any failure had consequences for the work in general. The first of these two challenges extended the list of objectives to include matters which were so fundamental that any signal of hesitation was reason enough for the Governments to back off and the second introduced a new extreme into the scale of interests which had to be reconciled: the United Kingdom. The combined effect was volatile.

The accession of the United Kingdom, Ireland, and Denmark in 1973 strengthened the hope that the Community would be given a fresh lease of life. But in spite of that, the first year after enlargement came to be characterized by 'brutal change and rapid transformation.' Perhaps most disheartening, the already serious financial situation was exacerbated by an oil crisis. Even if there was a strong awareness that this required common action the Community failed to react. One of the most painful expressions of this could be found in the project for creation of economic and monetary union. Although able for some time to keep their exchange rates within the margins of the so-called snake arrangement, most Governments refused to renounce the use of any major national policy instrument and the project was put on ice. There is no better way to describe the state in which the Community found itself than as a fear to engage in common action. Clearly, this would have been less hard to cope with if ideas for the right way forward had been more convergent. But over the years it had become apparent that some of the Governments were not only far from each other but held ideas which were impossible to reconcile. The dilemma this presented was certainly not going to be easier to resolve after enlargement.

The malaise which gripped the Community forced attention to be paid to the question of how decisions were taken or, all too often, not taken. The first important initiative in this direction was an 'emergency plan' presented in 1974 which called upon the Governments to make it their business to enable decisions to be reached in the Council without formal voting, thus avoiding the veto, and make extensive use of the power to confer implementing powers on the Commission. To make the latter less difficult to accept, the Governments were reminded that 'co-operation between the Commission and the competent national authorities would be ensured by procedures which are based on those of the management or other existing committees in the Community.'

Parallel to this emergency plan, the Belgium Prime Minster, Leo Tindemans, was invited to examine the possibility of converting the Community into some form of European Union. The hope was that this would help to shift the focus away from old disagreements and to consolidate those fields of common interest where the willingness and, indeed, ability to proceed had been manifested most strongly.

One year later Tindemans presented his report. Here the overall conclusion was drawn that it was too early to talk about a European Union. This was something which had to be developed over time and, importantly, progress could only be made to the extent it was possible to arrive at a political consensus. To overcome the present crisis, an overall approach would have to be agreed which could provide a framework for further action. The 'overall approach' would be accompanied by a number of 'practical measures' to be adopted simultaneously in the various directions entailed by the overall approach. The key proposals for such measures were that the Council would let decision-making by qualified majority become normal practice and make 'delegation of executive powers' to the Commission the general rule.

Tindemans' proposals were soon to be built on by others. Of particular importance in this respect was a series of reports in which the need for procedural and institutional improvements was addressed in the light of a second and third enlargement. None of the reports examined in this book was more important than the 1979 Report of the inter-governmental Committee of Three Wise Men. Similarly to Tindemans, this report emphasized that the deeper causes for failures lay 'in political circumstances and attitudes that sometimes produced conflicting conceptions of the right way forward, and sometimes produced no clear conception at all.' Against the background of that finding, a number of proposals were presented for practical measures which could create the best possible conditions for dealing with existing problems. This time the central proposals focused on the use of qualified majority voting in the Council and the exercise of implementing powers.

As suggested by the Committee of Three Wise Men a 'working principle' would be introduced in the Council according to which voting would be the normal practice in all cases where the veto did not apply. This, it was explained, did not mean that an actual vote would always be taken but above all that the mere prospect of resort to vote would encourage the Governments to join in a compromise. But the most important step which could be taken to restore efficiency was to apply a greater selectivity in the choice of cases for action in the Council and make better use of 'delegation' to the Commission. This, indeed, was a suggestion which had been made many times before. But now the focus was on the role of committees.

After the adoption of the 1974 emergency plan, the number of committees with which the Commission was required to co-operate increased drastically. According to the Committee of Three Wise Men, the anxieties underlying the development were not hard to understand. Even if the Governments had understood that it was necessary to make an effort to improve the preconditions for common action, the political basis was far from solid. Therefore, they were more sensitive than ever to the risk that delegation of implementing powers to the Commission could create political difficulties or alter the impact of the policy itself in unforeseen ways.

The finding this led the Committee of Three Wise Men to was that without committees no delegation would take place at all. But at the same time a warning finger was pointed at the time-consuming discussions on the type of procedure the committees should follow. Therefore, in order to ensure that the power to 'delegate' implementing powers to the Commission could be used to enhance efficiency in the Council, the proposal was advanced that a few 'stock formulae' should be worked out which could then be selected for insertion without dispute in each individual case.

In spite of all suggestions problems persisted and after the accession of Greece in 1981 new reports were presented in which the need for procedural and institutional improvements was addressed. This time the central proposals focused on the use of qualified majority voting in the Council and the exercise of implementing powers.

Over the next few years, there were several events which took the Community closer to an institutional reform. Of particular significance in that respect was the initiative taken by the European Parliament in 1984 through the adoption of a Draft Treaty on European Union. This, indeed, was a provocation but it was also an excuse for others to press for a revision of the EEC Treaty. Noteworthy, in that respect, was a promise by the French President, François Mitterand, to make sure that 'the main Treaty that binds the European countries together and constitutes their fundamental law' would be consolidated through amendments. Even if there was reasonable scepticism about Mitterand's intentions, the debate gathered speed and thanks to an unexpected French willingness to make concessions, the decision was taken to stage 'a strong revival' of the Community through a reform intended to give it an economic impulse similar to that given by the old programme for establishment of a common market: the 'internal market' project. Even if this was less ambitious than envisaged by European Parliament, it signalled a new kind of momentum and triggered a sequence of events which, in due time, would lead to the full transformation of the Community into a European Union.

During the period between 1970 and 1980 the number of comitology committees grew from 27 in 1970 to 85 in 1980. In the run-up to the 1985

Intergovernmental Conference the number grew to 154. Even if this could be seen as a sign of success, that the Council had been willing to follow the advice to distribute the burden to others, it was also evidence that the cure was becoming a cause. As a result of the constant attempts 'to limit a little bit more here or there' the implementing powers of the Commission, there were more than 30 different variants of the basic committee procedures in operation. In order to come to terms with this, the Commission presented proposals to the 1985 Intergovernmental Conference for a reform of the system for delegation of implementing powers which, above all, would strengthen its own autonomy. But the conclusion was reached in the Intergovernmental Conference that a more cautious construction had to be opted for. The result was manifested in an amendment to Article 145 EEC which codified previous practice in the form of a general rule which required the Council to 'confer on the Commission, in the acts which the Council adopts, powers for the implementation of the rules which the Council lays down.' Only in 'specific cases' would the Council be permitted to reserve the right to exercise such powers itself. No attempt was made to define the sub-stantive meaning of implementation. Therefore, the potential scope of these powers would remain extremely wide. Another feature of the same amendment was that the Council would continue to require the Com-mission to follow committee procedures ('impose certain requirements'). But, importantly, these procedures had to be consonant with 'principles and rules to be laid down in advance by the Council, acting unanimously on a proposal from the Commission and after obtaining the opinion of the European Parliament.'

The proposal for such 'principles and rules' was presented by the Commission immediately after the conclusion of the Intergovernmental Conference and before the new Treaty—the Single European Act—entered into force. Essentially, the content of the proposal was such as to fix three basic types of advisory, management, and regulatory committee procedures and to make sure that no other procedures would be used. But after lengthy discussions in the Council the envisaged procedures were not only enriched by the inclusion of variants but, with respect to committees already in operation, the existing range of procedures was explicitly preserved.

Over the next few years, the Commission often took the opportunity to express its discontent with the new arrangement for exercise of implementing powers and stated itself to be deeply concerned by the development. One of the problems addressed most clearly was the Council's preference for the most restrictive variant of the regulatory committee procedure over the advisory committee procedure.

The next opportunity for reform came with the 1991 Intergovernmental Conference. Basing itself on ideas which had already been set out by the European Parliament in its 1984 Draft Treaty on European Union, the Commission presented a proposal for a hierarchy of legal acts which would lead to a fundamental overhaul of the arrangement for exercise of implementing powers. The proposal envisaged a number of amendments which would make it possible to distinguish between different types of legal acts in accordance with their substance or quality and to link this to the procedure for their adoption. Clearly, the proposal had been designed to ensure the Commission a greater autonomy with respect to the adoption of implementing measures of general and permanent effect. But when trying to 'sell' the idea, the Commission emphasized that it would strengthen the role of the European Parliament by removing 'matters of detail' from its agenda.

The most central element of the proposal was found in the notion of implementation which was negatively, and indeed vaguely, defined. The new 'laws' (renamed directives) were to be used to lay down 'the fundamental principles, general guidelines and basic elements of the measures to be taken for their implementation.' Everything else should be considered as 'implementation' and would be dealt with in regulations or decisions. The significance of this was above all a procedural one: whereas the adoption of laws should be reserved for the Council and the European Parliament, the adoption of regulations and decisions would be left to the Commission. The Council would still be permitted to prescribe the use of advisory or management committee procedures but the regulatory committee procedure would be replaced by a new substitution mechanism which would enable the Council and the European Parliament to block the entry into force of a regulation if they considered that the Commission was exceeding its powers.

When the result of the 1991 Intergovernmental Conference—the Treaty on European Union—was presented it became clear that the Governments had been far from willing to accept the proposal for a hierarchy of legal acts. Not only had the amendments suggested by the Commission been completely ignored but a declaration had been included in which it was emphasized 'that it must be for each Member State to determine how the provisions of Community law can best be enforced in the light of its own particular institutions, legal system and other circumstances.' Clear as this may seem, the Governments were obviously aware of the likelihood that a number of problems would persist. Therefore, a provision had been included in the new Treaty in which it was explained that another Intergovernmental Conference would be convened in 1996. This would permit them to make a new examination of the question: 'to what extent might it be possible to review the classification of Community acts with a view to establishing an appropriate hierarchy between the different categories of act?'

Even if it had left the arrangement for exercise of implementing powers untouched, the Treaty on European Union was to have far-reaching implications for the future development. The reason for this was to be found in the establishment of the new co-decision procedure, which granted the European Parliament a genuine right to participate in the decision-making process and, if necessary, block legislation from being adopted. For the first time, therefore, the European Parliament was in a position to assert its demands.

As early as 1961, when the regulations were negotiated which were to provide the basis for a common agricultural policy, the European Parliament had manifested its discontent with the 'creation of new organs' to assist the Commission in the exercise of implementing powers. Even if the solution eventually opted for was less drastic than at first feared, the European Parliament was suspicious. This, indeed, was seen in the 1962 Deringer Report in which concerns were expressed that the use of committees would make it difficult, or even impossible, for the European Parliament to perform its duties. Parallel to the establishment of new committees, the European Parliament came to focus much of its work on the preconditions for exercise of implementing powers. None of the reports this led to was more important than the 1968 Jozeau-Marigné Report. This confirmed the previous suspicion: that the establishment of committees was one facet in a general trend characterized by the fact that an increasing number of matters with a legislative bearing were being dealt with in the form of implementing measures, in accordance with procedures from which the European Parliament was excluded. Even if the Report reached the conclusion that no legal objections could be made against the delegation of powers or against the use of committees it expressed a 'legitimate concern with an institutional evolution which . . . could very well be dangerous on the political plane.' Therefore, the claim was made that there was a need to grant the European Parliament a *droit de regard*: a right to be kept informed and to render an opinion when matters of notable importance were being dealt with.

However reasonable the demands of the European Parliament may have been, they found no or little support and much time would pass before any form of concession was made by the Council or, indeed, the Commission. For much of the Dark Ages, the European Parliament was exiled into a rather anonymous existence. But this was only a passing state of affairs and the revival of the Community was also that of the European Parliament. During the 1980s, the delegation of implementing powers and the rather drastic increase in the number of committees became a major pre-occupation for the European Parliament.

Somewhat paradoxically, the Treaty on European Union strengthened the role of the European Parliament in the legislative process but ignored its demands with respect to the exercise of implementing powers. Therefore, shortly after the entry into force of the Treaty on European Union a resolution was adopted in which the European Parliament emphasized that it was no longer acceptable for the Council to reserve the responsibility for political supervision over the exercise of implementing powers for itself. In particular, it was argued that the exercise of implementing powers with respect to acts adopted under the co-decision procedure could not be considered to fall within the scope of Article 145 EC, since this referred only to 'acts which the Council adopts' alone. According to the European Parliament, this was an omission which had to be dealt with in the next Intergovernmental Conference. Pending that a 'general decision' would be adopted which could provide a temporary solution.

Not surprisingly, the European Parliament had a rather clear idea of what the contents of that decision ought to be. First, it would only permit use of the advisory committee procedure. Then, the European Parliament would be granted a legally enforceable right to be informed about matters expected to lead to the adoption of implementing measures with a legislative bearing and to state its opinion. Parallel to this *droit de regard*, a substitution mechanism would be introduced which would enable the Council and the European Parliament to require the Commission 'to formulate a new decision, taking account of any guidelines approved by the two arms of the legislative authority'.

The demands were well received by the Commission, which had envisaged a similar solution as part of its proposal for a hierarchy of legal acts, and it promised to look into the possibility of revising existing rules.

But weary of waiting for whatever miracle the Commission might be hoped to perform, the European Parliament decided to launch an offensive which would force everyone to take it seriously. During the first year of operation of the co-decision procedure disputes over 'comitology' became a central feature of most negotiations and the issue was fought out on each individual item of legislation. The precedent was set in the very first matter dealt with under the co-decision procedure: the proposal for a Council Directive on the application of open network provision (ONP) to voice telephony.

At an early stage of the negotiations on the ONP-proposal, there was a general awareness that this would only be the first in a series of similar events and, attempting to prevent that, the Commission had presented a draft inter-institutional agreement on the rules for exercise of implementing powers with respect to acts adopted under the co-decision procedure. This supported the European Parliament's argument that the matter was not covered by Article 145 EC and that a temporary solution had to be found pending the next Intergovernmental Conference.

The key element of the draft inter-institutional agreement was found in a qualitative distinction between implementing acts as containing either 'legislative' or 'non-legislative' measures. For the adoption of the prior type of implementing acts a new type of procedure would be introduced which provided that a draft measure would be submitted to both an advisory committee (and no other type of committee) and the European Parliament. Then, taking 'full account' of their respective opinions, the Commission would adopt the measure which would apply immediately. Supplementary to this, a substitution mechanism would be introduced which would make it possible for the Council and the European Parliament to agree to repeal the measure in question. The solution was presented as a pragmatic attempt to resolve the 'differences of opinion' that were impeding the operation of the co-decision procedure. But, if accepted, it would have enabled the Commission to secure largely uncontrolled powers to itself. This, indeed, was a development which the Governments were not very enthusiastic about and not surprisingly, therefore, the draft agreement was rejected.

However clear it may seem that the Commission was trying to use the battle over comitology to move its own position forward, there was a growing risk of permanent conflict which needed to be avoided and, following a period of intense discussion, the Council finally managed to come up with the terms for a cease-fire which were acceptable to everyone. First of all, the Governments promised to examine the question of the exercise of implementing powers in respect of acts adopted under the co-decision procedure in the Intergovernmental Conference scheduled for 1996. Then, for the intermediate period, a *Modus Vivendi* would be established which would meet some of the European Parliament's demands but leave the existing arrangements for exercise of implementing powers intact.

The content of this *Modus Vivendi* was focused on a set of guidelines for the adoption of 'draft implementing acts of a general nature'. These provided, first and foremost, that the Commission would take account as far as possible of any comments by the European Parliament and keep it informed of the action which it intended to take on them. For this reason the Commission would send the European Parliament the relevant acts under the same conditions as they were sent to committees. It would also inform the European Parliament about those instances where a matter had to be referred to the Council. The Council, on its part, would not adopt a draft act which had been referred to it without first informing the European Parliament, setting a reasonable time limit for obtaining its opinion, and, in the event of an unfavourable opinion, taking due account of its point of view. The European Parliament, finally, would respect every time limit and, where necessary, undertake to use an urgent procedure.

It is clear that these guidelines included elements which had not been formalized before. Noteworthy, in that respect, was the undertaking by the Council not to adopt a draft act which had been referred to it without first informing the European Parliament and providing it with a genuine opportunity to state its opinion. Even if the situations to which this was to apply were extremely rare, the symbolic significance was considerable: for the first time the Council had agreed to place itself under a direct obligation to the European Parliament.

Less than a year after the entry into force of the Treaty on European Union a decision was taken by the European Council to set up a 'reflection group' to prepare the Intergovernmental Conference scheduled for 1996. The result was presented in a report submitted to the European Council. Of particular relevance for present purposes are the findings relating to the demand for revision of the arrangement for exercise of implementing powers and, intimately linked to that, the old proposal for a hierarchy of legal acts.

Two conflicting positions had emerged in the Reflection Group. The first position was that embraced by those representatives who favoured the introduction of a formal hierarchy of legal acts and were willing, therefore, to replace the existing rules for exercise of implementing powers with rules that would give the Commission full implementing powers subject to control by both the Council and the European Parliament. In their view, this would above all serve to clarify the functions of the Community Institutions. The second position was that taken by those who were opposed to the introduction of a hierarchy of legal acts. Although not denying that this could bring clarity, they refuted the logic which they felt was based on the idea of separation of powers within a state. Those who took this position were also refusing to grant the Commission its own 'executive' powers since this would disturb the institutional balance. But admitting that existing committee procedures were complicated they declared themselves prepared to consider a simplification 'which would not undermine the Council's executive functions.' This would not require a reform of the EC Treaty, but only a revision of the Comitology Decision.

Even if the result of the 1996 Intergovernmental Conference—the Treaty of Amsterdam—was more humble than that of the previous ones, it was certainly not insignificant. Perhaps most remarkably, a number of changes were agreed which would strengthen the role of the European Parliament in the process for adoption of legislation. But, as in 1991, nothing had been done to meet its demand with respect to the arrangement for exercise of implementing powers. The Governments restricted themselves to the solution which had already won support within the Reflection Group: a revision of the Comitology Decision.

The proposal for revision of the Comitology Decision was presented by the Commission in 1998. The content of the proposal would be divided into three different categories. The first included provisions aimed at making the committee system less complex by simplification of the fixed procedures, in particular through the abolition of all variants, and the adjustment of existing committees to the new model. Furthermore, the proposal envisaged that certain modifications should be made to the procedures. Overall these were rather modest. An important exception were the modifications to the regulatory committee procedure. These constituted the second category of content, intended to make the system more open to parliamentary control. As proposed by the Commission, its duty to place a proposal for implementing measures before the Council if it had not been approved by a committee would be replaced by a right to make a proposal within the normal legislative process. The third category of content consisted of provisions aimed to make the committee system less opaque. Essentially, two different aspects were dealt with.

Firstly, certain principles or 'criteria' would be introduced for the choice between different procedures. The idea was to link the choice of one committee procedure or another to the substantive scope or quality of the measures to be taken. Even if it was not stated clearly by the Commission, the underlying logic was similar to that of its proposal for a hierarchy of legal acts: the substantive scope of the measures to be taken would also determine how the balance between 'the legislative authority' and 'the executive authority' would be struck. This time the notion of implementation and, therefore, the substantive scope of the measures to be taken by the executive authority were very wide. Secondly, the European Parliament would be granted a right to information which was more limited than asked for: to receive information but not to be given an opportunity to act on the basis of that information.

The European Parliament's lifelong demand for a *droit de regard* had been refined parallel with the strengthening of its legislative powers and in 1993 it was finally absorbed by the proposal for a 'substitution mechanism' (which would enable the Council and the European Parliament to repeal an implementing measure on equal terms). In spite of the fact that the Commission had previously shown some sign of support for that suggestion, in its proposal an entirely different solution had been opted for: the reform of the regulatory committee procedure. This reform did not foresee any power to contest an implementing measure other than that left to the committee. Only in situations where the committee made use of that power could the European Parliament hope to be able to exercise some influence. The practical significance was minimal. Not only were these situations virtually non-existent, but if, exceptionally, they did occur, the matter would still not come before the European Parliament by default but only as the result of a decision by the Commission to present a normal proposal for legislation.

Shortly after the Commission had submitted the proposal for revision of the Comitology Decision, the process was initiated for consultation of the European Parliament. As immediately pointed out by its Committee on Institutional Affairs, the most important reason to change the arrangement for exercise of implementing powers was the risk that it would undermine the co-decision procedure: many matters which the European Parliament felt it should have a say on were dealt with in the form of implementing measures and, therefore, the scope for action under the co-decision procedure was increasingly restricted to the adoption of measures with a very general content. Against this background, it was not possible for the Committee on Institutional Affairs to reach any other conclusion than that the proposal presented by the Commission was far from sufficient and that the main concerns and requests from the European Parliament had been sidestepped. Two particular points were emphasized: that the notion of implementation enshrined in the proposal was too wide and that a substitution mechanism would have to be introduced which would give the European Parliament a real power to intervene.

In its final report, the Committee on Institutional Affairs advised the MEPs to approve the proposal subject only to a number of amendments. These envisaged, in addition to a more limited notion of implementation and a mechanism for control, a wider right to information and the complete abolition of the regulatory committee procedure. But after debate in plenary that final amendment was reformulated to insist on the abolition of the regulatory committee procedure *unless* it was simplified (by deleting the controversial *contre-filet* mechanism). This, indeed, was evidence that the MEPs were not only competent to make demands but also to bargain. Once they had voted an opinion, the discussions within the Council were intensified and, then, the new Comitology Decision was adopted. The contents of the Decision could be split into the same three categories as the proposal on which it was based.

The first category contained provisions which were intended to make the committee system less complex. The most substantial changes were those relating to the regulatory committee procedure. Like the old procedure the new one was based on the idea that the committee should actively approve a draft implementing measure before the Commission could adopt it. If not, the Commission had to submit a proposal which the Council could adopt, amend, or oppose by qualified majority. The latter was a novelty which had been introduced in place of the *contre-filet* mechanism. If the Council should oppose the proposal, the Commission would have to re-examine it and either re-submit its proposal—in original or amended version—or present a new proposal within the normal legislative process. In addition to the above a provision had been included in a declaration in which it was stated that the Council agreed that the adoption of the new Comitology Decision would be followed by adjustment of old procedures in the course of normal revision of legislation.

The second category of contents included provisions which were expected to make the system more open to parliamentary control. Quite clearly, the demands of the European Parliament for equality in the exercise of powers of political supervision had been the most difficult matter to deal with. After stubborn resistance, the Council finally surrendered and the European Parliament won its most important victory. According to the solution adopted, the European Parliament would be permitted to 'blow the whistle' if it felt that a draft implementing measure or a proposal submitted to the Council under the regulatory committee procedure was exceeding the powers conferred on the Commission in a basic instrument adopted under the co-decision procedure. The meaning of this was explained, most clearly, with respect to the first case. Here the Commission would have to re-examine the measure in the light of the European Parliament's opinion and either submit a new draft measure, continue with the procedure, or present a proposal for normal legislation. With respect to the second case, concerning a proposal submitted under the regulatory committee procedure, it was stated that the Council should only act on the proposal (i.e. adopt it or object to it) if this was appropriate 'in view of' the parliamentary position. The exact meaning of that was far from clear.

The third category of content contained provisions which were aimed to make the committee system less opaque or, in other words, more transparent. Noteworthy, first, was the establishment of criteria relating to the choice of committee procedure. Apparently, the objective had been to provide, at least some, consistency and predictability and, at the same time, avoid the risk of 'unnecessary opportunities for challenge on legal grounds.' The trick which made this possible was to insert an explanation that the criteria should only be of a non-binding nature. Most important were the criteria relating to the regulatory committee procedure, intended for the adoption of 'measures of general scope designed to apply essential provisions of basic instruments' or to 'adapt or update' certain non-essential provisions of basic instruments. This was more narrow than proposed by the Commission and a concession to the demands of the European Parliament. But at the same time it was clear that the criteria would be wide enough to ensure that the regulatory committee procedure could be used for the adoption measures of legislative bearing.

Furthermore, some provisions were included which aimed to secure the European Parliament's right to information. The basic idea was that previous promises would be replaced by a legally-binding commitment. Accordingly, the European Parliament would be entitled to receive agendas for committee meetings, draft implementing measures submitted to committees within fields of application of the co-decision procedure, and the results of voting. It would also be kept informed about matters transferred from the Commission to the Council. This was exactly the type of improvement upon which the Council and the Governments had been hoping to focus. In the negotiations, therefore, there was little or no objection. Instead the European Parliament was encouraged to ask for more. When the new Comitology Decision was finally adopted the list of items which it would now be entitled to receive had been extended. Significantly, it was also explained that the responsibility for providing information would rest with the Commission. Supplementary to the European Parliament's right to information, rules were inserted on information to the public.

The European Parliament's determination to fight an inter-institutional battle had been a strong incentive for the other parties to consider its demands and negotiate the new Comitology Decision. This had been seen, first, in the agreement on a *Modus Vivendi* and, then, in the final discussions in the Council, where the prospect of avoiding 'any further inter-institutional conflict' was so tempting that even its most resistant members could be convinced to give up the insistence on the *contre-filet* mechanism. The question which now remained to be answered was whether the result which had been achieved was sufficient to bring the battle to an end? Even if the European Parliament had received the new Comitology Decision as a great step forward, it had certainly not managed to satisfy all its demands. For this reason, it had been emphasized that the endorsement by the European Parliament of the new Decision did not prejudge its positions on matters of principle. But exactly what these positions were was no longer clear: this, indeed, was the object with which the European Parliament had been trading in the negotiations. No better example can be found than its sudden willingness to reconsider the life-long demand for abolition of the regulatory committee procedure. In contrast to the initial situation, where the MEPs had been standing united, there were now signs of a split between those who felt that the fight was over, and the old school of hard-liners who knew that it would soon be necessary again to take up arms.

5.2.2   *The judicial development*

The first ruling discussed is that in Case 9/56 *Meroni & Co. S.p.A. v High Authority of the ECSC*. Here the Court emphasized the significance of the idea of an institutional balance and said that it was only prepared to accept a delegation of powers to organs other than institutions if very strict requirements were complied with (with respect both to the manner in which the delegation had to be made and the substantive scope of the powers involved). But most importantly, it explained that those requirements would not need to be complied with in a situation where an institution was permitted to take over the deliberations of such an organ as its own. According to the Court, this would not constitute an instance of 'delegation' but merely 'the granting of a power to draw up resolutions' for which an institution would retain full responsibility.

Clearly, the Court's ruling in Case 9/56 was taken into consideration in 1961 when the Council discarded a proposal that powers to take the decisions needed for management of the common agricultural policy should not be left to the Commission but to specialized organs with their own secretariats. The solution finally arrived at was that which was to become the basis for the committee system: the management committees. In full compliance with the reasoning of the Court, this solution only entailed delegation from the Council to the Commission. The role of the new committees was confined to the deliberations. If everything worked well, the Commission would take over the deliberations as its own. If not, if the Commission would disregard the deliberations, the Council would still be in a position to step in to correct the result.

The second and third rulings were both given in 1970, a year characterized by a political awareness of the need for delegation of powers, not only in the Council and the Commission but also in the European Parliament, and a common understanding that this required use of committees. Against that background it is submitted that the ruling in Case 41/69 *Chemiefarma NV v Commission* represents a crucial point in the history of Community law: it was here that the Court of Justice made up its mind not to interfere with the development under way. Basing itself on a wide interpretation of Article 155 EEC, the Court explained that there was no prohibition against the Council delegating powers to the Commission which could be used to adopt implementing measures of a general nature.

Shortly after the ruling in Case 41/69, the Court was given an opportunity to demonstrate that it was prepared to accept the consequences. In Case 25/70 *Einfuhr- und Vorratsstelle für Getreide und Futtermittel v Köster, Berodt & Co.* the Court was called upon to resolve the question whether the procedure by which implementing powers were conferred on the Commission was compatible with the institutional balance. To some extent this question had already been answered in the affirmative in Case 41/69. But an important difference this time was the interposition between the Council and the Commission of a management committee.

There can be no doubt that the Court was very familiar with the reasoning in the European Parliament's Jozeau-Marigné Report. But in sharp contrast to that, the Court's view on the substantive scope of implementation was one aimed at maximizing the potential usefulness of delegation of powers to the Commission. According to the Court, if only 'the basic elements of the matter' had been established by the Council under a normal procedure for adoption of legislation, the provisions implementing that legislation could be decided under a simplified procedure, by the Council, reserving the exercise of implementing powers for itself, or by the Commission, subject to a delegation of powers.

In the Jozeau-Marigné Report the conclusion had been reached that the use of committees was an integral aspect of a general trend, characterized by 'an increase in the tasks facing the Commission.' Therefore, when the Court made up its mind not to oppose or complicate but to promote the transfer of implementing powers to the Commission, it must have been aware of the political reality: that there was little use for a principle of delegation of powers which could not accommodate the demand for political control. In this respect the use of management committees had proved to be a workable solution and, almost 10 years after they were first established, the Council and also the Commission and the European Parliament had come out in favour of them. Clearly, the Court cannot have been seriously expected to condemn them. Therefore, the most interesting aspect of the problem was what legal reasoning could be found to arrive at the conclusion everyone was expecting.

Enlarging upon the finding in the Jozeau-Marigné Report (that Article 155 EEC did not oblige but only permitted the Council to confer implementing powers on the Commission), the Court explained that '[t]he function of the management committee is to ensure permanent consultation in order to guide the Commission in the exercise of the powers conferred on it by the Council and to enable the latter to substitute its own action for that of the Commission. The management committee does not, therefore, have the power to take a decision in place of the Commission or the Council. Consequently, without distorting the institutional balance, the management committee machinery enables the Council to delegate to the Commission an implementing power of appreciable scope, subject to its power to take the decision itself if necessary.' The reasoning was not far-fetched but well in line with that applied in Case 9/56 *Meroni & Co. S.p.A. v High Authority of the ECSC.*

In Case 25/70 the Court manifested a striking responsiveness to the political need to provide the Commission with 'sufficient' powers and proved its awareness that there was little use for a principle of delegation of powers which could not accommodate the demand for participation by committees. A similar responsiveness was demonstrated in a number of cases heard during the period which followed the British demand for re-negotiation and the presentation of the 1974 emergency plan. Examples of this are found in the fourth and fifth rulings examined.

The fourth ruling looked at is that in Case 23/75 *Rey Soda v Cassa Conguaglio Zucchero.* Here the Court made it even more clear than before that it was aware of the functional link between its notion of implementation and the requirement for political control. In the words of the Court, the use of management committees made it possible for the Council 'to give the Commission an appreciably wide power of implementation whilst reserving where necessary its own right to intervene.'

Even if it was clear by now that the Court had no objections to management committees, its ruling in Case 25/70 *Einfuhr- und Vorratsstelle für Getreide und Futtermittel v Köster, Berodt & Co.* had fuelled some doubt with respect to regulatory committees. The reason for this was the apparent focus by the Court on the finding that the Commission was never obliged to follow the opinion of the committee and that the control-function only permitted the Council to react—*a posteriori*—to a measure which had already been adopted. Whatever the Court had intended or, indeed, not intended, to say by that, the answer to the question of the legality of regulatory committees was far from obvious and there was a need for clarification.

The fifth ruling discussed is that in Case 5/77 *Carlo Tedeschi v Denkavit Commerciale s.r.l.* Here the Court admitted that the most restrictive variant of the regulatory committee procedure (that including the *contre-filet* mechanism) made it possible to prevent the Commission 'from implementing the proposal rejected by the Council' even if the latter did not put forward an alternative solution. But somewhat surprisingly, this was not considered to have 'the effect of paralysing the Commission' since it was still able to issue 'any other measure which it considers appropriate.'

Therefore, in the end the conclusion was reached that no factor had been disclosed which could affect the validity of the procedure.

The ruling in Case 5/77 gave rise to much astonishment in the legal literature. What commentators found particularly difficult to understand was how the Court could say that the Commission was able to issue 'any other measure which it considers appropriate' when the contested procedure was based on the requirement that the Commission could only adopt the measure a qualified majority of the committee considered appropriate. The ambiguity was not lessened by the fact that the Court had based its previous approval of the procedure for co-operation with management committees on the finding that the Commission was never obliged to follow their opinion and that the control-function only enabled the Council to *react* by replacing a measure which had already been adopted.

The message was crystal clear: the Commission was obliged to ensure that the interests of the Member States were efficiently mediated between and that the machinery would function smoothly. If the Commission remained faithful to that objective, it would always consider appropriate the measure a qualified majority of the committee considered appropriate. It is submitted that the ruling in Case 5/77 provides one of the clearest expressions of the Court's result-oriented approach. In order to defend the future use of regulatory committees, the Court proved itself prepared to rephrase the previously so clear-cut principle of delegation of powers as a duty (for the Commission) to seek a swift end to problematic situations.

The sixth and seventh rulings discussed both related to the arrangement for exercise of implementing powers that was introduced by the Single European Act and, in particular, the question of the legality of the first Comitology Decision. Importantly, in these rulings the Court demonstrated that it was ready to accept the Council's interpretation of the new arrangement and refused to listen to the objections made by the European Parliament and the Commission.

In Case 302/87 *European Parliament v Council* the Court was faced with a challenge brought by the European Parliament. According to the European Parliament, the first Comitology Decision was an illegal attempt by the Council to restrict the meaning of Article 145 EEC and an interference with the institutional balance. But apparently the matter was too hot for the Court to handle: one year after the European Parliament had submitted the application it was dismissed on procedural grounds without anything being said about the substance. In the parallel Case 16/88 *Commission v Council* the Court was called upon to adjudicate in a long-standing dispute between the Commission and the Council over the use of the management committee procedure when implementing decisions were adopted involving budgetary spending. In its ruling the Court did not only erase every doubt with respect to the legality of the first Comitology Decision but it also made it clear that Article 145 EEC had become a central element of the constitutional legal order.

Within two years after its ruling in Case 302/87, the Court changed its mind with respect to the European Parliament's right to bring annulment actions and declared that this was admissible 'provided that the action seeks only to safeguard its prerogatives and that it is founded only on submissions alleging their infringement.' The European Parliament did not delay in responding. Of particular interest, in that respect, are a number of cases where the European Parliament sought to secure interpretations of the EC Treaty which would make it difficult for the Council and, indeed, the Commission to circumvent it by using simpli-fied procedures for adoption of implementing legislation.

Even if everyone was aware of the practical considerations underlying the wish to circumvent the European Parliament, from a legal point of view this was only tolerated if the matters dealt with did not go beyond the limits of what could reasonably be characterized as 'implementation' and if the requirement was respected that 'the basic elements of the matter' were established in accordance with the normal procedures for adoption of legislation. This meant that the possibility to use the sim-plified procedures for adoption of implementing legislation as a means of circumventing the European Parliament and, indeed, the ability of the European Parliament to resist this depended on a delicate balance, and the only one competent to strike that balance was the Court of Justice.

But the Court soon made it clear that it was not prepared to support the European Parliament's fight. Noteworthy, in that respect, were some rulings in which the Court struck the balance between the notion of implementation and the basic elements—requiring use of a normal procedure—in such a way as to encourage rather than prevent the Council and the Commission from outflanking the European Parliament. This, indeed, was seen in the eighth and ninth rulings: Case C-156/93 *European Parliament v Commission* and Case C-417/93 *European Parliament v Council.*

The implications of both these rulings were far-reaching. According to the Court, even if a provision was placed in legislation adopted under a normal procedure, it could be considered to be implementing in nature and, therefore, possible for the Commission and, indeed, the Council to modify under a simplified procedure which excluded participation of the European Parliament. The principal significance of this was not limited to those fields of activity where the consultation procedure applied but was general, thus extending also to those fields where the co-operation and co-decision procedures applied.

5.3   The actors and their positions: conclusions

5.3.1   *The Council: managing the inability to agree*

From the start it was clear that the new-born Community was bound to find its own ways of functioning and developing. Even if some concrete objectives had been formulated beforehand, most notably the establishment of a common market, it was far from obvious what this meant and how it should be achieved. The lack of precision was not the result of a slipshod preparatory work but of political disagreements. In spite of the fact that there were different national expectations and that some of the interests of the founding Governments were very difficult to reconcile the decision was taken to go ahead. It was expected that old problems would persist but, importantly, these were now to be dealt with within a new framework by new institutions. But the exact identity and role of these institutions was far from clear. This would have to be defined along the way.

Quite clearly, the lack of a clear destination, with respect both to political objectives and modes of operation, was something which would characterize the Community throughout its existence and, therefore, something with which it would have to learn to live. The motto which was to help the Community out of constant disagreements was pragmatism: to postpone any discussion on matters of principle and concentrate on compromise solutions to the specific problems that were most pressing at any given time. But over the years it became clear that some solutions worked better than others. Therefore, even if it was still regarded as the result of pragmatism rather than a settlement of matters of principle, a pattern emerged and, paradoxically, without choosing the Community still made its choice. It is striking that the driving force behind this development, the problems which were regarded as most pressing, was often found outside the Community: trade wars or armed conflicts and, linked to this, negotiations for accession of new members. The more peaceful the world in which the Community lived the more it could afford to do what it preferred the most: to disagree and avoid binding commitments.

In this book it has been seen that one of the central components of the pattern which emerged was that of delegation of decision-making powers to the Commission and, as an integral aspect of this, the committee system. This was born out of the Governments' awareness that they were not able to agree as much as they could agree was needed. Unwilling to choose a clear-cut solution with ideological implications—to entrust the necessary powers to the Commission, thus allowing it to become a truly supranational institution, or consolidate the prerogatives of those previously in charge: the national administrations—a mixed solution was opted for: the management committees. By providing that the Commission should work in close co-operation with the national administrations, the Governments had not only been able to postpone any discussion on matters of principle but they had discovered a miraculous medicine which would make it possible for them to manage their inability to agree.

During the transitional period it became evident to everyone that the inability to agree was not an infant disease but something which the Community would have to live with. This was manifested most strongly in the 1966 Luxembourg Compromise and the agreement which emerged from the 1969 Summit Meeting in The Hague. On both occasions the conclusion was reached by the Governments that it was their concurrent political wills, not supranational institutions, that would make co-operation possible and, therefore, that the policy objectives and procedural solutions aimed for had to be acceptable to all of them.

Parallel to the process which led the Governments to confess their belief in political wills rather than formal institutions, there was a growing pressure for common action. But the fundamental inability to agree persisted. During such circumstances the miraculous medicine transformed into a universal cure. The more difficult it was for the Governments themselves to decide in the Council what steps should be taken, the greater the responsibility transferred to the Commission and committees. Importantly, this made it possible to maintain flexibility: not to enter into far-reaching commitments and, at the same time, secure understandings on a case-by-case basis.

But, as the substantive scope of those 'implementing powers' grew wider, the Governments pressed for stronger mechanisms of political control. Therefore, from the tension between the need for action and the demand for control, a new form of committee was born which left the Commission even less room for exercise of autonomous powers. The functional identity of these committees was well reflected by their maiden name: 'legislative committees' (later to become regulatory committees). This time the medicine was successful. Therefore, after much hesitance, the Community was finally able to act in those fields where the inability to agree had been most costly: external and internal trade. The significance of this cannot be over-estimated. Even if it had been by a narrow margin, the Community was now able to state that it had passed the first test successfully: the establishment of a common market.

The general validity of this logic was to be confirmed again and again. While the Governments' inability to agree only became more evident after the first enlargement, the use of delegation and committees became a condition for living. No better illustration of this can be found than the steady increase in the number of committees. The final recognition of the pattern which had emerged came with the 1986 Single European Act. Here the mixed solution sprung out of pragmatism was finally given constitutional status.

Clearly, the amendments introduced by the Single European Act contained nothing really new and only codified existing practice. It is submitted that at least two important conclusions can be drawn from the fact that the Governments still bothered. First, that all of them, however unwilling they had once been to discuss comitology as a matter of principle, were now prepared to admit that it was a living part of the institutional system. This, indeed, confirmed the evolutionary nature of the Community; that without ever choosing it had still come to make a choice. Second, that there was a political intention to continue to use the possibility of delegation of powers, not less than before but more and also more systematically. That conclusion is supported by the fact that the potential scope of 'implementation' had been left undefined so as to secure maximum flexibility.

Both the above conclusions are affirmed by the first Comitology Decision, which was adopted immediately after the amendments introduced by the Single European Act entered into force. Contrary to what the Commission and the European Parliament had hoped for, the Decision did not bring about any radical changes of existing structures.

More than anything else, it could be seen as an unambiguous expression of the Council's insistence that delegation of implementing powers required mechanisms for political control. Therefore, even if there was an intention to make even better use of delegation than before, it was now clear that without mechanisms for control the Council would prefer not to make any delegation at all.

With the adoption of the first Comitology Decision the focus of attention was shifted away from the primary function of comitology, to provide a forum for co-operation (between the Commission and the national administrations and, even more importantly, between the national administrations *inter se*) toward the secondary, complementary, function, to provide mechanisms for political control over the Commission. Judging by the text of the Decision, it looked as if comitology was based on a conflict of interests between the Commission and the Council. This was deceptive, because the relationship between the Commission and the committees with which it was obliged to work was surprisingly friendly and also, because the conflicts comitology was primarily intended to counteract, or at least manage, were those that arose within the Council itself. Clearly, the formal mechanisms for control were not stated in the Decision to increase transparency—to explain how comitology functioned in a normal situation—but to provide a legal guarantee which would only be called into operation if things went wrong.

The continuous significance of this guarantee was affirmed during the years that followed. Perhaps most striking in that respect was the realization of the internal market programme, whose relative success was very much based on delegation and a rather generous interpretation of the substantive scope of implementing powers. The trick which made this possible was comitology and, above all, an increasing use of the regulatory committee procedure: the procedure that offered the best guarantee for political control. Apparently satisfied with the rather far-reaching opportunities which that procedure offered them to substitute and, sometimes, even block unwanted action, the Governments were now willing to let the Commission take those steps which they themselves had not been able to take before.

It follows from the above that the driving force behind the establishment and spread of the committee system was to be found in the Governments' fundamental inability to agree, their stubborn refusal to give up their belief in the power of concurrent political wills over supranational institutions, and their painful awareness of the need for common action. This became even more obvious after they had enlarged the circle of interests which had to be reconciled: by admitting new Governments into the Council and, eventually, granting the European Parliament a genuine right of participation. For each new interest that could claim a say in the process for adoption of legislation, the reasons to delegate and have matters dealt with under 'simplified' procedures only became more compelling.

But somewhat paradoxically, it was only the Council who could afford to delegate matters of significance and not lose influence and control. For the European Parliament the situation was entirely different. Its role in the development of the committee system will be discussed below. Sufficient, for now, is to note that the European Parliament had always looked upon the use of committees with suspicion. At the root of this suspicion was the fear of a sliding in powers: that more and more matters of political significance were to be dealt with outside the ordinary process for adoption of legislation, under procedures from which the European Parliament itself was excluded. There can be no doubt that the suspicion was well founded. The sad thing, for the European Parliament, was that the more it did to object (using its right of participation in the process for adoption of legislation) the more was done by the Council (and, indeed, the Commission) to have matters of potential controversy dealt with under 'simplified' procedures. For that reason it may be concluded, not only that the European Parliament itself became a driving force behind the very development it most wanted to resist but also that this had a healing effect on relations within the Council. Even if their fundamental inability to agree was to persist, the Governments were now forced to put up a common front.

It is at this stage of the development, when the European Parliament gets a real say, that comitology becomes a truly institutionalized phenomenon. This means, above all, that it was no longer possible for the Governments to treat the question of its function and design as a matter of its own convenience, without having to consider the interests of others: from now on the combined use of delegation and committees was to entail a lot more than a pragmatic solution for the Governments to manage their inability to agree. The transformation of comitology was well illustrated by the inter-institutional negotiations which led to the adoption of the second Comitology Decision in 1999. Even if it was not formally obliged to do so, the Council proved prepared to bargain with the European Parliament. Clearly, the result was far from revolutionary and most, if not all, essential parts of the old Decision were preserved in the new. But at the same time there were concrete expressions of the fact that all Governments, even some rather stubborn ones, had realized the importance of formal concessions. Probably most important, in that respect, was the inclusion of a right for the European Parliament to 'blow the whistle' when it felt that the Commission was exceeding its powers: in such cases the Commission would be compelled to re-examine the matter, taking the European Parliament's objections 'into account'. Even if this and other provisions included in the new Decision did only codify some existing routines and were not likely to have much practical significance, in the legal sense it meant that comitology had now been redefined so as to include the European Parliament.

5.3.2 The European Parliament: the fear of a sliding in powers

Throughout most of the history of the European Community and Union, the role of the European Parliament has been characterized by struggle: struggle with itself, to find an institutional identity, and struggle with others, to have that identity confirmed. Not many of the characteristics which make the European Parliament what it is today have been given to it for free, by birth, or blessing, but are the results of its refusal to content itself with what it has been given and an untiring struggle for more. The tactic of the European Parliament has been to wear its opponents down, by use and abuse of all means available, until the point has been reached where they realize that it will be less costly to make concessions than to resist.

It is difficult to conclude if this tactic has been successful. Clearly, it has led to changes: both the co-decision procedure and the reform of comitology are the results of life-long struggle. But perhaps these or similar changes would have come about anyway? Maybe, with a different tactic, the changes would have come about more quickly? Whatever answer should be given to those questions, there can be little doubt that the tactic applied by the European Parliament has become one more reason for the Governments not to give up comitology and to realize, even more clearly than before, how much they need it.

The logical starting point for the European Parliament is, and has always been, that the committee system poses a serious threat to its own role in the institutional system and, in particular, interferes with its fundamental rights to exercise political supervision (over the Commission) and to participate in political decision-making: the legislative process. In the view of the European Parliament, the Commission, and the Commission alone, should be given a clear-cut and autonomous responsibility for decision-making of an executive nature (as opposed to the responsibility for decision-making of a legislative nature which should remain with the Council and itself). As long as this is its view, the European Parliament is bound to be hostile to any arrangement which allows other organs, over which it has no right to exercise political supervision, to influence the outcome of executive decision-making.

In principle, as long as it holds this view, the European Parliament is also bound to favour a rather narrow definition of executive decision-making (cf. exercise of 'implementing' powers). Of course, at the time when its own right to participate in political decision-making was only that provided for under the consultation procedure, the European Parliament had little to lose from a definition of executive decision-making which opened up the substantive scope to matters with a legislative bearing (maybe, to some extent this was even something which it favoured, since this way its right to exercise political supervision only became more significant). But, undoubtedly, the step-by-step strengthening of the European Parliament's right to participate in political decision-making (replacing the consultation procedure, first, with the co-operation procedure and, then, with the co-decision procedure) has given it a strong reason to favour a strict definition of executive decision-making with a narrow substantive scope.

The committee system has come to interfere with the interests of the European Parliament in the worst possible way. Parallel to the strengthening of its right to participate in political decision-making, the Council and, indeed, the Commission (and the Court) demonstrated their wish to secure that the term 'implementation' was given the widest possible meaning and that an increasing number of matters of potential controversy would be dealt with in executive decision-making. At the same time the autonomous responsibility of the Commission was cut down rather drastically through the establishment of committees (and an intensified use of the regulatory committee procedure).

Throughout the years, the European Parliament's agenda with respect to comitology has been centred on its demand for a *droit de regard*: a right to be kept informed and to state its opinion. This dual right was set out, for the first time, in the early 1960s and, even if it has been refined, has been restated rather coherently for more than 40 years. But it is only during the last 10 years that there have been concrete results. This, indeed, is a telling example of the untiring struggle of the European Parliament. Today, the requirement that it should be kept fully informed about matters dealt with in committees and that it should be permitted to state its opinion (and have this opinion considered) is an integral part of the legal framework laid down in the second Comitology Decision. But, unsurprisingly, the European Parliament is refusing to content itself. Quite clearly, this is not only so for organic reasons but because in the last few years, the political need to delegate has only become more apparent.

The current agenda of the European Parliament, and most likely the agenda for the next few years, is not entirely clear. On the one hand, there are signals that the European Parliament will continue to defend its traditional position: to insist on a narrow definition of the notion of implementation and fight comitology. On the other hand, there are also signals that the European Parliament is becoming increasingly aware of the need for pragmatism: to admit the usefulness of wide delegation subject to mechanisms of political control. If this latter position is to prevail, it will bring the European Parliament's agenda closer to that of the Council. But, importantly, there will still be a fundamental difference of views with respect to the mechanisms for control. Even if they are more than satisfactory to the Council, in their present form, the mechanisms offered by comitology have little to offer the European Parliament. Therefore, it is unlikely that the European Parliament will ever fully admit the usefulness of the power to delegate without a reform of the committee system.

5.3.3   *The Commission: a mediator in its own interest*

It is difficult to avoid the impression that the Commission, throughout the history of the European Community and Union, has developed along lines very much opposite to those of the European Parliament: that it has had to learn not to struggle or fight for more but to adapt and try to keep as much as possible of all that it was originally given. Any expectations that the Commission should be allowed to lead the way towards a truly supranational co-existence were effectively erased by the other

Governments' acceptance of the French protest in 1965 (the Luxembourg Compromise). From that point onwards the Commission's political strength was to depend upon a collective mandate granted by the Council. It is submitted that, even if the mandate has been generously formulated (this, indeed, was the case with the Commission headed by Jacques Delors), it has never permitted the Commission to develop a truly autonomous position.

In this respect, the development of the committee system is but one example of a more general phenomenon. Even if the Commission itself preferred to emphasize the more practical benefits of co-operation with the national administrations, it is clear that the true reason for establishment of the management committee procedure was to be found in some Governments' wish to 'assure the effective direction.' It is equally clear that it was the belief that the management committee procedure could not provide a sufficient guarantee that the 'executive powers thus vested in the Commission should be precisely circumscribed and leave no room for discretion or autonomous responsibility' which was the true reason for the establishment of the regulatory committee procedure.

Whether the fear of what it could do if it was given its own responsibility was grounded or not, the Commission immediately proved that it was aware of the fact that without the control mechanisms offered by comitology there would be no delegation at all. Therefore, rather than objecting, it satisfied itself with a formal responsibility, the right to issue implementing measures, and adapted. In practice, this meant that the role of the Commission, with respect to the exercise of delegated powers, was to become that of a broker: not only between representatives of the national administrations but also between its own ambitions and the more modest needs of the Governments. It is impossible to judge whether the Commission's approach was the result of institutional vanity; the wish to keep up appearances, or the expression of a genuine feeling of responsibility; that it was its duty to make sure that things were done, one way or another. But it is evident that the Commission found comfort in the hope that the current state of affairs was only a passing moment and that sometime in the future, when things got better, it would be permitted to play a leading role.

The Commission's rather split attitude towards comitology became more pronounced during the process which was to lead to the first major reform of the institutional system. Here the massive support for extended use of delegation was exploited by the Commission to argue that the time had come to free it from existing constraints: to replace the case-by-case conferral of implementing powers with a constitutional birthright. At the same time the Commission assured the Governments that it was happy to continue to co-operate with the national administrations in accordance with 'the tried and tested procedures' and that its proposals for change would not affect their ability to exercise political control.

This argument did not manage to convince the Governments in 1985, when the Single European Act was negotiated. From a practical point of view, it seemed to have little significance. Only a few years after the reform, the Commission prided itself with the statistical fact that it had 'always been able to secure the backing of experts representing the Member States on the various committees.' On the one hand, the Commission pointed to the fact that co-operation with committees worked very well. At the same time, the Commission complained about co-operation with committees. The reason for complaining was not that there were practical problems with co-operation with committees but rather that the Commission did not like the idea behind that co-operation (as if to say: how come we are not allowed to do this alone, without having to co-operate with committees, do they not trust us?). As asked rhetorically by the Commission, if comitology and co-operation with the national administrations were working so well, why did the Council continue to insist on mechanisms for political control (the regulatory committee procedure was being used not less but more than before)? But that question could also be turned around so as to ask why did the Commission really care about the existence of formal mechanisms, if these were never called into operation? The answer to that question was to become clear during the following years.

When the Commission presented its ideas for reform of the arrangement for exercise of implementing powers to the 1985 Intergovernmental Conference, it had chosen to stress how vital these were for the success of the internal market programme. In 1991, more or less identical ideas were presented in the form of the proposal for introduction of a formal hierarchy of legal acts. This time they were styled as fundamental components in the constitutional construction of the new European Union. Only a few years later emphasis was put on citizens' need for simplification and transparency. Even if the wrapping changed, the content of the Commission's package remained the same: that it should be permitted to exercise widely (or rather vaguely) defined powers in its own right, without the need for prior delegation from the Council and, importantly, that there should be less room for use of the control mechanisms offered by comitology.

Parallel to the above, the Commission begun to justify its ideas for reform by reference to the concerns of the European Parliament. In particular, it was argued that the existing control mechanisms should be replaced by new mechanisms which would allow not only the Council but also the European Parliament to react (if they felt that the Commission was transgressing the border between executive and legislative decision-making). It is submitted that there are good reasons to be sceptical about the Commission's real intentions.

It is more than evident that the Commission was never very sensitive to the European Parliament's demand for a *droit de regard*. It was only after the European Parliament had learnt to make a rather aggressive use of its powers of budgetary control that the Commission proved itself prepared to provide the European Parliament with information about the operations of comitology. Once that point had been passed, the Commission transformed its vice into virtue and made several 'generous' offers. But the demand for a *droit de regard* also had a second component: that the European Parliament should be entitled to state its opinion. This, indeed, was the historical root of its more recent insistence on reform of comitology and the mechanisms for political control. With respect to this second, essential, component, nothing in the Commission's attitude is more striking than that it has always been very negative. A recent example of this can be found in the proposal for a second Comitology Decision. Here the Commission deliberately reduced the idea that the European Parliament should have a right to state its opinion into a formula for reform of the regulatory committee procedure which would have had no practical significance (for the European Parliament). It was only thanks to the European Parliament itself, far from content with the 'olive branches' held out by the Commission, and the Council that the final result was more advantageous.

On this occasion and others when the concerns of the European Parliament were interpreted by the Commission, there were always important nuances which all had in common that they were favourable to its own original position: wide powers and less room for effective use of mechanisms of political control. Since this position is impossible to reconcile with that of the European Parliament, it is difficult not to arrive at the conclusion that the purported support of the Commission to the European Parliament's cause has not been the result of ideological affinity but of tactical thinking. The full implication of this can only be appreciated in the light of the fact that the Commission's position was not only impossible to reconcile with that of the European Parliament but also with the position of the Council. But the reasons were the complete opposite. Therefore, if it could only play its cards successfully, offering itself to mediate between the other two, there was a chance that the Commission would end up with that which it had always wanted.

5.3.4   *The Court of Justice: a case of judicial inactivism*

It has been seen in this book that the Council, the European Parliament, and the Commission have all relied on the idea of an institutional balance of powers in order to defend their position in the development of the committee system. It has also been seen that their respective interpretations of what that idea really means have been rather divergent and, often, impossible to reconcile. Thus, for example, the Council has maintained that the use of committees to ensure influence and control is a necessary guarantee for its own 'constitutional' right to exercise executive powers. At the same time, the European Parliament has objected to the use of committees (other than purely advisory ones) as an illegal attempt by the Council to interfere with the powers of the Commission. This argument has been sustained by the Commission itself. Importantly, the European Parliament has also fought against a transfer of powers to adopt general measures with legislative bearing from the legislative sphere to the executive sphere on the ground that this undermines its right of participation.

As argued in Chapter 1, the fact that the idea of an institutional balance of powers has been so fundamental for the development of the committee system may be a reason to expect that an authoritative answer could be found in the rulings of the Court of Justice (see above 1.4.2). But, surprisingly, the role of the Court with respect to the development of the committee system has been far from active: not only has it proved itself unwilling to reduce the room for political negotiations but it has also demonstrated a surprising ability to adapt itself to their result. In order to test that argument, in this book a relatively small number of rulings involving comitology has been selected for a closer study. The basic submission is that the selected rulings are the most important ones from an inter-institutional or constitutional point of view: that they involve new matters of principal significance and were given at a crucial time in the development.

The overall conclusion that may be drawn from the rulings examined is that the role of the Court in the development of the committee system has been characterized, not so much by its notorious activism as by inactivism. But, importantly, this should not be taken to mean that the Court has not had a decisive influence. Instead its rulings may be seen as a crucial set of legal benedictions of the development already under way: by refraining from interfering, even if this has required it to avoid strict application of legal principles and sometimes even make sacrifices in the quality of reasoning, it has managed to secure the preconditions needed to push the Community out of political crises and forward. By giving leeway to others, most often the Council (the concurrent political wills of the Governments), the Court has proved its ability to respond to the serious efforts made on the political level thus promoting *l'effet utile.*

5.4   Prospects

5.4.1   *The debate on the future of the European Union*

On 14 February 2000, only one year after the entry into force of Council Decision 99/468/EC (see above 4.4.2), the Intergovernmental Conference was begun which led to the Treaty of Nice. Quite clearly, this was only intended to bring about the changes needed to conclude accession negotiations with the most advanced applicant countries. The most important matters addressed related to voting in the Council and the organization of the future Commission.[1] The Intergovernmental Conference was finalized on 11 December 2000 and the result was far from sufficient: much of what was hoped for had either been ignored completely or simply not discussed in any depth.[2] Therefore, already at the time of signature of the new Treaty, the call was made for another

---

[1]   See the Presidency Conclusions of the European Council meeting on 10 and 11 December 1999 (Helsinki), at internet www.europa.int.

[2]   Treaty of Nice of 26 February 2001 amending the Treaty on European Union, the Treaties establishing the European Communities and certain related acts (OJ 2001 C 80/1).

Intergovernmental Conference based on 'a deeper and wider debate about the future of the European Union.'[3]

This time the arrangement for exercise of implementing powers was expected to become a matter of central concern, all the more so because the political need for delegation of powers had become more pronounced. A major factor to consider in that respect was the parallel process for enlargement and the subsequent admission of 10 new members in the Council: the more interests that would have to be reconciled, the more difficult would it be to agree—even if decision-making by qualified majority voting was enforced—and the more useful the power to delegate. At the same time it had become obvious to everyone that delegation and, indeed, the conditions for delegation, could no longer be treated by the Governments as a matter of their own convenience. The inter-institutional negotiations which led to the adoption of Council Decision 99/468/EC demonstrated that all Governments had understood the need to make concessions to the European Parliament. Over the next few years it became clear that the relief with which the European Parliament had received the result of those negotiations did not mean that the battle over comitology had come to an end (see above 4.4.3.2). The best illustration of this can be found in the controversy surrounding the so-called Lamfalussy process for making progress in the market for financial securities.

Following calls that renewed efforts were urgently needed to build an integrated financial market, on 17 July 2000 the decision was taken by the Council to set up a committee of wise men under the chairmanship of the former President of the European Monetary Institute, Alexandre Lamfalussy. The final Lamfalussy Report was presented seven months later. Here the outline was presented of a procedural reform which would enable speedy adoption of legislation within the field of securities. Essentially, the reform was to be based on new framework legislation combined with delegation of powers to the Commission subject to comitology (typically, the regulatory committee procedure) and enhanced consultation of market actors. Against the background of previous failures and persistent disagreements within the Council

---

[3] See Declaration No 23 on the future of the Union, above Ch 4, n 16. For comments see e.g. Van Nuffel, P., Le traité de Nice: un commentaire (2001) 2 *RDUE* 329, Dashwood, A., The Constitution of the European Union after Nice: Law-making Procedures (2001) 26 *ELRev* 215, and Witte, B. de, The Nice Declaration: Time for a Constitutional Treaty of the European Union? (2001) 36 *IntSpec* 21.

(cf. above 4.3.4.1), the conclusion was drawn in the Report that there was 'no serious alternative available.'[4]

Even if the plan for reform was welcomed by the Council, the Commission, and the European Parliament it soon proved controversial. First some Governments indicated that they would not be willing to undertake any extensive delegation of powers to adopt implementing measures, now that committee procedures no longer made it so easy to block the Commission. Apparently, they only agreed to do so after the Commission had re-committed itself 'to avoid going against predominant views which might emerge within the Council, as to the appropriateness of such measures.'[5] Then the European Parliament made it clear that it would not approve the reform (in accordance with the co-decision procedure) unless it obtained a right to call-back delegation if dissatisfied, not just with the *scope* of implementing measures—as provided by Council Decision 99/468/EC—but with their *substance* (cf. above 4.4.2.3).[6] Not surprisingly, the European Parliament feared that the reform would give the Commission and comitology committees powers that were too wide and that there was a lack of adequate mechanisms of control.[7] It was only after one year of inter-institutional negotiations that a compromise was reached. The compromise was manifested, most clearly, in another undertaking of the Commission, read out to the European Parliament by Romano Prodi on 5 February 2002.[8]

---

[4] See Report of the Committee of Wise Men of 15 February 2001 on the regulation of European securities markets, at p. 8, at internet http://www.europa.eu.int.

[5] See European Council Resolution of 23 March 2001 on more effective securities market regulation in the European Union (OJ 2001 C 138/1). It may be noted that this commitment was included already in the statement by the Commission on Article 5 in Declarations on Council Decision 99/468/EC, above Ch 4, n 288.

[6] See the first Corbett Report of 29 April 2003, below Ch 5, n 10, at p. 18.

[7] It may be pointed out that Council Decision 99/468/EC recognized only that the European Parliament could claim (within one month) that an implementing measure exceeded the scope of powers delegated, in which case the measure had to be re-examined (see above 4.4.2.3). There was no recognized right to object to the substance. Cf. European Parliament Resolution of 17 February 2000 (above Ch 4, n 327), paragraph 3. Here the European Parliament stated 'that this agreement is without prejudice to its right to adopt any resolution on any subject, notably when it objects to the contents of a draft implementing measure.'

[8] See Implementation of financial services legislation in the context of the Lamfalussy Report, intervention by Commission President Romano Prodi to the European Parliament's plenary session in Strasbourg on 5 October 2002 (SPEEC/02/44).

According to President Prodi, the Commission accepted that the European Parliament's period in which to examine draft implementing measures in the field of securities would be extended (to three months instead of one) and promised that it would take 'utmost account' of the European Parliament's position, not just on *scope* but on *substance*. Furthermore, the Commission promised to include a so-called sunset clause in the proposals for framework legislation: a legal provision fixing a specific date when the delegation was automatically repealed.[9] The practical implication of this solution was that any further delegation beyond that date—and, thus, completion of the reform—would require fresh support from the European Parliament, something it would not be likely to give if it was not satisfied with the result.[10]

The fragile compromise on which the Lamfalussy process is currently resting shows that the European Parliament is ready to admit the need for pragmatism; to accept delegation and comitology, if it is only granted a real power to exercise its responsibility for political supervision. But, importantly, it also shows that the European Parliament has not given up the intention to insist on its old demands. This, indeed, was manifested in the statement made by the European Parliament when accepting the compromise, stressing that it was only a provisional solution pending an

---

[9] See e.g. Article 24(4) of European Parliament and Council Directive 03/71/EC of 4 November 2003 on the prospectus to be published when securities are offered to the public or admitted to trading and amending Directive 01/34/EC (OJ 2003 L 345/64). Here it is provided that 'the European Parliament and the Council may renew the provisions concerned in accordance with the procedure laid down in Article 251 of the Treaty and, to that end, shall review them prior to the expiry of the four-year period.'

[10] It may be noted that the European Parliament's Rules of Procedure were recently re-written to better reflect its position. As now stated in Rule 88(2): 'On a proposal from the committee responsible, Parliament may, within one month—or three months for financial services measures—of the date of receipt of the draft implementing measure, adopt a resolution objecting to the draft measure, in particular if it exceeds the implementing powers provided for in the basic instrument. Where there is no part-session before the deadline expires, or in cases where urgent action is required, the right of response shall be deemed to have been delegated to the committee responsible. This shall take the form of a letter from the committee chairman to the Member of the Commission responsible, and shall be brought to the attention of all Members of Parliament. If Parliament objects to the measure, the President shall request the Commission to withdraw or amend the measure or submit a proposal under the appropriate legislative procedure.' See Rule 88(2) of European Parliament Rules of Procedure of 5 March 2003 (OJ 2003 L 61/1). See also Report of 28 January 2002 drawn up on behalf of the Committee on Constitutional Affairs on the general revision of the Rules of Procedure (rapporteur: Richard Corbett) EP Doc A5-8/02.

amendment of Article 202 (ex 145) EC at the forthcoming Intergovernmental Conference.[11]

With respect to the debate on the future of the European Union that was launched by the Treaty of Nice and which followed upon the adoption of that Treaty there are two, parallel, initiatives which deserve to be mentioned: the Commission's White Paper on European Governance and the hierarchy of legal acts included in the Draft Treaty submitted by the so-called European Convention to the 2004 Intergovernmental Conference. The focus here will be on the latter. But before that a few words should be said about the White Paper on European Governance.

5.4.2   The White Paper on European Governance

5.4.2.1   A new system for exercise of delegated powers

The White Paper on European Governance, presented by the Commission on 25 July 2001 and subsequently refined in a number of documents, offers the most recent and, indeed, undisguised expression of its position with respect to delegation of powers and comitology.[12] Here the

---

[11] See European Parliament Resolution of 5 February 2002 on the implementation of financial services legislation (http://www.europarl.eu.int). The Resolution is based on the Report of 23 January 2002 drawn up on behalf of the Committee on Constitutional Affairs on the implementation of financial services (rapporteur: Karl von Wogau) EP Doc A5-11/02. Here it is explained that the European Parliament endorses the objective of establishing a securities market as quickly as possible and that it considers 'that the requisite measures must be taken to improve the effectiveness of the decision-making process and to speed up legislative procedures, in a manner entirely consistent with the provisions of the Treaties and the inter-institutional balance.' But at the same time it is emphasized 'that, according to Article 202 of the EC Treaty, the comitology procedure as set out in Council Decision 99/468/EC (see above Ch 4, n 275) is aimed at the adoption and application of implementing measures by the Commission in accordance with the relevant provisions of the basic instrument (directive or regulation), and cannot be regarded as a "simplified" or "delegated" system for the adoption of "secondary" legislation by that institution.' For an expression of the European Parliament's position within the context of the European Convention, see European Parliament Resolution of 17 December 2002 on the typology of acts and the hierarchy of legislation in the European Union (http://www.europarl.eu.int). Based on the Report of 3 December 2002 drawn up on behalf of the Committee on Constitutional Affairs on the typology of acts and the hierarchy of legislation in the European Union (rapporteur: Jean-Louis Bourlanges) EP Doc A5-425/02.

[12] See Commission White Paper of 25 July 2001: European Governance (COM (01) 428 final), in particular at pp. 31 and 34. See also the most recent follow-up Report on European

outlines are presented of a model for the European Union's future organization based on the idea of separation of powers. As envisaged by the Commission, legislation would be 'stripped back to essential principles and a framework setting out how they should be implemented.' The legislation would be adopted by the Council and the European Parliament jointly, and the regulations or decisions implementing that legislation would be adopted by the Commission.

At a first glance this seems to correspond quite well to the existing situation. But, importantly, the Commission argues that the conditions under which it currently adopts implementing measures would have to be reviewed. In the end, this would lead to a situation where legislation defines the limits within which the Commission carries out its 'executive' role and new mechanisms of control allow the 'legislature' (the Council and the European Parliament) to monitor the result. The centre-piece of the White Paper on European Governance is found in the call for a reform of the system for exercise of delegated powers in two stages: one temporary within the existing framework of Article 202 (ex 145) EC and another permanent, modifying that framework. Since the latter stage requires amendment of the Treaty, the White Paper clearly indicates the Commission's intention to take an active part in the debate on the future of the European Union and, indeed, make reform of the system for exercise of delegated powers a key objective:

This adjustment of the responsibility of the Institutions, giving control of executive competence to the two legislative bodies and reconsidering the existing regulatory and management committees touches the delicate question of the balance of power between the Institutions. It should lead to modifying Treaty article 202 which permits the Council alone to impose certain requirements on the way the Commission exercises its executive role. That article has become outdated given the co-decision procedure which puts Council and the European Parliament on an equal footing with regard to the adoption of legislation in many areas. Consequently, the Council and the European Parliament should have an equal role in supervising the way in which the Commission exercises its executive role. The Commission intends to launch a reflection on this topic in view of the next Intergovernmental Conference.[13]

Governance of 22 September 2004 (SEC (04) 1153). For an overview see Almer, J. and Rotkirch, M., *European Governance—An Overview of the Commission's Agenda for Reform*, Swedish Institute for European Policy Studies (Sieps) 2004:1u.

[13] The Commission White Paper, above Ch 5, n 12, at p. 31.

It follows from the above that the Commission's agenda for European Governance, in its most basic points, is not so new as it may sound. Instead it re-packages—once again—the old idea that Article 202 (ex 145) EC Treaty should be amended in order to provide the basis for a system for exercise of 'executive' powers which is based on a different logic than that of comitology (see above 5.3.3). It is noteworthy that the same idea was later taken up by the European Convention which prepared the work of the 2004 Intergovernmental Conference (see below 5.4.3). The most visible link between the White Paper on European Governance and the European Convention is found in a communication from 11 December 2002 where the Commission proposed 'to amend the Article 202 of the Treaty in order to establish a new system for delegating powers which more closely reflect the legal and political realities of the situation and the requirements for running an enlarged Union.'[14] Here the need was emphasized to include, in the new Treaty, a hierarchy of legal acts distinguishing between: 'institutional laws' and 'laws' adopted by the Council and the European Parliament under the co-decision procedure, and 'regulations' adopted by the Commission itself for the purposes of implementation. Importantly, the laws could make provision for extensive delegation of powers to the Commission subject to supervision by the Council and the European Parliament (for example through a call-back system): if the 'legislature' was to come out against a draft regulation, the Commission would have to withdraw it, amend it, or present a proposal under the co-decision procedure.

5.4.2.2   *The proposal for amendment of Council Decision 99/468/EC*

Pending the introduction of a new system for exercise of delegated powers, the White Paper on European Governance also envisages a first, temporary stage of reform. The meaning of this was clarified on 11 December 2002—the very same day as the Commission submitted its communication to the European Convention (see above 5.4.2.1)—when a

---

[14] See Commission Communication to the Convention of 11 December 2002 (below Ch 5, n 52, at 5.4.3.3). It may be noted that on the very same day the Commission presented its follow-up Report of 11 December 2002 on European Governance (COM (02) 705 final) and also its Proposal of 11 December 2002 for a Council Decision amending Decision 99/468/EC, see below Ch 5, n 15. The quotation is taken from the Explanatory Memorandum of that proposal, at p. 2.

proposal was presented for amendment of Council Decision 99/468/EC.[15] In full compliance with the White Paper on European Governance the proposal seeks to shift the logic of comitology from being national input into the exercise of implementing powers, to being supervision by the 'legislature' over the 'executive' and, in line with that, strengthen the autonomy of the Commission.[16] But according to the Commission itself, the main objective of its proposal is 'to take account of the European Parliament's position as a co-legislator . . . placing on an equal footing the European Parliament and the Council as supervisors of the Commission's exercise of the implementing powers.'[17]

The strongest expressions of the reform sought to be achieved are found in the proposed inclusion of a new Article 2a which shall operate alongside the existing Article 2, laying down criteria for the choice of committee procedure (see above 4.4.2.4) and a new Article 5a which shall operate alongside the existing Article 5, setting out the characteristics of the regulatory committee procedure (see above 4.4.2.3). In effect these changes mean that the current system for exercise of delegated powers is split into two parallel regimes: one for matters falling outside co-decision and another for matters falling inside. This, indeed, is what the European Parliament has been asking for since the birth of the co-decision procedure (see e.g. above 4.3.3.1 and 4.3.3.3).

In comparison with the existing Article 2, the new Article 2a applies more rigorous and legally binding criteria for determining the choice of committee procedure in fields of co-decision. The regulatory committee procedure should be used 'whenever the executive measures are designed to widely implement the essential aspects of the basic instrument or adapt certain other aspects of it' and the advisory committee procedure 'whenever the executive measures have an individual scope or concern the procedural arrangements for implementing basic instruments.' The management committee procedure would no longer be used (in fields of co-decision).

In comparison with the existing Article 5, the new Article 5a introduces a regulatory committee procedure which is based on a conceptualized

---

[15] Commission Proposal of 11 December 2002 for a Council Decision amending Decision 99/468/EC laying down the procedures for the exercise of implementing powers conferred on the Commission (COM (02) 719 final).

[16] For a thorough assessment of the proposal see House of Lords Select Committee on the European Union: Reforming Comitology, Session 2002–03, 31st Report (1 July 2003).

[17] See the Explanatory Memorandum of the Proposal of 11 December 2002 (above Ch 5, n 15), at p. 2.

distinction between two phases. The initial 'executive' phase is almost identical to the first stage of the existing procedure. The only difference can be found in a situation where a committee delivers an opinion which is unfavourable or where it does not deliver an opinion. According to the existing procedure, this means that the Commission will have to submit a proposal to the Council which it may adopt or oppose by qualified majority (see above 4.4.2.2). But according to the new, parallel, procedure a further period of one month will pass during which an attempt shall be made to find a solution for which a qualified majority can be obtained in the committee. At the end of the executive phase, the Commission shall propose a final draft, which may be amended to reflect the committee's opinion. According to the original proposal, the subsequent 'supervisory' phase would start with this final draft being submitted to the European Parliament and the Council. Then, if either of them raises any objections—by an absolute majority in the European Parliament and a qualified majority in the Council—within a period of one month (which may be extended by another month), the Commission would be left with two main options: either to enact the proposed measure, '*possibly* amending its draft to take account of the objections' (emphasis added), or to present a legislative proposal to be submitted to the co-decision procedure.

In addition to the above, a third feature should be pointed out: the deletion of the existing Article 8. Most importantly, this article allows the European Parliament to state its position that the scope of a draft measure falling within a field of co-decision exceeds the implementing powers provided for in the basic instrument, i.e. that the measure is *ultra vires*. In such a case the Commission will have to re-examine the measure, taking the position of the European Parliament 'into account' and either submit a new draft, continue with the procedure, or present a proposal for normal legislation (*cf.* above 4.4.3.2).[18] The Commission shall keep the European Parliament informed of the choice of action and its reasons. The deletion of Article 8 is justified by the inclusion of the new Article 5a which will enable the European Parliament to object to both the scope and substance of a draft implementing measure falling within a field of co-decision during the supervisory phase of the regulatory committee

---

[18]   See Article 8 of Council Decision 99/468/EC, above Ch 4, n 275. It was also explained that the parliamentary position should be stated in a resolution, setting out the grounds on which it was based.

procedure. But at the same time the European Parliament would lose its existing right to comment on the scope of a measure dealt with under the advisory committee procedure (the management committee procedure would no longer be used).

The Commission's proposal for amendment of Council Decision 99/468/EC was formally submitted to the Council on 11 December 2002 and on 10 January 2003 the process was initiated for consultation of the European Parliament. The matter was assigned to its Committee on Constitutional Affairs which appointed Richard Corbett as rapporteur. Less than four months later, the Committee on Constitutional Affairs adopted his first report broadly approving the proposal subject to a number of amendments.[19]

Most notably, a change was asked for in the new Article 5a to the effect that the Commission would be obliged to take into account objections expressed by the Council or the European Parliament to a final draft adopted under the regulatory committee procedure. Instead of the Commission 'possibly' amending its draft, the proposed amendment would require the Commission either to amend its draft to take account of the objections or else to 'withdraw its draft altogether.' As emphasized in the so-called Corbett Report, there must be no option for the Commission to disregard the objections and adopt its draft as it was.[20] Furthermore, the Committee on Constitutional Affairs proposed amendments re-instating the European Parliament's right to comment on the scope of a measure dealt with under the advisory committee procedure. In this respect the Report noted that the criteria for determining whether a matter should be dealt with under an advisory committee procedure or a regulatory committee procedure (the new Article 2a) were open to differing interpretations and, therefore, it was important for the European Parliament to have an input into both.

The amendments adopted by the Committee on Constitutional Affairs were discussed in the European Parliament at the sitting of 13 May 2003. This gave the rapporteur, Richard Corbett, an opportunity to clarify his views on the comitology system and the changes envisaged by the

---

[19] See Report of 29 April 2003 drawn up on behalf of the Committee on Constitutional Affairs on the proposal for a Council decision amending Decision 99/468/EC laying down the procedures for the exercise of implementing powers conferred on the Commission (rapporteur: Richard Corbett) EP Doc A5-128/03.

[20] See the Explanatory Statement of the first Corbett Report, above Ch 5, n 10, at p. 20.

Commission in its proposal:

The system was greatly improved in 1999 when the revised system was adopted by the Council: greater transparency, a greater guarantee that Parliament has access to all the proposals and all the documents. That is very good, but it has left two fundamental problems. Firstly, the Commission's powers are scrutinised only by committees of national civil servants, which alone have the power to block the Commission and call back the decision to the legislative authority. Secondly, if a decision is called back, it only goes to one branch of the legislative authority, namely the Council, even when it is co-decision legislation adopted in the first place by Parliament and the Council jointly. That is something we find unacceptable.

We want equal rights of call back for Parliament and the Council—Parliament by an absolute majority, the Council by a qualified majority, as is the bottom line now when a matter goes back to the Council. We should have the right to call back an implementing measure. If it is called back there should be equal rights of scrutiny for both Parliament and the Council.

The Commission proposal almost achieves that. It comes very close to doing that. The fly in the ointment is the word 'possibly', which is in the Commission's draft. In other words the Commission, if we object to a draft, will possibly amend it to take account of our objections or refer it to the legislative procedure. In my view and that of the committee, the word 'possibly' should go because only then will we really have a basis for a definitive solution to this issue.

Why does the Commission insist on the word 'possibly'? It says that the current legal basis of the Treaties does not allow it to go any further. I beg to disagree. If you look at the fact that the legislation is adopted anyway, in the first place, under co-decision by Parliament and the Council, it is up to Parliament and the Council to put in place any system, and any checks and balances that they want. If one argues that such checks and balances must conform to Article 202, then let us look at that article. It says: 'The Council may impose certain requirements in respect of the exercise of implementing powers.' 'Certain requirements' is the wording on which the whole comitology system is based. If such a complex system can be set up on the basis of that clause in the Treaty, there is absolutely nothing to prevent the Council from setting up a different system—the one which we are advocating—that gives the Council and Parliament equal rights to call back and equal rights to scrutinise. Article 202, in other words, is much more flexible than the Commission's legal service seems to believe.[21]

---

[21] See the statement by Richard Corbett in the Debates of the European Parliament on 13 May 2003, at internet http://www.europarl.eu.int.

But before the European Parliament was ready to proceed to the vote, Margot Wallström, the Commissioner responsible for Environment, was asked to explain the thinking which had guided the Commission when drafting the proposal and, indeed, comment on the Corbett Report. It is interesting to note, first, that according to Commissioner Wallström, it was hoped that a review of comitology would 'ultimately pave the way to a wider review based on Treaty changes.'[22] To this end, she said, the Commission had also made concrete proposals to amend Article 202 (ex 145) EC in the framework of the European Convention, notably by introducing the concept of delegation of legislative powers (see above 5.4.2.1). But at the same time she emphasized that a temporary reform of the system was all the more necessary as the uncertainty surrounding the ratification of the new Treaty was not inconsiderable. Addressing the concerns raised by Richard Corbett, Margot Wallström made it abundantly clear that the Commission could not accept the amendments asked for with respect to Article 5a and the new regulatory committee procedure. According to her, these amendments could not only 'complicate the Commission's negotiations with the Council' but they would tie the Commission's hands and prevent it from exercising its responsibility as the executive:

The withdrawal option, as formulated in Mr Corbett's Amendments Nos 3, 10 and 11, would effectively amount to replacing the freedom of adoption by the Commission by an explicit withdrawal or non-action by the Commission. If the Commission's views are not in line with those of the legislator, the Commission would be obliged to renounce the adoption of an implementing measure. Substitution of the Commission's responsibility and freedom to adopt an implementing measure via the non-action option would also send the wrong political signal to stakeholders.

The proposal is, on the contrary, based on the assumption that action is needed and that the Commission will take responsibility for it. Given the scope afforded by the current Treaty, these amendments are therefore not acceptable to the Commission. The proposal indeed goes as far as possible towards granting the European Parliament the control rights that, as a co-legislator, it should possess.

The reform, as I have just mentioned, cannot go as far as a more thoroughgoing reform conducted in the process of amending the Treaty. In the framework of the European Convention, the Commission has explicitly

---

[22] See the statement by Margot Wallström in the Debates of the European Parliament on 13 May 2003, at internet http://www.europarl.eu.int.

suggested that the Council and the European Parliament should, under delegation of legislative powers, have the possibility to oppose a text proposed by the Commission. In this scenario the latter would indeed either renounce its text, modify it or present a legislative proposal.

To conclude, I can assure you that the Commission will endeavour to achieve progress on this issue in the Council. I would like to conclude that the Commission needs Parliament's support in negotiating the strengthening of the European Parliament's prerogatives with the Council. I am confident that the Commission can count on Parliament's continued support in the process of clarifying the roles and competences of the executive and the legislator.

Not surprisingly, Margot Wallström's insistence on the Commission's freedom to adopt an implementing measure even if its 'views are not in line with those of the legislator' was unacceptable to the European Parliament. Therefore, the decision was taken to defer the final vote and refer the matter back to the Committee on Constitutional Affairs in order to allow the rapporteur the possibility to enter into talks with the Commission. Two months later the second Corbett Report was tabled.[23] Judging from the result, the talks had been rather one-sided.

The most interesting difference was found in the modified wording of the amendment to Article 5a. The word 'possibly' was still deleted but now the original reference to the Commission 'amending its draft to take account of the objections' of the European Parliament or the Council was changed to provide for the Commission simply 'taking account of the positions of the European Parliament and the Council'. Moreover, the amendment stipulated that the Commission could either amend its draft to take account of the objections or adopt the proposed 'draft of measures accompanied by an appropriate statement, or modify it, or withdraw its draft altogether.' This meant that even if the word 'possibly' disappeared the option would remain for the Commission to adopt its draft unchanged notwithstanding objections from the European Parliament or the Council. In addition to this it may be noted that the amendments re-instating the European Parliament's right to comment on the scope of matters dealt with under the advisory committee procedure were finally dropped. The reasons for this are shrouded in mystery.

---

[23] Report of 11 July 2003 drawn up on behalf of the Committee on Constitutional Affairs on the proposal for a Council decision amending Decision 99/468/EC laying down the procedures for the exercise of implementing powers conferred on the Commission (rapporteur: Richard Corbett) EP Doc A5-266/03.

As admitted by Richard Corbett to his fellow MEPs on 2 September 2003, before they voted to approve the proposal (subject to the amendments)[24]—and two months after the European Convention had adopted its Draft Treaty—the result was not ideal, but he still considered it 'suitable to tide us over until the new constitution comes into force, which will introduce a new category of delegated legislation giving us further powers under the terms of the constitution.' But this notwithstanding it is still difficult to understand why Corbett himself *and* the Committee on Constitutional Affairs *and* the European Parliament were all ready to give up their most central demand.[25] To the extent that this sudden change of position could perhaps be explained by a mistaken interpretation of the meaning of the final wording, this was corrected by the Commission on 22 April 2004, when it presented an amended proposal. Article 5a and the supervisory phase of the new regulatory committee procedure had now been revised in the light of the amendment voted by the European Parliament.[26] The change was explained accordingly:

The Commission recognises the reasons for Parliament's remarks concerning the Commission's options following possible objections by the legislature. It therefore proposes to amend its proposal accordingly. In the event

[24] See European Parliament Resolution of 2 September 2003 on the proposal for a Council decision on amending Decision 99/468/EC laying down the procedures for the exercise of implementing powers conferred on the Commission, at internet http://www.europarl.eu.int.

[25] The only trace of any explanation to be found in the second Corbett Report is that 'amendments are not necessarily the only way for the Commission to take account of Parliament's objections.' See the Explanatory Statement in the second Corbett Report of 11 July 2003 above Ch 5, n 23, at p. 13. See also the statement by Richard Corbett in the Debates of the European Parliament on 2 September 2003, at internet http://www.europarl.eu.int. Accordingly, '[i]f Parliament objects to an implementing measure adopted under comitology, then the Commission *must* either withdraw it, amend it or take account of Parliament's objection in some other way, or come before the House to make a statement to explain why it is taking any other course of action.' This, indeed, is difficult to reconcile with the justification for the amendment included in the Draft Resolution that the MEPs finally voted on: 'This means that in case of disagreement with the legislature the Commission must be placed in front of a threefold choice: Either it abandons the idea of implementing measures altogether, or it chooses the alternative of a fully fledged legislative procedure by proposing an act to modify or supplement the basic act, or it takes on board the objections raised by Parliament or Council and adopts the draft measures accordingly.' See the second Corbett Report of 11 July 2003, above Ch 5, n 23, at pp. 10 and 8.

[26] See Amended proposal of 22 April 2004 for a Council decision amending Decision 99/468/ EC laying down the procedures for the exercise of implementing powers conferred on the Commission (COM (04) 324 final).

of objections from Parliament and/or the Council to a draft for measures, the Commission may, taking account of the legislature's positions, choose between four options:

—*Modification of its draft;*
—*Presentation of a legislative proposal;*
—*Adoption of its draft without changes.* In this case, Parliament proposes that the draft for measures be accompanied by an 'appropriate statement'. The Commission must be able to apply its executive responsibility autonomously and therefore cannot be bound by the legislature's position. Consequently, this statement could not be regarded as the equivalent of an interpretative statement which would require the Commission to interpret the measure adopted in the manner desired by one branch or both branches of the legislature.
—*Withdrawal of the draft measure.* As suggested by Parliament, in certain exceptional cases the Commission must be able to decide that measures which were the subject of a draft are no longer appropriate. In such cases the Commission would retain the option to withdraw its draft.

In the event of objections from one branch or both branches of the legislature, the Commission undertakes to inform the legislature of how it intends to follow them up, and of the reasons.[27]

Touching briefly on the question of the future of the Commission's proposal for amendment of Council Decision 99/468/EC it should be noted, first, that at least one member of the Council, the British Government, has already voiced concerns. These range from 'doubts' that Article 202 (ex 145) EC provides a sufficient legal basis to outright rejection of the idea that there is any need for a new Article 5a and, in particular, a regulatory committee procedure which will enable the Commission to adopt implementing measures regardless of objections from the Council or the European Parliament.[28] As noted by the British Minister for Europe, Denis MacShane, the Commission has tried in the past 'to secure this licence' but the Governments have always resisted

[27] See the Explanatory Memorandum of the Commission's amended proposal of 22 April 2004, above Ch 5, n 26, at p. 2.

[28] See e.g. House of Commons European Scrutiny Committee, Session 2002–03, 32nd Report (17 September 2003, paragraphs 10.3–10.6; House of Commons European Scrutiny Committee, Session 2003–04, 23rd Report (16 June 2004), paragraphs 7.14 and 7.15; and House of Lords Select Committee on the European Union, Session 2003–4, 7th Report, Remaining Government Responses for Session 2002–03 (22 March 2004), at pp. 20–21.

it.[29] Not very surprisingly, the Council does not seem eager to proceed with any temporary reform of the system for exercise of delegated powers but prefers to wait until the future of the Constitutional Treaty is known.[30] For this reason one may wonder why the Commission chose to present the proposal and to present it when it did? Perhaps the answer lies not so much in a serious belief that the proposal would bring about a temporary order as in the hope that it should have a positive spin-off for the parallel work in the European Convention.[31] Irrespective of the answer to that question, the future of the proposal for amendment of Council Decision 99/468/EC depends very much on the future of the Constitutional Treaty. If the Treaty is successfully ratified, the proposal is likely to be taken over by the proposal(s) which will be needed for establishment of mechanisms of control for the new implementing acts (see below 5.4.4.1). But if the Constitutional Treaty is not successfully ratified, the proposal may very well be re-activated.

5.4.3 The European Convention and the proposal for a hierarchy of legal acts

5.4.3.1 A quest for simplification

The terms of reference for the work leading up to the next Inter-governmental Conference were laid down by the European Council on 15 December 2001, in its so-called Laeken Declaration.[32] Here it was stated that the European Union was standing 'at a crossroads, a defining moment in its existence' and that the decision had been taken to convene a convention composed of the main parties involved in the debate on the future. The European Convention would have as its task to consider the key issues arising from the European Union's future development and try to identify the various possible responses. The findings were to be presented in a final document which could 'comprise either different options, indicating the degree of support which they received, or

---

[29] See House of Lords Select Committee on the European Union (22 March 2004), above Ch 5, n 28.

[30] See House of Commons European Scrutiny Committee (16 June 2004), above Ch 5, n 28.

[31] Cf. the first Corbett Report of 29 April 2003, above Ch 5, n 10, at p. 21.

[32] See the Presidency Conclusions of the European Council meeting on 14–15 December 2001 (Laeken), at internet http://www.europa.eu.int (SN 300/1/01 REV 1).

recommendations if consensus is achieved.' Together with the outcome of the national debates that were expected to take place, this final document was to provide a starting point for discussions in the Inter-governmental Conference, which would then take the ultimate decisions. Of all matters addressed in the Laeken Declaration those which are most relevant for our present purposes were listed under the heading 'simplification of legal instruments'. The key questions were if a distinction should be introduced between 'legislative' and 'executive' measures and if the number of instruments should be reduced?

5.4.3.2   *The Report of the Working Group*

The European Convention began its work on 28 February 2002. But it was not before 23 May 2002 that questions relating to simplification were discussed. The overall conclusion was clear from the outset: there was a real need for simplification of both instruments and procedures. In response to that, the Convention Praesidium decided to assign a specific working group with the task of devising a method for simplification, 'bearing in mind the point made during the debate that we must sacrifice neither democracy nor efficiency in our quest for simplicity.'[33] Two types of questions were addressed: the first relating to procedures for decision-making in the Council and the European Parliament and, above all, the potential for streamlining; and the second, which is most relevant for our present purposes, relating to the current complexity of legal instruments.

    According to the Praesidium, there was a broad consensus in the Convention on the need to reduce the number of instruments and awareness that this would serve no purpose unless a genuine effort was made to rationalize the instruments by redefining them.[34] Apparently, many members of the Convention called for a classification of instruments that was clear to the public and there were suggestions that basic acts could be called 'laws' and 'framework laws' with the names 'regulations' and 'decisions' being reserved for implementing measures. As was emphasized, there were also some members who linked the result of such an exercise; the introduction of a hierarchy of legal acts, to the issue of a clear-cut separation of powers. Therefore, there was a specific need to clarify *who* adopts implementing rules. According to the Praesidium,

[33] See the Mandate of Working Group IX on the simplification of legislative procedures and instruments (CONV 271/02), in particular at pp. 6–8.

[34] See the Mandate of Working Group IX, above Ch 5, n 33.

this meant that the arrangement in Article 202 (ex 145) EC and, in particular, the existing mechanisms of control were something which would have to be studied closely.

The deliberations of the Working Group (IX) on simplification were begun on 19 September 2002 and only two months later the result was presented in a final report. In the report a series of proposals was advanced on the basis of conclusions that had enjoyed a wide support from the Working Group's members (headed by the Vice-Chairman of the Convention Praesidium, Professor Giuliano Amato). The key proposal concerned the establishment of a new system for legislation based on a hierarchy of legal acts. But before that proposal is examined it is useful to note that the Working Group had based its deliberations on the views stated by three legal experts: Jean-Claude Piris, Director-General of the Council Legal Service, Michel Petite, Director-General of the Commission Legal Service, and Koen Lenaerts, Judge of the Court of First Instance. Quite strikingly, the experts all agreed that simplification of legal instruments was a highly political exercise which was bound to have repercussions for the institutional balance. But the conclusions this led them to diverged greatly.

According to Jean-Claude Piris, the powers of the institutions were so convoluted that a distinction between legislative and executive *authority* could not be made without upsetting the institutional balance.[35] This did not mean that he was not aware of existing problems. In this respect comitology was identified specifically. As admitted by Piris, comitology is 'one area where the problem of the distinction between legislative and executive authority arises acutely and gives rise to differences between the European Parliament and the Council.' But, importantly, since the problem of the distinction between legislative and executive authority was so closely linked to the institutional balance, he felt that it should be addressed in a different forum. According to him, it was 'certainly open to the Treaty's authors should they see fit, to undertake such a project' but it was not a matter for the European Convention. The only thing he was prepared to accept, in principle, was a simple renaming of existing legal instruments. But this, he felt, was something which should be avoided since it could create more confusion than clarity and 'even rob the

---

[35] See Simplification of Legislative Procedures and Instruments, paper submitted by Jean-Claude Piris to Working Group IX on 17 October 2002 (Working Document 6), at pp. 2 and 20–23.

institutions of instruments which are invaluable in the day-to-day exercise of their functions.'[36]

The views presented by the expert from the Commission, Michel Petite, were quite different from those of Jean-Claude Piris and certainly did not reflect any fear of upsetting the institutional balance.[37] Quite the contrary, Petite expressed himself very much in favour of the idea of separation of powers and the introduction, therefore, of a hierarchy of legal acts based on the distinction between 'laws' and implementing acts. This, indeed, is what the Commission has sought to achieve for a long time (see above 4.3.2.2, 4.3.7.1, 4.4.1.1, and 5.4.2.1), a fact which he did not omit to mention. As recalled by Michel Petite, 'the Commission has, since Maastricht and through Amsterdam, taken a rather consistent position on simplifying the instruments of the Union. On those two occasions, the time was simply not ripe for its proposals to be taken up.' In compliance with those previous proposals, the solution advanced by Petite was based on the idea that the Commission alone should be permitted to adopt implementing measures (in the form of regulations or decisions) subject to mechanisms of control which were operated by the Council and European Parliament on equal conditions. The exact design of the envisaged mechanisms was not specified.

Clearly, the views stated by both Jean-Claude Piris and Michel Petite did not depart substantially from the positions taken by their respective institutions on previous occasions. For that reason, the views of the third expert, Koen Lenaerts, were particularly interesting.[38] In comparison with the other two experts (representing the two main political actors: the Council and the Commission) the views of Koen Lenaerts (a judge in the Court of First Instance) must be presumed to be less 'coloured' and he was therefore able to offer a more nuanced answer to the quest for simplification. Like the other two Lenaerts also based his reasoning on the

---

[36] As argued by Piris, '[t]he "classic" instruments (regulation, directive, decision) would probably have to be retained so that they could continue to be used for regulatory and executive powers as well as for implementing powers... given this complexity and the institutional balances underlying it, it is hard to argue that a given form of legal instrument should be associated always and exclusively with a particular adoption procedure.'

[37] See Simplifying Legislative Procedures and Instruments, paper submitted by Michel Petite to Working Group IX on 17 October 2002 (Working Document 8), in particular at pp. 2 and 7–8.

[38] See How to Simplify the Instruments of the Union? Paper submitted by Koen Lenaerts to Working Group IX on 17 October 2002 (Working Document 7).

conclusion that it was not possible to achieve any real simplification of legal instruments without a clear distinction between legislative and executive acts. But according to him the distinction should be based not on the identity of the author of a legal act, but on the type of procedure followed for its adoption. This made it possible for him to distance himself from the rather contentious question of pros and cons of a clear-cut separation of powers and to focus, instead, on the necessity to identify what procedures are best suited for the exercise of the legislative and executive *functions* of the institutions of the Union.[39]

Lenaerts' conclusion was that a simplification of legal instruments could be organized by reference to two categories of acts: legislative acts and executive acts. The legislative acts would be those containing the essential elements of an area (or 'the basic policy options'). According to him these should be adopted by the Council together with the European Parliament in compliance with the co-decision procedure. The executive acts, then, would be those containing either delegated legislation or executive acts in the strict sense. This, indeed, was the centre-piece of Lenaerts' proposal. In principle it meant that all acts currently embraced by the very wide notion of implementation would be split into two more specific subcategories.

The first subcategory, he said, could be used to update and modify legislative acts, for example for reasons of technical adaptation, and would be adopted by the Commission (and sometimes the Council) on the basis of powers granted in legislative acts. The second subcategory, which he only defined very vaguely, would be used for day-to-day management and would be adopted by the Commission. Importantly, comitology would continue to apply to both subcategories. For executive acts in the strict sense a 'light comitology' would suffice. But for delegated legislation it would be necessary to provide for a 'heavy comitology' coupled with a strict control by the European Parliament (which could include a right of 'call back' in certain cases).[40]

As a result of the discussions which ensued within the Working Group after the experts had stated their views, a final report was

---

[39] See Lenaerts, above Ch 5, n 38, at pp. 2–3.

[40] It may be noted that Lenaerts has later expressed his preference, in the first place, for 'a "simple" and balanced legislative call-back system, as opposed to the complicated and biased comitology system.' See Lenaerts, K. and Desomer, M., Simplification of the Union's Instruments, in de Witte, B. (Ed.), *Ten Reflections on the Constitutional Treaty for Europe* (European University Institute 2003), at p. 117. See also Lenaerts, K., A Unified Set of Instruments (2005) 1 *EuConst* 57.

presented on 29 November 2002.[41] Here it was admitted that 'it is difficult to make a crystal-clear distinction, as is done in national systems, between matters falling to the legislative arm and those falling to the executive.' But the Working Group thought that it was still possible to make a clearer distinction than the existing one. Quite obviously, in this respect, the members of the Working Group were inspired by Koen Lenaerts. In their report the proposal was advanced to specify a hierarchy of legal acts by demarcating 'legislative acts' as acts containing the essential elements of an area[42] and split all 'non-legislative acts' currently embraced by the notion of implementation into two more specific sub-categories: 'delegated acts' or 'implementing acts'. The legislative acts would be adopted by the Council together with the European Parliament and the non-legislative acts by the Commission (and, exceptionally, the Council).[43]

Thereby subscribing to suggestions for which support had already been won in the European Convention, the Working Group envisaged that legislative acts should be adopted in the form of 'laws' and 'framework laws' with the names 'regulations' and 'decisions' being reserved for delegated and implementing acts. The definition of 'laws' and 'framework laws' would be identical to that of 'regulations' and 'directives' as that which is currently established in Article 249 EC (but including also 'decisions' and 'framework decisions' from the field of police and judicial co-operation in criminal matters). Somewhat confusingly, the definition of the new regulations would continue to be that of the existing ones. This meant that both laws and regulations, as they would appear after reform, would have exactly the same legal characteristics. The definition of decisions introduced the new element that they would be generally binding and not only binding upon those to whom they are addressed.

---

[41] See Final Report of Working Group IX on Simplification of 29 November 2002 (CONV 424/02).

[42] As explained by Giuliano Amato, 'the Working Group had focussed on defining the concept of a legislative act as containing essential elements in a given field or new policy choices. The legislature would still have some degree of discretion in interpreting this concept.' See Summary Report on the plenary session on 5 and 6 December 2002 (CONV 449/02), at p. 2.

[43] See Final Report of Working Group IX, above Ch 5, n 41, at pp. 10 and 12. It may be noted that the Working Group had 'broached the idea' of introducing into the new Treaty the possibility of assigning decentralized agencies (or 'regulatory authorities') the task of adopting certain implementing acts.

That is quite remarkable since it would transform decisions into something very similar to regulations (and, thus, also laws).[44]

As had been the case with the simplification envisaged by Lenaerts, the most radical part of the reform was found in the first subcategory of executive acts. When presented by the Working Group, the delegated acts were styled as a *new* category. But this was misleading: everything that would be possible to do in these acts is already possible to do in acts covered by the notion of implementation: to flesh out the detail or amend certain elements of a legislative act.[45] The only novelty was that the delegated acts entailed a different logic for exercise of political supervision. Accordingly, comitology and the privileges it grants the national administrations or, strictly speaking, the Member States would be replaced by mechanisms which enable 'the legislator' to delegate whilst

---

[44] It may be noted that this problem and a number of other technical or legal problems are addressed in House of Lords Select Committee on the European Union, The Future of Europe: Constitutional Treaty—Draft Articles 24–22, Session 2002–03, 12th Report.

[45] See Summary Report of the plenary session on 17 and 18 March 2003 (CONV 630/03), at p. 3: 'Several speakers voiced their perplexity at what they viewed as a new development: the possibility of adopting non-legislative acts. Vice-Chairman Amato stressed that this was not a new development and that such (directly applicable) non-legislative acts already existed in the European Union.' See also House of Lords Select Committee on the European Union: Reforming Comitology, Session 2002–03, 31st Report (1 July 2003), paragraph 36. Cf. Lenaerts, K., A Unified Set of Instruments (2005) 1 *EuConst* 57, at p. 61: 'Although Article I-32(1) does not expressly mention it, a careful reading of Article I-35 and of Part III of the Constitution suggests that the allotment between legislative and non-legislative acts has been realized in agreement with the jurisprudential *acquis*, in particular, by saving the qualification of "legislative acts" for those laying down the "basic elements of the matter to be dealt with" and containing fundamental policy choices.' It may be recalled in that respect that the Court of Justice has made it abundantly clear, first, that not all provisions in basic legislation (adopted by the Council in collaboration with the European Parliament) qualify as containing the 'essential elements' of the relevant subject matter and, second, that those provisions which do not qualify as containing essential elements, are covered by the wide notion implementation. For those reasons they may also be amended by the Commission or by the Council (in 'specific cases'). See, in particular, the rulings of the Court of Justice in Case 156/93, above Ch 4, n 169; and Case C-417/93, above Ch 4, n 180. For some recent examples of existing 'delegated' acts, see Commission Directive 02/41/EC of 17 May 2002 adapting to technical progress European Parliament and Council Directive 95/1/EC on the maximum design speed, maximum torque and maximum net engine power of two- or three-wheel motor vehicles (OJ 2002 L 133/17); and Commission Directive 01/101/EC of 26 November 2001 amending European Parliament and Council Directive 00/13/EC on the approximation of the laws of the Member States relating to the labelling, presentation and advertising of foodstuffs (OJ 2001 L 310/19). Finally, it should be pointed out that those measures currently embraced by the wide notion of implementation which cannot be considered to fall within the 'new' subcategory of delegated acts will fall within the more general subcategory of implementing acts.

retaining control. The shift was explained accordingly:

At present there is no mechanism which enables the legislator to delegate the technical aspects or details of legislation whilst retaining control over such delegation. As things stand, the legislator is obliged either to go into minute detail in the provisions it adopts, or to entrust to the Commission the more technical or detailed aspects of the legislation as if they were implementing measures, subject to the control of the Member States, in accordance with the provisions of Article 202 TEC.

To remedy this situation, the Group proposes a new type of 'delegated' act which, accompanied by strong control mechanisms, could encourage the legislator to look solely to the essential elements of an act and to delegate the more technical aspects to the executive, provided that it had the guarantee that it would be able to retrieve, as it were, its power to legislate.[46]

Despite all other similarities, this solution seemed rather different from the one foreseen by Koen Lenaerts, who had sought to avoid a solution which rested on the highly controversial idea of a separation of powers. But apparently the members of the Working Group had not let themselves be discouraged.[47] Clearly, the findings and, indeed, preferences presented in the report of the Working Group were to have much influence on the result finally embraced by the European Convention and, eventually, the Intergovernmental Conference.

5.4.3.3   The Praesidium's draft articles

Three months after the Working Group had finalized its report, on 26 February 2003, a series of draft articles were presented by the Praesidium, for inclusion in the new Treaty.[48] According to the Praesidium, there was a broad consensus in the European Convention in favour of the Working Group's proposal to reduce the number of legal instruments and give them names which were readily understandable to the public: laws, framework laws, regulations, and decisions.[49] Apparently, many

---

[46] See Final Report of Working Group IX, above Ch 5, n 41, at pp. 8–9. Cf. the Praesidium's Draft of Articles, below Ch 5, n 48, at p. 3: 'The aim is to encourage the legislator to concentrate on the fundamental aspects, preventing laws and framework laws from being over-detailed.'

[47] See the paper submitted by Paolo Ponzano, below Ch 5, n 52, at p. 2.

[48] See the Praesidium's Draft of Articles 24 to 33 of the Constitutional Treaty (CONV 571/03).

[49] See Draft Article 24, above Ch 5, n 48. These legal instruments would apply in all areas, including those which currently fall under the second and third pillars. But they could be subject to special rules (to be specified in the light of the conclusions of the other Working Groups and

members of the Convention had also accepted the idea that the Treaty should include a hierarchy of legal acts, with essential elements or basic policy options being the preserve of laws and framework laws (but opinion had been divided with respect to delegated acts).[50]

The hierarchy of legal acts resulting from the draft articles presented by the Praesidium did not depart substantially from that of the Working Group: a basic distinction between legislative and non-legislative acts with the latter including the two subcategories of 'delegated' and 'implementing' acts and also a third subcategory of acts to be adopted 'in cases specifically laid down in the Constitution' (see below 5.4.4.1). The legislative acts would have the form of laws or framework laws and the non-legislative acts would have the form of regulations or decisions.[51] In compliance with the solution advanced by Koen Lenaerts and embraced by the Working Group, the centre-piece of the reform was found in the first two subcategories of non-legislative acts and, particularly, in that of delegated acts ('delegated regulations'). The characteristics were set out in Draft Article 27. Accordingly:

Article 27

1   European laws and European framework laws may delegate to the Commission the power to enact delegated regulations in order to supplement or amend certain non-essential elements of the law or framework law. The objectives, content, scope and duration of the delegation shall be explicitly defined in the laws and framework laws. A delegation may not cover the essential elements of an area. These shall be reserved for the law or framework law.

2   The conditions of application to which the delegation is subject shall be explicitly determined in the law or framework law; they shall consist of one or more of the following possibilities:
    —the European Parliament and the Council may decide to revoke the delegation;

discussions in the Convention). In addition to the binding legal instruments there would also be two regular types of non-binding legal instruments: recommendations and opinions (as today). See the Praesidium's Draft above Ch 5, n 48, at pp. 1–2.

[50] See the Praesidium's Draft of Articles, above Ch 5, n 48, at p. 1. See also the Summary Report, above Ch 5, n 42, at pp. 5 and 8.

[51] It may be noted that non-binding 'recommendations' were later added to this category. See e.g. Article I-34(2) of the Draft Treaty of 18 July 2003 establishing a Constitution for Europe (CONV 850/03).

> —the delegated regulation may enter into force only if no objection has been expressed by the European Parliament or the Council within a period set by the law or framework law;
>
> —the provisions of the delegated regulation are to lapse after a period set by the law or framework law. They may be extended, on a proposal from the Commission, by decision of the European Parliament and of the Council.

For the purposes of the preceding paragraph, the European Parliament shall act by a majority of its members, and the Council by a qualified majority.

For whatever reasons, the (ideo-)logical consequences of the rather bold conclusions reached by the Working Group were not clearly stated in its final report. But if anyone had failed to see them, this was soon corrected by the Commission and, then, the Praesidium. In the light of the fact that the European Convention was intended to offer a new and open method of deliberation, at least with respect to 'simplification' it is striking how closely its free minds were working to those of the thinkers behind the Commission's White Paper on European Governance (see above 5.4.2). Perhaps one should not underestimate the role of the invisible people in the Convention secretariat, such as Giuliano Amato's *aide-de-camp*, Hervé Bribosia (from the Commission Group of Policy Advisers). A more visible link between the White Paper on European Governance and the European Convention is found in the Commission Communication to the Convention on the institutional architecture, presented on the same days as the proposal for amendment of Council Decision 99/468/EC (see above 5.4.2.2). Here the Commission restated, in a somewhat simplified way, the need for a new system for exercise of delegated powers based on a conceptualized distinction between powers to be exercised by the legislature and powers to be exercised by the executive (see above 5.4.2.1).[52]

At the time the proposals elaborated by the Working Group had been translated into draft articles by the Praesidium they expressed its stance in favour of a shift from a system based on a flexible division of responsibility ('balance of powers') towards a system based on the idea of separation of powers. The most obvious sign of this stance was found in

---

[52] See Commission Communication to the Convention of 11 December 2002 on the institutional architecture—for the European Union: peace, freedom, solidarity (COM (02) 728 final/2, points 1.2 and 1.3 (in particular 1.3.4). See also Proposal to distinguish legislative and executive functions in the institutional system of the European Union, paper submitted by Paolo Ponzano to Working Group IX on 7 November 2002 (Working Document 16).

the submission that the co-decision procedure should be styled 'the legislative procedure' and that the Council and the European Parliament would be merged into 'the legislature'.[53] Another expression, certainly not less significant, was found in the conclusion that the Council's current ability to exercise executive powers itself would have to be abolished in the context of delegated acts (and kept to a minimum in the context of implementing acts).[54] This was based on the idea of separation of powers, where the activities of the Council are consumed by those of the legislature and, therefore, never permitted to provide an alternative to the activities of 'the executive': the Commission.

In order to ensure that the executive would not abuse its powers to adopt delegated acts, thus trespassing upon the domain of the legislature ('the essential elements of an area'), the legislature would have access to mechanisms of control which were to be determined on a case-by-case basis by reference to an exhaustive list laid down in Draft Article 27. Significantly, this construction was almost identical to that provided for in Article 202 (ex 145) EC (see above 3.4.2.2). The important difference, once again, was that the existing mechanisms of control, operated by the Council alone, would be replaced by mechanisms that were operated by both the Council and the European Parliament subject to qualified/ absolute majority voting. The exclusive list enshrined in Draft Article 27 included three types of mechanisms of control for delegated acts:

- a right of call-back: a power to prescribe that the legislature (the European Parliament and the Council[55]) shall be permitted to retrieve the right to legislate on a given subject;
- a period of tacit approval: a power to prescribe that delegated acts will only enter into force if the legislature (the European Parliament or the Council) has not expressed any objections;

---

[53] That this was very much a matter of 'styling' is clear from the fact that from the start, use of the co-decision procedure was intended to remain only as a general rule, i.e. unless a different procedure was specifically provided for. See Draft Article 25, above Ch 5, n 48.

[54] See Draft Articles 27 and 28(2). Cf. above 1.1.1.

[55] It is important to note that the word 'and' rather than 'or' makes an enormous difference. Since the preferences of the Council and the European Parliament are often quite the opposite, it is likely that they will find it difficult to agree when their right of call-back should be invoked. In practice, this means that they will block each other and, thus, the effective operation of this mechanism of control. The use of the word 'and' rather than 'or' is one of several nuances in the proposal which places it very much in line with the position taken by the Commission (see above 5.3.3 and 5.4.2).

- a sunset clause: a power to prescribe that provisions of delegated acts will have a limited period of duration which may be extended by the legislature (the European Parliament *and* the Council).

Yet another expression of the Praesidium's stance in favour of a shift towards a system based on the idea of separation of powers is found in Draft Article 28, setting out the specifics of the second subcategory of non-legislative acts: the implementing acts.[56] As envisaged by the Working Group, these were the only acts in respect of which comitology would continue to apply.[57] But according to the Praesidium, comitology could not continue to apply without adapting it to the logic that the operation of mechanisms of control of the executive was no longer a matter for the Council alone but for 'the legislature'. Therefore, the procedure for defining the 'principles and rules' on which comitology rested (currently laid down in Council Decision 99/468/EC) had to be shifted to co-decisions (see above 3.4.2.2). The implications were considerable. Not only had the most controversial group of matters handled under comitology been cut out and re-introduced in the form of 'delegated acts' (subject to a completely different type of mechanism of control) but also that which was left required principles and rules which the European Parliament could agree to. This meant that comitology was likely to be stripped of everything but its purely advisory functions (cf. above 3.4.2.2).

5.4.3.4   *The Draft Treaty establishing a Constitution for Europe*

Following the presentation of the Praesidium's draft articles (see above 5.4.3.3), several amendments were suggested by members of the European Convention. In the light of these amendments and comments made at

---

[56] See Draft Article 28(3): 'Implementing acts of the Union may be subject to control mechanisms which shall be consonant with principles and rules laid down in advance by the European Parliament and the Council in accordance with the legislative procedure.' It should be pointed out that the existing possibility for the Council to adopt implementing acts (in 'specific cases') would continue to apply. See Draft Article 28(2).

[57] See Final Report of Working Group IX above Ch 5, n 41, at p. 12. It may be noted, in this context, that the question of reform of comitology and the arrangement in Article 202 EC was something which the Working Group said went beyond its terms of reference. The reasoning behind that conclusion is rather mysterious. According to its mandate the arrangement in Article 202 EC and comitology (the mechanisms of control) was something which would 'need to be studied closely by the Working Group' (see above 5.4.3.2).

discussions in plenary, a revised version was presented by the Praesidium on 26 May 2003 which would enable it to hold consultations and 'assess the progress made in achieving consensus.'[58] In his conclusions, the Chairman of the Praesidium, former French President Valéry Giscard d'Estaing, noted that contributions by members of the European Convention had supported the general approach and that there was now broad agreement on the planned simplification, in particular the hierarchy of legal acts and the distinction between legislative and non-legislative acts.[59] But at the same time there were also many people who expressed differing and opposite views on the details. Many of these related to the new category of delegated regulations (altogether 51 written proposals for amendments). Thus, for example, some amendments sought to reclassify delegated regulations as legislative in character. There were also many amendments concerning the conditions for their application. Naturally, only some of the amendments had led the Praesidium to incorporate changes in its original draft articles.[60]

Starting off with the category of legislative acts, it should be noted that the description of the system for adoption of laws and framework laws (Draft Article 25, now renumbered Article I-33) was clarified through the introduction of an explicit distinction between the 'ordinary' legislative procedure, i.e. the co-decision, and the 'special' legislative procedures which should apply in the specific cases explicitly provided for. The reason for this was 'to avoid excluding the legislative nature of the very limited number of acts which might be adopted by the Parliament or by the Council with varying degrees of participation by the other arm of the legislative authority by virtue of procedures which, while undoubtedly legislative, are "special"'.[61] Most importantly, such special legislative procedures would allow the Council to act by unanimity after mere consultation of the European Parliament.[62] As later observed by

---

[58] See Revised text of Part One of the Draft Constitution of 26 May 2003 (CONV 724/03) and Summary Report of the plenary session on 15 and 16 May 2003 (CONV 748/03), at pp. 1–2.

[59] See Summary Report of the plenary session on 17 and 18 March 2003 (CONV 630/03), at pp. 2–5.

[60] See e.g. Reactions to draft Articles 24 to 33 of the Constitutional Treaty on 12 March 2003 (CONV 609/03), at p. 2.

[61] See Revised text of Part One (CONV 724/03), above Ch 5, n 58, at p. 90.

[62] See e.g. Article III-234(2) CT concerning a number of matters in the environmental field and Article III-277 CT concerning the establishment of the conditions under which the competent authorities of one Member State may operate in the territory of another Member State.

Koen Lenaerts, the continuous existence of special legislative procedures 'reflects a rather realist and pragmatic approach which tends to suffer from a lack of democratic legitimacy, but which simply testifies to the particular sensitivity of those matters to some, if not all, Member States.'[63]

Proceeding to the category of non-legislative acts, there are several changes which should be mentioned. Firstly, the instrument 'regulation' (Draft Article 24, now renumbered Article I-32) was redefined to incorporate the features of the existing directive, 'in order to be able to draw on a non-legislative instrument which is binding on Member States as to result, but flexible as to means.'[64] If the proposed text is adopted, the new legal instrument ('regulation') would be such that it could take either of two specific forms. The first form would be identical to the legal instrument 'regulation' as it is defined today and the second form would be identical to the legal instrument 'directive' as it is defined today.

Secondly, and most importantly for our present purposes, a few interesting changes were made with respect to the conditions for the application of delegated regulations (Draft Article 27, now renumbered Article I-35). The most obvious one was that the possibility to provide for a delegated regulation to lapse after a given deadline (sunset clause) had now been removed from the list setting out the alternative mechanisms of control. This had been requested in several amendments since it was felt, rightly, that it could be a source of uncertainty and cause legal insecurity.[65] A second change concerned the practical operation of the right of call-back. Here the requirement that this right should be exercised by the European Parliament *and* the Council jointly had been reconsidered so as to enable them to act separately (the European Parliament *or* the Council).[66] The final and, potentially, most important change concerned the legal nature of the list setting out the alternative mechanisms of control. In the original version, this list followed upon the explanation that '[t]he conditions of application to which the delegation is subject shall be explicitly determined in the law or framework law; they shall consist of one or more of the following possibilities: . . . '. But in the new

---

[63] See Lenaerts (2005), above Ch 5, n 45, at p. 58.

[64] See Revised text of Part One (CONV 724/03), above Ch 5, n 58, at p. 87. See also Reactions to draft Articles 24 to 33 (CONV 609/03), above Ch 5, n 60, at p. 2.

[65] A real example of this dilemma can be found in the context of the Lamfalussy process and the reform of the market in financial securities (see above 5.4.1).   [66] Cf. above Ch 5, n 55.

text those words had been reformulated so as to provide that '[t]he conditions of application to which the delegation is subject shall be explicitly determined in the *laws* and framework *laws*. They *may* consist of the following possibilities: . . .' (emphasis added). The reason given for this by the Praesidium was that it should make it clearer that these conditions would be determined case by case by the law or framework law which grants the delegation and that they would 'not constitute a mandatory element of such a law or framework law.'[67] The exact meaning of this and, indeed, the legal implications, whatever the intentions of its draftsmen, are far from clear. A question which immediately comes to mind is whether the fact that the listed conditions are not mandatory means that the legislature could choose not to use them or that they should only be seen as a few listed examples and, therefore, that the legislature would also be able to choose other, unlisted, conditions (i.e. mechanisms of control). It is noteworthy in this respect that some amendments had asked for a general clarification of the exact meaning of these conditions and also argued that the list should not be definitive but 'leave open the possibility of the legislators attaching further conditions to any delegation as they deem appropriate.'[68]

Finally, something should be said about implementing regulations and decisions (Draft Article 28, renumbered Article I-36). The only change made by the Praesidium was a rather minor attempt to bring about conceptual clarification to the end that it is 'Member States' rather than the legislature—or, indeed, any of the two arms of the legislature—who are bearers of the right to control the exercise of implementing powers on the European level. The idea was that this should serve to underline the general rule that the responsibility for exercise of implementing powers lies with the Member States. But as an attempt to bring about conceptual clarification the change was not entirely satisfactory and leads to questions about the logic of establishing the rules and general principles that will define the mechanisms of control in a law adopted by the legislature, presumably under the default 'ordinary' legislative procedure (cf. '[t]he law shall lay down in advance rules and general principles for the

---

[67] See Revised text of Part One (CONV 724/03), above Ch 5, n 58, at p. 93.

[68] See Summary report of the plenary session on 17 and 18 March 2003 (CONV 630/03), above Ch 5, n 59, at p. 3, and the suggestion for amendment of Draft Article 27 submitted by Dick Roche, Minister for State at the Irish Department of Foreign Affairs, at internet http://european-convention.eu.int.

mechanisms for control . . . ').[69] This and other aspects relating to the future system for control of the exercise of implementing powers had been addressed by a large number of amendments but the views expressed had often been contradictory: while some opposed the application of the ordinary legislative procedure for establishment of mechanisms of control for implementing acts, others were eager to simplify, or even eliminate, the current system for control (comitology).[70]

The final text of the Draft Treaty establishing a Constitution for Europe was adopted by the European Convention on 13 June and 10 July 2003.[71] Even though another list of amendments had been submitted, the provisions relating to delegated and implementing acts were, essentially, left unchanged. The only visible difference to be found was one concerning the procedure(s) for establishment of mechanisms of control for implementing acts. Here the word the 'law' had been substituted so as to provide that '[t]he European *laws* shall lay down in advance rules and general principles for the mechanisms for control . . .' (emphasis added). The reason for this change is far from clear and, unfortunately, is not explained in any document to be found in the internet-based archives of the European Convention. But the only reasonable interpretation is that parallel and different regimes may be permitted which must all still be adopted subject to the ordinary legislative procedure.[72]

---

[69] According to renumbered Article I-33, the 'ordinary' legislative procedure should be followed unless a different 'special' procedure was explicitly provided for.

[70] See Summary report of the plenary session on 17 and 18 March 2003 (CONV 630/03), above Ch 5, n 59, at pp. 3–5. Another question caused by the conceptual clarification (that it is 'Member States' who are bearers of the right to control the exercise of implementing powers) is whether intervention by the Council, as presently provided for under the management and regulatory comitology procedures, will be permitted in the future. See Petite, M. and Ladenburger, C., The Evolution in the Role of the European Commission, in *The EU Constitution: The Best Way Forward?* Conference Reader from 34th Session Asser Institute Colloquim on European Law on 13–16 October 2004, at p. 9.

[71] See Draft Treaty establishing a Constitution for Europe of 18 July 2003 (CONV 850/03).

[72] But at the same time it may be mentioned that there were a few last minute amendments submitted which opposed the application of the ordinary legislative procedure and insisted, sometimes repeatedly, that the current 'special' procedure must be kept, at least as one alternative. See Reactions to the draft Articles of the revised text of Part One (Volume I)—Analysis, 4 June 2003 (CONV 779/03), at pp. 14–15, and, in particular, the suggestions for amendment of Draft Article 28 and, later, Article I-36 submitted by Peter Hain, UK Minister for Europe, at internet http://european-convention.eu.int.

5.4.4   The Treaty establishing a Constitution for Europe

5.4.4.1   The 2004 Intergovernmental Conference and the new hierarchy of legal acts

On 1 May 2004 the European Union was enlarged from 15 to 25 members, to comprise also Cyprus, Estonia, Hungary, Latvia, Lithuania, Malta, Poland, Czech Republic, Slovakia, and Slovenia. This was not only the biggest ever increase in its size but a historic reunification of Europe 'after the travails of Communist dictatorship in Eastern and Central Europe.'[73] Only six weeks later the 2004 Intergovernmental Conference was concluded by the Heads of State or Government of all 25 Member States unanimously adopting the Treaty establishing a Constitution for Europe.[74] The Constitutional Treaty (CT) was signed on 29 October 2004[75] and the process for ratification is now pending. At the time of writing, it is far from certain what the result will be. Not only have several Governments announced that the future of the Constitutional Treaty will be decided in referenda but some of them have even put their own future within the European Union at stake. No better illustration can be found than the battle cry signalled by the British Prime Minister Tony Blair:

The electorate should be asked for their opinion when all our questions have been answered, when all the details are known, when the legislation has been finally tempered and scrutinised in the House, and when Parliament has debated and decided. The question will be on the Treaty. But the implications go far wider. It is time to resolve once and for all whether this country, Britain, wants to be at the centre and heart of European decision-making or not; time to decide whether our destiny lies as a leading partner and ally of Europe or on its margins. Let the Eurosceptics whose true agenda we will expose, make their case. Let those of us who believe in Britain in Europe not because we believe in Europe alone but because, above all we believe in Britain, make ours. Let the issue be put. Let the battle be joined.[76]

No attempt will be made in this book to summarize or assess the contents in general of the Constitutional Treaty. There is no shortage of such texts

---

[73] Quote from the statement by the British Prime Minister, Tony Blair, to the House of Commons on 20 April 2004, at internet http://www.fco.gov.uk, at p. 1.

[74] See the Presidency Conclusions of the European Council meeting on 17 and 18 June 2004 (Brussels), at internet http://www.europa.int.

[75] Treaty establishing a Constitution for Europe of 29 October 2004 (CIG 87/2/04 REV 2).

[76] See the statement by the British Prime Minister, Tony Blair, above Ch 5, n 73, at p. 1.

and new ones will be churned out at a steady rate. But one thing is sure, whether this was expected or not, the final result came close to that of the European Convention. The reasons for this and, indeed, its implications are also being explored by numerous scholars. But it is difficult to avoid the impression that the Heads of State or Government did not have the patience, or perhaps courage, to treat the text presented by the Convention as a mere 'starting point for discussions' and that this was a result of the fact that the text went far beyond the set of 'options' or 'recommendations' they originally asked for (see above 5.4.3.1). Only a few, rather symbolic issues seem to have taken up most of the time in the Intergovernmental Conference and the new hierarchy of legal acts was not one of them. In this respect, the only visible fingerprints left were a clarification that the future mechanisms for control of implementing powers would not apply in those specific cases where these powers were exercised by the Council and a renumbering of already renumbered articles.[77] Thus the provision born in the European Convention as Draft Article 27 was named Article I-36 and the provision born as Draft Article 28 was named Article I-37. In their final version these provisions now read:

Article I-36

1   European laws and framework laws may delegate to the Commission the power to adopt delegated European regulations to supplement or amend certain non-essential elements of the law or framework law. The objectives, content, scope and duration of the delegation of power shall be explicitly defined in the European laws and framework laws. The essential elements of an area shall be reserved for the European law or framework law and accordingly shall not be the subject of a delegation of power.

2   European laws and framework laws shall explicitly lay down the conditions to which the delegation is subject; these conditions may be as follows:
   (a) the European Parliament or the Council may decide to revoke the delegation;

---

[77] It should be pointed out also that a declaration was adopted by the Intergovernmental Conference which explicitly seeks to preserve the committee system in operation within the framework of the Lamfalussy process (see above 5.4.1). See Declaration on Article I-36 to be annexed to the Final Act of the Intergovernmental Conference of 25 October 2004 (ADD 2 CIG 87/04 REV 2). Here it is stated that: '[t]he Conference takes note of the Commission's intention to continue to consult experts appointed by the Member States in the preparation of draft delegated European regulations in the financial services area, in accordance with its established practice'. Apparently, the possibility has also been discussed of an inter-institutional agreement which would help determine which measures should be dealt with as delegated acts and which as implementing acts.

(b) the delegated European regulation may enter into force only if no objection has been expressed by the European Parliament or the Council within a period set by the European law or framework law.
'or the purposes of (a) and (b), the European Parliament shall act by a najority of its component members, and the Council by a qualified majority.

Article I-37

Member States shall adopt all measures of national law necessary to mplement legally binding Union acts.

Where uniform conditions for implementing legally binding Union acts re needed, those acts shall confer implementing powers on the Commission or, in duly justified specific cases and in the cases provided for in Article I-40, on the Council.

For the purposes of paragraph 2, European laws shall lay down in advance he rules and general principles concerning mechanisms for control by Member States of the Commission's exercise of implementing powers.

Union implementing acts shall take the form of European implementing egulations or European implementing decisions.

'erhaps most obviously, the new hierarchy of legal acts seeks to delimit he legislative acts which are needed to establish the 'essential elements' of an area. Like before, these acts will normally require a proposal, ubmitted by the Commission, and negotiations between the Govern-ments, within the Council, and then between the Council and the European Parliament. All other matters (i.e. everything but the essential elements) may be dealt with in non-legislative acts adopted under sim-plified procedures. Seemingly, with regard to the substantive scope, the listinction between legislative acts and those non-legislative acts which all into either of the two subcategories of delegated or implementing acts loes not amount to anything more than a codification of the existing ituation: those non-legislative acts are currently covered by the wide notion of implementation.[78] But it is difficult not to reach the rather listurbing conclusion that the third subcategory of non-legislative acts to be adopted, most notably by the Council, directly on the basis of a number of specific provisions in the Constitutional Treaty) will not have to be confined to non-essential elements and, therefore, that these

---

[78] See e.g. above 1.1.1 and Ch 5, n 45.

non-legislative acts could and most likely will have the same substantive quality as legislative acts.[79]

In the light of the above conclusion that delegated and implementing acts do not introduce any change with regard to the substantive scope, the reform embraced by the new provisions must primarily be appreciated for its ambition to 'encourage the legislature to look *solely* to the essential elements of an act and to delegate the more technical aspects to the executive' (emphasis added).[80] It has been seen in this book that the ambition is far from new. The trick, this time, is to style the most controversial group of measures currently covered by a very wide notion of implementation—those which supplement or amend non-essential elements of legislative acts—as a new subcategory to non-legislative acts: the delegated acts. But this is misleading. The matters to be dealt with in delegated acts are already dealt with in acts adopted under the arrangement in Article 202 (ex 145) EC.[81] Clearly, the fact that the new acts are not so new is something which a smaller group of people within the European Convention was well aware of but probably not the majority of its members.

The important difference between the existing type of delegated acts and those foreseen in the Constitutional Treaty relates to procedures and, in particular, the mechanisms of political control. Today, the acts are adopted, either by the Council itself (in 'specific cases') or, most commonly, by the Commission subject to comitology and the most restrictive procedure: the regulatory committee procedure. If and when the Constitutional Treaty enters into force, many of these acts will be adopted by the Commission alone (those which supplement or amend non-essential elements). Against that background, it must be concluded that the new hierarchy of legal acts stretches far beyond mere 'simplification' and that

---

[79] Cf. Article I-35 CT. It may be noted that this subcategory was largely deleted in the Draft Treaty that finally left the European Convention but re-introduced during the Intergovernmental Conference. Examples of such cases can be found in the field of economic policy (e.g. Article III-180), with respect to the organisation and operation of the European System of Central Banks (e.g. Articles III-187 and 190 CT), and in the field of agriculture (e.g. Article III-231 CT). For comments see Dougan, M., The Convention's Draft Constitutional Treaty: Bringing Europe Closer to its Lawyers? (2003) 28 *ELRev* 763, at pp. 783–784; Lenaerts above Ch 5, n 45, at p. 61; and Bogdandy, A. von and Bast, J., New Legal Instruments, in *The EU Constitution: The Best Way Forward?* Conference Reader from 34th Session Asser Institute Colloquim on European Law on 13–16 October 2004.   [80] See above 5.4.3.2.

[81] For some recent examples, see above Ch 5, n 45.

it will have the effect of bringing about a fundamental reform of the arrangement in Article 202 (ex 145) EC. This, indeed, is what the European Parliament and the Commission have always asked for but the Council rejected.

5.4.4.2 *An ambiguous and inconsistent terminology*

Quite clearly, there is much support for the submission that the Council and the European Parliament will have to focus their own efforts and make better use of the power to delegate to the Commission. This is especially so in the light of the recent enlargement and the resulting increase in the number of interests represented in the Council. But experience shows that the potential for full use of the possibility to delegate is hampered by political concerns, within both the Council and the European Parliament. Therefore, any attempt to encourage them to make better use of the power to delegate will only be successful if it can satisfy these concerns.

The solution now embraced by the Constitutional Treaty is to introduce a hierarchy of legal acts based on the idea of a separation of powers. Here, the label 'implementing' acts is reserved for the less controversial group of acts that the Commission may be authorized to adopt. The principal responsibility for implementing acts rests with the Member States rather than the Council and the European Parliament (the legislature). As argued, therefore, it is reasonable that these acts continue to be subject to comitology (defined as 'monitoring by committees made up of representatives of the Member States'[82]). The most controversial type of acts—those which are intended to release the Council and the European Parliament from some of their legislative burden—are branded 'delegated' acts. Here, the reasoning with respect to control is the reverse: since the principal responsibility for delegated acts rests with the Council and the European Parliament (the legislature), comitology—as we know it—is inappropriate and replaced, therefore, by a new type of mechanism of control operated by the Council and the European Parliament on equal conditions.

From a logical or, at least, aesthetical point of view, this solution is quite attractive. But, unfortunately, there are many problems with respect to its function. Perhaps most strikingly, the new provisions are based on

---

[82] See, in particular, the Praesidium's Draft of Articles, above Ch 5, n 48, at p. 17.

an ambiguous and rather inconsistent terminology. This will inevitably cause problems. An example can be found in the re-definition of legal instruments: regulations will have the same legal effect as laws or framework laws, and decisions will (as a general rule) have the same legal effect as those regulations which have the same legal effect as laws (see above 5.4.3.2). There are several other examples. The most unsatisfying ones relate to the distinction between legislative and non-legislative acts and, within the latter category, between delegated acts and implementing acts.

It has already been noted above that non-legislative acts can be adopted, not only after a conferral of powers (delegated and implementing acts), but also directly on the basis of specific provisions in the Constitutional Treaty and that these non-legislative acts could and most likely will have the same substantive quality as legislative acts (see above 5.4.4.1). Even if this construction, to some extent, was foreseen all along, it largely escaped attention in the European Convention. Perhaps this can be explained by the fact that the consequences of this third, less obvious subcategory of non-legislative acts could only be fully understood after Part III of the Treaty, comprising the provisions on policies and functioning, had been drafted. But this was saved for last and dealt with in a rush, during the Convention's very last moments of life. The result as it now appears in the Constitutional Treaty is a rather arbitrary division between legislative and non-legislative acts which 'produces similarly arbitrary knock-on effects' for provisions on, for example, national parliaments' right to object to legislative proposals on grounds of subsidiarity.[83]

Proceeding to some problems regarding the distinction between delegated and implementing acts, it may be observed, first, that the word 'delegated' relates to the origin of an act and that the word 'implementing' relates to its function. In principle, the envisaged implementing acts will also be delegated (or, in other words, acts resulting from a conferral of powers). Therefore, if an attempt should be made to distinguish between these acts, it would be more consistent and, indeed, clear if delegated acts were also given a label which would relate to their function (for example 'complementary acts').

However, the confusion with respect to the distinction between delegated and implementing acts goes far beyond their names into their

---

[83] See Dougan, above Ch 5, n 79, at p. 784.

substance. None of those who have had a decisive influence over the new hierarchy of legal acts has managed to come up with a substantive definition of delegated and implementing acts and none of those has managed to clarify on what grounds the choice should be made between the two of them. The only trace of an indication to be found in the Constitutional Treaty is the explanation that a delegated regulation may be used to 'supplement or amend certain non-essential elements' of a law or framework law and that '[t]he objectives, content, scope and duration of the delegation of power shall be explicitly defined' in that law or framework law.[84] But with respect to the envisaged and, indeed, permitted scope of implementing acts the new Treaty is silent. Even if it must be presumed that the 'new' delegated acts are intended to be used in the type of cases which are likely to cause most controversy it is far from certain that this will be the result. Hitherto the Council has insisted that such cases must be dealt with under the regulatory committee procedure. But it is noteworthy that according to the guidelines currently laid down in Council Decision 99/468/EC, the regulatory committee procedure should be used, not only to 'adapt or update' non-essential provisions of basic instruments but also to adopt 'measures of general scope designed to apply essential provisions'. It is difficult to avoid the conclusion that this latter task, which clearly is not insignificant, falls outside the remit of the new delegated acts and that in the future it will only be possible to deal with it in implementing acts (if at all). The lack of a substantive definition of delegated and implementing acts is particularly problematic since the choice between them entails fundamentally different procedures. In practice, this means that the Commission will have a considerable discretion to pick and choose: both when making its proposals for laws or framework laws and when adopting its regulations.

5.4.4.3 *The new mechanisms of control: operative disadvantages*

The legal or technical problems are added to by operative disadvantages. In order to fully understand these problems it should be recalled that delegation is not only an inter-institutional matter but also, and perhaps primarily, an inter-governmental matter. The history of the European Union tells us that delegation of powers is not the product of a constitutional choice but of the need to manage an inability to agree *within*

---

[84] See Article I-36(2) CT.

the Council (see above 5.3.1). The same history tells us that delegation of powers had never been permitted to become what it is today without comitology (see above 5.3.1).

To abolish comitology in the context of delegated acts for the reason that committee-members are representatives of the Member States and not of the Council (whose members are representatives of the same Member States) is unnecessarily formalistic and rather strained. Both committee-members and members of the Council are designated by the Governments and, ultimately, it is the interests of the Governments that they are all set to protect (cf. above 1.1.2 and 1.3.2). This, in fact, explains why comitology was invented in the first place. To abolish comitology in the context of delegated acts (and reduce it in the context of implementing acts) will deprive all members of the Council—the Governments—of their most valuable means for influence and continuous control. This, in turn, is likely to have a negative effect on their readiness to entrust the Commission with any potentially significant powers to adopt delegated acts. If so, the reform will fail in its most fundamental objective: to encourage the legislature to look solely to the essential elements and to delegate more (see above 5.4.3.2).

Of course, one must not ignore the fact that the Constitutional Treaty provides for use of new types of mechanism for control over delegated acts. This, indeed, is the most significant novelty (see above 5.4.3.3). The main advantage of the new types of mechanism is that they seem to satisfy the European Parliament's demand for equality and, at the same time, give the Governments a feeling that the Council will not lose control. But compared with comitology, which is very much based on the idea that any disagreements are sorted out at the stage of drafting, the new mechanisms appear to be a lot less flexible and quite difficult to operate. Essentially, they all leave the two arms of the legislature with a right to react but not to participate at the stage of drafting. From the Governments' perspective, the 'new' delegated acts entail a shift from a regime which enabled them to delegate—or perhaps decentralize— rather extensive responsibilities without losing their right to participate in the deliberations to one which will only enable them to supervise the Commission *ex posteriore* via the Council acting by a qualified majority (and always shared with the European Parliament as co-legislator). This may lead to an increasing number of situations where the need is felt to let the mechanisms of control enter into force (cf. above 1.1.3 and 1.3.2). At the same time, it should be remembered that this will require a qualified or absolute majority. After enlargement this cannot be taken for granted. Judging from the past, it is not unlikely that a mere suspicion that mechanisms of control will be difficult to set in motion will become a reason in the future to avoid delegation of any potentially significant powers.

5.4.4.4   A highly political exercise

Yet another problem, of political and even ideological significance, relates to the vagueness with respect to the substantive scope of delegated acts. As hoped for by the European Convention, these acts 'could encourage the legislator to look solely to the essential elements of an act and to delegate the more technical aspects to the executive . . . '[85] But this evades the fact that there is a huge grey-zone between the two extremes 'essential elements' and 'more technical aspects'. The existing forms of delegated and, indeed, implementing acts may very well concern matters which are felt to have political implications. This, indeed, is the key to understanding why:

- the Council has only been prepared to delegate subject to comitology and has often insisted on the most restrictive procedure: the regulatory committee procedure;
- the Council is sometimes unable to agree to delegate and prefers to reserve the responsibility to itself;
- the European Parliament is objecting so stubbornly: the way it sees things, the normal procedures for adoption of legislation are currently being drained away by a systematic transferral of important matters to simplified procedures.

Naturally, the existence of such a grey-zone should have been admitted when the members of the Working Group sat down to come up with their proposals for simplification. But, for some reason, the Working Group and, indeed, the Praesidium preferred not to address the grey-zone and, thus, the most central aspect of a long-lasting inter-institutional conflict.

The most forceful criticism which can be made against comitology and the existing arrangement for delegation in Article 202 EC is not that it

---

[85] See Final Report of Working Group IX, above Ch 5, n 41, at p. 9. See also the Praesidium's Draft of Articles, above Ch 5, n 48, at p. 3: 'The aim is to encourage the legislator to concentrate on the fundamental aspects, preventing laws and framework laws from being over-detailed.'

grants the national administrations a privileged position in the adoption of acts which concern 'the more technical aspects' of legislation but that it gives national experts and bureaucrats an effective right to participate in political decision-making. This, indeed, is a matter which deserves to be taken seriously. But the criticism against comitology does not justify a reform where much of the responsibility of the national administrations is automatically transferred to the Commission. An obvious risk with this is that the role of national experts and bureaucrats will merely be taken over by other experts and bureaucrats (who might be even less suited to participate in political decision-making).

The reasoning above supports the conclusion that simplification, such as that which was attempted in the European Convention and not in the 2004 Intergovernmental Conference, is a highly political exercise which is bound to have serious repercussions on the institutional balance. If the Council and, indeed, the European Parliament do effectuate the new hierarchy of legal acts in accordance with the intentions of those who designed it, this is likely to become the single most important change brought about by the Constitutional Treaty: a significant strengthening of the Commission's powers combined with a mandate to really make use of them. One immediate result will be that the number of non-legislative acts with a legislative bearing will continue to increase. But even if this may enhance effectiveness in the future European Union, many important questions are left unanswered. In particular, there is still a need to know on what political or ideological ground the main beneficiary of the simplified system for exercise of delegated powers—the Commission— can claim a right to exercise powers of political decision-making with much greater autonomy than today.[86]

5.4.4.5 An alternative interpretation?

The merits of the new hierarchy of legal acts are, above all, that it clarifies a number of existing practices and that it seeks to establish a system for exercise of delegated powers which will encourage both the Council and

---

[86] See e.g. Weiler, J. H. H., The Commission as Euro-Sceptic: A Task Oriented Commission for a Project-Based Union, and Scharpf, W. F., European Governance: Common Concerns vs. The Challenge of Diversity, both in Jean Monnet Programme Working Paper No 6/01, *Symposium: Mountain or Molehill? A Critical Appraisal of the Commission White Paper on Governance* (at internet www.jeanmonnetprogram.org); and Joerges, C., The Commission's White Paper on Governance in the EU—A Symptom of Crisis? (2002) 39 *CMLRev* 444.

the European Parliament to focus their infra- and inter-institutional negotiations on basic policy options. The need to have such priorities follows, in particular, from the recent enlargement of the European Union and the resulting increase of interests represented in the Council. Furthermore, there is solid evidence that the extended use of the co-decision procedure necessitates a system for exercise of delegated powers which will not only satisfy the demands of the Council and, thus, the Governments but also the demands of the European Parliament. Unless the European Parliament feels satisfied every attempt to enhance effectiveness will fail.

The most serious flaws in the new hierarchy of legal acts are caused by oversimplification—a wish to clarify more than is absolutely needed—and over-ambition with respect to (ideo-)logical thinking. To a considerable extent this is a result of the fact that the neat solutions originally envisaged had a long way to travel before they made it into the Constitutional Treaty. Even if the final product looks—and sounds—very much like the prototype, it is different. Perhaps most importantly, it is difficult to avoid the conclusion that there will be two parallel regimes for adoption of legislative and non-legislative acts: one 'ordinary' and one 'special'. The ordinary one embodies the idea of separation of powers on the supranational level and is hoped to bring Europe closer to its citizens. But the price which has to be paid for this 'constitutional component' is the re-introduction of a number of elements from the old treaty-based order in the form of a less transparent regime of special legislative *and* non-legislative procedures. All these procedures reinforce the inter-governmental powers of the Council without there being any real need to conceptualize in terms of legislative and executive authority. The special regime is unlikely to appear in colourful leaflets but this is okay for those who need it as long as it will continue to decide how things are really done in matters of vital national interest.

The best or perhaps worst examples of the special regime can be found in those non-legislative acts of a legislative bearing which are likely to be adopted directly on the basis of specific provisions in the Constitutional Treaty (see above 5.4.4.2) but arguably also in the lack of precision with respect to the operation of delegated and implementing acts. For that reason, in particular, it should not be taken for granted that the intentions of those who designed the new hierarchy of legal acts will be decisive for the way in which the reform is actually effectuated if and when the Constitutional Treaty enters into force. The most obvious 'scenario' in this respect is that the Heads of State or Government did not necessarily commit themselves (or, indeed, their successors) to the spirit of the reform when they signed up to it. Another 'scenario' is that the Heads of State or Government did believe in the spirit of the reform but that they did not fully realize its implications. In either case the need may arise to exploit the wording and search for an interpretation which will enable them to jump from the ordinary regime into the special.

It is noteworthy, in this respect, that the rules regulating the use of implementing regulations and decisions leave a considerable room for manoeuvre. Even if the rules and general principles concerning mechanisms for control will be specified, there is nothing in the wording of Article I-37 CT that prevents implementing regulations and decisions from becoming a more flexible instrument than delegated regulations. There are no explicit restrictions with respect to the substantive scope and the conferral of powers to adopt implementing acts can be made, not only in legislative acts by ordinary and special legislative procedures, but in other non-legislative acts.

Finally it should be pointed out that the rules regulating the use of delegated regulations do not, strictly speaking, exclude operation of old mechanisms of control which enable the Council or the Governments to participate *ex ante* in the deliberations on substance.[87] Even if this may be against the spirit of the reform it is possible to interpret Article I-36 CT so that the listed mechanisms of control, in particular 'call-back', pre-serves or even codifies the right to use existing or re-invented committee procedures. These procedures are, indeed, characterized by the fact that they enable one arm of the legislature to call back delegated powers. It is not unlikely that the other arm of the legislature, the European Parliament, would tolerate the use of committee procedures if only it was given a sufficiently strong right to call-back itself, organized in a way which would suit its own purposes. Should this happen, the major change stemming from the reform would not be that the Council loses influence, but that the European Parliament gains a genuine right to participate. Furthermore, one must not forget that the wording of Article I-36 CT does no longer exclude the use of other mechanisms of control than those listed (the shift from 'shall' to 'may'). Once again, to look for other

---

[87] Petite, M. and Ladenburger, C., The Evolution in the Role of the European Commission, in *The EU Constitution: The Best Way Forward?* Conference Reader from 34th Session Asser Institute Colloquim on European Law on 13–16 October 2004, at p. 8.

alternatives may be against the spirit of the reform. But at the same time it is clear that situations will occur which are not necessarily covered by the simplified arrangement. What applies, for example, to the use of delegated regulations within the remit of laws and framework laws adopted under special legislative procedures? Is it really reasonable or politically conceivable to grant the European Parliament co-legislator rights to interfere in other fields than co-decision? And is this something anyone has ever asked for? Somewhat sadly, the process which the European Union will have to get into before these questions are answered will be very similar to the one it got out of in 1989.

REFERENCES

Resolutions and Declarations

Résolution (Parlement européen) du 20 décembre 1961 sur les attributions de la Commission européenne dans la mise en œuvre de la politique agricole commune (Annuaire-Manuel du Parlement européen 1961–62/468)

European Parliament Resolution of 9 March 1966 concerning the present situation of the European Community adopted by the European Parliament (OJ 1966 769/66)

European Parliament Resolution of 17 October 1967 on the legal problems connected with the consultation of the European Parliament (*Bulletin EC* 12-1967/51)

Résolution (Parlement européen) du 19 octobre 1967 sur la proposition relative à une directive concernant l'introduction de modes de prélèvement d'échantillons et de méthodes d'analyse communautaires pour le contrôle officiel des aliments des animaux, complété par le noveau projet de décision concernant l'institution d'un Comité permanent des aliments des animaux (OJ 1967 268/20)

Council Resolution of 12 March 1968 on Community measures to be taken in the veterinary sector (OJ 1968 C 22/18)

Résolution (Parlement européen) du 2 octobre 1968 sur les procedures communautaires d'exécution du droit communautaire dérivé (OJ 1968 C 108/37)

Council Resolution of 28 May 1969 drawing up a programme for the elimination of technical barriers to trade in industrial products which result from disparities between the provisions laid down by Law, Regulation or Administrative Action in Member States (OJ 1969 C 76/1-5)

Council Resolution of 28 May 1969 drawing up a programme for the elimination of technical barriers to trade in foodstuffs which result from disparities between the provisions laid down by Law, Regulation or Administrative Action in Member States (OJ 1969 C 76/5-7)

Council Resolution of 28 May 1969 on the adaptation to technical progress of the Directives for the elimination of technical barriers to trade which result from disparities between the provisions laid down by Law, Regulation or Administrative Action in Member States (OJ 1969 C 76/8)

Council Resolution of 9 May 1971 concerning the monetary situation (OJ 1971 C 58/1)

Resolution of the Council and of the Representatives of the Governments of the Member States of 22 March 1971 on the attainment by stages of economic and monetary union in the Community (OJ 1971 C 28/1)

Resolution of the Council and of the Representatives of the Governments of the Member States of 21 March 1972 on the application of the Resolution of 22 March 1971 on the attainment by stages of economic and monetary union in the Community (OJ 1972 C 38/3)

Joint Declaration of the European Parliament, the Council and the Commission of 4 March 1975 concerning the institution of a conciliation procedure between the European Parliament and the Council (OJ 1975 C 89/1)

Council Resolution of 15 July 1975 on the adaptation to technical progress of Directives or other Community rules on the protection and improvement of the environment (OJ 1975 C 168/5)

Resolution of the European Council of 5 December 1978 on the establishment of the European Monetary System (EMS) and related matters (*Bulletin EC* 12-1978, point 1.1.11)

European Parliament Resolution of 17 April 1980 on the relations between the European Parliament and the Commission with a view to the forthcoming appointment of a new Commission (OJ 1980 C 117/53)

European Parliament Resolution of 10 July 1981 embodying the opinion of the European Parliament on the proposal from the Commission to the Council for a financial regulation on the application of the agreement concerning the implementation of pre-accession aid for Portugal (OJ 1981 C 234/100)

European Parliament Resolution of 20 November 1981 embodying the opinion of the European Parliament on the modified proposal from the Commission to the Council for a regulation establishing a Community system for the conservation and management of fishery resources (OJ 1981 C 327/132)

Council Resolution of 7 February 1983 on the continuation and implementation of a policy and action programme on the environment (OJ 1983 C 46/1)

European Parliament Resolution of 17 May 1983 closing the procedure of consultation of the European Parliament on the proposal from the Commission to the Council for a regulation to implement a Council decision on the tasks of the European Social Fund (OJ 1983 C 161/51)

European Parliament Resolution of 16 September 1983 on the cost to the EC budget and effectiveness of committees of a management, advisory and consultative nature (OJ 1983 C 277/195)

European Parliament Resolution of 14 February 1984 on the Draft Treaty establishing the European Union (OJ 1984 C 77/53)

Council Resolution of 27 February 1984 on a programme of action on safety and health at work (OJ 1984 C 67/2)

European Parliament Resolution of 10 April 1984 on the rationalisation of the operations of management, advisory and consultative committees, groups of experts and similar bodies financed from the EC budget (OJ 1984 C 127/56)

European Parliament Resolution of 21 May 1984 on committees for the adaptation of directives to technical and scientific progress (OJ 1984 C 172/6)

Council Resolution of 7 May 1985 on a new approach to technical harmonisation and standards (OJ 1985 C 136/1)

European Parliament Resolution of 16 January 1986 on the position of the European Parliament on the Single Act approved by the Intergovernmental Conference on 16 and 17 December 1985 (OJ 1986 C 36/144)

Declaration No 1 annexed to the Single European Act of 28 February 1986 on the powers of implementation of the Commission (OJ 1987 L 169/24)

European Parliament Resolution of 23 October 1986 closing the procedure for consultation of the European Parliament on the proposal from the Commission to the Council for a regulation laying down the procedures for the exercise of implementing powers conferred on the Commission (OJ 1986 C 297/94)

European Parliament Resolution of 17 June 1987 on the Single European Act (OJ 1987 C 190/75)

European Parliament Resolution of 8 July 1987 on the Council Decision of 22 June 1987 on the implementing powers of the Commission (OJ 1987 C 246/42)

European Parliament Resolution of 26 May 1989 embodying the opinion of the European Parliament on the proposal from the Commission to the Council for a directive on the establishment of the internal market for telecommunications services through the implementation of Open Network Provision (OJ 1989 C 158/300)

European Parliament Resolution of 11 July 1990 on the Intergovernmental Conference in the context of the Parliament's strategy for European Union (OJ 1990 C 231/97)

European Parliament Resolution of 12 December 1990 on the constitutional basis of European Union (OJ 1991 C 19/65)

European Parliament Resolution of 13 December 1990 on the executive powers of the Commission (commitology) and the role of the Commission in the Community's external relations (OJ 1991 C 19/273)

European Parliament Resolution of 12 March 1991 embodying the opinion of the European Parliament on the Commission proposal for a Council regulation on organic production of agricultural products and indications referring thereto on agricultural products and foodstuffs (OJ 1991 C 106/27)

European Parliament Resolution of 19 April 1991 on infant formulae and follow-up milks (OJ 1991 C 129/226)

European Parliament Resolution of 23 October 1991 embodying the opinion of the European Parliament on the Commission proposal for a Council Directive on the application of open network provision to leased lines (OJ 1991 C 305/61)

Declaration No 16 annexed to the Treaty of 7 February 1992 on European Union on the hierarchy of Community Acts (OJ 1992 C 191/101)

Declaration No 19 annexed to the Treaty of 7 February 1992 on European Union on the implementation of Community law (OJ 1992 C 191/102)

Council Resolution of 17 December 1992 on the assessment of the situation in the Community telecommunications sector (OJ 1993 C 2/5)

European Parliament Resolution of 14 July 1993 embodying Parliament's opinion on the proposal for a Council regulation concerning the provision of technical assistance to economic reform and recovery in the independent States of the former Union of Soviet Socialist Republics and Mongolia (OJ 1993 C 255/81)

Council Resolution of 22 July 1993 on the review of the situation in the telecommunications sector and the need for further development in that market (OJ 1993 C 213/1)

European Parliament Resolution of 16 December 1993 on questions of commitology relating to the entry into force of the Maastricht Treaty (OJ 1994 C 20/176)

European Parliament Resolution of 19 January 1994 embodying the opinion of the European Parliament on the common position established by the Council with a view to the adoption of a European Parliament and Council directive on the application of open network provision (ONP) to voice telephony (OJ 1994 C 44/93)

European Parliament Resolution of 30 September 1994 on the need for further action by the Community in the field of ONP-voice telephony (OJ 1994 C 305/147)

European Parliament Resolution of 15 December 1994 on the draft general budget of the European Communities for the 1995 financial year (OJ 1995 C 18/145)

European Parliament Resolution of 18 January 1995 on a decision of the European Parliament, the Council and the Commission on the detailed provisions governing the exercise of the European Parliament's right of inquiry and a *modus vivendi* between the European Parliament, the Council and the Commission concerning the implementing measures for acts adopted in accordance with the procedure laid down in Article 189b of the EC Treaty (OJ 1995 C 43/37)

European Parliament Resolution of 17 May 1995 on the functioning of the Treaty on European Union with a view to the 1996 Intergovernmental Conference (OJ 1995 C 151/56)

European Parliament Resolution of 26 October 1995 on the Commission's response to Parliament's request for information on the 1994 activities of executive committees (OJ 1995 C 308/133)

European Parliament Resolution of 13 March 1996 embodying (i) Parliament's opinion on the convening of the Intergovernmental Conference, and (ii) an evaluation of the work of the Reflection Group and a definition of the political priorities of the European Parliament with a view to the Intergovernmental Conference (OJ 1996 C 96/77)

European Parliament Resolution of 24 October 1996 on the draft general budget of the European Communities for the financial year 1997 (OJ 1996 C 347/125)

European Parliament Resolution of 16 January 1997 on the general outline for a draft revision of the Treaties (OJ 1997 C 33/66)

European Parliament Resolution of 11 June 1997 on the draft treaty drawn up by the Dutch Presidency (OJ 1997 C 200/70)

European Parliament Resolution of 26 June 1997 on the meeting of the European Council on 16 and 17 June in Amsterdam (OJ 1997 C 222/17)

Declaration No 31 annexed to the Treaty of Amsterdam of 2 October 1997 on the Council Decision of 13 July 1987 (OJ 1997 C 340/137)

European Parliament Resolution of 19 November 1997 on the Amsterdam Treaty (OJ 1997 C 371/99)

European Parliament Resolution of 14 May 1998 embodying Parliament's opinion on the proposal for a Council Regulation concerning the compulsory indication on the labelling of certain foodstuffs produced from genetically modified organisms (OJ 1998 C 167/187)

European Parliament Resolution of 16 September 1998 on the modification of the procedures for the exercise of implementing powers conferred on the Commission—commitology (OJ 1998 C 313/101)

European Parliament Resolution of 17 December 1998 on the draft general budget of the European Union for the financial year 1999 as modified by the Council (OJ 1999 C 98/212)

European Parliament Resolution of 5 May 1999 on the nomination of the Commission President (OJ 1999 C 279/171)

European Parliament Resolution of 6 May 1999 embodying Parliament's opinion on the proposal for a Council Decision laying down the procedures for the exercise of implementing powers conferred on the Commission (OJ 1999 C 279/404)

Declarations on Council Decision 1999/468/EC of 28 June 1999 laying down the procedures for the exercise of implementing powers conferred on the Commission (OJ 1999 C 203/1)

European Parliament Resolution of 17 February 2000 on the agreement between the European Parliament and the Commission on procedures for implementing Council Decision 1999/468/EC of 28 June 1999 laying down the procedures for the exercise of implementing powers conferred on the Commission (OJ 2000 C 339/269)

European Council Resolution of 23 March 2001 on more effective securities market regulation in the European Union (OJ 2001 C 138/1)

European Parliament Resolution of 5 February 2002 on the implementation of financial services legislation (http://www.europarl.eu.int)

European Parliament Resolution of 17 December 2002 on the typology of acts and the hierarchy of legislation in the European Union (http://www.europarl.eu.int)

Declaration No 23 annexed to the Treaty of Nice of 26 February 2001 on the future of the Union (OJ 2001 C 80/85)

European Parliament Resolution of 2 September 2003 on the proposal for a Council decision on amending Decision 1999/468/EC laying down the procedures for the exercise of implementing powers conferred on the Commission, at internet www.europarl.eu.int

Declaration on Article I-36 to be annexed to the Final Act of the Intergovernmental Conference of 25 October 2004 (ADD 2 CIG 87/04 REV 2)

Institutional agreements and codes of conduct

Code of Conduct of 12 July 1993 on the implementation of structural policies by the Commission (OJ 1993 C 255/19)

Code of Conduct of 6 December 1993 concerning public access to Council and Commission documents (OJ 1993 L 340/41)

Draft Inter-Institutional Agreement between the European Parliament, the Council and the Commission of 19 April 1994 on the rules for exercising the powers to implement acts adopted jointly by the European Parliament and the Council in accordance with the procedure laid down in Article 189b of the Treaty establishing the European Community (SEC (94) 645 final)

Modus Vivendi between the European Parliament, the Council and the Commission of 20 December 1994 concerning the implementing measures for acts adopted in accordance with the procedure laid down in Article 189b of the Treaty establishing the European Community (OJ 1996 C 102/1)

Code of Conduct annexed to the Resolution of 15 March 1995 on the Commission's annual programme of work (OJ 1995 C 89/69)

Agreement between the European Parliament and the Commission of 17 February 2000 on procedures for implementing Council Decision 1999/468/EC of 28 June 1999 laying down the procedures for the exercise of implementing powers conferred on the Commission (OJ 2000 L 256/19)

Other official documents

Council/European Council

Statutes of the Euratom Supply Agency of 6 November 1958 (OJ 1958 B 27/534)

Internal Agreement EEC/64/354 of the Representatives of the Governments of the Member States, meeting within the Council, on the measures to take and procedures to follow in the application of the Convention of association between the European Economic Community and the Associated African States and Madagascar (OJ 1964 93/1490)

Process-verbal de la session extraordinaire du Conseil de la Communauté Economique Européenne tenue à Luxembourg, 17–18 et 27–28 janvier 1966, no C/12 f/66 (AE 1) final

General Programme of 28 May 1969 for the elimination of technical barriers to trade which result from disparities between the provisions laid down by law, regulation or administrative action in Member States (OJ 1969 C 76/1)

Amendment of Rules of Procedure of 20 July 1987 (OJ 1987 L 291/27)

Presidency Conclusions of the European Council meeting in Corfu on 24 and 25 June 1994 (internet www.europa.eu.int)

Presidency Conclusions of the European Council meeting in Essen on 9 and 10 December 1994 (www.europa.eu.int)

Presidency Conclusions of the European Council meeting in Cannes on 26 and 27 June 1995 (internet www.europa.eu.int)

Presidency Conclusions of the European Council meeting in Madrid on 15 and 16 December 1995 (internet www.europa.eu.int)

Council meeting (General Affairs) of 31 May 1999 on Comitology (Presse 171-G No 8657/99)

Council meeting (General Affairs) of 21–22 June 1999 on Comitology (Presse 198 No 9008/99)

Presidency Conclusions of the European Council meeting in Helsinki on 10 and 11 December 1999 (internet www.europa.int)

Presidency Conclusions of the European Council meeting in Laeken on 14–15 December 2001 (internet www.europa.eu.int)

Presidency Conclusions of the European Council meeting in Brussels on 17 and 18 June 2004 (internet www.europa.int)

European Parliament

Rapport du 20 décembre 1961 fait au nom de la commission de l'agriculture sur les attributions de la Commission européenne dans la mise en œuvre de la politique agricole commune (rapporteur: Käthe Strobel) PE Doc 119/61

Rapport du 5 octobre 1962 fait au nom du comité des présidents sur le cinquième Rapport général sur l'activité de la Communauté économique européenne (rapporteur: Arved Deringer) PE Doc 74/62

Rapport du 17 octobre 1967 fait au nom de la commission de l'agriculture sur la proposition de la Commission de la C.E.E. au Conseil relative à une directive concernant l'introduction de modes de prélèvement d'échantillons et de méthodes d'analyse communautaires pour le contrôle officiel des aliments des animaus, complété par le nouveau projet de décision concernant l'intstitution d'un Comité permanent des aliments des animaux (rapporteur: Astrid Lulling) PE Doc 129/67

Rapport du 19 juin 1968 fait au nom de la commission des affaires sociales et de la santé publique sur la proposition de la Commission des Communautés européennes au Conseil relative à un règlement concernant le traitement du saccharose destiné à la consommation humaine (rapporteur: Josef Müller) PE Doc 76/68

Rapport du 24 juin 1968 fait au nom du comité de rédaction institué par la résolution du 12 mars 1968 sur le premier rapport général de la Commission des Communautés européennes sur l'activité des Communautés (rapporteur: Hans August Lücker) PE Doc 58/68

Rapport du 30 septembre 1968 fait au nom de la commission juridique sur les procédures communautaires d'exécution du droit communautaire dérivé (rapporteur: Léon Jozeau-Marigné) PE Doc 115/68

Final adoption of the General Budget of the European Communities for the financial year 1984 (OJ 1984 L 12/1)

Debates of the European Parliament on 28 March 1984 (OJ 1984 Annex 1–312/93)

Report of 5 May 1984 drawn up on behalf of the Legal Affairs Committee on Committees for the Adaptation of Directives to Technical and Scientific Progress (rapporteur: Alan Tyrrell) EP Doc A1-205/84

Debates of the European Parliament on 24 May 1984 (OJ 1984 Annex 1-314/262)

Debates of the European Parliament on 9 July 1986 (OJ 1986 Annex 2-341/130)

Report of 2 July 1986 drawn up on behalf of the Political Affairs Committee on the proposal from the Commission of the European Communities to the Council for a regulation laying down the procedures for the exercise of implementing powers conferred on the Commission (rapporteur: Klaus Hänsch) EP Doc A2-78/86

Report of 20 October 1986 drawn up on behalf of the Political Affairs Committee on the proposal from the Commission for a Council regulation laying down the procedures for the exercise of implementing powers conferred on the Commission (rapporteur: Klaus Hänsch) EP Doc A2-138/86

Report of 19 November 1990 drawn up on behalf of the Committee on Agriculture and Fisheries and Rural Development on the proposal from the Commission to the Council for a regulation on organic production of agricultural products and indications referring thereto on agricultural products and foodstuffs (COM (89) 552 final—C3-249/89) (rapporteur: Solange Fernex) EP Doc A3-311/90

Report of 19 November 1990 drawn up on behalf of the Committee on Institutional Affairs on the executive powers of the Commission (comitology) and the role of the Commission in the Community's external relations (rapporteur: Panayolis Roumeliotis) EP Doc A3-310/90

Report of 6 December 1993 drawn up on behalf of the Committee on Institutional Affairs on questions of committology relating to the entry into force of the Maastricht Treaty (rapporteur: Biagio de Giovanni) EP Doc A3-417/93

Report of 15 July 1994 drawn up on behalf of the delegation to the Conciliation Committee on the text confirmed by the Council following the conciliation procedure on the proposal for a European Parliament and Council Directive on the application of Open Network Provision (ONP) to voice telephony (rapporteur: Imelda Read) EP Doc A4-1/94

Report of 25 July 1995 drawn up on behalf of the Committee on Budgets on the Commission's response to Parliament's request for information on the 1994 activities of executive committees (rapporteur: Terence Wynn) EP Doc A4-189/95

Report of 5 March 1996 drawn up on behalf of the Committee on Institutional Affairs on (i) Parliament's Opinion on the convening of the IGC and (ii) evaluation of the work of the Reflection Group and definition of the political priorities of the European Parliament with a view to the Intergovernmental Conference (rapporteurs: Raymonde Dury and Hanja Maij-Weggen) EP Doc A4-68/96

White Paper of 29 March 1996 on the 1996 Intergovernmental Conference: Summary of the positions of the Member States of the European Union with a view to the 1996 Intergovernmental Conference, at internet www.europa.eu.int

Working Document of the Committee on Budgets of 30 April 1996 on developments on the Comitology dossier (PE 216.965)

Working Document of the Institutional Committee of 12 September 1996 on the *Modus Vivendi* concerning the implementing measures for acts (PE 218.255)

Final adoption of the General Budget of the European Union for the financial year 1998 (OJ 1998 L 44/1)

Report of 3 August 1998 drawn up on behalf of the Committee on Institutional Affairs on the modification of the procedures for the exercise of implementing powers conferred on the Commission—commitology (rapporteur: Maria Adelaide Aglietta) EP Doc A4-292/98

Debates of the European Parliament on 15 September 1998 (OJ 1998 C 313/17)

Report of 10 December 1998 drawn up on behalf of the Committee on Budgets on the draft general budget of the European Union for the financial year 1999 (rapporteur: Barbara Dührkop Dührkop) EP Doc A4-500/98

Report of 24 March 1999 drawn up on behalf of the Committee on Institutional Affairs on the proposal for a Council Decision laying down the procedures for the exercise of implementing powers conferred on the Commission (rapporteur: Maria Adelaide Aglietta) EP Doc A4-169/99

Debates of the European Parliament on 5 May 1999 (OJ 1999 C 279/160)

Report of 30 March 1999 drawn up on behalf of the Committee on Institutional Affairs on the proposal for a Council Decision laying down the procedures for the exercise of implementing powers conferred on the Commission (rapporteur: Maria Adelaide Aglietta) EP Doc A4-169/99

Final adoption of the General Budget of the European Union for the financial year 2000 (OJ 2000 L 40/1)

Report of 31 January 2000 drawn up on behalf of the Committee on Constitutional Affairs on the agreement between the European Parliament and the Commission on procedures for implementing the new Council Decision of 28 June 1999—commitology (rapporteur: Monica Frassoni) EP Doc A5-21/00

Debates of the European Parliament on 16 February 2000 (OJ 2000 C 339/57)

Report of 23 January 2002 drawn up on behalf of the Committee on Constitutional Affairs on the implementation of financial services (rapporteur: Karl von Wogau) EP Doc A5-11/02

Report of 28 January 2002 drawn up on behalf of the Committee on Constitutional Affairs on the general revision of the Rules of Procedure (rapporteur: Richard Corbett) EP Doc A5-8/02

Implementation of financial services legislation in the context of the Lamfalussy Report, intervention by Commission President Romano Prodi to the European Parliament's plenary session in Strasbourg on 5 October 2002 (SPEEC/02/44)

Report of 3 December 2002 drawn up on behalf of the Committee on Constitutional Affairs on the typology of acts and the hierarchy of legislation in the European Union (rapporteur: Jean-Louis Bourlanges) EP Doc A5-425/02

European Parliament Rules of Procedure of 5 March 2003 (OJ 2003 L 61/1)

Report of 29 April 2003 drawn up on behalf of the Committee on Constitutional Affairs on the proposal for a Council decision amending Decision 99/468/EC laying down the procedures for the exercise of implementing powers conferred on the Commission (rapporteur: Richard Corbett) EP Doc A5-128/03

Debates of the European Parliament on 13 May 2003 (internet www.europarl.eu.int)

Report of 11 July 2003 drawn up on behalf of the Committee on Constitutional Affairs on the proposal for a Council decision amending Decision 99/468/EC laying down the procedures for the exercise of implementing powers conferred on the Commission (rapporteur: Richard Corbett) EP Doc A5-266/03

Debates of the European Parliament on 2 September 2003 (internet www.europarl. eu.int)

Commission

First General Report on the Activities of the European Economic Community 1958 (Office for Official Publications 1959)

Fourth General Report on the Activities of the European Economic Community 1961 (Office for Official Publications 1962)

Sixth General Report on the Activities of the European Economic Community 1963 (Office for Official Publications 1964)

Seventh General Report on the Activities of the European Economic Community 1964 (Office for Official Publications 1965)

Ninth General Report on the Activities of the European Economic Community 1966 (Office for Official Publications 1967)

First General Report on the Activities of the European Communities 1967 (Office for Official Publications 1968)

Second General Report on the Activities of the European Communities 1968 (Office for Official Publications 1969)

Memorandum of 12 February 1969 to the Council on the co-ordination of the economic policies and the monetary co-operation within the Community (COM (69) 150)

Third General Report on the Activities of the European Communities 1969 (Office for Official Publications 1970)

Memorandum of 4 March 1970: a plan for the phased establishment of an economic and monetary union (*Bulletin EC* Supplement 3-1970)

Fourth General Report on the Activities of the European Communities 1970 (Office for Official Publications 1971)

Report on Enlarged Community—Outcome of the Negotiations with the Applicant States (*Bulletin EC* Supplement 1-1972)

Fifth General Report on the Activities of the European Communities 1971 (Office for Official Publications 1972)

Communication to the Council of 7 November 1973 on the transition to the second stage of economic and monetary union (OJ 1973 C 114/33)

Seventh General Report on the Activities of the European Communities 1973 (Office for Official Publications 1974)

Eighth General Report on the Activities of the European Communities (Office for Official Publications 1974)

Communication to the Council on 20 April 1978 entitled the transitional period and the institutional implications of enlargement (*Bulletin EC* Supplement 2-1978)

Communication to the Council on 24 September 1979 entitled Proposals for reform of the Commission of the European Communities and its services (*Bulletin EC* 9-1979, point 1.3.1 *et seq.*)

Thirteenth General Report on the Activities of the European Communities 1979 (Office for Official Publications 1980)

Communication to the European Council on 12 November 1982 entitled Problems of Enlargement—Taking Stock and Proposals (COM (82) 757 final)

Communication to the Council on 1 March 1983 entitled Institutional Implications of Enlargement: More Flexibility in Decision-Making (COM (83) 116 final)

Proposals to the IGC 1985 (*Bulletin EC* 9-1985, point 1.1.1 *et seq.*)

White Paper of 14 June 1985: Completing the Internal Market (COM (85) 310 final)

Nineteenth General Report on the Activities of the European Communities 1985 (Office for Official Publications 1986)

Proposal of 3 March 1986 for a Council Regulation laying down the procedures for the exercise of implementing powers conferred on the Commission (COM (86) 35 final)

Twentieth General Report on the Activities of the European Communities 1986 (Office for Official Publications 1987)

Proposal of 3 December 1986 for a Council Regulation laying down the procedures for the exercise of implementing powers conferred on the Commission (COM (86) 702 final)

Twenty-first General Report on the Activities of the European Communities 1987 (Office for Official Publications 1988)

Budget 1995 Comitology—Decisions taken in 1994 by committees listed in Annex I to Part A of section III of the General Budget for the European Union for 1994 (Commission Documents XIX/A7/0067/95 and XIX/A7/117/95 (addendum))

Communication to the Council of 10 July 1989: the Council's delegation of executive powers to the Commission (SEC (89) 1143 final)

Report to the European Parliament of 28 September 1989: delegation of executive powers to the Commission (SEC (89) 1591 final)

Proposal of 4 December 1989 for a Council Regulation on organic production of agricultural products and indications referring thereto on agricultural products and foodstuffs (OJ 1990 C 4/4)

Twenty-fourth General Report on the Activities of the European Communities 1990 (Office for Official Publications 1991)

Communication to the Council of 10 January 1991: conferment of implementing powers on the Commission (SEC (90) 2589 final)

Proposal of 28 August 1992 for a Council Directive on the application of open network provision (ONP) to voice telephony (OJ 1992 C 263/20)

Proposal of 25 November 1992 for a Council Regulation concerning the provision of technical assistance to economic reform and recovery in the independent States of the former Union of Soviet Socialist Republics and Mongolia (OJ 1993 C 48/13)

Proposal of 7 May 1993 for a Council Directive on the application of open network provision (ONP) to voice telephony (OJ 1993 C 147/12)

List of proposals pending before the Council on 31 October 1993 for which entry into force of the Treaty on European Union will require a change in the legal base and/or a change in procedure (COM (93) 570 final)

Opinion of 1 March 1994 on the European Parliament's amendments to the Council's common position regarding the proposal for a European Parliament and Council Directive on the application of open network provision (ONP) to voice telephony (COM (94) 48 final)

General Report on the Activities of the European Union 1994 (Office for Official Publications 1995)

Proposal of 4 July 1994 for a Council Directive on Ambient Air Quality Assessment and Management (OJ 1994 C 216/4)

Proposal of 1 February 1995 for a European Parliament and Council Directive on the application of open network provision (ONP) to voice telephony (OJ 1995 C 122/4)

General Report on the Activities of the European Union 1995 (Office for Official Publications 1996)

Report of 10 May 1995 on the Operation of the Treaty on European Union (SEC (95) 731)

Proposal of 17 July 1995 for a European Parliament and Council Directive amending Council Directive 93/6/EEC of 15 March 1993 on the capital adequacy of investment firms and credit institutions and Council Directive 93/22/EEC of 10 May 1993 on investment services in the securities field (OJ 1995 C 253/19)

Opinion of 29 February 1996: Reinforcing Political Union and Preparing for Enlargement (COM (96) 90 final)

General Report on the Activities of the European Union 1996 (Office for Official Publications 1997)

Draft Regulation of 25 February 1997 concerning the compulsory indication on the labelling of certain foodstuffs produced from genetically modified organisms of particulars other than those provided for in Directive 79/112/EEC (SEC (97) 2253)

Better Law Making Report 1997 (COM (97) 626 final)

General Report on the Activities of the European Union 1998 (Office for Official Publications 1999)

Proposal of 24 June 1998 for a Council Decision laying down the procedures for the exercise of implementing powers conferred on the Commission (OJ 1998 C 279/5)

General Report on the Activities of the European Union 1999 (Office for Official Publications 2000)

General Report on the Activities of the European Union 2000 (Office for Official Publications 2001)

Information from the Commission of 8 August 2000—List of committees which assist the Commission in the exercise of its implementing powers (OJ 2000 C 225/2)

Standard Rules of Procedure of 6 February 2001 for committees set up under Council Decision 99/468/EC (OJ 2001 C 38/3)

White Paper of 25 July 2001 on European Governance (COM (01) 428 final)

Report of 11 December 2002 on European Governance (COM (02) 705 final)

Report of 13 December 2002 on the working of the committees during 2001 (COM (2002) 733 final)

Communication to the Convention of 11 December 2002 on the institutional architecture—for the European Union: peace, freedom, solidarity (COM (02) 728 final/2

Proposal of 11 December 2002 for a Council Decision amending Decision 99/468/EC laying down the procedures for the exercise of implementing powers conferred on the Commission (COM (02) 719 final)

Amended proposal of 22 April 2004 for a Council decision amending Decision 1999/468/EC laying down the procedures for the exercise of implementing powers conferred on the Commission (COM (04) 324 final)

Report on European Governance of 22 September 2004 (SEC (04) 1153)

European Convention

Mandate of Working Group IX on the simplification of legislative procedures and instruments (CONV 271/02)

Simplification of Legislative Procedures and Instruments, paper submitted by Jean-Claude Piris to Working Group IX on 17 October 2002 (Working Document 06)

Simplifying Legislative Procedures and Instruments, paper submitted by Michel Petite to Working Group IX on 17 October 2002 (Working Document 08)

How to Simplify the Instruments of the Union? Paper submitted by Koen Lenaerts submitted to Working Group IX on 17 October 2002 (Working Document 07)

Proposal to distinguish legislative and executive functions in the institutional system of the European Union, paper submitted by Paolo Ponzano to Working Group IX on 7 November 2002 (Working Document 16)

Final Report of Working Group IX on Simplification of 29 November 2002 (CONV 424/02)

Summary Report of the plenary session on 5 and 6 December 2002 (CONV 449/02)

Draft of Articles 24 to 33 of the Constitutional Treaty (CONV 571/03)

Suggestion for amendment of Draft Article 27 submitted by Dick Roche, Minister for State at the Irish Department of Foreign Affairs (internet www.european-convention.eu.int)

Suggestions for amendment of Draft Article 28 and, later, Article I-36 submitted by Peter Hain, UK Minister for Europe (internet www.european-convention.eu.int)

Reactions to draft Articles 24 to 33 of the Constitutional Treaty on 12 March 2003 (CONV 609/03)

Summary Report of the plenary session on 17 and 18 March 2003 (CONV 630/03)

Summary Report of the plenary session on 15 and 16 May 2003 (CONV 748/03)

Revised text of Part One of the Draft Constitution of 26 May 2003 (CONV 724/03)

Reactions to the draft Articles of the revised text of Part One (Volume I)— Analysis, 4 June 2003 (CONV 779/03)

Draft Treaty of 18 July 2003 establishing a Constitution for Europe (CONV 850/03)

Special reports

Report of the Werner Group to the Council and the Commission of 8 October 1970 concerning the realisation by stages of the economic and monetary union in the Community (OJ 1970 C 136/1)

Report by Leo Tindemans to the European Council on 29 December 1975 entitled European Union (*Bulletin EC* Supplement 1-1976)

Report on European institutions of 8 November 1979 presented by the Committee of Three to the European Council (Office for Official Publications 1979)

Report by the Independent Review Body to the Commission on 24 September 1979 entitled Proposals for a reform of the Commission of the European Communities and its Services (*Bulletin EC* 9-1979/16)

Report of the Ad Hoc Committee on Institutional Affairs to the European Council of 19 March 1985 (*Bulletin EC* 3-1985, point 3.5.1 *et seq.*)

Report from the Chairman of the Reflection Group of 5 December 1995 on the 1996 Intergovernmental Conference: A Strategy for Europe (Office for Official Publications 1995)

Report of the Committee of Wise Men of 15 February 2001 on the regulation of European securities markets (at internet www.europa.eu.int)

National documents

Representation permanente de la Belgique auprès des Communautes europeennes, No C/QC/130A/15.259 (Conseil extraordinaire CEE; Luxembourg 17–18 janvier 1966)

Representation permanente de la Belgique auprès des Communautes europeennes, no C/QC/130/15.369 (Conseil extraordinaire CEE; Luxembourg 28–29 janvier 1966)

Debates of the House of Commons on 24 May 1971 (Hansard), Session 1970–71, Volume 818 (HMSO 1971)

Debates of the House of Commons on 23 January 1975 (Hansard), Session 1974–75 Volume 884 (HMSO 1975)

House of Lords Select Committee on the European Communities, Delegation of Powers to the Commission (final report) Session 1986–87, 3rd Report (16 December 1986)

Positions des Etats membres sur les thèmes à l'ordre du jour de la Conférence intergouvernementale 1996 (internet www.europa.eu.int)

Swedish Ministry of Foreign Affairs, Position PM of 20 November 1998 on the Commission Proposal for a Council Decision laying down the procedures for the exercise of implementing powers conferred on the Commission (internet www.regeringen.se)

House of Lords Select Committee on European Communities, Delegation of Powers to the Commission: Reforming Comitology, Session 1998–99, 3rd Report (2 February 1999)

House of Lords Select Committee on the European Union, The Future of Europe: Constitutional Treaty—Draft Articles 24–22, Session 2002–03, 12th Report (13 March 2003)

House of Lords Select Committee on the European Union: Reforming Comitology, Session 2002–03, 31st Report (1 July 2003)

House of Commons European Scrutiny Committee, Session 2002–03, 32nd Report (17 September 2003)

Swedish Ministry of Foreign Affairs, Riktlinjer för handläggningen av EU-frågor, UD PM 2003:5 (internet www.regeringen.se)

House of Lords Select Committee on the European Union, Session 2003–04, 7th Report, Remaining Government Responses for Session 2002–03 (22 March 2004)

Statement by the British Prime Minister, Tony Blair, to the House of Commons on 20 April 2004 (internet www.fco.gov.uk)

House of Commons European Scrutiny Committee, Session 2003–04, 23rd Report (16 June 2004)

Monographs

ALMER, J. and ROTKIRCH, M., *European Governance: an Overview of the Commission's Agenda for Reform,* Swedish Institute for European Policy Studies, Sieps 2004:1u

ANDENAES, M. and TÜRK, A. (Eds.), *Delegated Legislation and the Role of Committees in the EC* (Kluwer Law International 2000)

BERGSTRÖM, C. F., *Genomförandekommittéer: En expertstudie av svenska departements och myndigheters ansvar för antagande av gemenskapslagstiftning*, Swedish Agency for Public Management, Statskontoret 2000:20C

BERTRAM, C., *Das Verwaltungsausschussverfahren: Ein neuartiges Rechtsetzungs-verfahren der Europäischen Wirtschaftgemeinschaft* (Rheinischen Friedrich-Willhelms-Universität zu Bonn 1967)

BIEBER, R., DEHOUSSE, R., PINDER, J., and WEILER J. H. H. (Eds.), *1992: One European Market? A Critical Analysis of the Commission's Internal Market Strategy* (Nomos 1988)

BULMER, S. and WESSEL, W., *The European Council* (Macmillan Press 1987)

CAPPELLETTI, M., SECCOMBE, M., and WEILER, J. H. H. (Eds.), *Integration Through Law: Methods, Tools and Institutions* (De Gruyter 1986)

CHAPSAL, J., *La vie politique sous la V° Republique* (Paris Presses Universitaires de France 1990)

CHURCHILL, W. S., *Europe Unite* (Cassel 1950)

CORBETT, R., JACOBS, F., and SHACKLETON, M., *The European Parliament* (Harlow 1992)

CORBETT, R., JACOBS, F., and SHACKLETON, M., *The European Parliament* (John Harper Publishing 2000)

CORBETT, R., *The European Parliament's Role in Closer EU Integration* (Macmillan Press 1998)

CRAIG, P. and BÚRCA, G. de (Eds.), *The Evolution of EU Law* (Oxford University Press 1999)

CRAIG, P. and BÚRCA, G. de, *EU Law—Text, Cases and Materials* (Oxford University Press 2003)

CRAIG, P. and HARLOW C. (Eds.), *Lawmaking in the European Union* (Kluwer Law International 1998)

DEHOUSSE, R. (Ed.), *Une constitution pour l'Europe?* (Presses de Sciences Po 2002)

Encarta World English Dictionary (Microsoft 1999)

ENDO, K., *Presidency of the European Commission under Jacques Delors: the Politics of Shared Leadership* (Saint Martin's Press 2000)

FARRELL, H. and HÉRITIER, A., *The Invisible Transformation of Codecision: Problems of Democratic Legitimacy*, Sieps 2003:7 (Swedish Institute for European Policy Studies 2003)

FENNELL, R., *The Common Agricultural Policy of the European Community* (Granada 1979)

From Rome to Maastricht: a brief history of EMU (internet www.europa.eu.int)

GAZZO, M. (Ed.), *Towards European Union: from 'Crocodile' to the European Council in Milan* (Agence Europe 1985)

GROEBEN, W. von der, *The European Community: the Formative Years* (European Perspectives 1985)

HARTLEY, T.C., *The Foundations of European Community Law: an introduction to the constitutional and administrative law of the European Community* (Clarendon Press 1994)

Historique de la Conference Intergouvernementale 1996 (internet www.europa.eu.int)

JOERGES, C., LADEUR, K.-H., and VOS, E. (Eds.), *Integrating Scientific Expertise into Regulatory Decision-Making: National Traditions and European Innovations* (Nomos 1997)

JOERGES, C. and VOS, E. (Eds.), *EU Committees: Social Regulation, Law and Politics* (Hart Publishing 1999)

KAPTEYN, P. J. G. and VERLOREN van THEMAAT, P., *Introduction to the Law of the European Communities* (Kluwer Law International 1990)

KAPTEYN, P. J. G. and VERLOREN van THEMAAT, P., *Introduction to the Law of the European Communities* (Kluwer Law International 1998)

KELLERMAN, A. E. (Ed.), *The Treaty on European Union: Suggestions for Revision* (T.M.C. Asser Instituut 1996)

La Commission des Communautés Européennes e l'élargissement de l'Europe, colloque organisé les 23–24–25 novembre 1972 par l'Institut d'etudes européennes (Editions de l'Université de Bruxelles 1974)

LARSSON, T., *Precooking in the European Union—the World of Expert Groups*, Swedish Expert Group on Public Finance Ds 2003:16 (internet www.regeringen.se/eso)

LENAERTS, K. and NUFFEL, P. van, *Constitutional Law of the European Union* (Sweet & Maxwell 1999)

LINDBERG, L., *The Political Dynamics of European Integration* (Oxford University Press 1963)

LOTH, W., WALLANCE, W., and WESSELS, W. (Eds.), *Walter Hallstein: the Forgotten European?* (Macmillan Press 1998)

LYNCH, F., *De Gaulle's First Veto: France, the Rebuff and the Free Trade Area*, EUI Working Paper HEC No 98/8 (European University Institute 1998)

MALMBORG, M. af, *Den ståndaktiga nationalstaten: Sverige och den västeuropeiska integrationen 1945–1959* (Lund University Press 1994)

MILLER, V., *Qualified Majority Voting and the Blocking Minority*, House of Commons Research Paper 94/47, at pp. 11–12

MILWARD, A. (Ed.), *The Rise and Fall of a National Strategy* (Frank Cass 2002), at pp. 145–163

NOËL, É., *Working Together* (Office for Official Publications 1987)

NORTHCOTE PARKINSON, C., *Parkinson's Law or The Pursuit of Progress* (John Murray 1958)

Oxford Concise Dictionary of English Etymology (Oxford University Press 1996)

PEDLER, R. H. and SCHAEFER, G. F. (Eds.), *Shaping European Law and Policy: the Role of Committees and Comitology in the Political Process* (European Institute of Public Administration 1996)

RUYT, J. de, L'Acte Unique Européen: commentaire (Editions de l'Université de Bruxelles 1989)

SCHMITT von SYDOW, H. and von ROSENBACH, G., *Organe der Erweiterten Europäischen Gemeinschaften: Die Kommission* (Nomos 1980)
SCHWARZE, J., *European Administrative Law* (Sweet & Maxwell 1992)
THATCHER, M., *The Downing Street Years* (HarperCollins 1993)
TIBERG, H. and STERZEL, F. (Eds.), *Swedish Law—a Survey* (Juristförlaget 1994)
VOS, E., Institutional Frameworks of Community Health and Safety Legislation: Committees, Agencies, and Private Bodies (Hart Publishing 1999)
WADE, W., RAGNEMALM, H., and STRAUSS, P. L., *Administrative Law: the Problem of Justice Volume I* (Giuffrè 1991)
WALLACE, H., WALLACE, W., and WEBB, C. (Eds.), *Policy Making in the European Community* (Wiley 1983)
WEATHERILL, S. and BEAUMONT, P., *EU Law: the Essential Guide to the Legal Workings of the European Union* (Penguin Books 1999)
WEILER, J. H. H., *European Democracy and Its Critics: Five Uneasy Pieces,* Jean Monnet Working Paper 1/95 (at internet www.jeanmonnetprogram.org)
WEILER, J. H. H. *et al., Mountain or Molehill? A Critical Appraisal of the Commission White Paper on Governance,* Jean Monnet Working Paper 6/01 (at internet www.jeanmonnetprogram.org)
WERTS, J., *The European Council* (North Holland 1992)
WHITE, R. and SMYTHE, B. (Eds.), *Current Issues in European and International Law: Essays in Memory of Frank Dowick* (Sweet & Maxwell 1990)
WINTER, G., *Sources and Categories of European Union Law: a comparative and reform perspective* (Nomos 1996)
WITTE, B. de (Ed.), *Ten Reflections on the Constitutional Treaty for Europe* (European University Institute 2003)
YOUNG, H., *This Blessed Plot: Britain and Europe from Churchill to Blair* (Macmillan Press 1998)

Articles

ALLOTT, P., Britain and Europe: a Political Analysis (1975) 13 *JCMS* 203
BAARDMAN, B., annotation (1971) 8 *CMLRev* 89
BARENTS, R., The Internal Market Unlimited: Some Observations on the Legal Basis of Community Legislation (1993) 30 *CMLRev* 85
BERNITZ, U., Sweden and the European Union: on Sweden's implementation and application of European law (2001) 38 *CMLRev* 903
BERTRAM, C., Decision Making in the EEC: the Management Committee Procedure (1967–68) 5 *CMLRev* 246
BIEBER, R. and SALOMÉ, I., Hierarchy of Norms in European Law (1996) 33 *CMLRev* 907
BLUMANN, C., Le pouvoir exécutif de la Commission à la lumière de l'Acte unique européen (1988) 24 *RTDE* 23

BLUMANN, C., Le Parlement européen et la comitologie: une complication pour la Conférence intergouvernmentale de 1996 (1996) 32 *RTDE* 1

BLUMANN, C., annotation (1990) 26 *RTDE* 173

BOGDANDY, A. von and BAST, J., *New Legal Instruments*, in *The EU Constitution: The Best Way Forward?* Conference Reader from 34th Session Asser Institute Colloquim on European Law on 13–16 October 2004

BRADLEY, K., Maintaining the Balance: the Role of the Court of Justice in Defining the Institutional Position of the European Parliament (1987) 24 *CMLRev* 41

BRADLEY, K., The Variable Evolution of the Standing of the European Parliament in Proceedings before the Court of Justice (1988) 8 *YBEL* 27

BRADLEY, K., Sense and Sensibility: Parliament v. Council Continued (1991) 16 *ELRev* 245

BRADLEY, K., Comitology and the Law: Through a Glass Darkly (1992) 29 *CMLRev* 693

BRADLEY, K., The European Parliament and Comitology: On the Road to Nowhere? (1997) 3 *ELJ* 230

BRUCE, L., The EC's Lord Cockfield: Bullying Europe Towards Unity (1987) 42 *IntMan* 20

BÚRCA, G. de, annotation (1996) 33 *CMLRev* 1051

CATALANO, N., annotation (1976) 4 *GiustCiv* 6

CHRISTIANSEN, T., Intra-Institutional Politics and Inter-Institutional Relations in the EU: Towards Coherent Governance (2001) 8 *JEPP* 747

CONSTANTINESCO, V., annotation (1996) 123 *JDrInt* 459

CULLEN, H. and Worth, A. C., Diplomacy by Other Means: the Use of Legal Basis Litigation as a Political Strategy by the European Parliament and Member States (1999) 36 *CMLRev* 1243

DASHWOOD, A., The Constitution of the European Union after Nice: Law-making Procedures (2001) 26 *ELRev* 215

DEMARET, P., Ferri, M., Dewost, J. L., and Ehlermann, C.-D., L'avenir institutionnel des Communautés européennes (1984) 29 *AnnDL* 271

DOUGAN, M., The Convention's Draft Constitutional Treaty: Bringing Europe Closer to its Lawyers? (2003) 28 *ELRev* 763

DRAKE, H., Political Leadership and European Integration: The Case of Jacques Delors (1995) 18 *WEP* 140

ECKERT, D., annotation (1967) 11 *NJurW* 473

Editorial Comments (1965–66) 3 *CMLRev* 1

Editorial Comments (1965–66) 3 *CMLRev* 189

Editorial Comments (1966–67) 4 *CMLRev* 373

Editorial Comments (1968–69) 6 *CMLRev* 355

Editorial Comments (1968–69) 6 *CMLRev* 430

Editorial Comments (1970) 7 *CMLRev* 1

Editorial Comments (1970) 7 *CMLRev* 103

Editorial Comments (1970) 7 *CMLRev* 254

EDWARD, D., The Impact of the Single Act on the Institutions (1987) 24 *CMLRev* 19

EHLERMANN, C.-D., The Internal Market Following the Single European Act (1987) 24 *CMLRev* 361

EHLERMANN, C.-D., Differentiation, Flexibility, Closer Co-operation: The New Provisions of the Amsterdam Treaty (1998) 4 *ELJ* 246

EHLERMANN, C.-D., annotation (1971) 6 *EuR* 250

EHLERMANN, C.-D. and MINCH, M., Conflicts between the Community Institutions within the Budgetary Procedure: Article 205 of the EEC Treaty (1981) 16 *EuR* 23

EHLERMANN, C.-D., Compétences d'exécution conférées à la Commission—la nouvelle décision-cadre du Conseil (1988) 316 *RMC* 232

EVERLING, U., Legal Problems of the Common Commercial Policy in the European Economic Community (1966–67) 4 *CMLRev* 141

FORMAN, J., annotation (1990) 27 *CMLRev* 872

GLAESNER, H. J., Die Einheitliche Europäische Akte (1986) 21 *EuR* 2

GOZI, S., Does the EU Institutional Triangle have a Future? (2001) 36 *IntSpec* 39

HILF, M., annotation (1990) 25 *EuR* 273

IRVING, R. E. M., The United Kingdom Referendum, June 1975 (1976) 1 *ELRev* 3

JACQUÉ, J.-P., annotation (1989) 25 *RTDE* 225

JACQUÉ, J.-P., L'Acte unique européen (1986) 22 *RTDE* 595

JENKINS, R., Thatcher: a Satisfactory Alternative to Delors? (1990) 4 *EurAff* 53

JOERGES, C. and NEYER, J., From Intergovernmental Bargaining to Deliberative Political Processes: The Constitutionalisation of Comitology (1997) 3 *ELJ* 273

JOERGES, C., The Commission's White Paper on Governance in the EU: a Symptom of Crisis? (2002) 39 *CMLRev* 444

JORNA, M., The Accession Negotiations with Austria, Sweden, Finland and Norway: a Guided Tour (1995) 20 *ELRev* 131

KAISER, J. K., Das Europarecht in der Krise der Gemeinschaften (1966) 1 *EuR* 14

KORTENBERG, H., Comitologie: le retour (1998) 34 *RTDE* 317

LAMBERT, J., The Constitutional Crisis 1965–1966 (1966) 4 *JCMS* 195

LASOK, D., Some Legal Aspects of Fundamental Renegotiations (1976) 1 *ELRev* 375

LENAERTS, K., Constitutionalism and the Many Facets of Federalism (1990) 38 *AJCL* 205

LENAERTS, K., Regulating the Regulatory Process: 'Delegation of Powers' in the European Community (1993) 18 *ELRev* 23

LENAERTS, K. and VERHOEVEN, A., Towards a Legal Framework for Executive Rule-Making in the EU? The Contribution of the New Comitology Decision (2000) 37 *CMLRev* 645

LENAERTS, K., A Unified Set of Instruments (2005) 1 *EuConst* 57

LINDBERG, L., Integration as a Source of Stress on the European Community System (1966) 10 *IO* 233

LODGE, J., The Role of EEC Summit Conferences (1973–74) 12 *JCMS* 337

MAAS, H. H., The Administrative Commission for the Social Security of Migrant Workers: an Institutional Curiosity (1966–67) 4 *CMLRev* 51

MAN, G. de, The Economic and Monetary Union after Four Years: Results and Prospects (1975) 12 *CMLRev* 193

MARKERT, K., annotation (1971) 6 *EuR* 54

MONAR, J., Interinstitutional Agreements: the Phenomenon and its New Dynamics after Maastricht (1994) 31 *CMLRev* 693

MORAVCSIK, A., Negotiating the Single European Act: National Interests and Conventional Statecraft in the European Community (1991) 45 *IO* 19

NICOLL, W., The Luxembourg Compromise (1984) 22 *JCMS* 35

NICOLL, W., Qu'est-ce que la comitologie? (1987) 306 *RMC* 168

NOËL, É., The Single European Act (1988) 24 *GO* 3

NUFFEL, P. van, annotation (1995) 1 *ColJEL* 530

NUFFEL, P. van, Le traité de Nice: un commentaire (2001) 2 *RDUE* 329

OLMI, G., La mise en œuvre par la C.E.E. de l'organisation commune des marchés agricoles (1963) 6 *RMC* 420

OLMI, G., The Agricultural Policy of the Community (1963–64) 1 *CMLRev* 118

OLMI, G., Common Organisation of Agricultural Markets at the Stage of the Single Market (1967–69) 5 *CMLRev* 359

OLSEN, J. P., Reforming European Institutions of Governance (2002) 40 *JCMS* 581

PETITE, M. and LADENBURGER, C., The Evolution in the Role of the European Commission, in *The EU Constitution: The Best Way Forward?* Conference Reader from 34th Session Asser Institute Colloquim on European Law on 13–16 October 2004

RAMBOW, G., The End of the Transitional Period (1968–69) 6 *CMLRev* 434

SCHINDLER, P., The Problems of Decision Making by Way of the Management Committee Procedure in the EEC (1971) 8 *CMLRev* 184

SCHLACKE, S., annotation (1995) 110 *DVer* 1288

SCHØNBERG, S. and FRICK, K., Finishing, Refining, Polishing: on the Use of *travaux préparatoires* as an Aid to the Interpretation of Community Legislation (2003) 28 *ELRev* 149

SMIJTER, F. de, annotation (1995) 1 *RMUE* 203

TEASDALE, A. L., The Life and Death of the Luxembourg Compromise (1993) 31 *JCMS* 567

TIZZANO, A., annotation (1971) 4 *ForoIt* 33

VASEY, M., Decision Making in the Agriculture Council and the Luxembourg Compromise (1988) 25 *CMLRev* 725

VOS, E., The Rise of Committees (1997) 3 *ELJ* 210

WEBER, J. H., The Financing of the Common Agricultural Policy (1966–67) 4 *CMLRev* 263

WEILER, J. H. H., Pride and Prejudice: Parliament v. Council (1989) 14 *ELRev* 334

WEILER, J. H. H., The Transformation of Europe (1991) 100 *YaleLJ* 2403

WEILER, J. H. H. and Modrall, J., Institutional Reform: Consensus or Majority? (1985) 10 *ELRev* 316

WITTE, B. de, The Nice Declaration: Time for a Constitutional Treaty of the European Union? (2001) 36 *IntSpec* 21

ZWAAN, J. W. de, The Single European Act: Conclusion of a Unique Document (1986) 23 *CMLRev* 747

Bulletins

Office for Official Publications

Bulletin EEC 2-1959
Bulletin EEC 3-1959
Bulletin EEC 5-1959
Bulletin EEC 5-1960
Bulletin EEC 10-1960
Bulletin EEC 9/10-1961
Bulletin EEC 9/10-1962
Bulletin EEC 11-1962
Bulletin EEC 6-1964
Bulletin EEC 8-1965
Bulletin EEC 12-1965
Bulletin EEC 3-1966
Bulletin EEC 8-1967
Bulletin EEC 9/10-1967
Bulletin EC 2-1968
Bulletin EC 7-1968
Bulletin EC 8-1968
Bulletin EC 12-1968
Bulletin EC 1-1969
Bulletin EC 2-1969
Bulletin EC 8-1969
Bulletin EC 1-1970
Bulletin EC 2-1970
Bulletin EC 3-1970
Bulletin EC Supplement 11-1970
Bulletin EC 1-1971
Bulletin EC 3-1971
Bulletin EC 4-1971
Bulletin EC 6-1971
Bulletin EC 7-1971
Bulletin EC 11-1971
Bulletin EC 4-1972
Bulletin EC 8-1972

Bulletin EC 10-1972
Bulletin EC 5-1973
Bulletin EC 7/8-1973
Bulletin EC 12-1973
Bulletin EC 1-1974
Bulletin EC 3-1974
Bulletin EC 6-1974
Bulletin EC 12-1974
Bulletin EC 3-1975
Bulletin EC Supplement 2-1978
Bulletin EC 12-1978
Bulletin EC 9-1979
Bulletin EC 11-1979
Bulletin EC Supplement 2-1980
Bulletin EC Supplement 8-1982
Bulletin EC 6-1983
Bulletin EC 11-1983
Bulletin EC 1-1984
Bulletin EC 3-1984
Bulletin EC 6-1984
Bulletin EC 1-1985
Bulletin EC 3-1985
Bulletin EC 6-1985
Bulletin EC 9-1985
Bulletin EC 10-1985
Bulletin EC 11-1985
Bulletin EC 12-1985
Bulletin EC 1-1986
Bulletin EC 10-1986
Bulletin EC 6-1987
Bulletin EC Supplement 2-1991
Bulletin EC 7/8-1992
Bulletin EC 11-1992
Bulletin EC 3-1993
Bulletin EC 5-1993
Bulletin EC 6-1993
Bulletin EU 12-1993
Bulletin EU 1/2-1994
Bulletin EU 3-1994
Bulletin EU 7/8-1994
Bulletin EU 12-1994
Bulletin EU 1/2-1995
Bulletin EU 4-1997

Bulletin EU 6-1998
Bulletin EU 9-1998
Bulletin EU 10-1998
Bulletin EU 11-1998
Bulletin EU 12-1998
Bulletin EU 3-1999
Bulletin EU 5-1999
Bulletin EU 6-1999
Bulletin EU 1/2-2000
Bulletin EU 7/8-2000

Agence Europe

Europe (bulletin quotidien) 29 July 1960
Europe (bulletin quotidien) 12 September 1960
Europe (bulletin quotidien) 13 September 1960
Europe (bulletin quotidien) 10 October 1960
Europe (documents) 31 December 1960
Europe (bulletin quotidien) 28 November 1961
Europe (bulletin quotidien) 30 November 1961
Europe (bulletin quotidien) 13 December 1961
Europe (bulletin quotidien) 22 December 1961
Europe (bulletin quotidien) 14 January 1962
Europe (bulletin quotidien) 15 January 1962
Europe (bulletin quotidien) 22 December 1962
Europe (bulletin quotidien) 23 March 1965
Europe (bulletin quotidien) 24 March 1965
Europe (bulletin quotidien) 10 November 1965
Europe (bulletin quotidien) 21 December 1965
Europe (la journée politique européenne) 18 January 1966
Europe (bulletin quotidien) 31 January 1966
Europe (bulletin quotidien) 2 April 1966
Europe (bulletin quotidien) 4 April 1966
Europe (bulletin quotidien) 6 April 1966
Europe (bulletin quotidien) 4 May 1966
Europe (bulletin quotidien) 10 June 1966
Europe (bulletin quotidien) 25 July 1966
Europe (bulletin quotidien) 27 July 1966
Europe (bulletin quotidien) 22 January 1968
Europe (bulletin quotidien) 7 February 1968
Europe (bulletin quotidien) 9 February 1968
Europe (bulletin quotidien) 27 February 1968
Europe (bulletin quotidien) 28 February 1968

Europe (*bulletin quotidien*) 1 March 1968
Europe (*bulletin quotidien*) 4 March 1968
Europe (*bulletin quotidien*) 6 March 1968
Europe (*bulletin quotidien*) 13 March 1968
Europe (*bulletin quotidien*) 29 March 1968
Europe (*bulletin quotidien*) 1 April 1968
Europe (*bulletin quotidien*) 2 April 1968
Europe (*bulletin quotidien*) 8 April 1968
Europe (*bulletin quotidien*) 9 April 1968
Europe (*bulletin quotidien*) 16 April 1968
Europe (*bulletin quotidien*) 17 May 1968
Europe (*bulletin quotidien*) 20 May 1968
Europe (*bulletin quotidien*) 21 May 1968
Europe (*bulletin quotidien*) 22 May 1968
Europe (*bulletin quotidien*) 31 May 1968
Europe (*bulletin quotidien*) 10 June 1968
Europe (*bulletin quotidien*) 13 June 1968
Europe (*bulletin quotidien*) 17 June 1968
Europe (*bulletin quotidien*) 26 June 1968
Europe (*bulletin quotidien*) 28 June 1968
Europe (*bulletin quotidien*) 1 July 1968
Europe (*bulletin quotidien*) 2 July 1968
Europe (*bulletin quotidien*) 4 July 1968
Europe (*bulletin quotidien*) 12 July 1968
Europe (*bulletin quotidien*) 17 July 1968
Europe (*bulletin quotidien*) 19 July 1968
Europe (*bulletin quotidien*) 22 July 1968
Europe (*bulletin quotidien*) 23 July 1968
Europe (*bulletin quotidien*) 30 August 1968
Europe (*bulletin quotidien*) 3 October 1968
Europe (*bulletin quotidien*) 26 November 1968
Europe (*bulletin quotidien*) 19 December 1968
Europe (*bulletin quotidien*) 19 January 1994

INDEX

Lightning Source UK Ltd.
Milton Keynes UK
18 June 2010

155774UK00004B/4/P